1st Workshop on Computational Approaches to Discourse 2020

Online
20 November 2020

ISBN: 978-1-7138-1984-4

Printed from e-media with permission by:

Curran Associates, Inc.
57 Morehouse Lane
Red Hook, NY 12571

Some format issues inherent in the e-media version may also appear in this print version.

Copyright© (2020) by the Association for Computational Linguistics
All rights reserved.

Printed with permission by Curran Associates, Inc. (2021)

For permission requests, please contact the Association for Computational Linguistics
at the address below.

Association for Computational Linguistics
209 N. Eighth Street
Stroudsburg, Pennsylvania 18360

Phone: 1-570-476-8006
Fax: 1-570-476-0860

acl@aclweb.org

Additional copies of this publication are available from:

Curran Associates, Inc.
57 Morehouse Lane
Red Hook, NY 12571 USA
Phone: 845-758-0400
Fax: 845-758-2633
Email: curran@proceedings.com
Web: www.proceedings.com

EMNLP 2020

The First Workshop on Computational Approaches to Discourse

Proceedings of the Workshop

November 20, 2020
Online

©2020 The Association for Computational Linguistics

Introduction

Welcome to the first Workshop on Computational Approaches to Discourse, CODI! While there have been previous workshops on specific topics in discourse processing, CODI is intended to provide a venue for researchers working on all aspects of discourse. Our aim is to provide a venue for the entire discourse processing community where we can present and exchange our theories, algorithms, software, datasets, and tools.

The workshop consists of invited talks, contributed paper presentation, and discussion sessions. It also features several "Findings Papers" from EMNLP which are presented and discussed like regular workshop papers. We received paper submissions that span a wide range of topics, addressing issues related to discourse representation and parsing, argumentation, reference and coreference resolution, and more. As the workshop is virtual this year, papers are presented as prerecorded videos and discussed during live Q&A sessions. The workshop also includes a discussion on future shared tasks, special sessions on discourse representation and parsing, coreference resolution, and discourse and machine translation.

We thank our invited speakers **Eunsol Choi**, University of Texas at Austin, who works on language understanding and question answering in context, and **Eduard Hovy**, Carnegie Mellon University, who works on text analytics in its broadest sense. We would also like to thank our reviewers for their thoughtful and instructive comments. They helped us to prepare an inclusive workshop program.

The CODI Organizers,

Chloé Braud, Christian Hardmeier, Junyi Jessy Li, Annie Louis, and Michael Strube

Organizers:

Chloé Braud, CNRS - IRIT
Christian Hardmeier, University of Edinburgh and Uppsala University
Junyi Jessy Li, The University of Texas at Austin
Annie Louis, Google
Michael Strube, Heidelberg Institute for Theoretical Studies

Program Committee:

Giuseppe Carenini, University of British Columbia, Canada
Jackie Chi Kit Cheung, McGill University, Canada
Vera Demberg, Saarland University, Germany
Pascal Denis, Inria Lille, France
Elisa Ferracane, Abridge, USA
Mark Finlayson, Florida International University, USA
Zhengxian Gong, Soochow University, China
Yulia Grishina, Amazon, USA
Ruihong Huang, Texas A&M University, USA
Kentaro Inui, Tohoku University, Japan
Mohit Iyyer, University of Massachusetts Amherst, USA
Yangfeng Ji, The University of Virginia, USA
Sadao Kurohashi, Kyoto University, USA
Ekaterina Lapshinova-Koltunski, Saarland University, Germany
Yang Liu, The University of Edinburgh, UK
Qun Liu, Huawei Noah's Ark Lab, China
Sharid Loáiciga, University of Potsdam, Germany
Ana Marasović, Allen Institute of AI, USA
Katja Markert, Heidelberg University, Germany
Philippe Muller, University of Toulouse, France
Mark-Christoph Müller, Heidelberg Institute for Theoretical Studies, Germany
Anna Nedoluzhko, Charles University, Czech Republic
Vincent Ng, The University of Texas at Dallas, USA
Maciej Ogrodniczuk, Polish Academy of Sciences, Poland
Massimo Poesio, Queen Mary University of London, UK
Marta Recasens, Google, USA
Hannah Rohde, The University of Edinburgh, UK
Attapol Rutherford, Chulalongkorn University, Thailand
Manfred Stede, University of Potsdam, Germany
Don Tuggener, University of Zurich, Switzerland
Bonnie Webber, The University of Edinburgh, UK
Deyi Xiong, Tianjin University, China
Nianwen Xue, Brandeis University, USA
Amir Zeldes, Georgetown University, USA
Heike Zinsmeister, Hamburg University, Germany

Invited Speakers:

Eunsol Choi, The University of Texas at Austin, USA
Eduard Hovy, Carnegie Mellon University, USA

Table of Contents

Workshop Program

How does discourse affect Spanish-Chinese Translation? A case study based on a Spanish-Chinese parallel corpus

Shuyuan Cao

Grupo COLE, Departamento de Informática
Universidade de Vigo
Campus As Lagoas, Ourense 32004, Spain
`shuyuan.cao@uvigo.es`

Abstract

With their huge speaking populations in the world, Spanish and Chinese occupy important positions in linguistic studies. Since the two languages come from different language systems, the translation between Spanish and Chinese is complicated. A comparative study for the language pair can discover the discourse differences between Spanish and Chinese, and can benefit the Spanish-Chinese translation. In this work, based on a Spanish-Chinese parallel corpus annotated with discourse information, we compare the annotation results between the language pair and analyze how discourse affects Spanish-Chinese translation. The research results in our study can help human translators who work with the language pair.

1 Introduction

From the early history, people began to apply Natural Language Processing (NLP) techniques to language researches (Burstein, 2009). Different NLP studies make a great advance in different language aspects, such as pragmatics, semantics, speech, etc.

Among different NLP studies, the emphasis on the idea that discourse information may be useful for Natural Language Processing (NLP) has become increasingly popular. Discourse analysis is an unsolved problem in this field, although discourse information is crucial for many NLP tasks (Zhou et al., 2014). Plus, the greater the linguistic distance is between a pair of languages, the greater the number of differences in their syntax and discourse structure. Therefore, the translation between two very different languages can be potentially more difficult. Comparative or contrastive studies of discourse structures offer clues to identify properly equivalent discourse elements in two languages. These clues can be useful for human translation. The following examples show some of the discourse differences between Spanish and Chinese.

Example 1[1]:
(1.1) *Spanish*: [**Aunque** aún no contamos con resultados,]Unit₁ [intuimos que el modelo será más amplio que el del sintagma nominal.]Unit₂
[DM[2] still not get results,]Unit₁ [we consider that the model will be more extensive than the sentence group nominal.]Unit₂
(1.2) *Spanish*: [Intuimos que el modelo será más amplio que el del sintagma nominal,]Unit₁ [**aunque** aún no contamos con resultados.]Unit₂
[we consider that the model will be more extensive than the sentence group nominal.]Unit₁ [DM still not get results.]Unit₂
(1.3) *Chinese*: [尽管还没有取得最终结果，]Unit₁ [但是我们认为该模型已囊括了语段模型涉及的内容。]Unit₂
[DM1 still no get results,]Unit₁ [DM2 we consider that the model contains the sentence group nominal.]Unit₂
(1.4) *English*: Although we haven' t got the results yet, we consider that the model will be more extensive than the nominal sentence group.

In Example 1, we can see that the Spanish passage (1.1) and the Chinese passage (1.3) have a similar discourse structure. Both passages start with a discourse marker in the first unit. However, the DMs are used differently to show the same meaning in both languages. In Chinese, it is mandatory to include two DMs: the first one is *jinguan* (尽管), and it is located at the beginning of the first unit, and the other marker is *danshi* (但是), which is placed at the beginning of the second unit.

---

[1]We give an English literature translation for each example in this work.

[2]DM means discourse marker. We will give the specific definition of discourse marker in the methodology section.

Proceedings of the First Workshop on Computational Approaches to Discourse, pages 1–10
Online, November 20, 2020. ©2020 Association for Computational Linguistics
https://doi.org/10.18653/v1/P17

These two discourse markers (DMs) are equivalent to the English DM 'although'. By contrast, in Spanish, just one DM *aunque* is needed to express the same meaning. Besides, as we can see in another Spanish passage (1.2), the order of the discourse units in can be changed and it makes sense syntactically, so the DM can appear both at the beginning of the first or the second unit. By contrast, the order cannot be changed in the Chinese passage, because neither syntactically nor grammatically makes sense.

Due to the certain considerable discourse differences between the two languages, it is essential to carry out a discourse comparative study for Spanish and Chinese. Therefore, based on a Spanish-Chinese parallel corpus, this work aims to give a discourse analysis with the intention to analyze how Spanish-Chinese translation can be affected from discourse level. This analysis can be beneficial for human translators who work with the language pair.

In the second section, we present the theoretical framework of this study. In the third section, we talk about some related works. In the fourth section, we give detailed information on the methodology of this work. In the fifth section, we evaluate the research results and give a qualitative analysis. In the last section, we conclude our work and look ahead at future work.

2 Theoretical Framework

The Rhetorical Structure Theory (RST) (Mann and Thompson, 1988) is a theory that was created especially for discourse analysis. It focuses on the hierarchical structure of a whole text, where discourse relations can be annotated within a sentence (intra-sentence style) and between sentences (inter-sentence style). Intra-sentence and inter-sentence annotation styles help to inform how discourse elements are being expressed in a language, and translation strategies (if any) can be detected in different levels of an RS-tree (da Cunha and Iruskieta, 2010; Iruskieta et al., 2015).

RST addresses both hierarchical and relational aspects of text structures for discourse analysis. Elementary Discourse Units (EDUs) (Marcu, 2000) and coherence relations are established in RST. Relations are recursive in RST and are held between EDUs, which can be Nuclei or Satellites, denoted by N and S. Satellites offer additional information about nuclei. EDUs can be linked among them holding a nucleus-satellite (e.g. Cause, Justify, Evidence) function or a multinuclear (e.g. Conjunction, List, Sequence) function. As relations are recursive, all the discourse units of the text have a function in a treelike structure, if and only if the text is coherent.

3 State of the Art

Some previous researches using RST for comparative discourse are, for instance, Chinese and English (Ramsay, 2000, 2001), Japanese and Spanish (Kumpf, 1986; Marcu et al., 2000), Arabic and English (Mohamed and Omer, 1999), French and English (Delin et al., 1994; Salkie and Oates, 1999), Dutch and English (Abelen et al., 1993), Spanish and Basque (da Cunha and Iruskieta, 2010; Imaz and Iruskieta, 2017).

RST contrastive studies that use more than two languages are not common; those that have included work on Portuguese-French-English (Salkie and Oates, 1999) and Basque-English-Spanish (Iruskieta et al., 2015).

Currently, only three works use RST for Spanish-Chinese discourse analysis. One work is from (Cao et al., 2016). They explore sentences that contain the Spanish discourse marker *aunque* ('although' in English) and their Chinese parallel sentences in the UN subcorpus. Another work is the creation of the language teaching and learning resources for Spanish-Chinese by (Cao and Gete, 2018). In their work, they create a system that gives tests to check the Spanish-Chinese students language level through erased DMs in texts. But, they only analyze the single sentences in the corpus, not the whole discourse structure of each text in the corpus. The last work talks about the Spanish-Chinese discourse analysis taking RST as framework is the the RST Spanish-Chinese Treebank (Cao et al., 2018). Cao et al. (2018) establish the first Spanish-Chinese discourse treebank with annotated discourse information under RST. Although the treebank can be useful for different NLP tasks, Cao et al. (2018) only create the treebank without any practical use.

To our knowledge, our work is the first one that analyzes the discourse structures of a whole text for both Spanish and Chinese and apply the analysis results to a language translation task.

4　Methodology

In this section, we present the methodology of this study. In the first subsection, we introduce the research corpus. In the second subsection, we explain how we carry out our analysis.

4.1　Corpus

In this research, we use the RST Spanish-Chinese Treebank created by Cao et al. (2018), a corpus annotated with discourse information under RST. As Cao et al. (2018) indicate, The RST Spanish-Chinese Treebank is the first Spanish-Chinese parallel corpus that guarantees the discourse structure diversity for the language pair. In their corpus, the texts are from different sources. The genres and topics of the corpus are different. Totally, 50 Spanish texts and their translated Chinese texts are selected.

Concerning the corpus annotation, Cao et al. (2018) make three annotation steps. All the annotations are completed by linguists with RST annotation training. As the initial step, they segment the corpus based on the elaborated criteria. After the segmentation work, authors annotate the discourse structure of the whole corpus following the method proposed by Pardo (2005).

Towards the annotation quality of the corpus, Cao et al. (2018) use Kappa to measure the segmentation part. For the evaluation of discourse structure annotation, they use a qualitative method (Iruskieta et al., 2015). Under the qualitative method, four elements are being examined by using F-measure: Nuclearity(N), Relation(R), Composition(C) and Attachment(A).

The K results of the segmentation annotation in the Spanish subcorpus is from 0.716 to 0.945 while the results of the Chinese subcorpus is from 0.616 to 0.815. The F results of the discourse structure annotation in the Spanish subcorpus are: N (from 0.761 to 1), R (from 0.641 to 1), C (from 0.761 to 0.933) and A (from 0.731 to 0.933). For the Chinese subcorpus discourse structure annotation, the F results are: N (from 0.864 to 0.978), R (from 0.727 to 0.844), C (from 0.864 to 0.978) and A (from 0.84 to 0.978).

The full annotation of the RST Spanish-Chinese Treebank can be find at ixa2.si.ehu.es/rst/zh/index.php. It is a free open access to the research community and all the corpus texts and annotations can be downloaded for research purposes. Moreover, in their corpus, authors give the part-of-speech (pos) information for each text.

The evaluation results for each annotation step show that the corpus is annotated with high quality. Based on the the reliable annotation results, we decide to use the RST Spanish-Chinese as the research corpus.

4.2　Discourse differences in translation strategies

In the study of Iruskieta et al. (2015), besides of creating the qualitative method for the discourse annotation evaluation, they also find how discourse elements affect language translation and the causes are defined as translation strategies.

- Marker change. Marker change means for the parallel passages, the DMs in both texts are different.

- Clause structure change. During the translation process, a non-finite verb phrase is changed to finite verb structure.

- Unit shift. In the parallel passages, the punctuations are different.

Therefore, we follow the method of Iruskieta et al. (2015) to detect the possible translation strategies which can affect translation Spanish and Chinese from discourse level.

Additionally, for the marker change case, we confirm the definition of DM in our analysis. One of the DM definitions that address RST is from Eckle-Kohler et al. (2015). They consider that, from textual level, DMs are used to signal discourse relations in a text segment, as cohesive relationships between the utterances. Specifically, under RST, da Cunha (2013) proposes three types of DMs: (i) Traditional markers; (ii) Markers including lexical units; and (iii) Markers including verbal structures. Adopting the definitions from the two works, we use the concept of traditional markers and markers including verbal structures. Both types of markers signal a discourse relation in a segmented text.

5　Evaluation and Analysis

In this section we analyze the results based on the discourse differences. Based on the annotation of each text in the corpus, we compare all the parallel passages and find the following differences discourse differences in the corpus:

- Marker change. Marker change means for the parallel passages, the DMs in both texts are different.

- Unit shift. In the parallel passages, the punctuations in the original passage and the translated passage are different.

- Unit shift plus marker change. For the parallel passages, the punctuation and the DM in the translated passage are different from the original passage.

- Different order EDUs. Although the Spanish passage and its Chinese parallel passage include the same content, the order of the expressions are different in two languages.

- Added discourse. A new discourse is added in the translated passage and causes the relation change between the parallel parts.

Figure 1 concludes the statistical information of the translation strategies in our study. We can see that, among the 26 cases that we collected from the annotated corpus, marker change is the most frequent translation strategy.

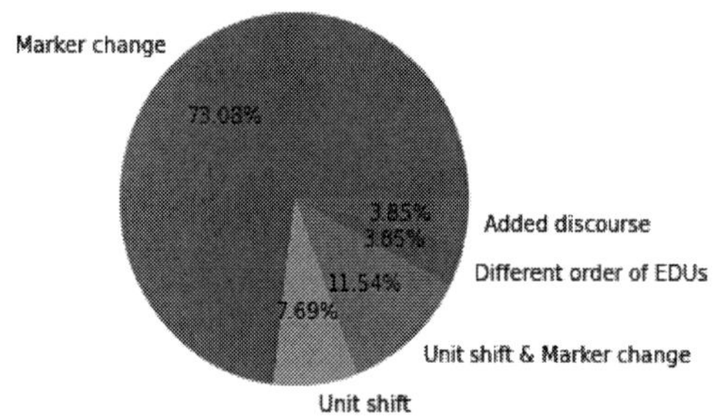

Figure 1: Statistical conclusion of the translation strategies in the corpus

5.1 Marker change

Totally, there are 19 cases related to marker change. There are 6 cases that the DMs in the Spanish passages are changed in their Chinese parallel passages. For the other 13 collected cases, the Spanish passages don't contain any DM. In contrast, there is a DM in each of their Chinese parallel passages. Table 1 sums up the cases of the change of the DMs. Meanwhile, Table 2 summarizes the facts of the cases whose Spanish passages

don't contain any DM but their parallel Chinese passages contain DMs.

From Table 1 we can see that, the types of discourse relations in the parallel passages can be same or different when there is a marker change process. In Table 2, we realize that with the new added DM, the type of the discourse relations between the parallel passages are all changed. For example, in the text EEP2, the discourse relation in the Spanish is implicit (Elaboration) because of the lack of the DM. The relation Elaboration is beyond to N-S type under RST. Notwithstanding, in its Chinese parallel passage, the DM *lingyifangmian* (另一方面) represents a List relation, and the relation is beyond to N-N type under RST.

The change of DMs causes changes of relation definition and relation type. As a result, the sentence meaning can be different between the parallel parts. In this work, we assume that the semantics of a discourse relation should transfer from source to target language, as indicated in da Cunha and Iruskieta (2010) and Laali and Kosseim (2014). For this reason, we consider that the semantic aspect doesn't affect the discourse meaning when the translation strategies are used for the Spanish-Chinese translation.

5.2 Unit Shift

As regards the translation strategy of unit shift, we only find 2 cases in total. Below, are the 2 cases and our analysis.

Text name: BMCS2
Spanish: [Metodología actual.]^{3}S_Interpretation [El material de enseñanaza procede de España, ...]N_Interpretation
English: [Methodology current.] [The material of teaching comes from Spain, ...]
Chinese: [领先的教学方法]S_Preparation [我们的教材为西班牙原版教材]N_Preparation
English: [Leading teaching method] [Our material is the Spanish original]

In this case, there is a period between two EDUs in the Spanish passage. But in its Chinese passage, the two EDUs don't contain any punctuation, and the relation definition between the two EDUs in the Chinese text is different from the Spanish passage. Yet, both Spanish and Chinese passages show the information of the teaching method.

---

[3]In our work, for some comparison analysis, we use color blue to detect the discourse differences.

Marker change (A DM → Another DM)				
	DM		Relation (Relation type)	
Text name	Spanish	Chinese	Spanish	Chinese
BMCS3	y (eng: and)	huozhe (或者) (eng: or)	List (N-N)	Disjunction (N-N)
FCEC1	y (eng: and)	zhizai (旨在) (eng: aims to)	List (N-N)	Purpose (N-S)
TERM31	igualmente (eng: and)	tongshi (同时) (eng: at the same time)	List (N-N)	Conjunction (N-N)
TERM18	para (eng: for)	ruo (若) (eng: if)	Purpose (N-S)	Condition (N-S)
TERM32	para que (eng: for)	ruo (若) (eng: if)	Purpose (N-S)	Condition (N-S)
TERM38	por lo tanto (eng: therefore)	dan (但) (eng: but)	Result (N-S)	Concession (N-S)

Table 1: Summary of cases that the DMS are different in the parallel passages

Text name: EEP7

Spanish: [La muestra de este año ha sido un reflejo de los desafíos a los que se enfrenta el cine español en la actualidad.]N_Evidence [Las tendencias globalizadas exigen a los renovados autores y talentos que incorporen las nuevas tecnologías y que desarrollen una innovadora experimentación genérica.]S_Evidence

English: [The show of this year has been a reflection of the challenges that facing the film Spanish today.] [The tendency globalized requires the renewed authors and talents to incorporate the new technologies and to develop a innovative experimentation generic.]

Chinese: [此次挑选的这一系列影片流派各异，]N_Evaluation [体现了西班牙电影界国内市场的繁荣和与时俱进的气象，反映了西班牙电影向国外市场扩张的趋势及其国际威望。]S_Evaluation

English: [The selection of this series of films varies in genres,] [showing the Spanish film industry's prosperity of the domestic market and the trend of advancing with the times, reflecting the Spanish films to foreign market's trend of expanding and their international prestige.]

In the above case, the period splits the Spanish passage into two sentences, and the relation between the two sentences is Evidence. Concurrently, there is a comma between the two EDUs in the Chinese passage. The two EDUs hold a Evaluation relation. Same as the prior case, the two different relations in the parallel passages doesn't affect the text idea, we can get the information about the Spanish film industry from both Spanish and Chinese passages.

5.3 Unit shift plus marker change

Comparing to Iruskieta et al. (2015), the first work that analyzes the language translation strategies from discourse level, unit shift plus marker change in our study is a newly discovered translation strategy. We find 3 cases corresponding to this phenomenon.

Text name: ICP3

Spanish: [Los actores son en su mayoría gratuitos]S_Concession [**pero** para las actividades que se realizan en nuestro auditorio se recomienda acudir unos minutos antes del cominezo, ya que el aforo de la sala es limitado a 90 personas.]N_Concession

English: [The acts are mainly free] [but for the

Marker change (No DM → A DM)				
	DM		**Relation** **(Relation type)**	
Text name	Spanish	Chinese	Spanish	Chinese
CCICE3	/	yinci (因此) (eng: therefore)	Elaboration (N-S)	Reault (N-S)
FCEC1	/	yinci (因此) (eng: therefore)	Elaboration (N-S)	Result (N-S)
TERM31	/	yinci (因此) (eng: therefore)	Elaboration (N-S)	Result (N-S)
TERM18	/	bing (并) (eng: and)	Condition (N-S)	List (N-N)
TERM32	/	bing (并) (eng: and)	Condition (N-S)	List (N-N)
TERM38	/	bing (并) (eng: and)	Condition (N-S)	List (N-N)
BMCS2	/	wei (为) (eng: and)	Elaboration (N-S)	Purpose (N-S)
EEP2	/	lingyifangmian (另一方面) (eng: on the other hand)	Elaboration (N-S)	List (N-N)
ICP5	/	yucitongshi (与此同时) (eng: meanwhile)	Summary (N-S)	Conjunction (N-N)
TERM31	/	ruo (若) (eng: if)	Evaluation (N-S)	Condition (N-S)
TERM31	/	ye (也) (eng: and)	Elaboration (N-S)	List (N-N)
TERM50	/	dang (当) (eng: when)	Contrast (N-N)	Circumstance (N-S)
TERM50	/	er (而) (eng: however)	Contrast (N-N)	Contrast (N-N)

Table 2: Summary of cases that add a new DM in the Chinese passages

activities that take place in our auditorium it is recommended to go a few minutes before the start, as the capacity of the room is limited to 90 people.]

Chinese: [我们的绝大部分文化活动面向公众免费开放。]N_Elaboration [由于场地有限（多功能厅限 90 人），建议大家在每次活动开始前，提前几分钟入场。]S_Elaboration

English: [Our most cultural activities are open to public for free.] [Due to the space limited (multi-function hall limited to 90 people), we recommend that in each activity start before, you present yourself a few minutes early.]

In the text ICP3, the Spanish passage is an independent sentence and is divided into two EDUs. The relation between the two EDUs is Concession because of the DM *pero* ('but' in English), which is at the beginning of the second EDU. Nevertheless, in the Chinese passage, there is a comma at the end of the first EDU, which makes the Chinese passage contain two sentences. Besides, in the Chinese passage, the DM is erased during the translation process. In the Chinese passage, the relation is Elaboration, which is different from the relation in the Spanish passage.

Text name: TERM31

Spanish: [En las lenguas de flexión compleja,

el tratar solamente el tratar solamente el aspecto formal de las palabras acarrerá malos resulta-dos]N_List [y será necesaria la lematización.]N_List
English: [In the languages of bending complex, treating only the aspect formal of the words will lead to poor results] [and will be necessary the lemmatization.]
Chinese: [对于词尾有复杂变化的语言来说，仅看单词表面就进行分析只会造成很糟糕的局面。]N_Circumstance [**此时**词根分析就变得更为不可或缺。]S_Elaboration
English: [For words that have complex variations of a language, only check the word at the surface to carry out the analysis can bring a bad situation.] [At this time, the stemming analysis becomes more essential.]

In the Spanish passage, we can see that the DM *y* splits the sentence into two parts. And the two EDUs hold a List relation. In its parallel Chinese passage, there is a comma at the end of the first EDU. Moreover, the DM in the Chinese passage is *cishi* (此时), whose meaning is 'when' in English and represents a Circumstance relation under RST.

Text name: ICP5
Spanish: [Estudiar español en nuestro instituto no es solo aprender el idioma,]N_List [sino que **también** da la oportunidad de conocer.]N_List [**y** descubrir las diferentes culturas del mundo hispánico.]N_List
English: [Studying Spanish in our institute is not only learning the language,] [but also gives the opportunity of knowing] [and discovering the differences cultural of the world Hispanic.]
Chinese: [[在我们学院学习西班牙语，不仅仅是学习语言本身，]N_List [**同时**也是学习西语世界的文化。]N_List]N_Summary [给予你一个了解和发掘西班牙西语世界不同文化的机会。]S_Summary
English: [In our institute study Spanish, is not only about learning the language itself,] [at the same time it is also about learning Spanish-speaking culture.] [Giving you an knowing and exploring Hispanic world different cultures opportunity.]

In this case, the Spanish passage is divided into three parts by the DMs *también* ('also' in English) and *y* ('and' in English). The three EDUs form a List relation[4]. Differently, although the parallel

Chinese passage also contains three EDUs, due to the comma at the end of the second EDU, the Chinese passage contains two sentences. The first two EDUs form a sentence and the last EDU is a single sentence. Like the Spanish passage, the first two EDUs in the Chinese passage hold a List relation because of the DM *tongshi* (同时) ('at the same time' in English). Unlike the Spanish passage, the third EDU in the Chinese passage doesn't contain any DMs and is an additional information of the first two EDUs. The relation between the first two EDUs and third EDU is Summary.

5.4 Different order of EDUs

Different order of EDUs is another new translation strategy that doesn't exist in the work of Iruskieta et al. (2015). Based on the annotation results, we detect a case of this translation strategy.

Text name: CCICE1
Spanish: [En 2015, por la primera vez, la región de Norteamérica se convierte en el tercer feudo por primas de Mafre,]N_Cause [desplazando en esa posición a Latam Sur.]S_Cause
English: [In 2015, for the first time, the region of North America becomes the third premium fief of Mapfre,] [displacing in this position to Latam Sur.]
Chinese: [在保险方面，北美已超越南美，]S_Cause [上升为西班牙保险公司 Mafre 第三大市场。]N_Cause
English: [In insurance, North America has surpassed South America,] [rose to the Spanish insurance company Mapfre third largest market.]

In this example, the translation of the first EDU in the Spanish passage is the second EDU of the Chinese passage. In the meantime, the second EDU in the Spanish passage matches the first EDU in the Chinese parallel passage.

5.5 Added discourse

Added discourse is also a new identified translation strategy in this study. During the analysis process, we find only one case about added discourse.

Text name: FICB2
Spanish: [Como conclusión de la formación,

---

[4]Although the three EDUs are annotated at different discourse level (see Figure 2 in the Appendices part), following van Kuppevelt and Smith (2012), EDUs that form the multi-nuclear relation type are at the same discourse level, so as in this study.

los asistentes compartieron dudas y experiencias.]N_Elaboration [Todos los asistentes recibieron los certificados de participación de Hanban y de la FICB.]S_Elaboration
English: [As the conclusion of the training, the assistants shared doubts and experiences.] [All the attendees received the certificate of the participation of Hanban and the FICB.]
Chinese: [... 之后进行了圆桌会议的讨论，全体与会教师就汉字书写问题等进行了讨论，并就海外汉语教学中的疑惑和经验展开了深入的交流。]N_Sequence [**培训结束之后**，我院为参加本次培训的每位教师颁发了汉办制作和巴塞罗那孔子学院制作的教学培训证书。]N_Sequence
English: [After that, held the roundtable discussion, all the participating teachers Chinese characters writing and other problems discussed, and oversea Chinese teaching process of doubts and experiences further communication.] [After the training, our institute awarded each teacher with Hanban and the FICB made certificate.]

In this case we can see both Spanish and Chinese passages include 4 EDUs. Notwithstanding, in the Chinese passage, a new discourse *peixun jieshu hou* (培训结束后) is inserted at the beginning of the last EDU. The phrase *peixun jieshu hou* (培训结束后) means 'after the training' in English, which composes a Sequence relation with other EDUs. Concurrently, the last EDU in the Spanish passage is an additional information of the third EDU and the relation between the two EDUs is Elaboration (see Figure 3).

6 Conclusion

In this paper, based on the annotations from the RST Spanish-Chinese Treebank, we compare all the annotated parts to find the discourse differences between Spanish and Chinese. The comparison results in this study match the conclusions in Iruskieta et al. (2015). Furthermore, we find some new translation strategies under RST: **unit shift plus marker change**, **different order of EDUs**, and **added discourse**. The research results can help the Spanish-Chinese human translation.

Regarding future work, we will apply our results to the shallow discourse parsing for Spanish and Chinese, with the intention to improve the Spanish-Chinese machine translation (MT) from discourse level.

Acknowledgments

We thank Dr. Iria da Cunha and Dr. Mikel Iruskieta for their insightful comments on this work. This work is partially funded by the Spanish Ministry of Economy and Competitiveness through project TIN2017-85160-C2-2-R, and by the Galician Regional Government under project ED431D 2017/12.

References

Eric Abelen, Gisela Redeker, and Sandra A Thompson. 1993. The rhetorical structure of us-american and dutch fund-raising letters. *Text-Interdisciplinary Journal for the Study of Discourse*, 13(3):323–350.

Jill Burstein. 2009. Opportunities for natural language processing research in education. In *International Conference on Intelligent Text Processing and Computational Linguistics*, pages 6–27. Springer.

Shuyuan Cao, Iria da Cunha, and Nuria Bel. 2016. An analysis of the concession relation based on the discourse marker aunque in a spanish-chinese parallel corpus. *Procesamiento del Lenguaje Natural*, (56):81–88.

Shuyuan Cao, Iria da Cunha, and Mikel Iruskieta. 2018. The rst spanish-chinese treebank. In *Proceedings of the Joint Workshop on Linguistic Annotation, Multiword Expressions and Constructions (LAW-MWE-CxG-2018)*, pages 156–166.

Shuyuan Cao and Harritxu Gete. 2018. Using discourse information for education with a spanish-chinese parallel corpus. In *Proceedings of the Eleventh International Conference on Language Resources and Evaluation (LREC 2018)*, pages 2254–2261.

Iria da Cunha. 2013. A symbolic corpus-based approach to detect and solve the ambiguity of discourse markers. *Research in Computer Science*, 70:95–106.

Iria da Cunha and Mikel Iruskieta. 2010. Comparing rhetorical structures in different languages: The influence of translation strategies. *Discourse Studies*, 12(5):563–598.

Judy Delin, Anthony Hartley, Cécile Paris, Donia Scott, and Keith Vander Linden. 1994. Expressing procedural relationships in multilingual instructions. In *Proceedings of the Seventh International Workshop on Natural Language Generation*.

Judith Eckle-Kohler, Roland Kluge, and Iryna Gurevych. 2015. On the role of discourse markers for discriminating claims and premises in argumentative discourse. In *Proceedings of the 2015 Conference on Empirical Methods in Natural Language Processing*, pages 2236–2242.

Oier Imaz and Mikel Iruskieta. 2017. Deliberation as genre: Mapping argumentation through relational discourse structure. In *Proceedings of the 6th Workshop on Recent Advances in RST and Related Formalisms*, pages 1–10.

Mikel Iruskieta, Iria da Cunha, and Maite Taboada. 2015. A qualitative comparison method for rhetorical structures: identifying different discourse structures in multilingual corpora. *Language resources and evaluation*, 49(2):263–309.

Lorraine Edith Kumpf. 1986. Structuring narratives in a second language : descriptions of rhetoric and grammar.

Jan CJ van Kuppevelt and Ronnie W Smith. 2012. *Current and new Directions in Discourse and Dialogue*, volume 22. Springer Science & Business Media.

Majid Laali and Leila Kosseim. 2014. Inducing discourse connectives from parallel texts. In *Proceedings of COLING 2014, the 25th International Conference on Computational Linguistics: Technical Papers*, pages 610–619.

William C Mann and Sandra A Thompson. 1988. Rhetorical structure theory: Toward a functional theory of text organization. *Text*, 8(3):243–281.

Daniel Marcu. 2000. The rhetorical parsing of unrestricted texts: A surface-based approach. *Computational linguistics*, 26(3):395–448.

Daniel Marcu, Lynn Carlson, and Maki Watanabe. 2000. The automatic translation of discourse structures. In *1st Meeting of the North American Chapter of the Association for Computational Linguistics*.

Aysha H Mohamed and Majzoub R Omer. 1999. Syntax as a marker of rhetorical organization in written texts: Arabic and english. *IRAL, International Review of Applied Linguistics in Language Teaching*, 37(4):291.

Thiago Alexandre Salgueiro Pardo. 2005. *Métodos para análise discursiva automática*. Ph.D. thesis, Universidade de São Paulo.

Guy Ramsay. 2000. Linearity in rhetorical organisation: a comparative cross-cultural analysis of newstext from the people's republic of china and australia. *International Journal of Applied Linguistics*, 10(2):241–256.

Guy Ramsay. 2001. What are they getting at? placement of important ideas in lengthy chinese newstext: A contrastive analysis with australian newstext. *Australian Review of Applied Linguistics*, 24(2):17–34.

Raphael Salkie and Sarah Louise Oates. 1999. Contrast and concession in french and english. *Languages in Contrast*, 2(1):27–56.

Lanjun Zhou, Binyang Li, Zhongyu Wei, and Kam-Fai Wong. 2014. The cuhk discourse treebank for chinese: Annotating explicit discourse connectives for the chinese treebank. In *LREC*, pages 942–949.

A Appendices

Supplied material 1: Figure 2 reflects the annotation case that, although EDU3, EDU4 and EDU5 are annotated at different discourse level, since they hold a multinuclear relation (List), the three EDUs can be considered as the same-discourse level EDUs.

Supplied material 2: Figure 3 shows the annotation of the added discourse case. From the annotation we can see that, in the Chinese passage, the last EDU starts with the added phrase *peixun jieshu hou* (培训结束后) changes the discourse level of the last EDU. Also, the new added discourse changes the relation between the last EDU and its previous EDUs, comparing to the Spanish parallel passage.

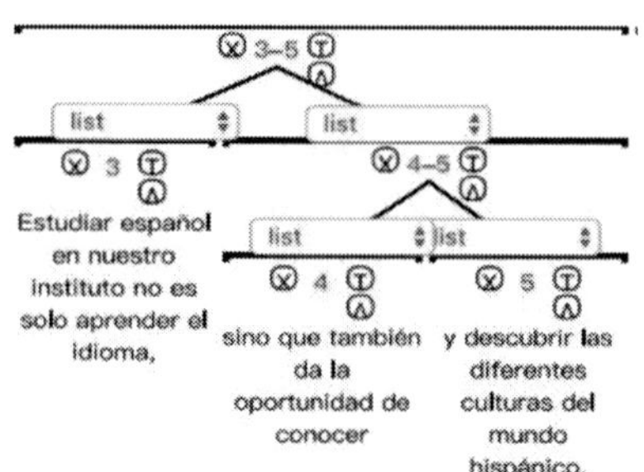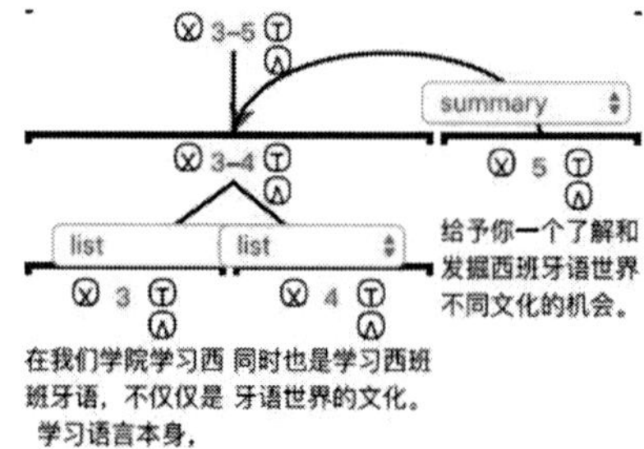

Figure 2: The annotation of the parallel parts of text ICP5

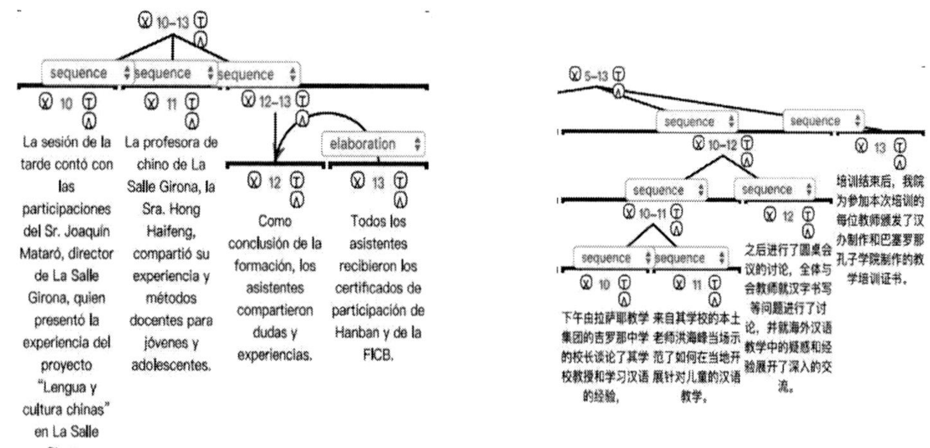

Figure 3: The annotation of the parallel parts of text FICB2

Beyond Adjacency Pairs: Hierarchical Clustering of Long Sequences for Human-Machine Dialogues

Maitreyee Tewari
Department of Computing Science
Umeå University
Umeå, Sweden
`maittewa@cs.umu.se`

Abstract

This work proposes a framework to predict sequences in dialogues, using turn based syntactic features and dialogue control functions. Syntactic features were extracted using dependency parsing, while dialogue control functions were manually labelled. These features were transformed using tf-idf and word embedding; feature selection was done using Principal Component Analysis (PCA). We ran experiments on six combinations of features to predict sequences with Hierarchical Agglomerative Clustering. An analysis of the clustering results indicate that using word-embeddings and syntactic features, significantly improved the results.

1 Introduction

Dialogues between humans is not a solitary activity of words, rather the involved participants have certain desires/goals that they want to achieve. In order to do that, they co-create understanding, by aligning aspects of their believes/knowledge to achieve their goals and reach a consensus using dialogue control functions. Dialogues between humans and machines can be facilitated by dialogue management systems (DMS). A basic DMS operates by coordinating natural language understanding (NLU), natural language generation (NLG) and a dialogue manager (DM). A DM employs either learned or hand-crafted strategies to the output from the NLU and sends its decisions to NLG that carries forward the interaction with the human participant.

A DM's flexibility can be partially attributed to the incoming knowledge from the NLU. By DM's flexibility we mean to have functions for anaphora resolution, co-referencing, keeping track of topic shifts and being able to return to previous topics (McTear et al., 2016).

The **motivation** behind this work is to explore sequences (Nicholas et al., 2016) in dialogues that can improve the NLU's knowledge. A well explored dialogue sequencing method (Palomar and Patricio, 2000; Boyer et al., 2009) with-in conversation analysis (CA) are studied as *adjacency pairs* (Schegloff and Sacks, 1973) such as *(Question-Answer, Request-Accept, Greeting-Greeting etc.)*, where the first one in the pair is called first pair part (FPP_{base}) and the second one is called second pair part (SPP_{base}). For exploring long sequences, CA provides a relevant framework of *sequence expansion* (Stivers, 2012) allowing the prior mentioned base parts to be expanded with preceding parts (FPP_{pre}, SPP_{pre}), insertion parts (FPP_{insert}, SPP_{insert}) or succeeding parts by (FPP_{post}, SPP_{post}).

This work proposes to use sequence expansion to analyse how much long sequences can be predicted by the machine learning models in order to build the knowledge for NLU. As an initial step, this work uses above mentioned sequence expansion labels to study the dendrograms and sequences of nodes longer than adjacency pairs.

The paper is structured as follows: Section 2 presents a summary of related literature and provides the necessary background. The Methodology and the clustering model is presented in Section 3, and Section 4 presents the results of our proposed model. Section 5 concludes this article.

2 Literature and Background

Structuring in dialogues have been explored by many researches utilising different sequencing theories: discourse representation theory (Kamp et al., 2011), conversation analysis (CA) (Sidnell and Stivers, 2012), and Rhetorical sequence theory (Hou et al., 2020) to name a few. Detailing these theories is beyond the scope of this work, but

Proceedings of the First Workshop on Computational Approaches to Discourse, pages 11–19
Online, November 20, 2020. ©2020 Association for Computational Linguistics
https://doi.org/10.18653/v1/P17

we will briefly explain some of their use-cases.

For instance, (Stent, 2000) used rhetorical sequence theory for sequencing task-driven dialogues and report several issues such as, deciding a minimal unit for annotation, overlap between subject-matter and presentational relations. In (Asher and Lascarides, 2003), the authors presented a novel theory called Segmented Discourse Interpretation Theory (SDRT), combining the knowledge from dynamic semantics, common sense reasoning, and speech act theory. The authors claimed SDRT to be the most formally mature and linguistically grounded theory.

While, the above mentioned works focused more on strengthening the theoretical foundations for dialogue sequencing, the authors (Boyer et al., 2009) identified themselves with solving practical matters of extracting sequences. Their corpus of human-human tutorial dialogues were manually annotated with dialogue acts and trained on a hidden Markov model (HMM) on adjacency pairs. More recently, the authors in (Nicholas et al., 2016) presented a multi-party corpus annotated with discourse sequence relations following SDRT mentioned earlier. Authors in (Gupta et al., 2018) proposed a hierarchical annotation scheme for query systems such as travel booking, in order to determine intents from complex nested queries compared to a single intent for each slot. In (Shi et al., 2019), the authors used a variational recurrent neural network (VRNN) and variational inference for dialogue sequence in task-oriented dialogues (finding restaurant and getting weather report).

The proposed work here is closely in line with (Zacharie et al., 2018; Duran and Battle, 2018; Tewari and Bensch, 2018), where in prior work the authors proposed a two step methodology of extracting two dimensional patterns in dialogues, followed by clustering. Their dialogues are manually annotated with emotion, gaze and dialogue act. In the latter work, the authors demonstrated the significance of dialogue sequencing for building domain agnostic dialogue models using CA. They explored sequence expansion and developed an annotation tool to annotate dialogues with sub-sequences based on CA and dialogue control functions. In the final work the authors used syntactic, communicative and CA based features and formalised them by extending the cooperating distributed grammar system.

The biggest difference of this work from the above mentioned prior works is in the definition of the task, i.e, the dialogue corpus. All the prior work has utilised either publicly available corpora based on query systems, while this work aimed to gather as diverse genres of task-driven query/reservation (booking laundry, ordering food), collaboration (cooking, taking medications, going to the flower shop) dialogues and chit-chat dialogues. The other difference is in the annotation approach and the training input, where, we neither use only manually labelled or the entire utterance as the input. Instead, we combine manually labelled and automatically extracted features.

The next section briefly provides some background on adjacency pairs and CA based sequence expansion.

2.1 Sequences in Dialogues

Adjacency pairs (Schegloff and Sacks, 1973) can be defined as utterances produced by two different participants and are adjacently placed. Instances of typically used adjacency pairs are greeting greeting, request accept/reject, offer accept/reject, question answer etc.

However, adjacency pairs allow *one-shot conversations* (McTear et al., 2016), where the human asks a question or queries a system and the system responds. Moving towards long and complex interactions which may include (pronoun resolution, topic management, etc) would leave adjacency pairs insufficient for the purpose. In the example below, we explain our scenario, labelled with dialogue control functions (Bunt, 1999), mentioned later.

Turn1 A1: Where is Eiffel Tower? Question

Turn2 Siri: Here is what I found. (displays information about Eiffel Tower) Answer

Turn3 A1: What are some of the good restaurants around it? Question

Turn4 Siri: Here is what I found. (displays restaurants around its current location) Incorrect Answer

Turn5 A1: Last year I had lot of fun in Scotland highlands. Can you tell me where is Windsor castle? Inform, Question

Turn6 Siri: I am sorry. Negative Feedback

This scenario poses at-least two challenges that motivates this work: *a)* at Turn3 'it' couldn't be be resolved by Siri and *b)* at Turn5 multiple dialogue control functions are present, where Siri fails to respond.

Research has been done already with regard to anaphora resolution using adjacency pairs (Palomar and Patricio, 2000), we propose to use sequence expansion for the problem *a)* above and for *b)* the annotation scheme proposed by Bunt et al. (Bunt et al., 2019). Next we explain the concept of sequence expansion (SE) to understand what do we mean by longer sequences.

Sequence Expansion (SE) (Stivers, 2012) constitutes labels that can precede, be inserted, or followed by the base adjacency pairs (introduced in Section 1). The above mentioned example can be translated with SE labels as in Table 1, and instead of knowledge from just a pair of turns, the machine can extract from multiple turns. Following such schemes allows machines, to have a longer window/slot for information. The other benefit is, it can optimise its knowledge and strategy, For example, if a machine observes that an SPP_{insert} is present in its slot, and its the machine's turn then it can switch the topic back to the base topic introduced at FPP_{base} if it hasn't been fulfilled by an SPP_{base}, etc.

To this end, SE labels are used to analyse the results of the clustering and to compare the amount of knowledge captured and the comprehensiveness they provide compared to adjacency pairs. The next section provides some details on the methodology employed by this work to predict distinctive clusters representing longer sequences.

3 Methodology

The method employed by this work to predict long sequences uses feature engineering and unsupervised clustering method on $n-$grams of syntactic features and dialogue control functions. The next sections provide details on the features used and the components of the model.

Overall, our framework consists of following stages represented in Figure 1:

1. Preparation of the corpus– consists of determining which genres should be considered, then merging of the samples from different sources was done, then the corpus was preprocessed by performing data cleaning, missing imputation, and assignment of unique-identifier.

2. Manual Annotation: transforming utterances to segments and labelling them with dialogue control function.

3. Extraction of features: next, a dependency parser was used on the corpus of dialogue segments to extract syntactic features ($uni-$grams and $tri-$grams).

4. Feature Transformation: employs a *tf-idf* when the feature consists of only dialogue control functions, and *GloVe* embeddings are used for different combinations of syntactic features and dialogue control functions.

5. Selection of features: we perform feature selection using PCA on the transformed features received from the previous stage.

6. Training of the model: the selected features are clustered with hierarchical agglomerative clustering.

7. Evaluation was done by computing Calinski Harabasz index, Silhouette score, Davies Bouldin score and Cophenetic Coefficient Correlation (Cophnet) for the clustering model.

3.1 Corpus

We conduct experiments on a collection of 78 dialogues of which 41 were synthetically created dialogues between an older adult H and a robot R. We used the scenario that R is situated in H's home to assist in daily tasks such as: meal reminders, playing board games, taking care of hazardous items etc.

The synthetic dialogues were combined with 9 dialogues from Dialog Bank [1] which already came with gold standard labels of ISO $24617-2$ scheme (Bunt et al., 2017) and 28 dialogues from dialogue breakdown detection challenge (DBDC3) (Higashinaka et al., 2017).

The synthetic dialogues and DBDC3 dialogues were hand labelled by the author with dialogue control functions following the ISO $24617-2$ annotation scheme. Since, this work is aimed towards extracting generic sequences hence, we combined different domains (taks-driven and chit-chat) and participant types (human-human, human-machine).

____

[1] https://dialogbank.uvt.nl/annotated dialogues/

Turn No./Participant	Utterances	DCF	SE
Turn1 A1:	Where is Eiffel Tower?	Question	$\mathbf{FPP}_{base}$
Turn2 Siri:	Here is what I found.	Answer	$\mathbf{SPP}_{base}$
Turn3 A1:	What are some of the good restaurants around it?	Question	$\mathbf{FPP}_{post}$
Turn4 Siri:	Here is what I found.	Incorrect Answer	$\mathbf{SPP}_{post}$
Turn5 A1:	Last year I had lot of fun in Scotland highlands.	Inform	$\mathbf{FPP}_{pre}$
Turn5 A1:	Can you tell me where is Windsor castle?	Question	$\mathbf{FPP}_{base}$
Turn6 Siri:	I am sorry.	Negative feedback	$\mathbf{FPP}_{insert}$

Table 1: The first column consists of the information about the turn and the participant, the second column provides one or more utterances with-in each turn, followed by the dialogue control functions (DCF) and sequence expansion (SE)

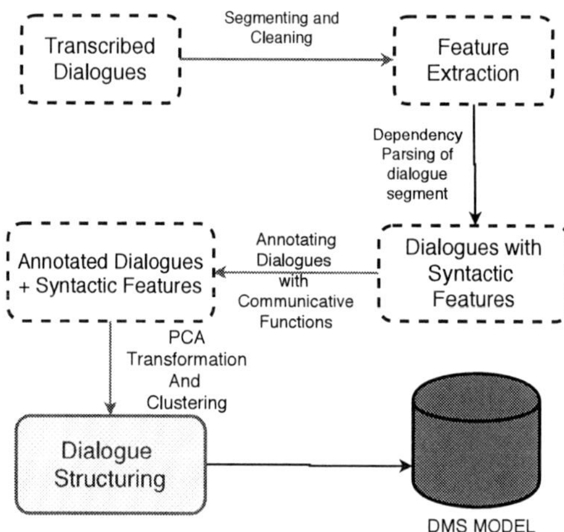

Figure 1: The workflow to obtain dialogue patterns for sequencing dialogues to build natural flows in DMS.

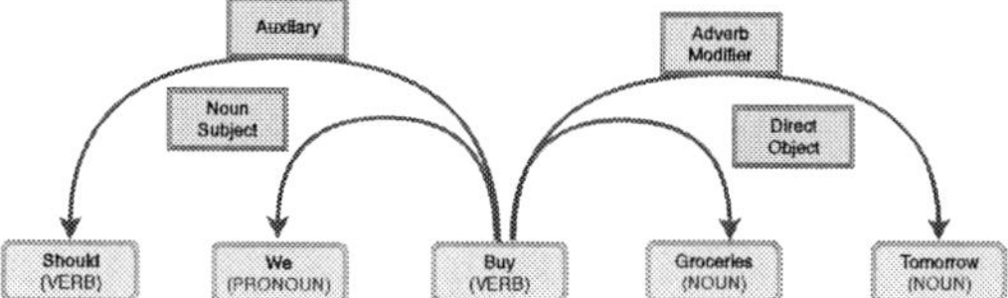

Figure 2: Dependency graph for an utterance, where coloured text in brackets are the POS tags associated to each lexical item (words). The arcs indicate the asymmetric dependency relation (auxiliary, noun subject, direct object and so on) between the head(arc orgins) and dependants(arc pointers).

3.2 Syntactic Features and Dialogue Control Functions

We use dependency parsing for extracting syntactic features of types, $uni-$gram and $tri-$gram with dependency relationship. Dependency parsing generates syntactic sequences between **lexical** elements i.e(words), which are linked by binary *asymmetrical* relation called *dependencies*. Figure 2 illustrates a dependency parsing graph with syntactic sequence. This work uses Spacy dependency parser proposed in (Honnibal and Johnson, 2015).

Based on a manual analysis of dependency graphs on randomly selected samples from the corpus, we decided to use POS tags as $uni-$gram syntactic features: pronouns, proper nouns, direct object, indirect objects, coordinating conjunction, and interjection. For tri-gram syntactic features *(subject-object-verb)* tuples and dependency graphs

of *(auxiliary verb)* and its right two neighbours were used.

Utterances in dialogues, have one to many relationship with functions to either provide or require information from an addressee and such functions are referred as dialogue control functions (Bunt et al., 2019). For instance in an utterance 'Hi John, Please get ready for some exercise' can be segmented into **'Hi John'** with dialogue control function (greeting) and **'Please get ready for some exercise'** with dialogue control function (request) and each of these segments are referred as *functional segments*. List of dialogue control functions used in this work are provided in Table 2.

3.3 Data Transformation and Reduction

Data transformation is an essential step for all machine learning algorithms and here we use two different transformation techniques for the two features used in this work.

Term Frequency Inverse Document Frequency tf-idf (Church and Gale, 1999) determines the relative frequency of terms in a document compared to the inverse proportion of that term over the collection of documents. Dialogue control functions are of categorical type and hence were trans-

Communicative Functions	Dialogue Control Functions
1.General Functions	Proposition, Set, Choice, Check Question, Inform, Agree, Disagree, Correction, Answer, Confirm, Dis-confirm, Promise, Offer, Address, Accept, Decline (Request, Suggest), Request, Instruct, Offer, Address, Accept, Decline (Offer).
2.Feedback Functs.	Auto-Positive, Allo-Positive, Auto-Negative, Allo-Negative, Feedback Elicitation.
3.Turn/Time Mgmt.	Accept-Turn, Grab-Turn, Assign-Turn, Keep-Turn, Release-Turn, Take-Turn, Stalling, Pausing.
5.Own/ Partner Comm. Mgmt.	Completion, Correct Misspeaking, Self-Error, Retraction, Self-correction.
6.Discourse Structuring	Interaction Structuring, Opening.
7.Social Obligation Mgmt.	Initial, Return (Greeting, Self-introduction, Goodbye), Apology, Thanking, Accept (Apology, Thanking).

Table 2: Different dialogue control functions corresponding to their respective Communicative functions

formed using tf-idf technique. Intuitively, it determines how significant a term is for a given document. Consider the corpus as a document collection D, with a term (dialogue control function) t, and document (a dialogue) $d \in D$, tf-idf can be calculated as (Ramos, 2003): $t_d = f_{t,d} \times \log(|D|/f_{t,D})$ Where, $f_{t,d}$ is the frequency of (dialogue control function) t in the given dialogue d, $|D|$ is the size of the corpus, and $f_{t,D}$ is the number of dialogues in which the dialogue control function t appears in the corpus D.

Word-embedding (Mikolov et al., 2013) transform words to vectors in a higher dimensional space to derive linear syntactic and/or semantic relationships between them. dc_t is the dialogue control function and $sf_t = [w_{1,t}, w_{2,t}...w_{n,t}]$ are the $n-$gram syntactic features for each segment, where w is a single syntactic feature. The concatenation of these two features $F = [dc_t, sf_t]$ is the variable. dc_t and sf_t were averaged for each segment of an utterance resulting into $\bar{sf_t}$, $\bar{dc_t}$ and transformed using pre-trained GloVe (Pennington et al., 2014) embedding with 300 features providing $\bar{F} = [\bar{dc_t}, \bar{sf_t}]$, which is then given to PCA for feature selection, explained next.

Principal Component Analysis (PCA) reduces higher dimensional feature space to lower dimension, by selecting the features with highest variance (Shlens, 2014). PCA receives the above trans-

formed features: tf-idf t_d and word-embedding $\bar{F}$. The linear transformations can be represented as a matrix computation: $P_1 t_d = T$ and $P_2 \bar{F} = F_{new}$. Where, the input to the HAC model are the rows of P_1 for only dialogue control functions and P_2 for combination of the features.

3.4 Hierarchical Agglomerative Clustering (HAC)

HAC is an unsupervised machine learning method (Murtagh and Contreras, 2012), that partitions the corpora into n singleton nodes and keeps merging mutually close pair of nodes until one final node is generated.

Let S_0 be the initial set of data points, at each step n_i is the new node formed by merging a_i and b_i with a given distance δ_i. It runs for $N1$ turns, resulting into a final state of only one node with all N initial nodes. Next we briefly describe the steps a HAC algorithm follows: *(i)* Generation of priority queue with nearest neighbours and minimal distances. *(ii)* Find the closest pair of nodes based on computed values for nearest neighbours and minimal distance, and append them to a list L to generate the dendrogram. *(iii)* Ensure the minimal distance between two nearest neighbours holds true till the end, and updates the minimum distance at every time step of the merging.

3.5 Model Definition

We experimented with four different HAC models and compared it for *Euclidean* and *Manhattan* distance measures for finding out the minimum distance between two feature combinations in order to merge them into clusters. To generate *dendrograms* we used *Ward* linkage and *complete* linkage. The four HAC models we experimented for different feature combinations: *(i)* Pre-defined number of clusters $n = 6$, distance metric: *Euclidean* distance, merging of clusters: *Ward*. *(ii)* Pre defined number of clusters $n = 5$, distance metric: *Euclidean* distance, merging of clusters: *Ward*. *(iii)* Pre defined number of clusters $n = 5$, distance metric: *Manhattan* distance, merging of clusters: *complete*. *(iv)* Pre defined number of clusters $n = 3$, distance metric: *Euclidean* distance, merging of clusters: *Ward*.

We ran the HAC models on tuple of features for each segment of an utterance. Following tuple of features were selected for running the experiment:

(i) only dialogue control functions *(DCF)*.

(ii) dialogue control functions and syntactic feature ($tri-$grams–subject-object-verb) as *(DCF,SS1)*.

(iii) dialogue control functions and syntactic feature ($tri-$grams–auxiliary verb, right neighbour1, right neighbour2) as *(DCF,SS2)*.

(iv) dialogue control functions and $uni-$gram syntactic features (Nouns, Direct object, Indirect object, Interjection and Coordinating Conjunction) *(DCF,ST)*.

(v) dialogue control functions and $tri-$gram syntactic features (auxiliary right neighbour1 Right neighbour2 and subject object verb) as (DCF,SS1,SS2).

(vi) dialogue control function and syntactic features, $uni-$grams and $tri-$grams as (DCF,ST,SS1,SS2).

4   Results

To evaluate the HAC model on different combination of features, we compute the silhouette coefficient, Calinski Harabasz index and Davies Bouldin score, these metrics illustrate if the model generated well defined clusters. In Statistics Cophnet, measures how well the *dendro-gram* preserves the pair wise distances of original data points (Saraçli et al., 2013). We use *Cophnet* to measure the correlation between original and the predicted data points.

The evaluation of the HAC model is illustrated in the Table 3. The overall performance of the HAC model is good on specific combination of features **DCF, SS1, SS2** and **DCF, ST** as highlighted in bold with high Calinski Harabasz Index, Silhouette score, and Davies Bouldin score. The Cophnet score is high for half of the combination of features i.e, **DCF, SS1, DCF, ST**, and **DCF, SS1, SS2**. We can see that the performance of the HAC model on only **DCF** is also high, however it is not a relevant result for us because it doesn't convey any information about the sequence.

4.1   Empirical Analysis of HAC Model

In order to identify the sequence expansions we manually analysed random sample of dendrograms, for all the six combination of features mentioned above with 200 nodes. We provide here five such examples of the analysed dendrograms, which are manually labelled with sequence expansion labels, in-order to see if such labelling can help to capture and build more knowledge.

Table 4 provides two examples extracted from one of the generated dendrograms, for (dialogue control functions and $uni-$gram syntactic feature). In the first sample, *Instruct* node with the syntactic feature *mill* was adjacent to *Question* node with the syntactic feature *picket*, other adjacent nodes without any syntactic feature was a positive feedback and an answer. Indicating that this example could possibly be a part of a navigation instruction, while the other dialogue seems to be a part of a chit-chat dialogue. For each example, each subsequent line represents the closest node while browsing the dendrogram from top to bottom if its vertically drawn. As it can be seen in these examples, the model doesn't predict the nodes to be in perfect pairs, hence highlighting that using adjacency pairs will be insufficient in extracting knowledge that is not distributed with-in pairs.

Three examples from the analysed dendrograms are presented in Table 5 representing the combination of features (dialogue control function and $tri-$gram syntactic feature). Also, for this case we manually labelled them with SE labels. The example number 1 seems to be about finding glasses, while the others indicate towards them being a part of a dialogue on machines and stealing of the jobs.

Sr.No	Feature Combination	Calinski Harabasz Index	Silhouette score	Cophnet score	Davies Bouldin
1.	DCF	*81333*	*0.77*	*0.40*	*0.35*
2.	DCF SS1	*3910*	*0.51*	***0.76***	*0.59*
3.	DCF SS2	***16454***	*0.60*	*0.56*	*0.54*
4.	DCF ST	***11002***	***0.73***	***0.80***	***0.20***
5.	DCF SS1 SS2	***22096***	***0.66***	***0.75***	*0.50*
6.	DCF ST SS1 SS2	*3550*	*0.60*	*0.64*	*0.56*

Table 3: Evaluation of HAC Model on eight combination of features with communication and syntax features.

S.No	Feature Combination	Sequence Expansion
1.	Positive feedback, uh huh	FPP_{pre}
	Instruct, mill	SPP_{pre}
	Check question, picket, fence	FPP_{base}
	Positive feedback, answer, picket	SPP_{base}
	Positive feedback, uh huh	FPP_{post}
2.	Inform, school	FPP_{pre}
	Question, kids	FPP_{base}
	Stalling, uh	FPP_{insert}

Table 4: Some clusters from HAC model for the combination of features *dialogue control functions and syntactic features*

Here, it can be found in Example 2 third line that there is no FPP_{base} for the SPP_{base}, indicating that the parts for the same pair (base, pre, post, insert) can sometimes be very far away or possibly the model places them far because of the dissimilarities between them.

The analysis also showed that among the syntactic features, $uni-$grams were present dominantly around 84% of the times, while $tri-$grams of subject-object-verb tuples constituted 50% of the segments and auxiliary verbs were 20% of the segments.

5 Conclusion, Discussion and Future Work

This work explored combination of features (syntactic features and dialogue control functions) in order to find sequences in dialogues, such that we can build NLU functions for capturing information distributed over turns longer than two for DMs to possibly conduct flexible dialogues. Dependency parsing was used for extracting syntactic features ($uni-$grams and $tri-$grams) and dialogue control functions were labelled manually using ISO $24617-2$ scheme. The feature transformation was done using tf-idf (when using only dialogue control function training the model), and GloVe embedding were used for combination of features (dialogue control functions and syntactic features), for both the cases feature selection was done with PCA. The selected features were modelled with hierarchical agglomerative clustering, the results validated our assumption that capturing longer sequences using syntactic features can provide knowledge that adjacency pairs would fall short in.

This work being at a preliminary stage doesn't provide any concrete solution yet for building flexible dialogue strategies and rich knowledge sources, however it can be seen as more of a proof-of-concept for using syntactic features and sequence expansion labels for dialogue sequencing. The benefit of using syntactic features is that they can be extracted automatically from the raw data and state-of-the-art methods are robust enough. This work explored tuples of syntactic features, instead trees or graphs must be explored. Syntactic features provides flexibility to a machine, in the sense that it can select and prioritise to accomplish a topic (objects, nouns, etc) depending on the goals and/or the domain it is employed for. For pronoun resolution, relationship between prior mentioned proper noun/s and incoming pronouns can be established

S.No	Feature Combination	Sequence Expansion
1.	Inform, cant see anything	FPP_{pre}
	Question, do you remember	FPP_{base}
	Inform, on the bedside	FPP_{insert}
	Inform, did't find glasses	SPP_{insert}
2.	Turn keep, don't you see	FPP_{insert}
	Confirm, they do not	SPP_{insert}
	Accept, machines steal jobs	SPP_{base}
	Inform, a set people	FPP_{pre}
3.	Retract, it does not, steals jobs	SPP_{base}
	Inform, machines	FPP_{pre}
	Question, work that does	FPP_{base}

Table 5: Selection of clusters from HAC model indicating sequence expansions for feature combination *dialogue control function and $tri-gram$ syntactic features.*

using extraction of uni-gram syntactic features delimited by SE labels. For managing multiple dialogue control functions, coordinating conjunctions and interjections can be used for identifying response generation.

This work also comes with its limitations, where the first is related to the corpus, which could be biased due to a large number of samples being synthetically prepared by the author. Another limitation is the size of the corpus. The author is currently working on both of these limitations and in the future we have planned to combine different genres of dialogues from publicly available sources. Another limitation of this work is that it doesn't use any dialogue features such as intents, semantics, context, etc. Other limitations include selection and model of the syntactic features, where some of the features such as auxiliary verbs should be dropped because of their low frequency, it could be also a bias from the corpus that was used. A common assumption that dialogues are about subjects objects and verbs could not be held by this work.

Whether dialogues are task-driven or open ended or chit-chat– one commonality is that they all are directed towards activities fulfilling human needs (both tangible or intangible) More abstract models such as BDI models (Rao et al., 1995) and/or Activity theory (Leontiev, 1978) should be considered and be complemented with syntactic and pragmatic features mentioned here.

6   Acknowledgement

I would like to thank Associate Prof. Suna Bensch at the Department of Computing Science, Umeå University, Umeå, Sweden for her intellectual contribution towards ideation and refining of the research work done in this article.

This work has received funding from the European Union's Horizon 2020 research and innovation programme under the Marie Skłodowska-Curie grant agreement No 721619 for the SOCRATES project.

References

Nicholas-Michael Asher and Alex Lascarides. 2003. *Motivating Rhetorical Relations*, chapter 1. Cambridge University Press.

Kristy Boyer, Robert Phillips, Young Ha Eun, Michael Wallis, Mladen Vouk, and James Lester. 2009. Modeling dialogue structure with adjacency pair analysis and hidden markov models. In *Proceedings of Human Language Technologies: The 2009 Annual Conference of the North American Chapter of the Association for Computational Linguistics, Companion Volume: Short Papers*, pages 49–52. ACL.

Harry Bunt. 1999. Dynamic interpretation and dialogue theory. *The structure of multimodal dialogue*, 2:1–8.

Harry Bunt, Volha Petukhova, Andrei Malchanau, Alex Chengyu Fang, and Kars Wijnhoven. 2019. The dialogbank: dialogues with interoperable annotations. *Language Resources and Evaluation*, 53:213–249.

Harry Bunt, Volha Petukhova, David Traum, and Jan Alexandersson. 2017. *Dialogue Act Annotation with the ISO 24617-2 Standard*, pages 109–135. Springer International Publishing.

Kenneth Church and William Gale. 1999. Inverse document frequency (idf): A measure of deviations from poisson. In *Natural language processing using very large corpora*, pages 283–295. Springer.

Nathan Duran and Steve Battle. 2018. Conversation analysis structured dialogue for multi-domain dialogue management. *DEXAHAI*, pages 1–4.

Sonal Gupta, Rushin Shah, Mrinal Mohit, Anuj Kumar, and Mike Lewis. 2018. Semantic parsing for task oriented dialog using hierarchical representations. In *Conference on Empirical Methods in Natural Language Processing (EMNLP)*, page 6, Belgium. ACL.

Ryuichiro Higashinaka, Funakoshi Kotaro, Inab Michimasa, Tsunomori Yuiko, Takahashi Tetsuro, and Kaji Nobuhiro. 2017. Overview of dialogue breakdown detection challenge 3. *Proceedings of Dialogue System Technology Challenge*, page 14.

Matthew Honnibal and Mark Johnson. 2015. An improved non-monotonic transition system for dependency parsing. In *Proceedings of the 2015 Conference on Empirical Methods in Natural Language Processing*, pages 1373–1378, Lisbon, Portugal. Association for Computational Linguistics.

Shengluan Hou, Shuhan Zhang, and Chaoqun Fei. 2020. Rhetorical structure theory: A comprehensive review of theory, parsing methods and applications. *Expert Systems with Applications*, 157:113421.

Hans Kamp, Josef Van Genabith, and Uwe Reyle. 2011. *Discourse Representation Theory*, pages 125–394. Springer Netherlands, Dordrecht.

Aleksei Nikolaevich Leontiev. 1978. *Activity, consciousness, and personality*. Prentice-Hall, Moscow, Russia.

Michael McTear, Zoriada Callejas, and Davis Griol. 2016. Towards a technology of conversation. In *The Conversational Interface*, chapter 3, pages 25–45. Springer.

Tomas Mikolov, Ilya Sutskever, Kai Chen, Greg S Corrado, and Jeffrey Dean. 2013. Distributed representations of words and phrases and their compositionality. In *Proceedings of the 26th International Conference on Neural Information Processing Systems - Volume 2*, NIPS'13, pages 3111–3119, USA. Curran Associates Inc.

Fionn Murtagh and Pedro Contreras. 2012. Algorithms for hierarchical clustering: an overview. *Wiley Interdisciplinary Reviews: Data Mining and Knowledge Discovery*, 2(1):86–97.

Asher Nicholas, Hunter Julie, Morey Mathieu, Benamara Farah, and Afantenos Stergos. 2016. Discourse Structure and Dialogue Acts in Multiparty Dialogue: the STAC Corpus. In *10th International Conference on Language Resources and Evaluation (LREC 2016)*, pages 2721–2727, Portoroz, Slovenia.

Manuel Palomar and Martínez-Barco Patricio. 2000. Anaphora resolution through dialogue adjacency pairs and topics. In *Natural Language Processing — NLP 2000*, pages 196–203, Berlin, Heidelberg. Springer Berlin Heidelberg.

Jeffrey Pennington, Richard Socher, and Christopher D Manning. 2014. Glove: Global vectors for word representation. In *Empirical Methods in Natural Language Processing (EMNLP)*, pages 1532–1543, Doha, Qatar. ACL.

Juan Ramos. 2003. Using tf-idf to determine word relevance in document queries. volume 242, pages 133–142.

Anand S Rao, Michael P Georgeff, et al. 1995. Bdi agents: from theory to practice. In *ICMAS*, volume 95, pages 312–319, USA. MIT Press.

Sinan Saraçli, Nurhan Doğan, and İsmet Doğan. 2013. Comparison of hierarchical cluster analysis methods by cophenetic correlation. In *Journal of Inequalities and Applications*, 1, page 203. SpringerOpen.

Emanuel A Schegloff and Harvey Sacks. 1973. Opening up closings. In *Semiotica*, volume 8, pages 289–327. Walter de Gruyter.

Weiyan Shi, Tiancheng Zhao, and Zhou Yu. 2019. Unsupervised dialog structure learning.

Jonathon Shlens. 2014. A tutorial on principal component analysis. *arXiv preprint arXiv:1404.1100*, page 12.

Jack Sidnell and Tanya Stivers. 2012. *The Handbook of Conversation Analysis*. Wiley-Blackwell, UK.

Amanda Stent. 2000. Rhetorical structure in dialog. In *In Proceedings of the 2nd International Natural Language Generation Conference (INLG'2000*, pages 247–252.

Tanya Stivers. 2012. Sequence organization. In *The Handbook of Conversation Analysis*, chapter 10, pages 191–209. Wiley-Blackwell, UK.

Maitreyee Tewari and Suna Bensch. 2018. Natural language communication with social robots for assisted living. In *IROS Workshop in Robots for Assisted Living*, pages 1–4, Madrid, Spain.

Ales Zacharie, Pauchet Alexandre, and Knippel Arnaud. 2018. Extraction and clustering of two-dimensional dialogue patterns. *International Journal on Artificial Intelligence Tools*, 27(02):1850001.

Using Type Information to Improve Entity Coreference Resolution

Sopan Khosla   **Carolyn Rose**

Language Technologies Institute
Carnegie Mellon University, USA

{sopank, cprose}@cs.cmu.edu

Abstract

Coreference resolution (CR) is an essential part of discourse analysis. Most recently, neural approaches have been proposed to improve over SOTA models from earlier paradigms. So far none of the published neural models leverage external semantic knowledge such as type information. This paper offers the first such model and evaluation, demonstrating modest gains in accuracy by introducing either gold standard or predicted types. In the proposed approach, type information serves both to (1) improve mention representation and (2) create a soft type consistency check between coreference candidate mentions. Our evaluation covers two different grain sizes of types over four different benchmark corpora.

1   Introduction

Coreference resolution (CR) is an extensively studied problem in computational linguistics and NLP (Hobbs, 1978; Lappin and Leass, 1994; Mitkov, 1999; Ng, 2017; Clark and Manning, 2016; Lee et al., 2017). Solutions to this problem allow us to make meaningful links between concepts and entities within a discourse and therefore serves as a valuable pre-processing step for downstream tasks like summarization and question-answering (Steinberger et al., 2007; Dasigi et al., 2019; Sukthanker et al., 2020a).

Recently, multiple datasets including Ontonotes (Pradhan et al., 2012), Litbank (Bamman et al., 2020), EmailCoref (Dakle et al., 2020), and WikiCoref (Ghaddar and Langlais, 2016) have been proposed as benchmark datasets for CR, especially in the sub-area of entity anaphora (Sukthanker et al., 2020b). Entity anaphora is a simpler starting place for work on anaphora because unlike abstract anaphora (Webber, 1991), entity anaphora are pronouns or noun phrases that refer to an explicitly mentioned entity in the discourse rather than an abstract idea that must be constructed from a repackaging of information revealed over an extended text. An affordance of entity anaphora is that they have easily articulated semantic types. Most of the entity CR datasets are extensively annotated for syntactic features (like constituency parse etc.)   and semantic features (like entity-types). However, none of the published SOTA methods (Lee et al., 2017; Joshi et al., 2019, 2020) explicitly leverage the type information.

In this paper, we present a proof of concept to portray the benefits of using type information in neural approaches for CR. Named entities are generally divided generically (e.g.   person, organization etc.)   or in a domain-specific manner (e.g. symptom, drug, test etc.). In this work, we consider CR datasets that contain generic entity-types. One challenge is that the different corpora do not utilize the same set of type tags. For example, OntoNotes includes 18 types while EmailCoref includes only 4. Thus, we evaluate the performance of the proposed modeling approach on each dataset both with the set of type tags germaine to the dataset as well as a common set of four basic types (person, org, location, facility) inspired from research on Named Entity Recognition (NER) (Tjong Kim Sang, 2002; Tjong Kim Sang and De Meulder, 2003).

Our motivation is similar to (Durrett and Klein, 2014), which used a structured CRF with hand-curated features to jointly-model the tasks of CR, entity typing, and entity linking. Their joint architecture showed an improved performance on CR over the independent baseline. However, our work differs from there's as we show the benefits of entity-type information in neural models that use contextualized representations like BERT (Peters et al., 2018). Some prior art (Petroni et al., 2019; Roberts et al., 2020) argues that contextual-

Proceedings of the First Workshop on Computational Approaches to Discourse, pages 20–31
Online, November 20, 2020. ©2020 Association for Computational Linguistics
https://doi.org/10.18653/v1/P17

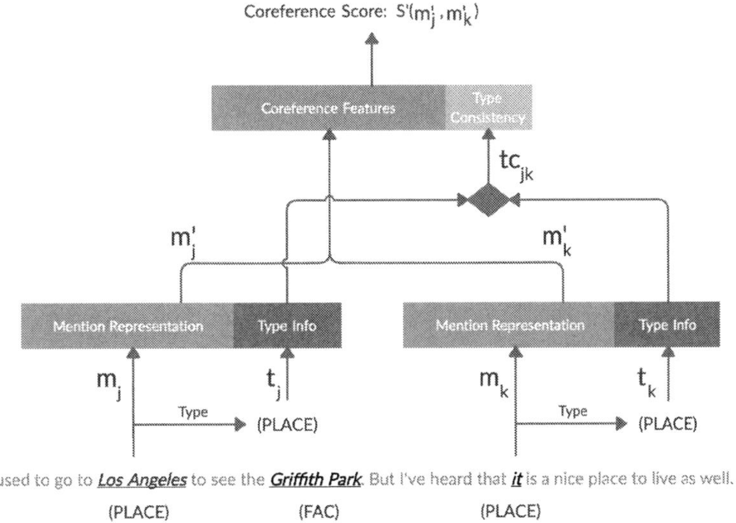

Figure 1: We improve Bamman et al. (2020) for entity coreference resolution by incorporating type information at two levels. (1) Type information is concatenated with the mention span representation created by their model; and (2) A consistency check is incorporated that compares the types of two mentions under consideration to calculate the coreference score. Please refer to Section 3 for details.

ized embeddings implicitly capture facts and relationships between real-world entities. However, in this work, we empirically show that access to explicit knowledge about entity-types benefits neural models that use BERT for CR. We show a consistent improvement in performance on four different coreference datasets from varied domains.

Our contribution is that we evaluate the impact of the introduction of type information in neural entity coreference at two different levels of granularity (which we refer to as original vs common), demonstrating their utility both in the case where gold standard type information is available, and the more typical case where it is predicted.

2 Related Work

Neural Coreference Resolution: Recently, neural approaches to coreference (Joshi et al., 2020, 2019; Lee et al., 2018, 2017) have begun to show their prowess. The SOTA models show impressive performance on state-of-the-art datasets like OntoNotes (Pradhan et al., 2012) and GAP (Webster et al., 2018). The notable architecture proposed by Lee et al. (2017) scores pairs of entity mentions independently and later uses a clustering algorithm to find coreference clusters. On the other hand, Lee et al. (2018) improve upon this foundation by introducing an approximated higher-order inference that iteratively updates the existing span representation using its antecedent distribution. Moreover, they propose a coarse-to-fine grained approach to pairwise scoring for tackling the computational challenges caused due to the iterative higher-order inference. More recently, Joshi et al. (2019, 2020) showed that use of contextual representations instead of word-embeddings like GloVe (Pennington et al., 2014) can further boost the results over and above those just mentioned. Our work offers additional improvement by building on the model proposed in Bamman et al. (2020), which is based on Lee et al. (2017), and adds additional nuanced information grounded in semantic types.

Type Information: Named Entity Recognition datasets (Tjong Kim Sang, 2002; Tjong Kim Sang and De Meulder, 2003; Li et al., 2016) often group entity mentions into different types (or categories) depending on the domain and the potential downstream applications of the corpus. For example, the medical corpus used in the i2b2 Challenge 2010 (Uzuner et al., 2011) annotates domain-specific types like *problem*, *test*, *symptom* etc., whereas, a more general-domain dataset like CoNLL-2002 (Tjong Kim Sang, 2002) uses generic types like *person*, *organization*, and *location*. Type information as a predictive signal has been shown to be beneficial for NLP tasks like relation extraction (Soares et al., 2019) and entity-linking (Chen et al., 2020). It affords some level of disambiguation, which assists models with filtering out some incorrect predictions in order to increase the probability of a correct prediction. In this work, we evaluate the benefits of using explicit type information for CR. We show that a model that leverages entity types associated with the anaphoric/ antecedent mentions significantly reduces the problem of type inconsistency in the output coreference clusters and thus improves the overall performance of the neural baseline on four datasets.

Type Information for CR: Multiple prior works have shown type-information to be a useful feature for shallow coreference resolution classifiers (Soon et al., 2001; Bengtson and Roth, 2008; Ponzetto and Strube, 2006; Haghighi and Klein, 2010; Durrett and Klein, 2014). (Soon et al., 2001) take the most frequent sense for each noun in WordNet as the semantic class for that noun and use a decision-tree for pairwise classification of whether two samples co-refer each other. (Bengtson and Roth, 2008) use a hypernym tree to extract the type information for different common nouns, and compare the proper names against a predefined list to determine if the mention is a person. They, then, pass this and many other features (like distance, agreement, etc.) through a regularized average perceptron for pairwise classification. This paper expands on these studies to show that entity-type information is also beneficial for neural models that use contextualized representations like BERT (Peters et al., 2018), which have been argued to implicitly capture facts and relationships between real-world entities (Petroni et al., 2019; Roberts et al., 2020).

3 Model

In this section, we explain how we introduce type information into a neural CR system.

3.1 Baseline

We use the model proposed in Bamman et al. (2020) as our baseline. The model gives state-of-the-art scores on the LitBank corpus (Bamman et al., 2020) and is an end-to-end mention ranking system based on Lee et al. (2017), which has shown competitive performance on the OntoNotes dataset. However, this model differs from Lee et al. (2017) as it uses BERT embeddings, omits author and genre information, and only focuses on the task of mention-linking. Since our main

goal is to evaluate the benefits of type information, we too separate mention-linking from mention-identification and only show results computed over gold-standard mentions. This controls for the effects of the mention-identification module's performance on our experiments. Impact of type-information incorporation in the real-world end-to-end CR setting (mention identification + linking) is left as future work.

The BERT embeddings for each token i are passed through a bi-directional LSTM (x_i). To represent a mention m with start and end positions s, e respectively, x_s, x_e, attention over $x_s, ..., x_e$, and features to represent the width (wi) and inclusion within quotations (qu) are concatenated.

$$m = [x_s; x_e; Att(x_s, .., x_e); wi; qu] \quad (1)$$

Finally, given the representation of two mentions m_j and m_k, their coreference score $\mathbf{S}(m_j, m_k)$ is computed by concatenating $m_j, m_k, m_j \odot m_k$, distance (d) between the mentions and whether one mention is nested (n) within the other, which are then passed through fully-connected layers ($\mathbf{FC}$).

$$\mathbf{S}(m_j, m_k) = \mathbf{FC}([m_j; m_k; m_j \odot m_k; d; n]) \quad (2)$$

We refer the reader to (Bamman et al., 2020; Lee et al., 2017) for more details about the architecture.

3.2 Entity Type Information

We improve the above model by including entity-type information on two levels (Figure 1). First, we concatenate the entity-type t of the mention to m (in Eq. 1) to improve the mention representation.

$$m' = [m; t] \quad (3)$$

This allows the model access to the entity type of the mention as an additional feature. We call this **+ET-self**. Second, to check the type consistency (softly) between any two mentions under consideration as possibly coreferent, we append a feature (tc) in Eq. 2, which takes the value 0 if both mentions have the same type, and 1 otherwise. For example, in Figure 1, since *Los Angeles* and *it* have the same entity-type PLACE, $tc_{jk} = 0$.

$$\mathbf{S}'(m'_j, m'_k) = \mathbf{FC}([m'_j; m'_k; m'_j \odot m'_k; d; n; tc_{jk}]) \quad (4)$$

This part of the approach is referred to as **+ET-cross** throughout the remainder of the paper. We decide against the use of a hard consistency check (which would filter out mentions which do not have the same type) as it might not generalize well to bridging anaphora (Clark, 1975) where the anaphor refers to an object that is associated with, but not identical to, the antecedent (Poesio et al., 2018). In such cases, the type of the anaphora and its antecedent may not match. Finally, our architecture combines both components together as **+ET** (ET = ET-self + ET-cross).

4 Datasets

We gauge the benefits of using entity-type information on the four datasets discussed below.

LitBank. This dataset (Bamman et al., 2020) contains coreference annotations for 100 literary texts.[1] This dataset limits the markable mentions to six entity-types, where majority of the mentions (83.1%) point to a person.

EmailCoref. This dataset (Dakle et al., 2020) comprises of 46 email threads with a total of 245 email messages.[2] Similar to LitBank, it considers a mention to be a span of text that refers to a real-world entity. In this work, we filter out pronouns that point towards multiple entities in the email (e.g. we, they) thus only focusing on singular mentions.

Ontonotes. From this multi-lingual dataset, we evaluate on the subset (english) from OntoNotes that was used in the CoNLL-2012 shared task (Pradhan et al., 2012).[3] It contains 2802 training, 343 development, and 348 test documents. The dataset differs from LitBank in its annotation scheme with the biggest difference being the fact that it does not annotate singletons.

It contains annotations for 18 different entity-types. However, unlike LitBank and EmailCoref, not all mentions have an associated entity-type. For example, none of the pronoun mentions are given a type even if they act as anaphors to typed entities. We partially ameliorate this issue by extracting gold coreference clusters that contain at least one typed mention and assigning the majority type in that cluster to all of its elements. For example, in Figure 1, if *Los Angeles* is typed PLACE, and *it* is in the gold coreference cluster of *Los Angeles* (no other element in the cluster), then *it* is also assigned the type PLACE.

Dataset	#Types	Categories
LitBank	6	PER, LOC, FAC, GPE, VEH, ORG
EmailCoref	4	PER, ORG, LOC, DIG
WikiCoref	8	ORG, PER, CORP, EVENT, PLACE, THING, OTHER, NA
OntoNotes	19	ORG, WOA, LOC, CARD, EVENT, NORP, GPE, DATE, PER, FAC, QUANT, ORD, TIME, PROD, PERC, MON, LAW, LANG, NA
Common	5	PER, ORG, LOC, FAC, OTHER

Table 1: Type statistics for corpora used in this study.

WikiCoref. This corpus, released by (Ghaddar and Langlais, 2016), comprises 30 documents from wikipedia annotated for coreference resolution.[4] The annotations contain additional metadata, like the associated freebase rdf link for each mention (if available). We use this rdf entry to extract the mention's entity types from freebase dump. Mentions that do not get any type are marked *NA*. The first 24 documents are chosen for training, the next 3 for development, and the rest for testing.

The above-discussed datasets differ in the number as well as the categories of entity-types they originally annotate (Table 1). Apart from a common list of types (like PER, ORG, LOC), they also include corpus-specific categories like DIGital (EmailCoref), MONey, and LANG (OntoNotes). We carry out experiments with two sets of types – original and common – for each dataset. The common set of types include the following 5 categories: PER, ORG, LOC, FAC, OTHER.

5 Experiments and Results

In this section, we provide the results of our empirical experiments.

Evaluation Metrics: We convert all three datasets into the CoNLL 2012 format and report the F1 score for MUC, B^3, and CEAF metrics using the CoNLL-2012 official scripts. The performances are compared on the average F1 of the above-mentioned metrics.

For EmailCoref, OntoNotes, and WikiCoref, we report the mean score of 5 independent runs of the model with different seeds. Whereas, for LitBank, we present the 10-fold cross-validation results.[5]

---

[1] https://github.com/dbamman/lrec2020-coref
[2] https://github.com/paragdakle/emailcoref
[3] https://catalog.ldc.upenn.edu/LDC2013T19

[4] http://rali.iro.umontreal.ca/rali/?q=en/wikicoref
[5] Hyperparameter values are provided in Appendix A.

Model	B^3	MUC	CEAFE	Avg. F1	#IC
LitBank (Bamman et al., 2020)					
Baseline	72.7	88.5	76.7	79.30	26
+ ET (orig)	**74.1**	**89.2**	**77.5**	**80.26**	**5**
+ ET (com)	73.3	89.1	77.5	79.97	13
EmailCoref (Dakle et al., 2020)					
Baseline	72.8	84.5	62.7	73.33	9
+ ET (orig)	**74.9**	86.7	**66.9**	**76.17**	**0**
+ ET (com)	74.8	**86.8**	66.7	76.10	2
WikiCoref (Ghaddar and Langlais, 2016)					
Baseline	70.7	80.0	54.7	68.45	133
+ ET (orig)	73.0	**82.8**	**58.3**	**71.35**	**70**
+ ET (com)	**73.4**	80.7	55.1	69.71	94
OntoNotes (Pradhan et al., 2012)					
Baseline	82.3	90.8	77.1	83.36	60
+ ET (orig)	84.4	**92.9**	**79.9**	**85.76**	**44**
+ ET (com)	**84.6**	92.6	79.8	85.68	46

Table 2: CR results with entity-type information (gold mentions). **IC** = Impure Clusters.

5.1 Performance with Original Types

In order to establish an upper bound for improvement through introduction of type information, our first experiment leverages the original list of entity-types annotated in different corpora (**+ ET (orig)**), using the gold standard labels for types. Inclusion of entity-type information improves over the baseline for all CR datasets. Table 2 presents the performance of the baseline model and the model with entity-type information.

We find that entity-type information gives a boost of 0.96 Avg. F1 ($p < 0.01$) on LitBank which is the new state-of-the-art score with gold-mentions. This suggests that type information is helpful for CR on LitBank despite the heavily skewed distribution of entity-types in this corpus. Similarly, type information also benefits Email-Coref and WikiCoref resulting in an absolute improvement of 1.67 and 2.9 Avg. F1 points respectively ($p < 0.01$). We also see a 2.4 Avg. F1 improvement ($p < 0.01$) on OntoNotes, the largest dataset in this study. This suggests that explicit access to type information is beneficial all over the board, despite the use of contextual representations which have been claimed to model real-world facts and relationships (Petroni et al., 2019).

Ablation Results: To understand the contribution of the inclusion of type information to improve mention representation (+ET-self) and type consistency check between candidate mentions (+ET-

Dataset	Baseline	+ ET-self	+ ET-cross	+ ET (orig)
LitBank	79.30	79.97	79.76	**80.26**
EmailCoref	73.33	73.98	74.32	**76.17**
WikiCoref	68.45	70.89	70.71	**71.35**
OntoNotes	83.36	85.55	85.69	**85.76**

Table 3: Ablation results (**ET = ET-self + ET-cross**).

cross), we perform an ablation study (Table 3). We find that both components consistently provide significant performance boosts over the baseline. However, their combination (+ET) performs the best across all datasets.

5.2 Performance with Common Types

The previous experiment leverages the original entity-types assigned by dataset annotators. Due to the differences in domain and annotation guidelines among these datasets, the annotators introduce several domain-specific entity types (e.g. DIGital, Work Of Art etc.) apart from the common four (PERson, ORGanization, LOCation, FACility) that are often used in the Named Entity Recognition literature (Tjong Kim Sang, 2002). The former can prove to be much more difficult to obtain/ learn due to dearth of relevant data. Therefore, to assess the worth of using a common entity-type list for all datasets, we map the original types (Table 1) to the above-mentioned four common types. [6] Categories that do not map to any common type are assigned *Other*. **+ET (com)** rows in Table 2 show the results for this experiment. Models trained with common types as features perform worse than **+ET (orig)** which was expected as several original types are now clubbed into a single category (e.g. LAW -> OTHER, LANG -> OTHER) thus somewhat reducing the effectiveness of the feature. One surprising observation is the small difference between the performance on OntoNotes dataset, despite the fact that the number of type categories reduce from 18 + Other (**+ET (orig)**) to 4 + Other (**+ET (com)**). This could either be because (1) the entities with corpus-specific types occur less frequently in Ontonotes, or (2) the baseline model does a good job in resolving them. Further research is required to understand this case which is out of scope for this work.

---

[6]We provide the mapping between the original types and the common types in Appendix B.

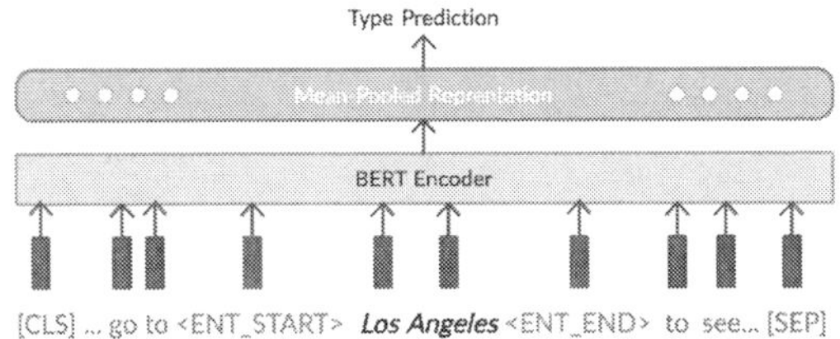

Figure 2: Type-prediction model.

5.3 # Impure Clusters (#IC)

Our hypothesis around the use of entity-types was to provide additional information to the model that could be leveraged to minimize errors due to type mismatch in CR. To evaluate if the F1 score improvements achieved by **+ET** models are because of fewer type mismatch errors, we report the number of coreference clusters detected by the model that contain at least one element with a type that is different from the others in the cluster. Since all of the datasets used in this work only consider identity coreferences (Recasens et al., 2011) - with potentially varied definitions of identity (Bamman et al., 2020; Pradhan et al., 2012) - where the mention is a linguistic "re-packaging" of its antecedent, this measure makes sense. As shown in Table 2, the models that score lower on the impurity measure get a higher Avg F1. This suggests that the aggregate performance improvements are at least partly due to the better mention-mention comparison in **+ET** systems.

6 Predicted Types

Results shown in the previous section assume the presence of gold standard types during training as well as inference, which is often impractical in the real-world. Most of the new samples that a CR model would encounter would not include type information about the candidate mentions. Therefore, we set up an additional experiment to gauge the benefits of type information using predicted types. We introduce a baseline approach to infer the type of the mentions and then use these predictions in the +ET models, in place of the gold types, for coreference resolution.

6.1 Type Prediction Model

Given the mention and its immediate context, i.e. the sentence it occurs in ($S = ..., c_{-2}, c_{-1}, \mathbf{e_1}, \mathbf{e_2}, ..., \mathbf{e_n}, c_1, c_2, ...$), we add markers <ENT_START>/ <ENT_END>

before/ after the beginning/ ending of the mention in the sentence. The new sequence ($S' = ..., c_{-2}, c_{-1},$ <ENT_START>, $\mathbf{e_1}, \mathbf{e_2}, ..., \mathbf{e_n},$ <ENT_END>, $c_1, c_2, ...$) is tokenized using BERT tokenizer and passed through the BERT encoder. The output from which is then mean-pooled and passed through a fully-connected layer for classification. This architecture is motivated from (Soares et al., 2019) who show that adding markers around entities before passing the sentence through BERT performs better for relation extraction.

6.2 Experiments and Results

Type Prediction: Our final evaluation of the use of types in coreference is perhaps the most important one as it uses predicted types rather than annotated types, thus demonstrating that the benefits can be achieved in practice. Here we use the Type Prediction Model described just above. We limit the length of the input sequence to 128 tokens and use BERT-base-cased model for our type-prediction experiments. We perform a five-fold cross-validation to predict the type for each mention in the dataset. Since all four datasets suffer from class-imbalance, we report both Macro F1 score as well as the accuracy for the model. The model is trained for 20 epochs, with early-stopping (patience = 10), and is fine-tuned on the development set for Macro F1 to give more importance to minority type categories. We do not consider NA as a separate class during type prediction for WikiCoref and OntoNotes. For evaluation of our type-prediction model, we ignore the mentions that do not have an associated gold type (NA) from the final numbers in Table 4.

As shown, our model performs well on Lit-Bank, EmailCoref, and Ontonotes due to their favorable size in terms of training samples for the BERT-based type predictor. WikiCoref, however, proves more challenging as the model only manages 38.0 Macro F1 points with original (orig) types and 45.0 with common types (com), portraying its lack of ability to learn minority type categories with less data. Furthermore, our model finds it easier to predict the common (com) set of types for each dataset as combining multiple corpus-specific types into one partially alleviates the problem of class-imbalance. In line with our expectation, the largest improvement due to common types is seen for OntoNotes where the prob-

Dataset (Types)	Macro F1	Accuracy					
	All	All	PRP (dem.)	PRP (pers.)	NP (len = 1)	NP (len = 2)	NP (len > 2)
LitBank (orig)	84.0	97.0	70.5 (207)	99.75 (6127)	96.5 (6477)	95.8 (5439)	94.03 (4443)
LitBank (com)	87.0	97.0	72.5 (207)	99.8 (6127)	97.2 (6477)	96.7 (5439)	94.8 (4443)
EmailCoref (orig)	83.0	91.0	77.1 (35)	83.8 (482)	93.6 (1635)	91.3 (484)	94.1 (1058)
EmailCoref (com)	85.0	92.0	65.7 (35)	84.6 (482)	93.5 (1635)	90.3 (484)	95.5 (1058)
WikiCoref (orig)	38.0	61.0	53.3 (75)	59.4 (340)	58.9 (1531)	55.1 (1223)	54.5 (1218)
WikiCoref (com)	45.0	74.0	82.7 (75)	56.5 (340)	64.3 (1531)	69.2 (1223)	68.7 (1218)
OntoNotes (orig)	74.0	95.0	80.2 (1698)	94.6 (8682)	96.2 (21589)	95.5 (13297)	94.0 (11951)
OntoNotes (com)	90.0	96.0	84.5 (1698)	94.3 (8682)	96.9 (21589)	96.4 (13297)	95.0 (11951)

Table 4: Performance of our BERT-based model for type-prediction. The last five columns show the accuracy (# samples) on demonstrative and personal pronouns, and noun phrases of different lengths. **PRP (dem.)** = Demonstrative Pronouns (this, that, it, these, those), **PRP (pers.)** = Personal Pronouns (she, he, they, me, you, we). The scores for WikiCoref and OntoNotes do not include mentions without an associated gold type (*NA*).

Dataset	Baseline	+ ET-pred (orig)	+ ET-pred (com)
LitBank	79.30	**79.58**	79.40
EmailCoref	73.33	**74.20**	**74.18**
WikiCoref	68.45	68.37	68.62
OntoNotes	83.36	**84.02**	83.65

Table 5: CR results with predicted types. Numbers in **bold** are significantly better ($p < 0.01$) than the baseline.

lem reduces from an 18-way classification to a 5-way classification.

Coreference Resolution: Each mention in the corpus occurs in the test-sets of the five-fold cross-validation type-prediction experiments exactly once. This allows us to infer the type of each mention using the model that is trained on a different subset of the dataset. These inferred types are used in the training and testing of the CR systems in a manner similar to the annotated types.

Empirically, we found that the above configuration performs better than using the **+ET** models trained with annotated types and testing with predicted types, as the former exposes the CR models to the noisy types during training thus allowing them to learn weights that take this noise into account. We report the results for both original (**+ ET-pred (orig)**) and common (**+ ET-pred (com)**) type categories on each dataset.

Table 5 shows the results for performance of the baseline and the type-informed models on the four datasets, where the types are inferred from the model described in Section 6.1. We find that the improvements from type-information persist across LitBank, EmailCoref, and OntoNotes despite the use of predicted types, but, quite expectedly, remain smaller than the improvements from the gold annotated types. Scores on WikiCoref show no significant improvement over the baseline, which could be explained by the poor performance of the type prediction model on this dataset which reduces the potency of the feature for CR.

7 Discussion

7.1 Genres of OntoNotes

Table 6 shows the most frequently occurring entity-types for each of the genres in OntoNotes. In line with our intuition, we find that enity-type information helps the baseline in *bc*, *bn*, *wb*, and *mz* genres which have less skew in their entity-type distribution. Genres like *bc*, *bn* and *wb*, although dominated by PER entities, contain a substantial minority of other entity-types like ORG and GPE. Along the same lines, *mz* contains a majority of GPE entities but also enough entities with type PER and ORG to make type information a potentially useful feature for CR. However, two exceptions to this are the improved performance of **+ET** **(orig)** on *tc* (highest skew) and no significant improvement on *nw* (lowest skew). These findings prompt further research in the future.

7.2 Type Prediction: PRP vs NP

Entity coreference in discourse often takes the surface form of pronouns (PRP) (like she, they, that, it etc.) or noun phrases (NP) (like LA, John's brother etc.) In Table 4, we compare the performance of our type prediction model on different types of pronouns, and noun phrases of varying length. We find that the model does well in predicting types for personal pronouns (PRP (pers.)) like *she*, *he* and noun phrases (NP). However, it consistently underperforms on demonstrative pro-

Genre	Baseline	+ET (orig)	Most Frequent Entity-Types (Ratio)
tc	81.15	**85.97**	PER (0.839), GPE (0.083)
bc	79.66	**83.25**	PER (0.456), GPE (0.277), NORP (0.098), ORG (0.089)
nw	84.91	85.26	ORG (0.411), GPE (0.232), PER (0.161), DATE (0.132)
pt	84.7	85.66	-
bn	84.22	**87.46**	PER (0.484), GPE (0.237), ORG (0.132), DATE (0.052)
wb	80.57	**83.52**	PER (0.744), GPE (0.130), ORG (0.092)
mz	89.21	**91.92**	GPE (0.513), PER (0.273), ORG (0.198)

Table 6: Type Distribution (excluding OTHER) for mentions within different Ontonotes genres after clustering based type-propagation. Numbers in **bold** are significantly better than the baseline ($p < 0.01$). - represents that none of the mentions in the genre are annotated with types.

	Example
Gold	Hi Chris **(0)** , I **(1)** will have {Tamara Utsch} **(2)** reply to you **(0)** on your **(0)** refund - I **(1)** believe she **(2)** updated you **(0)** last week , but we **(3)** 'll see if there 's new news this week . Can you **(0)** please send me **(1)** {your **(0)** current home address} **(4)** so we **(3)** can send you **(0)** {an organizer} **(5)** ? Thanks , {Judy Perdomo} **(1)** {PricewaterhouseCoopers Calgary} **(3)**
Baseline	Hi Chris **(0)** , I **(1)** will have {Tamara Utsch} **(2)** reply to you **(0)** on your **(0)** refund - I **(1)** believe she **(2)** updated you **(0)** last week , but we **(3)** 'll see if there 's new news this week . Can you **(0)** please send me **(1)** {your **(0)** current home address} **(4)** so we **(3)** can send you **(0)** {an organizer} *(4)* ? Thanks , {Judy Perdomo} **(1)** {PricewaterhouseCoopers Calgary} *(6)*
+ ET (orig)	Hi Chris **(0)** , I **(1)** will have {Tamara Utsch} **(2)** reply to you **(0)** on your **(0)** refund - I **(1)** believe she **(2)** updated you **(0)** last week , but we **(3)** 'll see if there 's new news this week . Can you **(0)** please send me **(1)** {your **(0)** current home address} **(4)** so we **(3)** can send you **(0)** {an organizer} **(5)** ? Thanks , {Judy Perdomo} **(1)** {PricewaterhouseCoopers Calgary} **(3)**
+ ET (com)	Hi Chris **(0)** , I **(1)** will have {Tamara Utsch} **(2)** reply to you **(0)** on your **(0)** refund - I **(1)** believe she **(2)** updated you **(0)** last week , but we **(3)** 'll see if there 's new news this week . Can you **(0)** please send me **(1)** {your **(0)** current home address} **(4)** so we **(3)** can send you **(0)** {an organizer} **(5)** ? Thanks , {Judy Perdomo} **(1)** {PricewaterhouseCoopers Calgary} **(3)**
+ ET-pred (orig)	Hi Chris **(0)** , I **(1)** will have {Tamara Utsch} **(2)** reply to you **(0)** on your **(0)** refund - I **(1)** believe she **(2)** updated you **(0)** last week , but we **(3)** 'll see if there 's new news this week . Can you **(0)** please send me **(1)** {your **(0)** current home address} **(4)** so we **(3)** can send you **(0)** {an organizer} **(5)** ? Thanks , {Judy Perdomo} **(1)** {PricewaterhouseCoopers Calgary} *(6)*

Table 7: An example email from EmailCoref corpus. Numbers in round brackets denote the cluster number of the mention. Red denotes incorrect predictions.

nouns (PRP (dem.)) like *this*, *that*, and *it* across all datasets.

This reduced performance could be due to the fact that demonstrative pronouns do not contain any signal about the type of the entity they refer to. Therefore, the type prediction model has to solely rely on the context to make that decision. However, this is not the case with PRPs (pers.) and NPs where the mention string is usually a strong indicator of the type. This problem is worsened by the imbalance due to the small presence of PRP (dem.) mentions in difference CR datasets. Since, the model does not encounter enough PRPs (dem.), it might not be able to learn to give high importance to context in these cases.

This could be partially alleviated by creating a separate type-prediction path for PRP (dem.) where the mention span is masked before it is passed through the model. A model that is trained with masked mentions would focus more on the context for type prediction and thus could lead to better performance on PRPs (dem.).

One could also experiment with training the type-prediction model on all of the mentions across the four datasets. The common list of types introduced in this work would allow for the creation of a larger training-set that includes mentions from multiple corpora (including external NER datasets) which could provide enough signal for the model to better learn the common types for PRPs (dem.).

Both these approaches could further boost the

results for CR with predicted entity-types, ultimately, reducing the gap between the scores in Table 2 and 5. However, they are left as future work as they are out of scope for this paper.

7.3 Case Study

Table 7 provides an excerpt of an email from EmailCoref corpus. As shown, the baseline model predicts the coreference clusters for *an organizer* (DIG) and *PricewaterhouseCoopers Calgary* (ORG) incorrectly. For the former, the model mistakes it as a reference to *your current home address* (LOC) which is corrected by the entity-type aware models. For the latter, the baseline considers *PricewaterhouseCoopers Calgary (PCC)* as part of a new coreference cluster, even though it refers to the organization of the email's sender which was previously referred to as *we* in the email. Models with access to gold type information (+ET (orig) and +ET (com)) are able to make that connection.

+ET-pred (orig), however, is unable to cluster *PCC* correctly which could be due to the fact that the type-prediction model incorrectly classifies the type of *we* as PER rather than ORG. This could lead to the CR model considering *PCC* (ORG) as a new entity in the discourse rather than a postcedent of *we*. This example demonstrates that sentence-level context might not be sufficient in some cases for mention type-disambiguation. We intend to experiment with models that capture long-term context and leverage external knowledge in the future.

8 Conclusion

In this work, we show the importance of using entity-type information in neural coreference resolution (CR) models with contextualized embeddings like BERT. Models which leverage type information, annotated in the corpus, substantially outperform the baseline on four CR datasets by reducing the number of type mismatches in detected coreference clusters. Since, these datasets vary in number and categories of the types they define, we also experiment with mapping the original corpus types to four common types (PER, ORG, LOC, FAC) based on previous NER research that can be learnt more easily through large NER datasets. Models which use these common types perform slightly worse than original types but still show significant improvements over the baseline systems.

The presence of gold standard types during CR inference is unlikely in practice. Therefore, we propose a model that infers the type of a mention given the mention span and its immediate context to use along side the proposed CR approach. In our evaluation, we find that using types predicted by our model for CR still performs significantly better than the baseline, thus offering stronger evidence that type information holds the potential for practical improvements for CR.

Acknowledgements

We thank the anonymous reviewers for their insightful comments. We are also grateful to the members of the TELEDIA group at LTI, CMU for the invaluable feedback. This work was funded in part by Dow Chemical, and Microsoft.

References

David Bamman, Olivia Lewke, and Anya Mansoor. 2020. An annotated dataset of coreference in english literature. In *Proceedings of The 12th Language Resources and Evaluation Conference*, pages 44–54.

Eric Bengtson and Dan Roth. 2008. Understanding the value of features for coreference resolution. In *Proceedings of the 2008 Conference on Empirical Methods in Natural Language Processing*, pages 294–303.

Shuang Chen, Jinpeng Wang, Feng Jiang, and Chin-Yew Lin. 2020. Improving entity linking by modeling latent entity type information. *arXiv preprint arXiv:2001.01447*.

H. H. Clark. 1975. Bridging. In *Proceedings of TIN-LAP*.

Kevin Clark and Christopher D Manning. 2016. Deep reinforcement learning for mention-ranking coreference models. In *Proceedings of the 2016 Conference on Empirical Methods in Natural Language Processing*, pages 2256–2262.

Parag Pravin Dakle, Takshak Desai, and Dan Moldovan. 2020. A study on entity resolution for email conversations. In *Proceedings of The 12th Language Resources and Evaluation Conference*, pages 65–73.

Pradeep Dasigi, Nelson F. Liu, Ana Marasović, Noah A. Smith, and Matt Gardner. 2019. Quoref: A reading comprehension dataset with questions requiring coreferential reasoning. In *Proc. of EMNLP-IJCNLP*.

Greg Durrett and Dan Klein. 2014. A joint model for entity analysis: Coreference, typing, and linking. *Transactions of the Association for Computational Linguistics*, 2:477–490.

Abbas Ghaddar and Philippe Langlais. 2016. Wikicoref: An english coreference-annotated corpus of wikipedia articles. In *Proceedings of the Tenth International Conference on Language Resources and Evaluation (LREC'16)*, pages 136–142.

Aria Haghighi and Dan Klein. 2010. Coreference resolution in a modular, entity-centered model. In *Human Language Technologies: The 2010 Annual Conference of the North American Chapter of the Association for Computational Linguistics*, pages 385–393.

Jerry R Hobbs. 1978. Resolving pronoun references. *Lingua*, 44(4):311–338.

Mandar Joshi, Danqi Chen, Yinhan Liu, Daniel S Weld, Luke Zettlemoyer, and Omer Levy. 2020. Spanbert: Improving pre-training by representing and predicting spans. *Transactions of the Association for Computational Linguistics*, 8:64–77.

Mandar Joshi, Omer Levy, Luke Zettlemoyer, and Daniel S Weld. 2019. Bert for coreference resolution: Baselines and analysis. In *Proceedings of the 2019 Conference on Empirical Methods in Natural Language Processing and the 9th International Joint Conference on Natural Language Processing (EMNLP-IJCNLP)*, pages 5807–5812.

Shalom Lappin and Herbert J Leass. 1994. An algorithm for pronominal anaphora resolution. *Computational linguistics*, 20(4):535–561.

Kenton Lee, Luheng He, Mike Lewis, and Luke Zettlemoyer. 2017. End-to-end neural coreference resolution. In *Proceedings of the 2017 Conference on Empirical Methods in Natural Language Processing*, pages 188–197.

Kenton Lee, Luheng He, and Luke Zettlemoyer. 2018. Higher-order coreference resolution with coarse-to-fine inference. In *Proceedings of the 2018 Conference of the North American Chapter of the Association for Computational Linguistics: Human Language Technologies, Volume 2 (Short Papers)*, pages 687–692.

Jiao Li, Yueping Sun, Robin J Johnson, Daniela Sciaky, Chih-Hsuan Wei, Robert Leaman, Allan Peter Davis, Carolyn J Mattingly, Thomas C Wiegers, and Zhiyong Lu. 2016. Biocreative v cdr task corpus: a resource for chemical disease relation extraction. *Database*, 2016.

Ruslan Mitkov. 1999. *Anaphora resolution: the state of the art*. Citeseer.

Vincent Ng. 2017. Machine learning for entity coreference resolution: A retrospective look at two decades of research. In *Thirty-First AAAI Conference on Artificial Intelligence*.

Jeffrey Pennington, Richard Socher, and Christopher D Manning. 2014. Glove: Global vectors for word representation. In *Proceedings of the 2014 conference on empirical methods in natural language processing (EMNLP)*, pages 1532–1543.

Matthew Peters, Mark Neumann, Mohit Iyyer, Matt Gardner, Christopher Clark, Kenton Lee, and Luke Zettlemoyer. 2018. Deep contextualized word representations. In *Proceedings of the 2018 Conference of the North American Chapter of the Association for Computational Linguistics: Human Language Technologies, Volume 1 (Long Papers)*, pages 2227–2237.

Fabio Petroni, Tim Rocktäschel, Sebastian Riedel, Patrick Lewis, Anton Bakhtin, Yuxiang Wu, and Alexander Miller. 2019. Language models as knowledge bases? In *Proceedings of the 2019 Conference on Empirical Methods in Natural Language Processing and the 9th International Joint Conference on Natural Language Processing (EMNLP-IJCNLP)*, pages 2463–2473.

Massimo Poesio, Yulia Grishina, Varada Kolhatkar, Nafise Sadat Moosavi, Ina Roesiger, Adam Roussel, Fabian Simonjetz, Alexandra Uma, Olga Uryupina, Juntao Yu, et al. 2018. Anaphora resolution with the arrau corpus. In *Proceedings of the First Workshop on Computational Models of Reference, Anaphora and Coreference*, pages 11–22.

Simone Paolo Ponzetto and Michael Strube. 2006. Exploiting semantic role labeling, wordnet and wikipedia for coreference resolution. In *Proceedings of the Human Language Technology Conference of the NAACL, Main Conference*, pages 192–199.

Sameer Pradhan, Alessandro Moschitti, Nianwen Xue, Olga Uryupina, and Yuchen Zhang. 2012. Conll-2012 shared task: Modeling multilingual unrestricted coreference in ontonotes. In *Joint Conference on EMNLP and CoNLL - Shared Task*, CoNLL '12, page 1–40, USA. Association for Computational Linguistics.

Marta Recasens, Eduard Hovy, and M Antònia Martí. 2011. Identity, non-identity, and near-identity: Addressing the complexity of coreference. *Lingua*, 121(6):1138–1152.

Adam Roberts, Colin Raffel, and Noam Shazeer. 2020. How much knowledge can you pack into the parameters of a language model? *arXiv preprint arXiv:2002.08910*.

Livio Baldini Soares, Nicholas FitzGerald, Jeffrey Ling, and Tom Kwiatkowski. 2019. Matching the blanks: Distributional similarity for relation learning. In *Proceedings of the 57th Annual Meeting of the Association for Computational Linguistics*, pages 2895–2905.

Wee Meng Soon, Hwee Tou Ng, and Daniel Chung Yong Lim. 2001. A machine learning approach to coreference resolution of noun phrases. *Computational linguistics*, 27(4):521–544.

Josef Steinberger, Massimo Poesio, Mijail A Kabadjov, and Karel Ježek. 2007. Two uses of anaphora resolution in summarization. *Information Processing and Management*, 6(43):1663–1680.

Rhea Sukthanker, Soujanya Poria, Erik Cambria, and Ramkumar Thirunavukarasu. 2020a. Anaphora and coreference resolution: A review. *Information Fusion*, 59:139–162.

Rhea Sukthanker, Soujanya Poria, Erik Cambria, and Ramkumar Thirunavukarasu. 2020b. Anaphora and coreference resolution: A review. *Information Fusion*, 59:139–162.

Erik F. Tjong Kim Sang. 2002. Introduction to the CoNLL-2002 shared task: Language-independent named entity recognition. In *COLING-02: The 6th Conference on Natural Language Learning 2002 (CoNLL-2002)*.

Erik F Tjong Kim Sang and Fien De Meulder. 2003. Introduction to the conll-2003 shared task: language-independent named entity recognition. In *Proceedings of the seventh conference on Natural language learning at HLT-NAACL 2003-Volume 4*, pages 142–147.

Özlem Uzuner, Brett R South, Shuying Shen, and Scott L DuVall. 2011. 2010 i2b2/va challenge on concepts, assertions, and relations in clinical text. *Journal of the American Medical Informatics Association*, 18(5):552–556.

Bonnie Lynn Webber. 1991. Structure and ostension in the interpretation of discourse deixis. *Language and Cognitive processes*, 6(2):107–135.

Kellie Webster, Marta Recasens, Vera Axelrod, and Jason Baldridge. 2018. Mind the gap: A balanced corpus of gendered ambiguous pronouns. *Transactions of the Association for Computational Linguistics*, 6:605–617.

Appendix

A Hyperparameters

Hyperparameter	Value
BERT	base-cased
BERT weights	freeze
BiLSTM hidden dim	200
Type embedding size	20
FC-layer 1 size	150
FC-layer 2 size	150
Dropout	0.2

Table A1: Hyperparameter values for our model. We refer the reader to `https://github.com/dbamman/lrec2020-coref` for the implementation of the baseline model.

B Original types to Common types

Corpus-level	Common
PER	PER
LOC	LOC
FAC	FAC
GPE	LOC
VEH	Other
ORG	ORG

Table A2: Litbank

Original	Common
PER	PER
ORG	ORG
LOC	LOC
DIG	Other

Table A3: EmailCoref

Original	Common
Organization	ORG
Person	PER
Corporation	FAC
Event	Other
Place	LOC
Thing	Other
OTHER	Other
NA	Other

Table A4: WikiCoref

We use four common types (PERson, LOCation, FACility, ORGanization) and *Other* in **+ET**

Original	Common
ORG	ORG
WORK_OF_ART	Other
LOC	LOC
CARDINAL	Other
EVENT	Other
NORP	Other
GPE	LOC
DATE	Other
PERSON	PER
FAC	FAC
QUANTITY	Other
ORDINAL	Other
TIME	Other
PRODUCT	Other
PERCENT	Other
MONEY	Other
LAW	Other
LANGUAGE	Other
NA	Other

Table A5: OntoNotes

(**com**) experiments. These types are annotated in most of the named-entity recognition datasets and therefore are easier to model and learn via machine learning approaches. Tables A2, A3, A4, A5 show the mapping between the original types of each coreference dataset used in our study to the reduced common types. The most drastic difference occurs for OntoNotes (19 -> 5) and WikiCoref (8 -> 5). *OTHER* type in WikiCoref is for freebase links that did not have an associated type stored in freebase, whereas *NA* is used for mentions which do not have a freebase link. For OntoNotes, *NA* refers to the mentions that did not get any type assigned to them even after the use of our cluster based type-propagation approach (explained in Section 4).

Exploring Span Representations in Neural Coreference Resolution

Patrick Kahardipraja[†], Olena Vyshnevska[†], Sharid Loáiciga
Computational Linguistics, Department of Linguistics
University of Potsdam, Germany
{kahardipraja,olena.vyshnevska,loaicigasanchez}@uni-potsdam.de

Abstract

In coreference resolution, span representations play a key role to predict coreference links accurately. We present a thorough examination of the span representation derived by applying BERT on coreference resolution (Joshi et al., 2019) using a probing model. Our results show that the span representation is able to encode a significant amount of coreference information. In addition, we find that the head-finding attention mechanism involved in creating the spans is crucial in encoding coreference knowledge. Last, our analysis shows that the span representation cannot capture non-local coreference as efficiently as local coreference.

1 Introduction

Coreference resolution, the task of grouping all referring expressions that point to the same entity into a cluster, plays a key role for various higher level NLP tasks that involve natural language understanding such as information extraction, question answering, machine translation, text summarisation, and textual entailment. Referring expressions or mentions can be common nouns, proper nouns, or pronouns, which refer to a real-world entity known as the referent.

With the breakthrough of end-to-end neural systems (Lee et al., 2017), current coreference resolution systems are for the most part neural based. Contrary to previous architectures which identified mentions and then took coreferential decisions in two separate steps, these systems jointly learn the two. A typical system requires different levels of semantic representation of the input sentences, usually done by computing representations at the span level given the word embeddings.

In another area, a wave of recent work has tried to inspect neural NLP models by associating neural network components with distinct linguistic phenomena by means of probing tasks (Shi et al., 2016; Liu et al., 2019a; Tenney et al., 2019).

Targeting the coreference task, in this paper, we build a probing model (Tenney et al., 2019; Liu et al., 2019a) to find out what degree of coreference information is encoded in the span representations as first proposed by Lee et al. (2017). Specifically, we generate mention-span representations with BERT embeddings fine-tuned on the OntoNotes dataset (Pradhan et al., 2012) and train a probing model to predict coreference arcs between two mentions from the mention-span representations alone. Moreover, we explore how fine-tuning BERT (Devlin et al., 2019) on coreference resolution affects the linguistic knowledge learned by the span representations. Given the well-documented difficulty in modelling long-distance coreference relations, we also measure the robustness of the span representations at different distance ranges between mentions.

Our probing models consistently achieve $> 90\%$ accuracy and F1, suggesting that span representations encode a significant amount of coreference information. Besides, they show that fine-tuning a BERT model greatly helps with encoding coreference relations. By ablating components of the span representation, we also find that the head-finding attention mechanism plays a crucial part in encoding important coreference information. Finally, we show that despite using a fine-tuned BERT, the span representations cannot capture non-local coreference relation efficiently. Our implementation is publicly available[1].

[†] Shared first authorship

[1] https://github.com/pkhdipraja/
exploring-span-representations

Proceedings of the First Workshop on Computational Approaches to Discourse, pages 32–41
Online, November 20, 2020. ©2020 Association for Computational Linguistics
https://doi.org/10.18653/v1/P17

2 Related Work

2.1 Span-Ranking Architecture

In this paper we focus on the span representation used in span-ranking models (Lee et al., 2017, 2018; Joshi et al., 2019) and examine their capability to encode the necessary information to make coreference decisions.

Lee et al. (2017) proposed an end-to-end coreference resolution model that learns to jointly model mention detection and coreference prediction using span-ranking. However, the model only computes scores between pairs of entity mentions. In an attempt to improve the weakness of this approach, Lee et al. (2018) proposed a model that captures higher-order interactions between mention spans in predicted coreference clusters. The model refines existing span representations iteratively with the antecedent distribution as an attention mechanism. We further refer to this model as *c2f-coref*.

Joshi et al. (2019) proposed to replace the bidirectional LSTM encoder in *c2f-coref* with BERT transformers and fine-tune it for coreference resolution. Although BERT improves the state-of-the-art results in other NLP tasks significantly (Devlin et al., 2019), coreference resolution still proves to be a challenging task, as the BERT encoder offers a marginal performance increase only. Furthermore, the model still struggles in modelling pronouns and resolving cases where mention paraphrasing is required. We further refer to this model as *BERT-coref*.

2.2 Probing Tasks

The most common method to explore linguistic properties in neural network components is by using the hidden state activations to predict the property of interest, also known as "probing tasks" (Conneau et al., 2018) or "auxiliary prediction tasks" (Adi et al., 2016). Shi et al. (2016) use the internal representations of an LSTM encoder as input to train a logistic regression classifier that predicts various syntactic properties. Conneau et al. (2018) study the linguistic properties of fixed-length sentence encoders with a bidirectional LSTM and gated convolutional networks.

Liu et al. (2019a) explore representations produced by pre-trained contextualisers and demonstrate that frozen contextual representations fed into linear models can show similar levels of performance as state-of-the-art task-specific models on many NLP tasks. They also used the coreference arc prediction task, whereby linear models are used to predict whether two mentions corefer. The coreference arc prediction was already used by Soon et al. (2001) as a part of the mention-pair model, where it is used with heuristic procedures to merge coreference chains.

Tenney et al. (2019), on their part, introduced the edge probing framework, which focuses on linguistic analysis on sub-sentence level. Their approach relies on a FFNN model with a projection layer and an attention mechanism on top of frozen contextual vectors to predict linguistic properties. Clark et al. (2019) further extended the probing-based approach by proposing attention-based probing classifiers and show that the attention heads in BERT correspond to linguistic notions of syntax and coreference.

Our approach is most similar to Liu et al. (2019a) and Tenney et al. (2019), but we use the span representation learned from Lee et al.'s 2017 coreference resolution model and focus on examining coreference phenomena. Note that we use the coreference arc prediction task as a tool to understand the span representation better, we do not do coreference resolution. Compared to Liu et al. (2019a) who consider single-token mentions only, we use mention-spans to predict coreference arcs. We also compare the span representation against a baseline span representation obtained from pre-trained contextual word embeddings (Tenney et al., 2019).

3 Probing Mention-Span Representations

3.1 Span Representations

Span representations are key in span-ranking models since they are used to compute a distribution over candidate antecedent spans. In order to predict coreference relations accurately, a span representation should also capture information about the span's internal structure and its surrounding context. For our experiments, we construct span representations as proposed by Lee et al. (2017), but with BERT embeddings (Devlin et al., 2019) instead of an LSTM-based encoder to encode the lexical information of a span and its context, following Joshi et al. (2019). A span representation is a vector embedding which consists of context-dependent boundary representations with an attentional representation of the head words over the span. The boundary representations are composed of the first and last wordpieces of the span itself.

The head words are automatically learned using additive attention (Bahdanau et al., 2015) over each wordpiece in a span:

$$\alpha_t = \boldsymbol{w}_\alpha \cdot \text{FFNN}_\alpha(\boldsymbol{x}_t^*)$$

$$a_{i,t} = \frac{\exp(\alpha_t)}{\sum\limits_{k=start(i)}^{end(i)} \exp(\alpha_k)}$$

$$\hat{\boldsymbol{x}}_i = \sum_{t=start(i)}^{end(i)} a_{i,t} \cdot \boldsymbol{x}_t$$

where $\hat{\boldsymbol{x}}_i$ is a weighted vector representation of wordpieces for span i. This representation is augmented by a $\mathbb{R}^d$ feature vector which encodes the size of span i with $d = 20$. The final representation $\boldsymbol{g}_i$ for span i is formulated as follows:

$$\boldsymbol{g}_i = [\boldsymbol{x}_{start(i)}^*, \boldsymbol{x}_{end(i)}^*, \hat{\boldsymbol{x}}_i, \phi_i]$$

where $\boldsymbol{x}_{start(i)}^*$ and $\boldsymbol{x}_{end(i)}^*$ are first and last wordpieces of a span, and ϕ_i is the span width embedding.

3.2 Coreference Arc Prediction

We focus on the coreference arc prediction task, which is a part of the probing tasks suite for contextual word embeddings. In this task, a probing model is trained to determine whether two mentions refer to the same entity. We produce negative samples following the approach by Liu et al. (2019a). For every pair of gold mentions (w_i, w_j), where they belong to the same gold coreference cluster and w_i is an antecedent of w_j, we generate a negative example (w_{random}, w_j) where w_{random} is randomly sampled from a different coreference cluster.

This method ensures a balanced ratio between positive and negative examples. The negative examples do not contain any singleton mentions, as in OntoNotes only coreferential mentions are annotated. We also follow the approach of Tenney et al. (2019) by using spans of wordpieces for mentions, as Liu et al.'s approach is limited to single-token mentions and therefore unable to fully exploit available information in a mention-span.

3.3 The Probing Model

Our probing model is a simple feed-forward neural network (FFNN), which is designed with a limited capacity to focus on the information that can be extracted from the span representations. As input to the model, we take a span representation for a pair of mention-spans $\boldsymbol{g}_1 = [\boldsymbol{x}_{start(1)}^*, \boldsymbol{x}_{end(1)}^*, \hat{\boldsymbol{x}}_1, \phi_1]$ and $\boldsymbol{g}_2 = [\boldsymbol{x}_{start(2)}^*, \boldsymbol{x}_{end(2)}^*, \hat{\boldsymbol{x}}_2, \phi_2]$, where both $\boldsymbol{g}_1$ and $\boldsymbol{g}_2$ are concatenated and passed to the FFNN. The FFNN consists of a single hidden layer followed by a sigmoid output layer. The model is trained to minimise binary cross-entropy with respect to the gold label $Y \in \{0, 1\}$. The probing architecture is depicted in Figure 1.

We obtained the mention-span representations from BERT, a language representation model based on the Transformer architecture (Vaswani et al., 2017), trained jointly with a masked language model and next sentence prediction objective. It enables significant improvement in many downstream tasks with relatively minimal task-specific fine-tuning. To study the quality of mention-span representations, we extract mention-span embeddings from BERT-base (12-layer Transformers, 768-hidden) and BERT-large (24-layer Transformers, 1024-hidden) pre-trained models. Furthermore, we compare these *original* BERT models with *fine-tuned* variants, with the purpose to assess any fine-tuning effect on the quality of the span representations.

4 Experiments

4.1 Dataset

We use the coreference resolution annotation from the CoNLL-2012 shared task based on the OntoNotes dataset (Pradhan et al., 2012). The dataset is split into 2,802 training documents, 343 validation documents, and 348 test documents. On average, the training documents contain 454 words. The largest document contains a maximum of 4,009 words. Since OntoNotes only provides annotations for positive examples, we generate our own negative examples (§3.2).

4.2 Implementation Details and Hyperparameters

We extend the original Tensorflow implementation of *BERT-coref*[2] in order to build our probing model with Keras frontend (Chollet et al., 2015). Our probing model is trained for 50 epochs, using early stopping with patience of 3 and batch size of 512. For optimisation, we use Adam (Kingma and Ba, 2015) with a learning rate of 0.001. The weights

---

[2] https://github.com/mandarjoshi90/coref

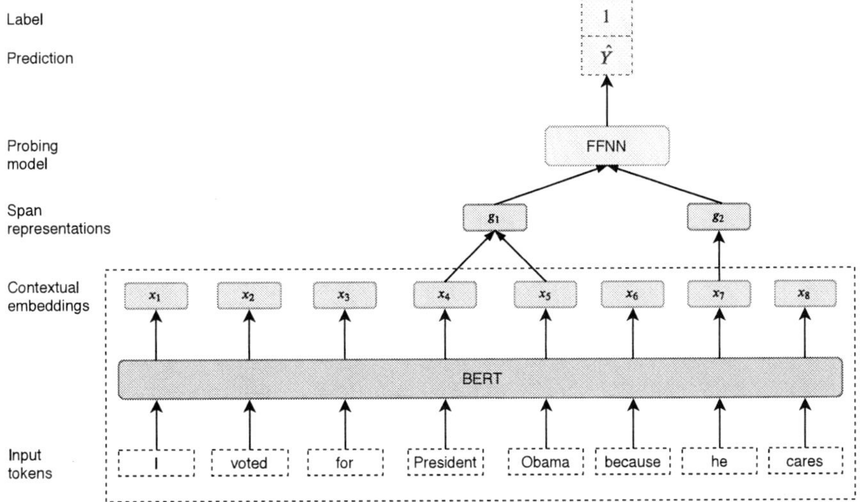

Figure 1: The probing architecture for span representations. The feed-forward neural network is trained to extract information from span representations g_1 and g_2, while all the parameters inside the dashed line are frozen. The example depicts a mention-pair, where g_1 corresponds to span representation of "President Obama", while g_2 corresponds to "he". We predict $\hat{Y}$ as positive for this example.

of the probing model are initialised with Kaiming initialisation (He et al., 2015) and the size of the hidden layer is $d = 1024$ with rectified linear units (Nair and Hinton, 2010). As mentioned previously, we use both a pre-trained BERT (original) model without fine-tuning the encoder weights and a BERT model that has been fine-tuned on the coreference resolution task (i.e., on OntoNotes annotations). For the fine-tuned BERT model, we take the models that yield the best performance for Joshi et al. (2019), which were trained using 128 wordpieces for BERT-base and 384 wordpieces for BERT-large. The fine-tuned model is trained using split OntoNotes documents where each segment non-overlaps and is fed as a separate instance. This is done as BERT can only accept sequences of at most 512 wordpieces and typically OntoNotes documents require multiple segments to be read entirely. In all of our experiments, we use the cased English BERT models. We will further refer to the base and large variants as *BERT-base c2f* and *BERT-large c2f* respectively.

4.3 Baseline

As our baseline, we use the span representation introduced in the edge probing framework (Tenney et al., 2019). First of all, we take concatenated contextual embeddings for a pair of mention-spans $e^{(1)} = [x_1^{(1)}, x_2^{(1)}, x_3^{(1)}, ..., x_n^{(1)}]$ and $e^{(2)} = [x_1^{(2)}, x_2^{(2)}, x_3^{(2)}, ..., x_n^{(2)}]$ as inputs. We then project

the concatenated contextual embeddings $e^{(1)}$ and $e^{(2)}$ to improve performance following Tenney et al. (2019):

$$e^{(i)} = Ae^{(i)} + b$$

where $i = (1, 2)$, A and b are weights of the projection layer. Afterwards, we apply the self-attentional pooling operator in §3.1 over the projected representations to yield fixed-length span representations.

This helps to model head words for each mention-span. These mention-span representations are then concatenated and passed to the probing model to predict whether they corefer or not. We use shared weights for both projection and self-attentional layer so that the model can learn the similarity between representations of mention-spans. It is important to note that the self-attention pooling is computed only using tokens within the boundary of the span. As a result, the model can only access information about the context surrounding the mention-span through the contextual embeddings. We take the contextual embeddings from activations of the original pre-trained BERT final layer, while freezing the encoder.

We compare the span representation used in the span-ranking model against the baseline, as it measures the performance that the probing model can achieve with representations that are constructed from lexical priors alone, without any access to the local context within the mention-spans. The resulting baseline span representation have a dimension of $d = 768$ for BERT-base and $d = 1024$ for BERT-large.

4.4 Long-range Coreference

In order to investigate whether the span representation is able to capture long-range coreference relations, we extend our baseline by introducing a convolutional layer to incorporate surrounding context and improve the baseline span representation, following Tenney et al. (2019).

We replace the projection layer in our probing architecture with a fully-connected 1D CNN layer with a kernel width of 3 and 5, stride of 1 and same padding to properly include contextual embeddings at the beginning and at the end of each mention-span. This is equivalent to seeing ± 1 and ± 3 tokens around the centre word respectively. We also initialise the weights of the CNN layer with Kaiming initialisation (He et al., 2015). Using this extended probing architecture with a CNN layer as another baseline, which we will refer to as *CNN-baseline*, enables us to examine the contribution of local and non-local context to the performance of the probing model.

We then test our probing model with various distances between mention-spans. We separate pairs of mention-spans that appear in the OntoNotes test set into several buckets, based on the distance between the last token of the mention-span w_i and the first token of the mention-span w_j, where w_j occurs after w_i. Each bucket contains at least 50 examples of pairs of mention-spans.

4.5 Control Tasks

To ensure that our probing model is robust, we compare its performance with a control task (Hewitt and Liang, 2019). For every pair of mention-spans (g_1, g_2), we replace one of the span representations g_i with another g_i' randomly sampled from the data set. Note that in this control task, some information of the original mention-pairs is still preserved as the other span representation in the pair is not replaced.

5 Results and Discussion

5.1 Comparison of Probing Models

Table 1 compares the performance of the probing model using span representations fine-tuned on the OntoNotes dataset against baseline span representations and a *CNN-baseline* that utilises the original pre-trained BERT encoder. The results of the control task are reported in the bottom two lines.

The probing model suggests that span representations in *BERT-coref* encode a significant amount of coreference information, as we are able to train the model to predict whether a pair of mention-spans corefer based on their span representations alone. Both *BERT-base c2f* and *BERT-large c2f* consistently score above 90% (accuracy and F1 score) on the OntoNotes test set.

We observe that both *BERT-base c2f* and *BERT-large c2f* perform better in predicting coreference arc between a pair of mention-spans compared to their respective baselines (by 2.37 points for accuracy and 2.18 F1 points on average). We find that, although training the contextual probing model to learn contextual features for coreference arc prediction helps to encode the necessary coreference information into the baseline span representations, it still cannot outperform the probing model that utilises span representations in *BERT-coref*. This is likely caused by better coreference-related features that are learned by the BERT encoder when it is fine-tuned on OntoNotes.

We also see that fine-tuning the span representations on coreference resolution task helps encode local and long-range context inside the mention-spans efficiently. This can be observed from the performance of *CNN-baseline*, where the probing model is trained using a 1D CNN layer with kernel width of 3 and 5 to allow the model to see the contribution of local and long-range dependencies, but ultimately still underperforms compared to *BERT-coref*.

Surprisingly, our baseline span representations which were constructed from only lexical priors perform better compared to the *CNN-baseline* span representations on both metrics. We attribute this to our decision of using contextual embeddings from the final layer of pre-trained BERT, as most transferable representations from contextual encoders trained with a language modelling objective tend to occur in the intermediate layers, and that the topmost layers might be overly specialised for next-word prediction (Liu et al., 2019a; Peters et al., 2018a,b; Blevins et al., 2018; Devlin et al., 2019). This might cause the CNN layer to learn suboptimal representations of the mention-spans. The probing model that we choose is also highly selective, with

	Accuracy	F1 Score
BERT-base c2f (fine-tuned)	92.93	93.02
BERT-large c2f (fine-tuned)	93.65*	93.68*
BERT-base CNN (original, K=3)	89.51	89.91
BERT-base CNN (original, K=5)	89.04	89.28
BERT-large CNN (original, K=3)	90.27	90.35
BERT-large CNN (original, K=5)	88.09	88.28
BERT-base (original) baseline	90.37	90.65
BERT-large (original) baseline	91.47	91.69
BERT-base c2f (random)	64.83	65.17
BERT-large c2f (random)	67.53	68.36

Table 1: Comparison of the probing model's performance with various mention-span representations evaluated on the OntoNotes test set. An asterisk (*) denotes the best performance on each metric. *BERT-large c2f* improves the accuracy and F1 score over the probing baseline by 3.28% and 3.03% for the base variant, while for BERT-large baseline the improvements are 2.18% and 1.99% respectively.

selectivity of 28.1 for *BERT-base c2f* and 26.1 for *BERT-large c2f*. This also means that to achieve high accuracy, the probes must rely on coreference information encoded in the span representation.

5.2 Ablations

To examine the importance of each component in *BERT-coref* span representation, we conduct an ablation study on each part of the representation and report the accuracy and the F1 score for the probing model on the test data (Table 2).[3]

The head-finding attention mechanism is crucial for coreference-arc prediction, as it contributes the highest to the final result with 0.98 and 0.95 points for accuracy and for F1 score on average, respectively. This is consistent with previous findings from Lee et al. (2017), who shows that the attention mechanism is able to learn representations important for coreference.

We also observe that span-width embeddings play an important role in determining a coreference relation, without them the performance degrades on average by 0.4 and 0.37 for accuracy and F1. Contrary to the head-finding attention and span-width embeddings, boundary representations did not contribute much to the model's performance. We hypothesise that although boundary representations may encode a large amount of information for coreference resolution, they are not significant for coreference arc prediction, as the model does not have to predict distribution over possible spans.

5.3 Encoding Long-range Coreference

We compare how our probing model performs on various separation distances between mention-spans. Figure 2 depicts F1 scores as a function of distance between pairs of mention-spans. Although performance with BERT models degrades with larger distances, the span representations in *BERT-coref* hold up better in general compared to the baseline or *CNN-baseline*. The BERT-base variant experiences a minor degradation in performance up to 5 points when $d = 125$ tokens, while for BERT-large the F1 score drops only by 7 points between $d = 0$ tokens and $d = 250$ tokens, which suggests that the depth of the Transformer layer helps to encode long-range coreference.

However, we lack sufficient evidence to suggest that the span representations are able to encode long-range coreference relations efficiently, seeing that although the encoder has been fine-tuned on OntoNotes, the model still cannot perform consistently across distant spans, with the lowest F1 score of 67% and 75% for BERT-base and BERT-large respectively, when $d = 451$ to 475 tokens.

5.4 Error Analysis

We provide qualitative error analysis for predicted coreference between mention-pairs. We look at the output of *BERT-base c2f* (cased, fine-tuned) and *BERT-large c2f* (cased, fine-tuned). The predictions of both models on the same subset of 1,250 predictions from the test set are analysed. Overall, we found 93 errors in the model with BERT-base embeddings and 84 for the model with BERT-large embeddings. The errors are grouped into: *Similar Word Forms, Anaphora, Gender, Mention Para-*

---

[3] Results for replication experiments after acceptance are reported in Appendix A.

	Accuracy	F1 Score	ΔAccuracy	ΔF1 Score
BERT-base c2f (fine-tuned)	92.93	93.02		
- boundary representations	92.88	92.96	-0.05	-0.06
- head-finding attention	92.05	92.16	-0.88	-0.86
- span-width embeddings	92.46	92.56	-0.47	-0.46
BERT-large c2f (fine-tuned)	93.65	93.68		
- boundary representations	93.47	93.49	-0.18	-0.19
- head-finding attention	92.57	92.65	-1.08	-1.03
- span-width embeddings	93.32	93.41	-0.33	-0.27

Table 2: Comparison of the probing models on the OntoNotes test set with various components removed. The head-finding attention and span-width embeddings contribute significantly to the performance of the probing model.

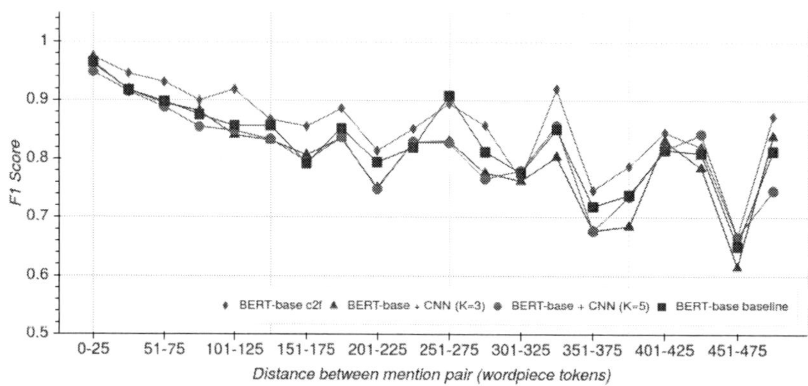

(a)

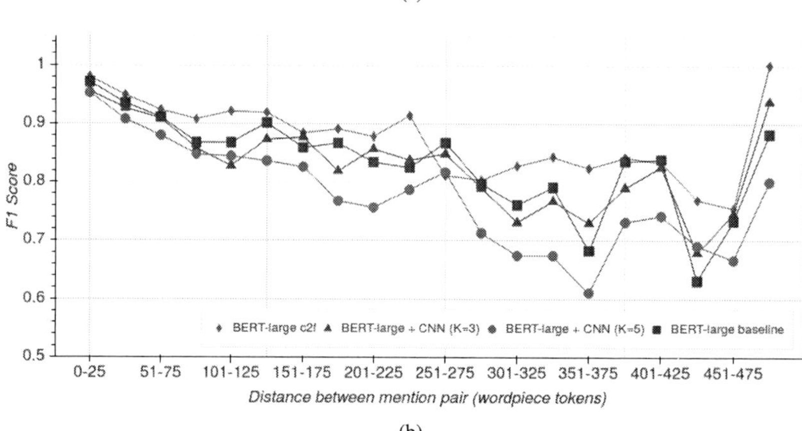

(b)

Figure 2: F1 scores of the probing model as a function of separating distance between two mention-spans with BERT-base (2a) and BERT-large (2b) on test set. The performance of the model with either BERT-base or BERT-large embeddings tends to decrease as the distance between wordpiece tokens increases.

phrasing, and *Temporal and Spacial Agreement*. Although *Gender* can be considered as a subcategory of *Anaphora*, we decided to separate it to check whether gender bias is present in the models.

Table 3 portrays an overview of the errors made by both models in each category. We note that mentions separated by a distance of more than 25 tokens have a higher error rate than mentions separated by smaller distances, suggesting that *BERT-base c2f*

and *BERT-large c2f* perform better when resolving coreference locally.

In the gender category, we only found one problematic example. The proper name *Scooter Libby* is consistently predicted to corefer with *she* and *her*, although the real world referent is male.

Consistent with Joshi et al. (2019), the most difficult case for both models is anaphora, even at very short distances between mentions, as in the follow-

Category	Snippet	BERT-base c2f	BERT-large c2f
Similar Word Forms	... in some of the questioning eh of *Miller*, I think ... you have *Judy Miller* there (13) ... this is the Dick Cheney aide she **agreed** to refer ... I think the **agreement** was strange (85)	17	13
Anaphora	... it was very prompt with *traffic management and emergency repair* ... ah, because *it* involved various (5) ... the news on the day of *the accident* ... instead of the east and *it* did not (277)	47	41
Gender	... killed a piece written by a reporter about **Scooter Libby** ... They didn' t say that you know until **she** walked out (58)	0	2
Mention Paraphrasing	When someone sews a patch over **a hole in an old coat,** they ... If they do, **the patch** will shrink (22) ... read a statement from **a Sixty Minutes spokesman** ... When **Mister Carson the representative** spoke ... (241)	20	19
Temporal and Spacial	... people from economic circles, who even predicted that in *1998* ... They pointed out that, *this year*, except ... (13) ... and only 582 million US dollars **last year**... momentum can not be restrained, **this year** ... (379)	9	9
Total		93	84

Table 3: Number of errors by the *BERT-base c2f* and *BERT-large c2f* fine-tuned models. The number of tokens between the highlighted mentions is given in the parenthesis. False positives are denoted **bold**, false negatives in *italic*.

ing example with a distance of only 5 tokens: "we should say it was very prompt with *traffic management and emergency repair*, ah, because *it* involved various [...]". Cases of coreference between two pronouns are also difficult for both models.

The similar word forms category concerns errors in mentions with morphologically related word forms which are identified as coreferent, for instance "[...] this is the Dick Cheney aide she *agreed* to refer [...]". I think the *agreement* was strange [...]". In contrast, together with anaphora, errors involving paraphrasing and temporal and spacial agreement have an extra level of complexity in that they involve real world knowledge. For instance, for humans it is trivial that *1996* and *1997* are years and that they are different ones. The systems, on the other hand, consistently label them as coreferent, as if they were morphologically related forms.

6   Conclusion and Future Work

In this paper, we quantify the coreference information in the span representation by how well they can do on the coreference arc prediction task. We demonstrate that using mention-span representations as inputs, a simple probing model can be used to predict coreference for pairs of mention spans with accuracy and F1 score over 90%. This suggests that a significant amount of coreference

information is encoded in mention-span representations obtained from BERT embeddings, which are fine-tuned on the OntoNotes dataset. Consistently with non-neural architectures, our analysis also shows that non-local coreference is challenging for span representations. Furthermore, we show that the head-finding attention mechanism encodes essential coreference-related features in span representations, even when using original pre-trained BERT embeddings.

The findings we report are solely based on an English corpus. Other pieces of research (Azerkovich, 2020; Hint et al., 2020) suggest that such positive results might be more challenging to achieve for morphologically or syntactically complex languages.

Although we work with the OntoNotes dataset, there are other challenging coreference resolution datasets that focus on ambiguous pronouns (GAP by Webster et al. (2018)) or commonsense reasoning (WinoGrande by Sakaguchi et al. (2019)), which can be used to understand coreference information in span representations better. Moreover, we would like to probe span representations derived from other pre-trained language models such as RoBERTa (Liu et al., 2019b) and SpanBERT (Joshi et al., 2020). Alternative Transformer-based architecture that is better at handling long sequences such as Longformer (Beltagy et al., 2020) also seems promising to explore, as it might improve span representations capability to model long-range coreference. Lastly, instead of building span representations from the final layer of a pre-trained BERT model, one can opt to use the activations from the intermediate layers as well as ELMo-style scalar mixing (Tenney et al., 2019; Peters et al., 2018a). We leave this to future work.

Acknowledgements

We thank the anonymous reviewers for their critical reading of our manuscript and their insightful comments and suggestions.

References

Yossi Adi, Einat Kermany, Yonatan Belinkov, Ofer Lavi, and Yoav Goldberg. 2016. Fine-grained analysis of sentence embeddings using auxiliary prediction tasks. *CoRR*, abs/1608.04207.

Ilya Azerkovich. 2020. Using semantic information for coreference resolution with neural networks in russian. In *Analysis of Images, Social Networks and Texts*, pages 85–93, Cham. Springer International Publishing.

Dzmitry Bahdanau, Kyunghyun Cho, and Yoshua Bengio. 2015. Neural machine translation by jointly learning to align and translate. In *3rd International Conference on Learning Representations, ICLR 2015, San Diego, CA, USA, May 7-9, 2015, Conference Track Proceedings*.

Iz Beltagy, Matthew E. Peters, and Arman Cohan. 2020. Longformer: The long-document transformer. *arXiv:2004.05150*.

Terra Blevins, Omer Levy, and Luke Zettlemoyer. 2018. Deep RNNs encode soft hierarchical syntax. In *Proceedings of the 56th Annual Meeting of the Association for Computational Linguistics (Volume 2: Short Papers)*, pages 14–19, Melbourne, Australia. Association for Computational Linguistics.

François Chollet et al. 2015. Keras. https://keras.io.

Kevin Clark, Urvashi Khandelwal, Omer Levy, and Christopher D. Manning. 2019. What does bert look at? an analysis of bert's attention. In *BlackBoxNLP@ACL*.

Alexis Conneau, German Kruszewski, Guillaume Lample, Loïc Barrault, and Marco Baroni. 2018. What you can cram into a single $&!#* vector: Probing sentence embeddings for linguistic properties. In *Proceedings of the 56th Annual Meeting of the Association for Computational Linguistics (Volume 1: Long Papers)*, pages 2126–2136, Melbourne, Australia. Association for Computational Linguistics.

Jacob Devlin, Ming-Wei Chang, Kenton Lee, and Kristina Toutanova. 2019. BERT: Pre-training of deep bidirectional transformers for language understanding. In *Proceedings of the 2019 Conference of the North American Chapter of the Association for Computational Linguistics: Human Language Technologies, Volume 1 (Long and Short Papers)*, pages 4171–4186, Minneapolis, Minnesota. Association for Computational Linguistics.

Kaiming He, Xiangyu Zhang, Shaoqing Ren, and Jian Sun. 2015. Delving deep into rectifiers: Surpassing human-level performance on imagenet classification. In *Proceedings of the 2015 IEEE International Conference on Computer Vision (ICCV)*, ICCV '15, page 1026–1034, USA. IEEE Computer Society.

John Hewitt and Percy Liang. 2019. Designing and interpreting probes with control tasks. In *Proceedings of the 2019 Conference on Empirical Methods in Natural Language Processing and the 9th International Joint Conference on Natural Language Processing (EMNLP-IJCNLP)*, pages 2733–2743, Hong Kong, China. Association for Computational Linguistics.

Helen Hint, Tiina Nahkola, and Renate Pajusalu. 2020. Pronouns as referential devices in estonian, finnish, and russian. *Journal of Pragmatics*, 155:43 – 63.

Mandar Joshi, Danqi Chen, Yinhan Liu, Daniel S Weld, Luke Zettlemoyer, and Omer Levy. 2020. Spanbert: Improving pre-training by representing and predicting spans. *Transactions of the Association for Computational Linguistics*, 8:64–77.

Mandar Joshi, Omer Levy, Daniel S. Weld, and Luke Zettlemoyer. 2019. BERT for coreference resolution: Baselines and analysis. In *Empirical Methods in Natural Language Processing (EMNLP)*.

Diederik P. Kingma and Jimmy Ba. 2015. Adam: A method for stochastic optimization. In *3rd International Conference on Learning Representations, ICLR 2015, San Diego, CA, USA, May 7-9, 2015, Conference Track Proceedings*.

Kenton Lee, Luheng He, Mike Lewis, and Luke Zettlemoyer. 2017. End-to-end neural coreference resolution. In *Proceedings of the 2017 Conference on Empirical Methods in Natural Language Processing*, pages 188–197, Copenhagen, Denmark. Association for Computational Linguistics.

Kenton Lee, Luheng He, and Luke Zettlemoyer. 2018. Higher-order coreference resolution with coarse-to-fine inference. In *Proceedings of the 2018 Conference of the North American Chapter of the Association for Computational Linguistics: Human Language Technologies, Volume 2 (Short Papers)*, pages 687–692, New Orleans, Louisiana. Association for Computational Linguistics.

Nelson F. Liu, Matt Gardner, Yonatan Belinkov, Matthew E. Peters, and Noah A. Smith. 2019a. Linguistic knowledge and transferability of contextual representations. In *Proceedings of the 2019 Conference of the North American Chapter of the Association for Computational Linguistics: Human Language Technologies, Volume 1 (Long and Short Papers)*, pages 1073–1094, Minneapolis, Minnesota. Association for Computational Linguistics.

Yinhan Liu, Myle Ott, Naman Goyal, Jingfei Du, Mandar Joshi, Danqi Chen, Omer Levy, Mike Lewis, Luke Zettlemoyer, and Veselin Stoyanov. 2019b. Roberta: A robustly optimized bert pretraining approach. *arXiv preprint arXiv:1907.11692*.

Vinod Nair and Geoffrey E. Hinton. 2010. Rectified linear units improve restricted boltzmann machines. In *Proceedings of the 27th International Conference on International Conference on Machine Learning*, ICML'10, page 807–814, Madison, WI, USA. Omnipress.

Matthew Peters, Mark Neumann, Mohit Iyyer, Matt Gardner, Christopher Clark, Kenton Lee, and Luke Zettlemoyer. 2018a. Deep contextualized word representations. In *Proceedings of the 2018 Conference of the North American Chapter of the Association for Computational Linguistics: Human Language Technologies, Volume 1 (Long Papers)*, pages 2227–2237, New Orleans, Louisiana. Association for Computational Linguistics.

Matthew Peters, Mark Neumann, Luke Zettlemoyer, and Wen-tau Yih. 2018b. Dissecting contextual word embeddings: Architecture and representation. In *Proceedings of the 2018 Conference on Empirical Methods in Natural Language Processing*, pages 1499–1509, Brussels, Belgium. Association for Computational Linguistics.

Sameer Pradhan, Alessandro Moschitti, Nianwen Xue, Olga Uryupina, and Yuchen Zhang. 2012. CoNLL-2012 shared task: Modeling multilingual unrestricted coreference in OntoNotes. In *Joint Conference on EMNLP and CoNLL - Shared Task*, pages 1–40, Jeju Island, Korea. Association for Computational Linguistics.

Keisuke Sakaguchi, Ronan Le Bras, Chandra Bhagavatula, and Yejin Choi. 2019. Winogrande: An adversarial winograd schema challenge at scale. *ArXiv*, abs/1907.10641.

Xing Shi, Inkit Padhi, and Kevin Knight. 2016. Does string-based neural MT learn source syntax? In *Proceedings of the 2016 Conference on Empirical Methods in Natural Language Processing*, pages 1526–1534, Austin, Texas. Association for Computational Linguistics.

Wee Meng Soon, Hwee Tou Ng, and Daniel Chung Yong Lim. 2001. A machine learning approach to coreference resolution of noun phrases. *Computational Linguistics*, 27(4):521–544.

Ian Tenney, Patrick Xia, Berlin Chen, Alex Wang, Adam Poliak, R. Thomas McCoy, Najoung Kim, Benjamin Van Durme, Samuel R. Bowman, Dipanjan Das, and Ellie Pavlick. 2019. What do you learn from context? probing for sentence structure in contextualized word representations. In *International Conference on Learning Representations*.

Ashish Vaswani, Noam Shazeer, Niki Parmar, Jakob Uszkoreit, Llion Jones, Aidan N Gomez, Ł ukasz Kaiser, and Illia Polosukhin. 2017. Attention is all you need. In I. Guyon, U. V. Luxburg, S. Bengio, H. Wallach, R. Fergus, S. Vishwanathan, and R. Garnett, editors, *Advances in Neural Information Processing Systems 30*, pages 5998–6008. Curran Associates, Inc.

Kellie Webster, Marta Recasens, Vera Axelrod, and Jason Baldridge. 2018. Mind the gap: A balanced corpus of gendered ambiguou. In *Transactions of the ACL*, page to appear.

A Appendix

A.1 Averaged Accuracy and F1 Score for Ablation Study

	Accuracy	ΔAccuracy
BERT-base c2f (fine-tuned)	92.93	
- boundary representations	92.77	-0.16
- head-finding attention	91.74	-1.19
- span-width embeddings	92.59	-0.34
BERT-large c2f (fine-tuned)	93.65	
- boundary representations	93.88	$+0.23$
- head-finding attention	92.65	-1.00
- span-width embeddings	93.43	-0.22

Table 4: Averaged accuracy for ablation on the OntoNotes test set. We take the average accuracy of 10 runs.

	F1 Score	ΔF1 Score
BERT-base c2f (fine-tuned)	93.02	
- boundary representations	92.89	-0.13
- head-finding attention	91.81	-1.21
- span-width embeddings	92.68	-0.34
BERT-large c2f (fine-tuned)	93.68	
- boundary representations	93.89	$+0.21$
- head-finding attention	92.64	-1.04
- span-width embeddings	93.44	-0.24

Table 5: Averaged F1 score for ablation on the OntoNotes test set. We take the average F1 score of 10 runs.

Supporting Comedy Writers: Predicting Audience's Response from Sketch Comedy and Crosstalk Scripts

Maolin Li
Independent Research[*]
maolin.li.cs@gmail.com

Abstract

Sketch comedy and crosstalk are two popular types of comedy. They can relieve people's stress and thus benefit their mental health, especially when performances and scripts are high-quality. However, writing a script is time-consuming and its quality is difficult to achieve. In order to minimise the time and effort needed for producing an excellent script, we explore ways of predicting the audience's response from the comedy scripts. For this task, we present a corpus of annotated scripts from popular television entertainment programmes in recent years. Annotations include a) text classification labels, indicating which actor's lines made the studio audience laugh; b) information extraction labels, i.e. the text spans that made the audience laughed immediately after the performers said them. The corpus will also be useful for dialogue systems and discourse analysis, since our annotations are based on entire scripts. In addition, we evaluate different baseline algorithms. Experimental results demonstrate that BERT models can achieve the best predictions among all the baseline methods. Furthermore, we conduct an error analysis and investigate predictions across scripts with different styles.[1]

1 Introduction

Comedy plays a major role in people's lives in that it relieves stress and anxiety (Williams et al., 2005; Sarıtaş et al., 2019). There are two popular types of comedy: sketch comedy and crosstalk. A sketch comedy usually presents a short story and is performed by multiple comedians in various short scenes; while in a crosstalk performance, which is similar to a talk show, there are usually two performers telling humorous stories behind a desk. Although these two types of comedy are different, both of them are performed based on scripts. A script breaks down a story into pieces along with the details that describe which performer should take what action or say which lines at a specific point (Blake, 2014). Therefore, the quality of the script is critical and it directly influences whether the audience enjoys the performance.

However, it is difficult for script writers to ensure a high-quality comedy script and be productive. Firstly, writers have to assess if audiences will react as expected, in particular laughing at specific points. It is necessary to rehearse multiple times to continuously improve the script, which is time-consuming and can be costly. Secondly, to develop laughter triggers, writers need to identify the potential points from the script where there are possibilities for performers to use funny body moves, tone or tell amusing stories to make the audience laugh. Thirdly, the more times a script is publicly performed, the less laughter it can bring, since the audience have become too familiar with it. Thus, it is essential for comedy writers to explore new laughter triggers constantly.

Since natural language processing (NLP) has been widely and successfully applied to a number of fields (Carrera-Ruvalcaba et al., 2019; Rao and McMahan, 2019), we investigate how NLP methods can support comedy writers to produce high-quality scripts more efficiently. This paper specifies this challenge as a new task, i.e. the prediction of the audience's response to sketch comedy and crosstalk scripts. To address this challenge, we explore the use of two different NLP methodologies: 1) Text Classification: we predict whether or

---

[*] The research was conducted during non-working time. The idea of this research was inspired by a discussion with my friend about an entertainment TV programme in which the comedians mentioned the difficulties of producing a high-quality script.

[1] The corpus and source code can be freely downloaded from https://github.com/createmomo/supporting-comedy-writers

Proceedings of the First Workshop on Computational Approaches to Discourse, pages 42–52
Online, November 20, 2020. ©2020 Association for Computational Linguistics
https://doi.org/10.18653/v1/P17

Label	Actor's Line	Source
1	宋小宝：我的人生格言是，在哪里跌倒，就在哪里睡一觉。 Xiaobao SONG: My life motto is to have a sleep where you've fallen.	碰瓷 (*An Incident-Faking Extortionist*) Joyful Comedians (Season 1), 2015
1	张小斐：我可能是洗的你藏私房钱的这条裤子。 Xiaofei ZHANG: The trousers I wash might be the ones you hide your secret purse.	幸福牛家村 (*Happy Niu Families' Village*) JSTV Chinese New Year Gala, 2019
0	沈腾：大妈，你好好回忆一下，真的没有撞你。 Teng SHEN: Please recall exactly what happened. I really did not hit you.	扶不扶 (*Help Her Up or Not*) CCTV Chinese New Year Gala, 2014

Table 1: Text classification annotation examples taken from different comedies in our corpus. In the *Label* column, *1* and *0* indicate whether or not this line makes audiences laugh respectively; In the ***Action Line*** column, we present the performer's names and their lines; The ***Source*** column indicates the title of the comedy and the venue where it is performed.

Actor's Line with Annotations	Source
贾玲：这种装修风格显得你家特别的大。（客厅几乎是空的） Ling JIA: With this decoration style, your house seems to be *incredibly big*. (The living room is almost empty)	懒汉相亲 (Idler's Blind Date) Ace VS Ace (Season 4), 2019
岳云鹏：不能，不退票是我们的服务宗旨。 Yunpeng YUE: No way! Our policy *is no refund*.	非一般的爱情 (*Unusual Love*) Joyful Comedians (Season 2), 2016
贾冰：恩。（贾冰乖乖地闭上了双眼） Bing JIA: Okay. (He duly *closes his eyes*)	贾总的演讲 (*Manager JIA's Presentation*) Legend of Laughter (Season 1), 2017

Table 2: Information extraction annotation examples taken from different comedies in our corpus. In the first column, we highlight the **text spans** that trigger laughs from audiences. Note that, we also collected the performer's moves (e.g., *"duly closes his eyes"* in the third example).

not an actor's lines[2] can make audiences laugh. In other words, we formulate the task of predicting as a binary text classification problem. 2) Information Extraction: we predict the text spans from an actor's lines indicating the specific words that trigger an audience's laughter.

Contributions Firstly, we introduce a Chinese corpus of annotated comedy scripts collected from popular TV entertainment programmes. Our annotations include both text classification and information extraction labels. Tables 1 and 2 present annotation examples. The corpus can be used to build an intelligent system to benefit the script writing for comedy writers. It may also be useful for dialogue system research and discourse analysis. Secondly, we evaluate a number of NLP methods and the results demonstrate that BERT models (Devlin et al., 2019) are able to achieve the best prediction performance among all methods. We also further conduct an error analysis which may be useful for further improving the performance. Lastly, we experimentally show that our corpus can also be used to predict laughter triggers for scripts which have very different styles compared to training data.

2 Related Work

Our work is closely related to humour detection, which has been widely studied for many years in natural language processing. Mihalcea and Strapparava (2006); Yang et al. (2015); Chen and Soo (2018); Blinov et al. (2019) investigated if a text fragment is a one-liner.[3] Zhang and Liu (2014); Ortega-Bueno et al. (2018); Chiruzzo et al. (2019) explored the humour classification task on tweets. Castro et al. (2018) collected humour values and funniness scores of Spanish tweets by using crowdsourcing. Chiruzzo et al. (2019) proposed a regression task that predicts the humour score for a tweet. Li et al. (2020) collected Chinese Internet slang expressions and combined them with a humor detecting method to analyse the sentiment of Weibo[4] posts. It should be noted that the examples in all of the corpora used or constructed in the above-mentioned studies are independent of each other. Since our corpus is based on entire scripts, the annotated lines and text spans might also benefit the researchers who are interested in modelling long-context-aware algorithms to understand humour. Apart from the studies on short text fragments, Bertero (2019) and Hasan et al. (2019) created corpora from television (TV) sitcoms such as *The Big Bang Theory*[5] and *TED talks*[6] respectively. Their goal is to predict whether or not a sequence of texts will trigger immediate laughter. Yang et al. (2015); Zhang et al. (2019) extracted the key words such as *sing*, *sign language* and *pretty handy* from jokes, which are similar to our information extraction annotations.

---

[2]The lines are from the dialogue of a comedy performance. Each line consists of an actor's name and the sentences this actor speaks in performance.

[3]A one-liner is a joke that is delivered in a single line which only contains a few words.

[4]Weibo is a Chinese micro-blogging website similar to Twitter: https://www.weibo.com/

[5]https://the-big-bang-theory.com/

[6]https://www.ted.com/talks

3 Corpus

3.1 Data Collection

Source Selection In order to ensure the high-quality of scripts, we carefully selected thirty performances (the total duration is approximately 473 minutes), including both sketch comedies and crosstalks, of which the leading roles are famous Chinese comedians. These performances were played on well-known Chinese TV entertainment programmes such as Chinese New Year Gala and *Ace VS Ace*[7]. Since there were many people in the audience present for the recording of these performances, the annotators can judge whether the audience laughed based on the performance videos. Please refer to the appendix for the full list of performances which gives details of their titles, leading comedians and sources. Lastly, we manually typed up actors' lines for each performance and completed thirty scripts. Although there may be differences between our scripts and the real scripts used by comedians in terms of format or content, we assume that our scripts contain the key information about the real scripts, i.e., the actors' lines. Therefore the corpus can be useful for the development of intelligence-assistant comedy script writing systems.

Diversity We also took the comedy style into consideration. In order to ensure the diversity and its balance: a) The performances were selected from three main different types of sources[8] as shown in Table 3, including the topic descriptions of selected performances. It can be observed that the corpus has a wide range of topics. b) As a preliminary study, we selected six popular Chinese comedians who have various and distinctive styles, and we chose five representative performances of each comedian.

Corpus Statistic Table 4 illustrates the statistics and Figure 1 shows the laughter rates of each script. The highest line-level and character-level rates are

---

[7] https://es.wikipedia.org/wiki/Ace_vs_Ace

[8] The three sources are: **Chinese New Year Galas**—the annual televised Chinese New Year celebrations which are the most viewed TV shows in China. The shows consist of various performances including sketch comedies and crosstalks; **Reality Shows**—the programmes that show the unscripted actions of participants such as playing games and talking. We selected the shows in which comedians were involved; **Comedy Competition Shows**—the programmes where different comedians present their comedy performances to a studio audience and the winners are selected based on the audience's votes.

Source	Topics
Chinese New Year Galas	- Love stories and blind dates between old people; - Reflecting social phenomena to call for a better society (e.g. avoid judging people by their appearances, do not spoil children, care more about lonely seniors, the woman builds a good relationship with her mother-in-law, spend more time with children, be wary of scams); - Funny family stories during spring festival;
Reality Shows	- Stories happened in ancient times; - Stories about young people (e.g. encounter ex-boyfriends or ex-girlfriends, relationships between best friends, blind dates); - Reflecting social phenomena to call for a better society (e.g. give seats to vulnerable people);
Comedy Competition Shows	- Love stories; - Hot topics (e.g. support the COVID-19 frontline fighters); - Funny stories that happened among friends and in families; - Reflecting social phenomena to call for a better society (e.g. be wary of scams, care more about orphans in orphanage);

Table 3: Topics of the selected comedies.

Statistics	Value
# of Comedy Scripts	30
Year Range	2014—2020
Total Duration	473.44 mins
Average Duration	15.78 mins
# of Actors' Lines	6087
Laughter Rate (Line-Level)	28.62%
# of Characters	120451
Laughter Rate (Character-Level)	8.16%

Table 4: Corpus statistics. ***# of Actors' Lines*** and ***Characters*** correspond to the total number of lines and characters in our corpus respectively. ***Laughter Rate*** is the rate of lines/characters that trigger laughter.

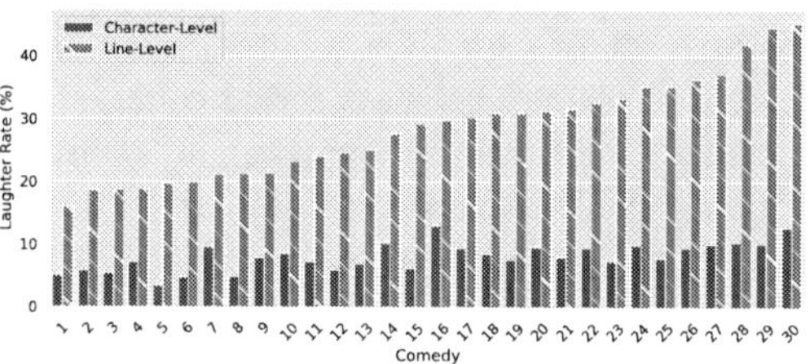

Figure 1: Each script's laughter rate in our corpus.

45.39% and 13.12%, while the lowest rates are 16.03% and 3.49%. We note that the character-level laughter rates vary in different scripts. This may be due to density of laughter triggers of a line or the topic of the script.

3.2 Annotation

The annotation was completed on *Doccano* platform (Nakayama et al., 2018) and the annotators are two native Chinese speakers. The annotations were produced based on the studio audiences' responses as observed in the videos, and are not based on the annotators' responses.

Annotation Instruction Annotating text classification labels is easy; annotators are requested to simply assigned label *1* to the lines that make audiences laugh, and *0* to the others. With regard to the information extraction annotations, annotators are requested to identify text spans which are usually phrases. The span consists of the words that immediately made the audience laugh after the comedians said them. For example, as indicated in Table 2, the span *incredibly big* was annotated. In this case, only annotating *big* would be considered as an incorrect annotation, because the comedian was using *incredibly* to strongly emphasise *big* which was her first impression of a man's house in a blind date. Only annotating *incredibly* would also be incorrect, because the main reason why the audience laughed was because the comedian said the house looked *big*.[9]

Annotation Process   The annotation process was as follows: Firstly, the annotators conducted discussions about the conflicting annotations after several attempts to annotate the same three scripts. Secondly, once agreements about how to solve the conflicts had been reached, they started to annotate their assigned scripts. Afterwards, since information extraction annotation is more complex than that of classification annotations, we measured its quality by computing three types of inter-annotator agreement. We asked the annotators to annotate the same six scripts having different styles and then calculated the Overall Percent Agreement (OPA), Fleiss's kappa (Fleiss, 1971) and Randolph's kappa (Randolph, 2005). We found that the agreement rates were high (OPA 98.09%, Fleiss's Kappa 0.85, Randolph's Kappa 0.96). This is due to the fact that the discussions about solving conflicts were in-depth and the laughter triggers were usually clear in the lines.

4   Baselines and Results Discussion

In order to understand how well the machine learning methods work on our corpus, we evaluate the performances of a number of models on 5-fold cross-validation random splits of the scripts in our corpus and report the average results in this section.[10] All the BERT models were pre-trained by using a mixture of large Chinese corpora.[11] Please

Model	P	R	F	Acc.
CNN (Kim, 2014)	42.53	64.14	51.07	66.29
RCNN (Lai et al., 2015)	41.21	**68.52**	50.89	63.54
BiLSTM (Liu et al., 2016)	41.17	57.13	47.66	65.69
+ Attention (Zhou et al., 2016)	39.97	59.91	47.44	63.94
FastText (Joulin et al., 2017)	40.61	66.26	50.12	63.72
DPCNN (Johnson and Zhang, 2017)	42.46	63.25	50.76	66.32
Transformer (Vaswani et al., 2017)	42.60	64.71	51.24	66.18
BERT-tiny (Jiao et al., 2019)	47.56	53.38	48.91	66.21
BERT-small (Turc et al., 2019)	47.29	56.21	51.21	70.78
BERT-base (Devlin et al., 2019)	**47.60**	56.64	**51.61**	**70.94**

Table 5: Text classification performance. *P*, *R*, *F* and *Acc.* are *Precision*, *Recall*, *F1-score* and *Accuracy* respectively.

Model	P	R	F
HMM (Rabiner and Juang, 1986)	22.19	7.43	11.04
CRF (Lafferty et al., 2001)	28.56	6.11	10.01
BiLSTM (Huang et al., 2015)	**31.21**	1.64	3.09
BiLSTM-CRF (Lample et al., 2016)	30.33	9.81	14.48
BERT-tiny (Jiao et al., 2019)	26.26	19.89	22.57
BERT-small (Turc et al., 2019)	28.82	17.52	21.56
BERT-base (Devlin et al., 2019)	30.15	**21.47**	**24.59**

Table 6: Information extraction performance. Relaxed metrics are used. The exact-match metric is over-strict because the length of text spans in this corpus is much longer than general named entities. The computation of these metrics can be found in (Nguyen et al., 2017).

refer to the appendix for the results of each fold, statistics of splits, computing infrastructure, each model's running time, parameter details and hyper-parameter settings.

Baselines   Tables 5 and 6 respectively present the results of text classification and information extraction. BERT-base has the best F1-scores among all the methods. We also note that the classification recall of RCNN (Lai et al., 2015) is much higher than other methods. Therefore, we suggest using this model if users prefer a classifier with a high recall. In addition, we observe that the scores are not high, especially for the information extraction task. The reason may be if the audience laughter highly depends on the conversation contexts which were not considered by baselines. Therefore, taking a longer conversation context of a line into consideration is a worthy research direction.

Prediction Errors   Tables 7 and 8 present examples incorrectly predicted by the BERT-base. The first 3 examples describe how the model failed to predict the laughter triggers, while the last 3 examples show false positive predictions. Incorporating the context information of lines may further reduce these errors.

Cross-Style Performance   We further investigate the performance of predicting laughter triggers on scripts with a totally different style compared to

---

[9]The house is actually small. Since there is almost no furniture in the house, the comedian said it looked big.

[10]Model implementations were adapted from `https://github.com/649453932/Chinese-Text-Classification-Pytorch`, `https://github.com/luopeixiang/named_entity_recognition` and Zhao et al. (2019).

[11]More details are listed in `https://github.com/dbiir/UER-py/wiki/Modelzoo`.

G	P	Actor's Line	Translation
1	0	(雷电、下雨)	(Thunder, Rain)
1	0	岳云鹏: 今天别开生面，我给大家说一段单口相声。	Yunpeng YUE: Today, to start with something new, I will present a monologue comic talk.
1	0	(马丽出场摔倒)	(Li MA falls down right after she comes on stage)
0	1	快递哥: (电话) 啊，开了。	Courier: (Phone) Yeah, the door opens.
0	1	张小斐: 哎呀，快快快。哎呀，这怎么弄呀，焦头烂额呀，快，擦擦。	Xiaofei ZHANG: Oops! Think quick quick quick. Oh no! What can I do? I'm in a dilemma. Clean it quickly.
0	1	何欢: 爷爷，我错了，我以后再也不撒谎了，我错了爷爷。	Huan HE: It's my fault, grandpa. I'll never lie again. My mistake, grandpa.

Table 7: Examples of incorrect classifications taken from different comedies in our corpus. *G* and *P* are *Gold* and *Predicted* labels, respectively.

Actor's Line	Translation
贾冰: 这事我不敢保证我现在还认不认字啊]。	Bing JIA: I can't guarantee *if I am still [able to read this]* now.
岳云鹏: 你什么时候来的啊	Yuepeng YUE: Huh? *When did you come?*
沈腾: 走肯定是不赶趟了，我得跑了。	Teng SHEN: Walking is not fast enough, *I have to run to escape this*.
快递哥: [散打那个]。	Courier: [The one who is good at free combat].
张小斐: 哎呀，这是善意的谎言，可问题是，老师也不会[演戏呀]！	Xiaofei ZHANG: Well, this is a white lie. But the problem is, I don't know how [to pretend]!
何欢: 不是，你[找谁呀]？	Huan HE: Eh? [Who are] you [looking for]?

Table 8: Examples of incomplete and incorrect extractions taken from different comedies in our corpus. Characters in **bold** and located in [ ] are the gold annotations and predicted results respectively.

the styles in the training data. Firstly, since the six comedians in the corpus have distinctive comedy styles, we split the entire corpus into a 6-fold cross-validation manner. The comedies in each fold are performed by the same leading comedian. Secondly, we train baseline models on five of the folds and evaluate the performance on the remaining fold. Tables 9 and 10 present the average results and the full results are available in the appendix. The results demonstrate that the laughter triggers can be detected even though the styles in the training data are very different compared to the testing data.

5 Conclusion and Future Work

We study the prediction of laughter triggers from comedy scripts by using text classification and information extraction methods. Firstly, we introduce a corpus including high-quality and annotated sketch comedy and crosstalk scripts. Secondly, we evaluate a number of baselines and find that BERT models achieve the best performance. We note that the information extraction performance was very low, indicating that this task is particularly challenging. We also conduct an error analysis of incorrect predictions. The errors suggest the incorporation of rich context information may further improve the performance. Therefore, it is worth investigating a model which can take such infor-

Model	P	R	F	Acc.
CNN (Kim, 2014)	42.75	65.69	51.63	65.04
RCNN (Lai et al., 2015)	42.32	**71.26**	**52.32**	62.79
BiLSTM (Liu et al., 2016)	41.35	60.76	48.81	63.71
+ Attention (Zhou et al., 2016)	43.20	53.76	47.57	66.55
FastText (Joulin et al., 2017)	40.86	67.43	50.70	62.62
DPCNN (Johnson and Zhang, 2017)	41.26	66.82	50.42	62.44
Transformer (Vaswani et al., 2017)	41.57	70.15	51.92	63.06
BERT-tiny (Jiao et al., 2019)	43.01	56.76	48.69	66.23
BERT-small (Turc et al., 2019)	44.95	55.59	49.09	67.38
BERT-base (Devlin et al., 2019)	**47.28**	58.13	51.72	**69.39**

Table 9: Cross-style text classification performance.

Model	P	R	F
HMM (Rabiner and Juang, 1986)	19.79	7.52	10.68
CRF (Lafferty et al., 2001)	25.29	5.03	8.35
BiLSTM (Huang et al., 2015)	29.05	2.90	5.23
BiLSTM-CRF (Lample et al., 2016)	**30.72**	8.77	12.56
BERT-tiny (Jiao et al., 2019)	26.30	19.20	22.14
BERT-small (Turc et al., 2019)	24.93	27.31	25.12
BERT-base (Devlin et al., 2019)	24.64	**31.65**	**26.51**

Table 10: Cross-style information extraction performance.

mation into consideration. Furthermore, it is also worth extending the corpus to a multimodal one by aligning scripts to corresponding audios or videos, because certain intonations or scenes can also make audiences laugh. The multimodal corpus can also benefit the creation of silent comedy. Enriching the corpus by including scripts in other languages may also be a potential direction. Lastly, the encouraging cross-style prediction performance shows the usefulness of our corpus for predicting new scripts with different styles.

Moreover, it is also interesting to explore human performances by asking annotators to make predictions based purely on the scripts of unwatched comedies, and to investigate if the script writers find the model predictions insightful.

We hope this study will benefit script writing by inspiring the community to develop intelligent systems for comedy writers and other artists in the field. The corpus might also be useful for researchers who are working on related or similar tasks, such as discourse analysis and humorous response generation for dialogue systems.

Acknowledgements

We would like to express our sincere appreciation to all comedians and backstage teams for their hard work to make audiences happy. We also sincerely appreciate the valuable comments of all anonymous reviewers. My deepest thanks should also be given to my best friend who inspired me to conduct such research and whose encouragement was important for me to be able to complete the work.

References

Dario Bertero. 2019. *Conversational humor recognition and generation through deep learning.* PhD dissertation, Hong Kong University of Science and Technology.

Marc Blake. 2014. *How to be a Comedy Writer*, volume 1. Andrews UK Limited.

Vladislav Blinov, Valeria Bolotova-Baranova, and Pavel Braslavski. 2019. Large dataset and language model fun-tuning for humor recognition. In *Proceedings of the 57th Annual Meeting of the Association for Computational Linguistics*, pages 4027–4032, Florence, Italy. Association for Computational Linguistics.

Ernesto Carrera-Ruvalcaba, Johnson Ekedum, Austin Hancock, and Ben Brock. 2019. Leveraging natural language processing applications and microblogging platform for increased transparency in crisis areas. *SMU Data Science Review*, 2(1):6.

Santiago Castro, Luis Chiruzzo, Aiala Rosá, Diego Garat, and Guillermo Moncecchi. 2018. A crowd-annotated Spanish corpus for humor analysis. In *Proceedings of the Sixth International Workshop on Natural Language Processing for Social Media*, pages 7–11, Melbourne, Australia. Association for Computational Linguistics.

Peng-Yu Chen and Von-Wun Soo. 2018. Humor recognition using deep learning. In *Proceedings of the 2018 Conference of the North American Chapter of the Association for Computational Linguistics: Human Language Technologies, Volume 2 (Short Papers)*, pages 113–117, New Orleans, Louisiana. Association for Computational Linguistics.

Luis Chiruzzo, S Castro, Mathias Etcheverry, Diego Garat, Juan José Prada, and Aiala Rosá. 2019. Overview of haha at iberlef 2019: Humor analysis based on human annotation. In *Proceedings of the Iberian Languages Evaluation Forum (IberLEF 2019). CEUR Workshop Proceedings, CEUR-WS*, Bilbao, Spain.

Jacob Devlin, Ming-Wei Chang, Kenton Lee, and Kristina Toutanova. 2019. BERT: Pre-training of deep bidirectional transformers for language understanding. In *Proceedings of the 2019 Conference of the North American Chapter of the Association for Computational Linguistics: Human Language Technologies, Volume 1 (Long and Short Papers)*, pages 4171–4186, Minneapolis, Minnesota. Association for Computational Linguistics.

Joseph L Fleiss. 1971. Measuring nominal scale agreement among many raters. *Psychometrika*, 76(5):378.

Md Kamrul Hasan, Wasifur Rahman, AmirAli Bagher Zadeh, Jianyuan Zhong, Md Iftekhar Tanveer, Louis-Philippe Morency, and Mohammed (Ehsan) Hoque. 2019. UR-FUNNY: A multimodal language dataset for understanding humor. In *Proceedings of the 2019 Conference on Empirical Methods in Natural Language Processing and the 9th International Joint Conference on Natural Language Processing (EMNLP-IJCNLP)*, pages 2046–2056, Hong Kong, China. Association for Computational Linguistics.

Zhiheng Huang, Wei Xu, and Kai Yu. 2015. Bidirectional lstm-crf models for sequence tagging. *arXiv preprint arXiv:1508.01991*.

Xiaoqi Jiao, Yichun Yin, Lifeng Shang, Xin Jiang, Xiao Chen, Linlin Li, Fang Wang, and Qun Liu. 2019. Tinybert: Distilling bert for natural language understanding. *arXiv preprint arXiv:1909.10351*.

Rie Johnson and Tong Zhang. 2017. Deep pyramid convolutional neural networks for text categorization. In *Proceedings of the 55th Annual Meeting of the Association for Computational Linguistics (Volume 1: Long Papers)*, pages 562–570, Vancouver, Canada. Association for Computational Linguistics.

Armand Joulin, Edouard Grave, Piotr Bojanowski, and Tomas Mikolov. 2017. Bag of tricks for efficient text classification. In *Proceedings of the 15th Conference of the European Chapter of the Association for Computational Linguistics: Volume 2, Short Papers*, pages 427–431, Valencia, Spain. Association for Computational Linguistics.

Yoon Kim. 2014. Convolutional neural networks for sentence classification. In *Proceedings of the 2014 Conference on Empirical Methods in Natural Language Processing (EMNLP)*, pages 1746–1751, Doha, Qatar. Association for Computational Linguistics.

John Lafferty, Andrew McCallum, and Fernando CN Pereira. 2001. Conditional random fields: Probabilistic models for segmenting and labeling sequence data. In *Proceedings of the 18th International Conference on Machine Learning*, San Francisco, CA, USA. Morgan Kaufmann Publishers Inc.

Siwei Lai, Liheng Xu, Kang Liu, and Jun Zhao. 2015. Recurrent convolutional neural networks for text classification. In *Proceedings of the Twenty-Ninth AAAI Conference on Artificial Intelligence*, AAAI'15, page 2267–2273. AAAI Press.

Guillaume Lample, Miguel Ballesteros, Sandeep Subramanian, Kazuya Kawakami, and Chris Dyer. 2016. Neural architectures for named entity recognition. In *Proceedings of the 2016 Conference of the North American Chapter of the Association for Computational Linguistics: Human Language Technologies*, pages 260–270, San Diego, California. Association for Computational Linguistics.

Da Li, Rafal Rzepka, Michal Ptaszynski, and Kenji Araki. 2020. Hemos: A novel deep learning-based fine-grained humor detecting method for sentiment analysis of social media. *Information Processing & Management*, 57(6):102290.

Pengfei Liu, Xipeng Qiu, and Xuanjing Huang. 2016. Recurrent neural network for text classification with multi-task learning. In *Proceedings of the Twenty-Fifth International Joint Conference on Artificial Intelligence*, IJCAI'16, page 2873–2879. AAAI Press.

Rada Mihalcea and Carlo Strapparava. 2006. Learning to laugh (automatically): Computational models for humor recognition. *Computational Intelligence*, 22(2):126–142.

Hiroki Nakayama, Takahiro Kubo, Junya Kamura, Yasufumi Taniguchi, and Xu Liang. 2018. doccano: Text annotation tool for human. Software available from https://github.com/doccano/doccano.

An Thanh Nguyen, Byron Wallace, Junyi Jessy Li, Ani Nenkova, and Matthew Lease. 2017. Aggregating and predicting sequence labels from crowd annotations. In *Proceedings of the 55th Annual Meeting of the Association for Computational Linguistics (Volume 1: Long Papers)*, pages 299–309, Vancouver, Canada. Association for Computational Linguistics.

Reynier Ortega-Bueno, Carlos E Muniz-Cuza, José E Medina Pagola, and Paolo Rosso. 2018. Uo upv: Deep linguistic humor detection in spanish social media. In *Proceedings of the Third Workshop on Evaluation of Human Language Technologies for Iberian Languages (IberEval 2018) co-located with 34th Conference of the Spanish Society for Natural Language Processing (SEPLN 2018)*, pages 203–213, Seville, Spain.

Lawrence Rabiner and B Juang. 1986. An introduction to hidden markov models. *IEEE ASSP Magazine*, 3(1):4–16.

JJ Randolph. 2005. Free-marginal multirater kappa: an alternative to fleiss' fixed-marginal multirater kappa. *Joensuu University Learning and Instruction Symposium*.

Delip Rao and Brian McMahan. 2019. *Natural language processing with PyTorch: build intelligent language applications using deep learning.* " O'Reilly Media, Inc.".

Serdar Sarıtaş, Hasan Genç, Şerafettin Okutan, Ramazan İnci, Ahmet Özdemir, and Gülnaz Kizilkaya. 2019. The effect of comedy films on postoperative pain and anxiety in surgical oncology patients. *Complementary Medicine Research*, 26(4):231–239.

Iulia Turc, Ming-Wei Chang, Kenton Lee, and Kristina Toutanova. 2019. Well-read students learn better: The impact of student initialization on knowledge distillation. *arXiv preprint arXiv:1908.08962*.

Ashish Vaswani, Noam Shazeer, Niki Parmar, Jakob Uszkoreit, Llion Jones, Aidan N Gomez, Ł ukasz Kaiser, and Illia Polosukhin. 2017. Attention is all you need. In I. Guyon, U. V. Luxburg, S. Bengio, H. Wallach, R. Fergus, S. Vishwanathan, and R. Garnett, editors, *Advances in Neural Information Processing Systems 30*, pages 5998–6008. Curran Associates, Inc.

Sandy M Williams, Pauline K Arnold, and Jennifer N Mills. 2005. Coping with stress: a survey of murdoch university veterinary students. *Journal of Veterinary Medical Education*, 32(2):201–212.

Diyi Yang, Alon Lavie, Chris Dyer, and Eduard Hovy. 2015. Humor recognition and humor anchor extraction. In *Proceedings of the 2015 Conference on Empirical Methods in Natural Language Processing*, pages 2367–2376, Lisbon, Portugal. Association for Computational Linguistics.

Dongyu Zhang, Heting Zhang, Xikai Liu, Hongfei Lin, and Feng Xia. 2019. Telling the whole story: A manually annotated Chinese dataset for the analysis of humor in jokes. In *Proceedings of the 2019 Conference on Empirical Methods in Natural Language Processing and the 9th International Joint Conference on Natural Language Processing (EMNLP-IJCNLP)*, pages 6402–6407, Hong Kong, China. Association for Computational Linguistics.

Renxian Zhang and Naishi Liu. 2014. Recognizing humor on twitter. In *Proceedings of the 23rd ACM International Conference on Conference on Information and Knowledge Management*, CIKM '14, page 889–898, New York, NY, USA. Association for Computing Machinery.

Zhe Zhao, Hui Chen, Jinbin Zhang, Xin Zhao, Tao Liu, Wei Lu, Xi Chen, Haotang Deng, Qi Ju, and Xiaoyong Du. 2019. UER: An open-source toolkit for pretraining models. In *Proceedings of the 2019 Conference on Empirical Methods in Natural Language Processing and the 9th International Joint Conference on Natural Language Processing (EMNLP-IJCNLP): System Demonstrations*, pages 241–246, Hong Kong, China. Association for Computational Linguistics.

Peng Zhou, Wei Shi, Jun Tian, Zhenyu Qi, Bingchen Li, Hongwei Hao, and Bo Xu. 2016. Attention-based bidirectional long short-term memory networks for relation classification. In *Proceedings of the 54th Annual Meeting of the Association for Computational Linguistics (Volume 2: Short Papers)*, pages 207–212, Berlin, Germany. Association for Computational Linguistics.

A Appendices

A.1 Computing Resources

Table 11 describes the details of the computing resources used for all of our experiments. These resources are freely available from *Paperspace*[12].

A.2 Model Details

Below we present **model hyper-parameter values**[13] and the **average running time of one epoch**.

---

[12] https://www.paperspace.com/

[13] The size of model's trainable parameters can be found in original papers.

Name	Description
CPU	8 vCPUs, 30GB RAM
GPU	NVIDIA Quadro P5000 Graphics Card, 16GB
Processor	Intel Xeon
Clock Speed	2.60 GHz

Table 11: Details of computing resources.

A.2.1 Text Classification Models

CNN (Kim, 2014) Dropout = 0.5, Number of Epochs = 20, Batch Size = 128, Learning Rate = 0.001, Number of Filters = 256, Filter Sizes = 2,3,4, Average Running Time = 5s.

RCNN (Lai et al., 2015) Dropout = 1.0, Number of Epochs = 10, Batch Size = 128, Learning Rate = 0.001, Hidden Size = 256, Number of Layers = 1, Average Running Time = 5s.

BiLSTM (Liu et al., 2016) Dropout = 0.5, Number of Epochs = 10, Batch Size = 128, Learning Rate = 0.001, Hidden Size = 128, Number of Layers = 2, Average Running Time = 5.4s.

+ Attention (Zhou et al., 2016) Dropout = 0.5, Number of Epochs = 10, Batch Size = 128, Learning Rate = 0.001, Hidden Size = 128 and 64 respectively, Number of Layers = 2, Average Running Time = 5.74s.

FastText (Joulin et al., 2017) Dropout = 0.5, Number of Epochs = 20, Batch Size = 128, Learning Rate = 0.001, Hidden Size = 256, Average Running Time = 22.5s.

DPCNN (Johnson and Zhang, 2017) Dropout = 0.5, Number of Epochs = 20, Batch Size = 128, Learning Rate = 0.001, Number of Filter = 250, Average Running Time = 5s.

Transformer (Vaswani et al., 2017) Dropout = 0.5, Number of Epochs = 20, Batch Size = 128, Learning Rate = 0.0005, Number of Head = 5, Number of Encoder = 2, Average Running Time = 6.528s.

BERT-tiny (Jiao et al., 2019) Dropout = 0.1, Number of Epoch = 20, Batch Size = 64, Learning Rate = 0.00002, Size of Embedding = 384, Feedforward Size = 1536, Hidden Size = 384, Number of Head = 6, Number of Layer = 3, Average Running Time = 20.63s.

BERT-small (Turc et al., 2019) Dropout = 0.5, Number of Epoch = 20, Batch Size = 64, Learning Rate = 0.00002, Size of Embedding = 512, Feedforward Size = 2048, Hidden Size = 512, Number of Head = 8, Number of Layer = 6, Average Running Time = 36.65.

BERT-base (Devlin et al., 2019) Dropout = 0.1, Number of Epoch = 10, Batch Size = 64, Learning Rate = 0.00002, Size of Embedding = 768, Feedforward Size = 3072, Hidden Size = 768, Number of Head = 12, Number of Layer = 12, Average Running Time = 99s.

A.2.2 Information Extraction Models

HMM (Rabiner and Juang, 1986) Uniform Distribution for Initialisation, Average Total Running Time = 8.47s.

CRF (Lafferty et al., 2001) LBFGS algorithm, c1 = 0.1, c2 = 0.1, Max Iteration = 100, Average Total Running Time = 11.72s.

BiLSTM (Huang et al., 2015) Number of Epoch = 30, Batch Size = 64, Learning Rate = 0.001, Size of Embedding = 128, Hidden Size = 128, Average Running Time = 8.43s.

BiLSTM-CRF (Lample et al., 2016) Number of Epoch = 30, Batch Size = 64, Learning Rate = 0.001, Size of Embedding = 128, Hidden Size = 128, Average Running Time = 9.35s.

BERT Models We use the same hyper-parameter settings as used in the text classification models with the exception of Batch Size = 16. The average running time of BERT-tiny, BERT-small and BERT-base for information extraction are 34.00s, 55.73s, and 120s respectively.

A.3 Details of Baseline Experiments

Table 12 shows the statistics of each fold.

Fold	Text Classification # of Lines	Total	Information Extraction # of Characters	Total
0	277/685	962	1666/20010	21676
1	290/854	1144	1703/19354	21057
2	285/789	1074	1666/19609	21275
3	358/909	1267	2251/23535	25786
4	459/1181	1640	2632/28025	30657

Table 12: Statistics of each fold in the baseline experiments. The number before slash indicates how many actor's lines or characters that make the audience laugh. The number after slash indicates the number of lines or characters without causing audiences laugh.

	Model	Fold-0	Fold-1	Fold-2	Fold-3	Fold-4	Average
P	CNN	42.64	40.43	42.61	42.27	44.68	42.53
	RCNN	43.47	38.30	43.93	35.44	44.93	41.21
	BiLSTM	43.56	37.80	40.19	42.20	42.12	41.17
	+Attention	39.53	38.93	41.75	37.62	42.01	39.97
	FastText	39.37	44.64	36.96	41.12	40.98	40.61
	DPCNN	42.44	41.67	41.73	41.86	44.61	42.46
	Transformer	**46.67**	38.17	42.43	42.08	43.66	42.60
	BERT-tiny	42.26	42.05	44.62	**54.43**	**54.43**	47.56
	BERT-small	44.74	46.13	**46.02**	52.35	47.22	47.29
	BERT-base	45.65	**47.73**	42.66	53.03	48.91	**47.60**
R	CNN	70.04	64.02	60.70	66.48	59.48	64.14
	RCNN	66.06	**70.08**	59.65	**86.03**	60.78	**68.52**
	BiLSTM	51.26	65.15	58.95	56.70	53.59	57.13
	+Attention	55.23	65.91	58.60	75.14	44.66	59.91
	FastText	68.23	56.82	**71.58**	63.41	**71.24**	66.26
	DPCNN	67.87	62.50	61.05	65.36	59.48	63.25
	Transformer	60.65	69.70	64.91	62.29	66.01	64.71
	BERT-tiny	62.09	41.03	59.65	49.72	54.43	53.38
	BERT-small	59.93	47.24	62.81	59.22	51.85	56.21
	BERT-base	62.45	50.69	55.09	61.17	53.81	56.64
F	CNN	53.01	49.56	50.07	51.68	51.03	51.07
	RCNN	52.44	49.53	50.60	50.20	51.67	50.89
	BiLSTM	47.10	47.84	47.80	48.39	47.17	47.66
	+Attention	46.08	48.95	48.76	50.14	43.29	47.44
	FastText	49.93	**50.00**	48.75	49.89	52.03	50.12
	DPCNN	52.22	**50.00**	49.57	51.04	50.98	50.76
	Transformer	**52.75**	49.33	51.32	50.23	**52.56**	51.24
	BERT-tiny	50.29	41.54	51.05	51.97	49.72	48.91
	BERT-small	51.23	46.68	**53.12**	55.57	49.43	51.21
	BERT-base	52.74	49.16	48.09	**56.81**	51.24	**51.61**
A	CNN	64.24	66.41	67.88	64.88	68.05	66.29
	RCNN	65.49	63.18	69.09	51.78	68.17	63.54
	BiLSTM	66.84	63.38	65.83	65.82	66.40	65.65
	+Attention	62.79	64.55	67.32	57.77	67.26	63.94
	FastText	60.60	70.70	60.06	64.01	63.23	63.72
	DPCNN	64.24	67.77	67.04	64.56	67.99	66.32
	Transformer	**68.71**	63.09	67.32	65.11	66.65	66.18
	BERT-tiny	64.66	70.72	69.65	74.03	51.97	66.21
	BERT-small	67.15	72.64	**70.58**	73.24	70.30	70.78
	BERT-base	67.78	**73.43**	68.44	**73.72**	**71.34**	**70.94**

Table 13: Each fold's text classification baseline experiments and their overall average performance. *P*, *R*, *F* and *A* are *Precision*, *Recall*, *F1-score* and *Accuracy* respectively.

Tables 13 and 14 describe the detailed performance of text classification and information extraction baseline experiments.

	Model	Fold-0	Fold-1	Fold-2	Fold-3	Fold-4	Average
P	HMM	18.26	21.15	26.37	19.46	25.70	22.19
	CRF	24.62	**30.86**	**34.17**	23.33	29.83	28.56
	BILSTM	26.25	37.14	26.00	**37.31**	29.35	**31.21**
	BiLSTM-CRF	30.50	24.43	32.46	29.71	**34.56**	30.33
	BERT-tiny	27.64	23.98	28.89	26.73	24.08	26.26
	BERT-small	31.71	24.12	30.83	28.04	29.38	28.82
	BERT-base	**36.23**	28.16	26.56	30.88	28.93	30.15
R	HMM	7.19	9.64	7.38	5.93	7.02	7.43
	CRF	6.49	5.49	6.32	6.47	5.76	6.11
	BILSTM	2.24	1.23	0.55	2.47	1.70	1.64
	BiLSTM-CRF	16.76	8.00	9.25	6.30	8.73	9.81
	BERT-tiny	17.37	19.54	20.96	**22.46**	19.10	19.89
	BERT-small	16.90	19.22	16.26	21.35	13.86	17.52
	BERT-base	**21.62**	**21.19**	**27.17**	21.02	**16.35**	**21.47**
F	HMM	10.32	13.24	11.53	9.09	11.03	11.04
	CRF	10.27	9.33	10.67	10.13	9.65	10.01
	BILSTM	4.13	2.37	1.08	4.63	3.22	3.09
	BiLSTM-CRF	21.63	12.05	14.40	10.39	13.94	14.48
	BERT-tiny	21.33	21.53	24.30	24.41	**21.30**	22.57
	BERT-small	22.05	21.40	21.29	24.24	18.83	21.56
	BERT-base	**26.01**	**24.18**	**26.86**	**25.02**	20.89	**24.59**

Table 14: Each fold's information extraction baseline experiments and their overall average performance.

A.4 Details of Cross-Style Experiments

Table 15 shows the statistics of the scripts performed by specific leading comedians. Tables 16 and 17 present the prediction results.

Comedian	Text Classification		Information Extraction	
	# of Lines	Total	# of Characters	Total
Xiaobao SONG	315/815	1150	2001/20366	22367
Yuepeng YUE	436/1547	1983	2362/25579	27941
Ling JIA	195/501	696	1135/14414	15549
Xiaofei ZHANG	190/495	685	1056/15946	17002
Teng SHEN	166/350	516	1071/13143	14214
Bing JIA	367/690	1057	2293/21085	23378

Table 15: Statistics of the scripts performed by specific leading comedians.

A.5 Full List of Selected Comedy Performances

Tables 18 and 19 show the full list of performances in our corpus with details.

	Model	0	1	2	3	4	5	Average
P	CNN	41.99	40.00	41.85	39.67	45.70	47.29	42.75
	BiLSTM	38.17	42.18	39.35	36.26	45.26	46.90	41.35
	+ Attention	42.70	38.16	**45.06**	38.49	48.02	46.78	43.20
	RCNN	**46.93**	44.01	36.36	37.23	46.26	43.10	42.32
	FastText	41.88	37.99	36.64	37.81	45.24	45.57	40.86
	DPCNN	42.01	42.21	36.03	35.25	45.33	46.71	41.26
	Transformer	41.97	36.32	36.94	41.30	46.50	46.41	41.57
	BERT-tiny	40.73	37.41	42.38	40.81	45.30	51.40	43.01
	BERT-small	39.08	39.67	42.97	48.40	43.22	56.38	44.95
	BERT-base	42.50	**44.40**	42.73	**48.68**	**48.05**	**57.31**	**47.28**
R	CNN	61.59	51.38	69.74	66.48	**80.61**	64.31	65.69
	BiLSTM	51.75	47.02	62.56	70.33	75.15	57.77	60.76
	+ Attention	36.19	55.05	53.85	53.30	58.79	65.40	53.76
	RCNN	55.87	51.38	82.05	**75.27**	78.79	**84.20**	**71.26**
	FastText	62.22	55.50	73.85	66.48	**80.61**	65.94	67.43
	DPCNN	60.95	47.25	75.38	74.18	79.39	63.76	66.82
	Transformer	62.22	**62.39**	**84.10**	66.48	**80.61**	65.12	70.15
	BERT-tiny	**67.62**	47.71	58.46	47.89	63.86	55.04	56.76
	BERT-small	61.90	44.50	56.41	47.89	71.08	51.77	55.59
	BERT-base	64.76	47.25	49.74	58.42	74.10	54.50	58.13
F	CNN	49.94	44.98	**52.31**	49.69	58.33	54.50	51.63
	BiLSTM	43.94	44.47	48.32	47.85	56.49	51.77	48.81
	+ Attention	39.18	45.07	49.07	44.70	52.86	54.55	47.57
	RCNN	51.01	**47.41**	50.39	49.82	58.30	**57.01**	**52.32**
	FastText	50.06	45.11	48.98	48.21	57.95	53.90	50.70
	DPCNN	49.74	44.59	48.76	47.79	57.71	53.92	50.42
	Transformer	50.13	45.91	51.33	50.95	**58.98**	54.20	51.92
	BERT-tiny	50.84	41.94	49.14	44.07	53.00	53.16	48.69
	BERT-small	47.91	41.95	48.78	48.15	53.76	53.98	49.09
	BERT-base	**51.32**	45.78	45.97	**53.11**	58.29	55.87	51.72
A	CNN	66.17	72.37	64.37	61.72	62.89	62.72	65.04
	BiLSTM	63.83	74.18	62.50	56.41	62.70	62.63	63.71
	+ Attention	69.22	70.50	**68.68**	62.50	66.21	62.16	66.55
	RCNN	**70.61**	74.94	54.74	56.87	63.67	55.91	62.79
	FastText	66.00	70.30	56.90	59.38	62.30	60.83	62.62
	DPCNN	66.26	74.18	55.60	53.91	62.50	62.16	62.44
	Transformer	66.09	67.68	55.32	63.59	63.87	61.78	63.06
	BERT-tiny	64.17	70.95	66.09	66.28	63.57	66.32	66.23
	BERT-small	63.13	72.92	66.81	**71.39**	60.66	69.35	67.38
	BERT-base	66.35	**75.39**	67.24	**71.39**	**65.89**	**70.10**	**69.39**

Table 16: Performance of text classification in predicting the scripts performed by specific leading comedians (*0*: Xiaobao SONG, *1*: Yuepeng YUE, *2*: Ling JIA, *3*: Xiaofei ZHANG, *4*: Teng SHEN, *5*: Bing JIA).

	Model	0	1	2	3	4	5	Average
P	HMM	21.67	19.47	22.03	16.69	14.61	24.25	19.79
	CRF	22.72	20.54	**39.79**	21.43	18.28	28.96	25.29
	BILSTM	**26.32**	21.48	31.70	24.53	**32.39**	37.89	29.05
	BiLSTM-CRF	**26.32**	**23.35**	33.08	**31.86**	25.71	**44.02**	**30.72**
	BERT-tiny	24.43	21.87	29.61	26.37	27.19	28.32	26.30
	BERT-small	23.93	20.19	26.01	23.85	22.80	32.81	24.93
	BERT-base	20.48	19.10	23.74	24.41	26.58	33.51	24.64
R	HMM	6.91	6.26	6.96	9.50	8.79	6.68	7.52
	CRF	5.80	4.87	7.47	4.41	3.13	4.48	5.03
	BILSTM	4.40	2.17	2.40	2.20	3.71	2.49	2.90
	BiLSTM-CRF	7.64	14.06	17.52	7.30	3.20	2.90	8.77
	BERT-tiny	16.88	19.89	22.26	19.15	19.06	**17.98**	19.20
	BERT-small	22.63	31.31	29.31	**32.78**	**32.42**	15.39	27.31
	BERT-base	**39.61**	**36.43**	35.25	32.01	28.64	17.95	**31.65**
F	HMM	10.48	9.48	10.58	12.11	10.97	10.47	10.68
	CRF	9.24	7.87	12.59	7.31	5.34	7.76	8.35
	BILSTM	7.60	3.94	4.46	4.04	6.65	4.67	5.23
	BiLSTM-CRF	11.87	17.55	22.90	11.88	5.70	5.44	12.56
	BERT-tiny	19.97	20.83	25.42	22.19	22.41	22.00	22.14
	BERT-small	23.26	24.55	27.56	27.61	26.77	20.95	25.12
	BERT-base	**27.00**	**25.06**	**28.37**	**27.70**	**27.57**	23.37	**26.51**

Table 17: Performance of information extraction in predicting the scripts performed by specific leading comedians.

Performance Title	Translation	Comedians	Source	Translation
扶不扶	Help Her Up or Not	Teng SHEN etc.	央视春晚	CCTV Chinese New Year Gala
碰瓷	An Incident-Faking Extortionist	Xiaobao SONG etc.	欢乐喜剧人(第一季)	Joyful Comedians (Season 1)
一念天堂	Heaven or Hell?	Teng SHEN etc.	欢乐喜剧人(第一季)	Joyful Comedians (Season 1)
纯闺蜜	We Are Pure Besties	Teng SHEN etc.	欢乐喜剧人(第一季)	Joyful Comedians (Season 1)
以貌取人	Judge By Appearances	Xiaobao SONG etc.	辽宁卫视春晚	LNTV Chinese New Year Gala
闺蜜小时代之怀孕	Story of My Bestie - Pregnancy	Xiaofei ZHANG etc.	喜剧班的春天(第一季)	Comedy Class of Spring (Season 1)
非一般的爱情	Unusual Love	Yunpeng YUE and Yue Sun	欢乐喜剧人(第二季)	Joyful Comedians (Season 2)
选妃记	Select Imperial Concubine	Xiaobao SONG etc.	王牌对王牌(第一季)	Ace VS Ace (Season 1)
暴走街区	Violent Teenagers	Xiaofei ZHANG etc.	欢乐喜剧人(第三季)	Joyful Comedians (Season 3)
前男友前女友	Ex-boyfriend and Ex-girlfriend	Xiaofei ZHANG etc.	喜剧班的春天(第二季)	Comedy Class of Spring (Season 2)
落跑姐妹之还债	Escapted Sisters - Repay a Debt	Ling JIA etc.	喜剧班的春天(第二季)	Comedy Class of Spring (Season 2)
公交故事之让座	Give Up Seats on a Bus	Ling JIA etc.	喜剧班的春天(第二季)	Comedy Class of Spring (Season 2)
贾总的演讲	Manager JIA's Presentation	Bing JIA etc.	笑声传奇(第一季)	Lengend of Laughter (Season 1)
一碗元宵	A Bowl of Yuanxiao	Xiaofei ZHANG etc.	湖南卫视元宵喜乐会	Mango TV Lantern Festival Party
非诚来扰	Blind Date with Me If You Are Not Sincere	Xiaobao SONG etc.	辽宁卫视春晚	LNTV Chinese New Year Gala
学车	Learn Driving	Bing JIA etc.	央视春晚	CCTV Chinese New Year Gala
爱回家	Love Back Home	Bing JIA etc.	东方卫视春晚	Tomato TV Chinese New Year Gala
幸福牛家村	Happy Niu Families' Village	Xiaofei ZHANG etc.	江苏卫视春晚	JSTV Chinese New Year Gala
关于爱情	Something About Love	Yunpeng YUE and Yue Sun	辽宁卫视春晚	LNTV Chinese New Year Gala
懒汉相亲	Idler's Blind Date	Ling JIA etc.	王牌对王牌(第4季)	Ace VS Ace (Season 4)
啼笑皆非	Not Know Whether to Laugh or Cry	Ling JIA etc.	央视春晚	CCTV Chinese New Year Gala
占位子	Grab The Best Seat In The Classroom for My Children	Teng SHEN etc.	央视春晚	CCTV Chinese New Year Gala
你膨胀了	Arrogant You	Yunpeng YUE and Yue Sun	东方卫视春晚	Tomato TV Chinese New Year Gala
乌龙快递	Express Delivery for COVID-19 Frontline Fighters	Bing JIA etc.	欢乐喜剧人(第六季)	Joyful Comedians (Season 6)
父与子	Father and Son	Bing JIA etc.	辽宁卫视春晚	LNTV Chinese New Year Gala
猜谜语	Guess Riddles	Yunpeng YUE and Yue Sun	辽宁卫视春晚	LNTV Chinese New Year Gala
想说爱你不容易	Not Easy to Say Love You	Xiaobao SONG etc.	山东卫视春晚	SDTV-1 Chinese New Year Gala
生活趣谈	Funny Stories in Life	Yunpeng YUE and Yue Sun	央视春晚	CCTV Chinese New Year Gala
婆婆妈妈	Husband's Mother	Ling JIA etc.	央视春晚	CCTV Chinese New Year Gala
走过场	Go Through The Motions	Teng SHEN etc.	央视春晚	CCTV Chinese New Year Gala

Table 18: Full list of the selected comedy performances with their titles, leading comedians and source.

Performance Title	Translation	Year	Duration (mins)	Number of Lines	Laughter Rate (Line-Level)	Number of Characters	Laugher Rate (Character-Level)
扶不扶	Help Her Up or Not	2014	14.75	114	44.74%	3411	10.29%
碰瓷	An Incident-Faking Extortionist	2015	16.07	202	23.27%	3902	8.69%
一念天堂	Heaven or Hell?	2015	10.92	55	32.73%	1518	9.55%
纯闺蜜	We Are Pure Besties	2015	11.3	85	35.29%	2468	7.86%
以貌取人	Judge By Appearances	2015	12.87	220	31.36%	3919	9.72%
闺蜜小时代之怀孕	Story of My Bestie - Pregnancy	2015	8.5	81	33.33%	1894	7.44%
非一般的爱情	Unusual Love	2016	41.68	317	27.76%	4836	10.36%
选妃记	Select Imperial Concubine	2016	12.62	141	21.28%	2522	9.79%
暴走街区	Violent Teenagers	2017	12.67	190	20%	4768	4.8%
前男友前女友	Ex-boyfriend and Ex-girlfriend	2017	10.43	106	19.81%	2723	3.49%
落跑姐妹之还债	Escapted Sisters - Repay a Debt	2017	12.27	135	25.19%	2894	6.91%
公交故事之让座	Give Up Seats on a Bus	2017	9.28	95	42.11%	1795	10.53%
贾总的演讲	Manager JIA's Presentation	2017	23.5	228	36.4%	5319	9.64%
一碗元宵	A Bowl of Yuanxiao	2018	17.58	177	31.07%	4465	7.57%
非诚来扰	Blind Date with Me If You Are Not Sincere	2018	31.3	357	35.29%	7854	10.06%
学车	Learn Driving	2018	14.83	165	30.3%	3306	9.5%
爱回家	Love Back Home	2019	15.31	152	45.39%	3738	12.79%
幸福牛家村	Happy Niu Families' Village	2019	12.18	131	31.7%	3152	8.03%
关于爱情	Something About Love	2019	21.83	590	21.53%	8044	7.91%
懒汉相亲	Idler's Blind Date	2019	8.77	101	18.81%	1946	5.4%
啼笑皆非	Not Know Whether to Laugh or Cry	2019	17.72	178	24.72%	4726	5.99%
占位子	Grab The Best Seat In The Classroom for My Children	2019	14	140	29.29%	3786	6.15%
你膨胀了	Arrogant You	2020	12.65	241	29.88%	3797	13.12%
乌龙快递	Express Delivery for COVID-19 Frontline Fighters	2020	15.43	195	24.1%	4672	7.3%
父与子	Father and Son	2020	23.33	317	37.22%	6343	10.2%
猜谜语	Guess Riddles	2020	19.4	523	18.93%	7142	7.24%
想说爱你不容易	Not Easy to Say Love You	2020	12.53	230	18.7%	4170	5.85%
生活趣谈	Funny Stories in Life	2020	11.5	312	16.03%	4122	5.09%
婆婆妈妈	Husband's Mother	2020	16.42	187	31.02%	4188	8.55%
走过场	Go Through The Motions	2020	11.8	122	21.31%	3031	4.88%

Table 19: Full list of the selected comedy performances with their titles, years, duration, number of lines/characters and laughter rate at line/character-level.

Exploring Coreference Features in Heterogeneous Data

Ekaterina Lapshinova-Koltunski
Saarland University and
University of Hildesheim
Saarbrücken Campus A2.2 Germany
`e.lapshinova@mx.uni-saarland.de`

Kerstin Anna Kunz
Heidelberg University
Plöck 57a, 69117 Heidelberg
`kerstin.kunz@`
`iued.uni-heidelberg.de`

Abstract

The present paper focuses on variation phenomena in coreference chains. We address the hypothesis that the degree of structural variation between chain elements depends on language-specific constraints and preferences and, even more, on the communicative situation of language production. We define coreference features that also include reference to abstract entities and events. These features are inspired through several sources – cognitive parameters, pragmatic factors and typological status. We pay attention to the distributions of these features in a dataset containing English and German texts of spoken and written discourse mode, which can be classified into seven different registers. We apply text classification and feature selection to find out how these variational dimensions (language, mode and register) impact on coreference features. Knowledge on the variation under analysis is valuable for contrastive linguistics, translation studies and multilingual natural language processing (NLP), e.g. machine translation or cross-lingual coreference resolution.

1 Introduction

The way in which coreference is realised in texts is governed by the mode of production, by typical contexts of situation and by language peculiarities. In this study, we are particularly concerned with coreference variation as a result of these three influencing factors. The production and reception of referring expressions in naturally occurring discourse is a reflection of discourse mode (spoken vs. written discourse, see Kibrik, 2011, 11). Another influence is exerted by discourse genres or registers[1] that correspond to standard configurations of communicative topics, goals and speaker interaction, typical of particular discourse communities. We know from register and genre studies (for instance Biber, 2012, 33) that register differences can be observed at all linguistic levels and be deduced from lexico-grammatical features. The production and reception of referring expressions is governed by language-specific factors, as coreference relations in different languages vary considerably in the range of linguistic means triggering these relations (Kunz and Steiner, 2012; Kunz and Lapshinova-Koltunski, 2015; Novák and Nedoluzhko, 2015). Moreover, there are language-specific preferences for using particular means over others.

Variational dimensions such as mode, register and language influence the choice and the frequency of referential expressions in language use. We therefore need to know how this influence is reflected in the kinds of coreference phenomena, their internal organisation (structure) and in their interplay with other related phenomena. Apart from answering linguistically motivated contrastive questions, this knowledge is also beneficial to the area of natural language processing, i.e. when designing features for coreference resolution tasks in multilingual heterogeneous data. The importance of the information on this variation is known, as for instance, the CoNLL-2012 shared task on coreference resolution included multiple languages, modes and registers within OntoNotes (Recasens and Pradhan, 2016). Information on language-driven variational mechanisms in coreference is valuable for multilingual coreference resolution systems (Rahman and Ng, 2012; Pradhan et al., 2012; Recasens et al., 2010; Harabagiu and Maiorano, 2000). Kübler and Zhekova (2016) describe difficulties and challenges of this task showing that many issues remain unsolved in multilingual coreference resolution. In coreference projection, when the annotation of coreference chains in a source lan-

---

[1] We prefer to use the term 'register' instead of 'genre', as register reflects functional variation of a language, whereas 'genre' rather refers to the cultural belonging of a text.

53

Proceedings of the First Workshop on Computational Approaches to Discourse, pages 53–64
Online, November 20, 2020. ©2020 Association for Computational Linguistics
https://doi.org/10.18653/v1/P17

guage is projected onto a target language (Novák et al., 2017; Grishina and Stede, 2015; Yarowsky et al., 2001), non-equivalences resulting from language contrasts cause numerous errors. Knowledge on the register and on mode differences is also useful for coreference resolution that requires domain adaptation (Rösiger and Teufel, 2014; Uryupina and Poesio, 2012; Yang et al., 2012; Apostolova et al., 2012). There are studies showing that register and mode impact on anaphora prediction models (see e.g. Zeldes, 2018).

In this paper, we define a number of coreference features that are inspired through several sources – cognitive parameters, pragmatic factors and typological status. We pay attention to the distributions of these features in a dataset containing English and German texts that belong to two different discourse modes (spoken and written) and can be classified into seven different registers (academic speeches, political essays, general interviews, literature, technical manuals, popular science and texts from company websites). As our main goal is to find out how these variational dimensions (language, mode and register) impact on coreference features, we apply data mining techniques focusing on the following research questions (RQs):

RQ1 Which coreference features are most informative in the three prediction tasks: (a) language, (b) mode, (3) register?

RQ2 Which parameters are distinctive for the languages, modes and registers under analysis?

2 Theoretical Background

In our study, coreference includes cohesive relations of identity, i.e. relations between coreferring expressions in a text pointing to the same extra-linguistic referent. This is illustrated in example (1).

(1)   *... what relativity is really about, is the question of what two different people, in motion with respect to another, relative to one another, when they look at something happening, or they measure something, the distance between two points or the time between two events, the question is what do these two guys get, if they're in relative motion...*

The first referring expression in the text is the `antecedent` (*two different people*) introducing the referent into the textual world. We account for antecedents referring to referents such as persons, objects, times and locations, and also to more complex semantic concepts such as actions or processes, as in example (2), or facts and events. Concepts relating to persons or objects are often expressed by simpler linguistic structures such as noun phrases, while complex concepts are typically reflected by less condensed structures such as sentences and even larger stretches of text and may therefore also function as antecedents in coreference chains. These are also included in our analysis.

All other subsequent expressions, referring to the same referent are `anaphors` – explicit linguistic triggers indicating an anaphoric relation to another stretch of text. They include personal and demonstrative pronouns (*it* and *this*), cohesive adverbs of place and time (e.g. *here*, *then*) and pronominal adverbs (e.g. *herewith* in English or *damit* in German), which are especially frequent in German. They all function as anaphoric heads. Moreover we include possessive and demonstrative determiners (*these* in *these two guys* in example (1)) and the definite article, functioning as modifiers within the anaphor. The antecedent and all subsequent anaphors pointing to the same referent occur in a `coreference chain`.

In our study, we account for variation of form and structure of coreferring expressions, their grammatical function and syntactic position, as well as variation with respect to the chain relation. Most studies on (automatic) anaphora resolution are based on the assumption that the reasons for differences in form, grammatical function and position of coreferring expressions in one and the same chain are related to differences in the degree of accessibility, givenness or salience that a referent has in the recipient's mind at a given point (Ariel, 2001; Prince, 1981; Gundel et al., 2003; Grosz et al., 1995; Eckert and Strube, 2000, among others). For instance, coreferring expressions that are realised as pronouns and occur as subjects in sentence-initial position typically signal a high degree of accessibility, whereas full lexical phrases that are non-subjects at sentence-final position typically reflect a lower degree of accessibility. Furthermore, the accessibility of a referent is related to chain features (e.g. Eckert and Strube, 2000): low distance in long coreference chains together with a low general number of different coreference chains is related to a high degree of accessibility.

Our main interest is functional variation of coreference that mainly stems from three variables of language use – mode of production, register variation and language contrast. We are aware of the fact that these variables interact with the general principles of cognitive processing mentioned above. However, the reflection of the cognitive status in coreference variation itself is not the focus of the current paper.

As mentioned above, the range of available and preferred linguistic structures for realising coreference chains differs across languages (Kunz and Steiner, 2012; Kunz and Lapshinova-Koltunski, 2015; Novák and Nedoluzhko, 2015). The two languages under analysis differ in the linguistic forms available to signal coreference: German has more fine-grained options for differentiating degrees of accessibility, such as pronominal adverbs or demonstrative articles, whereas the English language system provides less syntactic flexibility and is more restricted than German in the distribution of accessible or less accessible referents. Besides that, English prefers more lexical means for establishing cohesion, whereas German tends to use more grammatical means of coreference (Kunz et al., 2017). German also seems to tend towards explicitating coreference relations, especially by using more demonstratives than English. We therefore argue that English and German differ in how correferring expressions vary in their form, syntactic function and position if looking inside coreference chains. For instance, frequent alternations in the use of demonstrative and personal pronouns are common in German, whereas in English, the form of the anaphor generally does not often change.This is illustrated in examples (2) and (3).

(2) *We work for prosperity and opportunity because they're right. It's the right thing to do.*

(3) *Wir arbeiten für Wohlstand und Chancen, weil das richtig ist. Wir tun damit das Richtige. ("We work for prosperity and opportunity because that is right. We do thereby the right").*

In the English example, the personal pronoun *they* refers to the entities *prosperity and opportunity*, and the personal pronoun *It* – to the event *working for prosperity and opportunity*. In the translation into German, the demonstrative *das* and the pronominal adverbial *damit* refer to the event *working for prosperity and opportunity* in both cases. In the second case, an additional logico-semantic relation of instrument is encoded implying a change in terms of form, grammatical function as well as position of the anaphor.

High or low variation in the use of different coreference expressions in texts may not only by subject to language contrasts but may also be a reflection of register or/ and the type of language production:

(4) *I live in a town called called Reigate. It's between London and the countryside which is quite nice. It takes us about 25 minutes to get to London on the train. It's I say it's a town, it's more of a village. It's quite small. It's very nice actually, it's a nice place to live.*

Example (4) is an extract from our spoken register INTERVIEW. It not only shows no variation at all in terms of the form of anaphors used in one coreference chain but concerning their syntactic function and position. Moreover, high thematic continuity is reflected by a long coreference chain with small distance between all elements in the coreference chain. These features used in combination typically reflect spontaneous spoken language involving dialogue between at least to speech participants. Much more variation can be expected in particular written language registers of our corpus.

3 Feature Categories under Analysis

Our coreference features can be classified into several groups[2]. The first group (features 1-24) includes features that are related to the form, to functional and structural properties of coreferring expressions – categories motivated by various pragmatic factors.

1-5. Subtypes of antecedents: nominal phrases (**ant-np**), pronouns (**ant-pron**), fact sentences (**ant-fact-s**), verbal phrases representing events (**ant-event-vp**) and other structurally more complex segments such as complex sentences or paragraphs(**other**). This classification is based on the scope of the coreference relation: the distinction between entities and events / states is reflected in the distinction between nominal and verbal expressions (Kibrik, 2011, 7). Since languages, modes and registers show variation in terms of nominal

---

[2]Note that we count the total number of items per category instead of a boolean feature normally used in a coreference resolution system

and verbal expressions, we also expect that the scope of the coreference relation may vary depending on contextual influence.

6. ante-ttr The feature reflecting antecedent variability – 'type-token-ratio' of antecedents per text. We measure variability of antecedents – their structural complexity, i.e. pronouns, nominal phrases, event verbal phrases, fact sentences or bigger elements occurring as antecedents per text.

7-13. Morpho-syntactic subtypes of anaphors: personal pronoun *it* (**ana-pers-it**)[3], other third person personal pronouns (**ana-pers-head**), possessive pronouns triggering cohesiveness of the whole nominal phrase (**ana-pers-mod**), demonstrative pronouns such as *this* and *that* used as nominal heads (**ana-dem-head**), demonstrative pronominal adverbs, such as *hereby*, *herewith*(**ana-dem-pronadv**), definite articles triggering cohesiveness of the whole nominal phrase (**ana-dem-art**), demonstrative modifying pronouns triggering cohesiveness of the whole nominal phrase (e.g. *this* and *these*, as in *this project/ these projects* (**ana-dem-mod**). This classification is based on a two-fold motivation: On the one hand, it partly reflects the *Givenness Hierarchy* (Gundel et al., 1993, 275). On the other hand, this is related to the levels of *explicitness* of coreferential expressions proposed by Becher (2011) who distinguishes three degrees (low, medium and high) of explicitness that rise with the information provided by the referring element. This also goes along with the concept of Accessibility of cohesive referents by Ariel (1990) – a suitable means to measure coreferential explicitness, although Ariel (1990) does not make use of the term explicitness in her work.

14-15. Subtypes of anaphors referring to location (**ana-dem-local**) and time (**ana-dem-temp**). This is motivated by the fact that time and location are often conceptualised as referents in human languages (Kibrik, 2011). This kind of referent is captured by our classification of anaphor forms only.

16-17. Subtypes of comparative reference indicating the level of their specificity: general (**ana-comp-general**) and particular (**ana-comp-partic**). We here follow Halliday and Hasan (1976, 78) who argue that comparison (in terms of likeness or

unlikeness) is a form of reference as likeness is referential property. General comparison refers to general likeness, expressed by adjectives such as *same, similar, other*. Particular comparison concerns comparability between discourse units in terms of quantity (e.g. *more, fewer*) or quality (expressed by comparative adjectives and adverbs).

18-21. Grammatical functions of antecedents and anaphors: antecedent as a subject (**ant-subj**), antecedent as an object (**ant-obj**), anaphor as a subject (**ana-subj**), anaphor as an object (**ana-obj**). Grammatical functions were often used as a parameter of discourse salience in coreference resolution systems (Lappin and Leas, 1994; Mitkov et al., 2002; Klenner and Tuggener, 2011).

22-24. Total number of mentions: **mention** includes the total number of anaphors and antecedents, **anaphor** accounts for the total number of anaphors and **antecedent** for the total number of antecedents, respectively.

The other feature group is related to the properties of chains and includes the following categories.

25. Length of coreference chains measured in the number of chain elements within one chain (**length**), reflecting how coreference chains contribute to thematic continuity in a text - the longer the chain, the more continuity is explicitly expressed by cohesion.

26. Total number of coreference chains (**chain**). Higher frequencies of different chains per text reflect thematic progression or thematic variation in a text as opposed to continuity.

27. Distance between chain members within a coreference chain measured by tokens (**dist-t**). A similar feature was used by Aone and Bennett (1996) who included distance between anaphor and antecedent into their feature set[4].

28. Number of anaphors per chain that occur at sentence-initial position (**ana-p-start**).

29. Number of anaphors per chain that have a subject function (differs from ana-subj which indicates total number of subjects as anaphors) (**ana-is-subj**).

We also include features reflecting structural variation in chains measured by switch rates, as

---

[3]We include the pronoun *it/es* in a separate category, as it is ambiguous and semantically very vague, both in English and in German.

[4]Here, there is again a difference to features normally used by coreference systems, where distance is computed for a given mention pair.

well as variation in terms of parallel constructions and structural complexity of antecedents. The switch rates are calculated for the members of a chain in linear order. In example (1), there is a coreference chain of five members (*two different people – they – they – these two guys – they*). If the corresponding property of the first anaphor is the same as the second (in both cases *they*), there is no switch. If the property is different, as between the second and the third anaphor (*they* vs. *these two guys* in terms of form – personal pronoun vs. nominal phrase modified by a demonstrative), we observe a switch. The switch rate (*srate*) is calculated using Formula (1) where N_s is the number of switches and N_e the total number of elements in a chain.

$$srate = \frac{N_s}{N_e} \qquad (1)$$

30. Variation in the sentence position of the coreferring expression (**srate1**): sentence-initial vs. other positions – e.g. *srate*1 for the chain in example (4) equals 0, as we have no chain members at sentence start[5].

31. Variation in grammatical function (**srate2**): subjects vs. other functions. Both *srate*1 and *srate*2 are supposed to reflect variation in the degree of accessibility of coreferring expressions – the higher the observed values, the more variation and less standardisation we observe.

32. Variation in the form of anaphors (**srate3**): *srate*2 amounts to 0.5 in example (1), as there are two switches between *they* and *these two guys*, and *these two guys* and *they*.

33-34. Parallelism (**srate4.1** and **srate4.2**): Based on (Mitkov et al., 2002, 4), who used parallelism in the syntactic role of the nominal verb complements. If the property of all the mentions in a chain is the same, the chain is considered to be parallel and *srate* equals 0. Any difference in the properties of a chain member make a chain non-parallel. The proportion of chains being parallel and non-parallel is calculated for *srate*1 – chains in which all mentions occur at sentence-initial vs. non-initial position (*srate*4.1), and for *srate*2 – all mentions in a corresponding chain function as subjects vs. non-subjects in a

sentence (*srate*4.2). This is related to the general principles of priming and information distribution.

4 Data and Methods

4.1 Data

Since our main goal does not include automatic coreference resolution and we are interested in exploring different coreference preferences in heterogeneous data, we decided for a manually-annotated corpus of English and German comparable texts (EO and GO) that represent a variety of different registers representing both spoken and written discourse. We therefore use the corpus GECCo annotated for various cohesive devices, including coreference chains. The texts in the data represent seven different registers: five written and two spoken, see Table 1,. The written part was extracted from the corpus described by Hansen-Schirra et al. (2012) and contains popular-scientific articles (POPSCI), political essays (ESSAY), technical manuals (INSTR), texts from company websites (WEB) and fictional texts (FICTION). The latter register is considered to be at the borderline between written and spoken discourse, as it contains dialogues. The spoken part was extracted from the corpus described by Lapshinova-Koltunski et al. (2012) and includes academic speeches (ACADEMIC) and transcribed interviews on general topics (INTERVIEW)[6].

register	EO		GO	
	text	token	text	token
ACADEMIC	10	40,559	10	43,703
ESSAY	29	34,998	23	35,668
FICTION	10	36,996	10	36,778
INSTR	10	36,167	14	36,880
INTERVIEW	12	37,898	14	40,198
POPSCI	11	35,148	10	36,177
WEB	12	36,119	13	35,779
TOTAL	94	257,885	94	265,183

Table 1: Information on the corpus size.

The corpus contains annotations of various categories of textual cohesion elaborated for a multilingual dataset. They provide uniform coreference annotations capturing different types and subtypes of coreferring expressions existing in English and German. We select those corresponding to our features 7–15 described in Section 3 above. Besides that, the corpus contains various categories of antecedents reflecting their structural complexity that

---

[5] Please note that this feature is calculated for coreference relations beyond sentence borders

[6] More information about the corpus and how to gain access to it can be found at `http://fedora.clarin-d.uni-saarland.de/gecco`.

correspond to our features 1–5 described above. An overview of the anaphor and antecedent types annotated in GECCo are provided along with language illustrations in both languages in the Appendix.

4.2 Methods

For RQ1, we use a feature selection procedure, which is normally applied to automatically select attributes relevant to the predictive modeling problem (prediction of a class membership). We use Information Gain (IG) to reduce the number of the analysed coreference features to those relevant for a concrete prediction task – to see which coreference features are especially informative if we deal with the data that is influenced by different variation dimensions: (I) languages, (II) modes, (III) registers. IG measures the expected reduction in entropy – uncertainty associated with a random feature (Roobaert et al., 2006, 464–465), or in other words, the feature's contribution to reduce the entropy.

To answer the second research question, we apply text classification with Support Vector Machines (SVM, cf. Vapnik and Chervonenkis, 1974; Joachims, 1998) with a linear kernel to answer the the second research question. We label our data with the information on classes represented in our case by (I) languages, (II) modes and (III) registers, collect the information on the frequencies of cohesive categories from our corpus, and see if our corpus data support these classes. We apply separate binary classification tasks for languages, modes and registers. In case of both languages and modes, we have two classes only: English vs. German and spoken vs. written. However, we have a multi-class task in case of registers, as our dataset contains seven different registers. For this, we use a pairwise classification, i.e. one-versus-one classifiers are built for register distinction: ESSAY vs. FICTION, ESSAY vs. INSTR, etc. The performance scores of classifiers are judged in terms of precision, recall and f-measure. They are class-specific and indicate the results of automatic assignment of class labels to certain texts. Afterwards, we inspect in detail the whole range of features that make the pre-defined classes distinct from one another. For this, the SVM weights (representing the hyperplane and corresponding to the support vectors) are judged – the magnitude of the weights provides the information on the importance of each feature: the higher the weight of a feature, the more

distinctive it is for a particular class in the respective classification task.

5 Analyses and Results

5.1 RQ1: Distinctive feature selection

We use 188 instances (text-based) and start with 34 attributes. Our prediction tasks with IG depend on the dimension of variation under analysis as described above. In the task for language prediction (I), where we need to select the features from our dataset that are most informative in the distinction between English and German texts – the algorithm delivers 10 attributes. In the mode prediction task (II), the algorithm delivers 21 attributes features that are most informative in the distinction between spoken vs. written texts. And in the register prediction task (III), we receive a list of 24 features that are most informative in the distinction between several classes of registers: academic speeches vs fiction or essays, etc. In this last prediction task, almost all the features have higher scores if we compare them to the output of the two previous scenarios. We provide the resulting lists of features in Appendix, where the selected features are ranked according to their IG score.

Interestingly, four of the 34 features (**ana-pers-it**, **ana-dem-local**, **ant-fact-s**, **ana-obj**) are informative in all the three prediction tasks – the first one is related to the anaphor form and thus givenness/salience/accessibility parameters, the second and the third describe the nature of the referent (fact and location) and the last one is also associated with givenness/salience/accessibility. Apart from these, language and mode prediction scenarios share one feature only that reflects the nature of the referent represented here by time (**ana-dem-temporal**). Language and register do not share any features, whereas mode and register prediction task share 14 features, which is more than a half of the selected features in both tasks. This is not surprising as both mode and register are related to contextual, i.e. functional variation.

The features that are informative for the language prediction only include reference via pronominal adverbs (**ana-dem-pronadv**), both comparative subtypes (**ana-comp-partic and ana-comp-general**), parallelism in grammatical function (**sr4.2**) and the number of anaphors per chain that have a subject function (**ana-is-subj**). They are attributed to existing language contrasts (extensive use of pronominal adverbs in German, less flexible word order in English and others) and can be used for a language prediction task regardless of the mode and the register the texts belong to. In a multilingual coreference resolution task, the features reflecting language contrast should be used with caution, as they might be confounding if used for both languages involved.

The features that are informative for the distinction of modes only are related to the position in the sentence (**sr1** and **ana-p-start**). They can be attributed to the specific speech conditions such as constraints on working memory capacity, spontaneous and partially unreflected text production. We assume that such features should be excluded from a feature set, when a coreference system is trained on a dataset containing both spoken and written texts.

Grammatical function of antecedent (**ant-subj** and **ant-obj**), anaphors in the subject role (**ana-subj**), demonstrative modifiers triggering coreference (**ana-dem-mod**), pronominal antecedents (**ant-pron**) and the distance between the chain members (**dist_t**) are informative if we are predicting the register a text belongs to. They are related to the contextual parameters that may vary across registers, e.g. thematic progression or degree of accessibility of referents, and may also have something to do with textual functions. This kind of features could be confounding, when a coreference resolution system is trained on a dataset of texts from different registers.

5.2 RQ2: Automatic classification

(I) Language We start with the prediction for languages between two classes – English and German. As the size of our dataset is small, we evaluate the performance of the classifier in a 10-fold cross-validation step. We judge the performance scores in terms of precision, recall and f-measure. These scores are class (in our case, language) -specific and indicate the results of automatic assignment of language labels to certain texts in our data. The results of the classification performance are presented in Table 2.

	Precision	Recall	F
EO	88.7	100.0	94.0
GO	100.0	87.2	93.2
Weight.av.	94.3	93.6	93.6

Table 2: Classification results for language distinction.

Overall, we achieve a good classification result (93.62% of accuracy with an f-measure of 93.6%) predicting between English and German texts on the basis of coreference features. This confirms that coreference phenomena have language-specific properties. All the English texts in our data were assigned with the correct labels which consequently contributes to 100% of recall for EO and 100% of precision for GO. The confusion matrix reveals that 12 German texts were erroneously classified as being English.

EO	**GO**
ana-pers-it	ana-dem-pronadv
ana-comp-general	ana-dem-local
ana-comp-partic	ant-fact-s
ana-is-subj	ana-dem-temp

Table 3: Class-specific features for languages.

In Table 3, we list the top four distinctive features for English and German. The most prominent feature in English is coreference via the personal pronoun *it*, whereas pronominal adverbs are the most distinctive features in German. German pronominal adverbs can function as referring expressions or establish a conjunctive relation. Interestingly, the antecedent-related features such as extended referents (clauses or sentences) and reference to location and timeare distinctive for German only.

(II) Mode The same analysis steps are performed for the differentiation between spoken and written modes. The dataset is bilingual – we do not separate them according to their languages, as our task is to predict modes regardless of the language (language-independent classification)[7]. The results for the mode prediction (presented in Table 4) are better than those for the language prediction, as we achieve 96.81% of accuracy here (with an f-measure of 96.8%). Overall, mode prediction works better for the written texts. However, spoken texts are classified with better precision (97.6% vs. 96.6%).

In Table 5, we list the top four distinctive features for the prediction of spoken vs. written mode. Both lists contain features related to the sentence-initial position of chain members (**ana-p-start** and **srate1**). The first position in the list of distinctive spoken features is occupied by demonstrative func-

---

[7]This means that texts labelled as 'spoken' are in both English and German

	Precision	Recall	F
spoken	97.6	89.1	93.2
written	96.6	99.3	97.9
Weight.av.	96.8	96.8	96.8

Table 4: Classification results for mode distinction.

Spoken	**Written**
ana-dem-head	ana-obj
ana-pers-it	ana-pers-mod
ana-dem-local	srate1
ana-p-start	antecedent

Table 5: Class-specific features for modes.

tioning as heads in texts, e.g. *dies/this*, followed by *es/it* in the same function.

(III) Register   Here, we also perform classification on the bilingual dataset, as we did in the previous task. The results of the classification performance are presented in Table 6. This prediction task delivers the least satisfactory results, which is not unexpected, since we have here a multi-class task with a smaller number of items. However, the overall result is 90.88% of accuracy (with an f-measure of 66.1%). The best result was achieved for fictional texts and academic speeches, whereas the lowest scores were observed for websites and technical manuals.

	Precision	Recall	F
ESSAY	59.5	96.2	73.5
FICTION	85.0	85.0	85.0
INSTR	69.2	37.5	48.6
POPSCI	61.1	52.4	56.4
WEB	53.8	28.0	36.8
ACADEMIC	92.9	65.0	76.5
INTERVIEW	80.8	80.8	80.8
Weight.av.	69.4	68.1	66.1

Table 6: Classification results for register distinction.

We suggest that the registers whose texts are not misclassified possess very strong coreference features that distinguish them from other texts. This means that when building systems for coreference resolution, register adaptation for these registers is essential.

Most misclassified texts of various registers were labelled as ESSAY (34)[8]. Most distinctive features

---

[8]We provide the confusion matrix in Appendix.

of this register seem to be shared by other registers resulting in the high number of noisy texts in the ESSAY class. While erroneous assignment of 'foreign' classes is typical for ESSAY, ACADEMIC seems to be very different from all other register classes, with one exception of an interview text. Therefore, we decide to analyse the top distinctive features of these two registers in detail.

In Table 7, we summarise the top five features distinctive for ESSAY and for ACADEMIC, if classified against the other six registers. As seen from the table, the features of ESSAY are related to the distance between chain elements and the properties of antecedents: variation in the scope of relation and the subject/object function, which is a salience feature. In the prediction between FICTION and ESSAY, only two features turned out to be distinctive. The longest list was observed in the prediction between ESSAY and INSTR.

Most features in ACADEMIC are related either to the form of anaphors or the antecedent types Here, we observe a preference for events or states. Overall, the ESSAY features are more diverse in their categories. Moreover, the ACADEMIC lists are longer: the longest one contains 19 members (in the prediction between ACADEMIC and ESSAY).

6   Conclusion and Discussion

We used a set of coreference features of cognitive, pragmatic and typological nature to analyse their variation in heterogeneous data – texts that belong to two different languages, spoken and written modes classified into seven different registers. We used different methods to find out in which way the three variational dimensions that are present in our dataset (language, mode and register) influence the constellation of features.

The results show that depending on the variational dimension, we can have different sets of coreference features. The information on the nature of features derived from our analyses can be useful for studies that use heterogeneous datasets for automatic coreference resolution tasks and multilingual coreference projection. Depending on the dataset at hand, a feature adaptation is recommended.

Information on the features that are distinctive for certain classes included into our analysis provide us with patterns of systematic contrasts. The differences in position, grammatical function and forms of coreferring expressions in a source and a target text belonging to the same register cause

Features distinctive for ESSAY					
FICTION	dist-t	ant-ttr	NA	NA	NA
INSTR	dist-t	ant-subj	srate3	ant-other	ana-pers-mod
POPSCI	dist-t	ant-ttr	ana-dem-local	ant-other	length
WEB	dist-t	ant-ttr	ant-subj	srate4.1	ant-event-vp
ACADEMIC	dist-t	ant-subj	ana-pers-mod	ant-ttr	ana-obj
INTERVIEW	ant-subj	ant-obj	dist-t	ana-pers-mod	ana-obj
Features distinctive for ACADEMIC					
ESSAY	ana-dem-mod	ana-dem-local	ana-dem-head	ana-pers-it	srate4.1
FICTION	ana-dem-head	srate4.1	ana-dem-mod	ana-pers-it	ant-fact-s
INSTR	ana-dem-head	ana-dem-local	srate3	ana-pers-it	srate4.1
POPSCI	ana-dem-head	ana-dem-local	ant-other	ana-pers-it	srate4.1
WEB	ana-dem-head	srate4.1	ana-dem-local	ana-pers-it	ant-event-vp
INTERVIEW	ana-dem-mod	antecedent	chain	ant-obj	ant-subj

Table 7: Features distinctive for ESSAY in different classification tasks.

frequent problems in automatic alignment of the members of coreference chains which may result in erroneous coreference projection. The knowledge on systematic error sources can be used for an automatic improvement of alignment. In coreference resolution, the information on registerial differences may be helpful for domain adaptation. Political essays turn out to have the smallest number of prominent coreference features, which means that working with texts of this register does not require any domain adaptation. There is an opposite tendency for academic speeches – these texts differ strongly from other text types, and thus, domain adaptation is necessary. The knowledge on language, mode and register contrasts is also important for contrastive linguistics and translation studies. In the future, it would be interesting to test whether our assumptions about the correlation of specific types of features and variational dimensions may influence the performance of automatic coreference resolution systems and multilingual coreference projection tasks.

Acknowledgments

The present work was done within the GECCo project funded through the German Research Foundation (DFG). We would like to thank José Manuel Martínez Martínez for contributing to the extraction and calculation of a number of features used in the analyses. We would also like to thank our reviewers for their useful comments and suggestions.

References

Chinatsu Aone and Scott William Bennett. 1996. Applying machine learning to anaphora resolution. In Stefan Wermter, Ellen Riloff, and Gabriele Scheler, editors, *Connectionist, Statistical and Symbolic Approaches to Learning for Natural Language Processing*, pages 302–314. Springer, Berlin, Heidelberg.

Emilia Apostolova, Noriko Tomuro, Pattanasak Mongkolwat, and Dina Demner-Fushman. 2012. Domain adaptation of coreference resolution for radiology reports. In *Proceedings of the 2012 Workshop on Biomedical Natural Language Processing*, BioNLP '12, pages 118–121, Stroudsburg, PA, USA. Association for Computational Linguistics.

Mira Ariel. 1990. *Accessing noun-phrase antecedents*. Routledge, London.

Mira Ariel. 2001. Accessibility theory: an overview. In T. Sanders, J. Schilperoord, and W. Spooren, editors, *Text Representation*, pages 29–88. John Benjamins, Amsterdam/Philadelphia.

Victor Becher. 2011. *Explicitation and implicitation in translation: A corpus-based study of English-German and German-English translations of business texts*. Ph.D. thesis, Universität Hamburg.

Douglas Biber. 2012. Register as a predictor of linguistic variation. *Corpus Linguistics and Linguistic Theory*, 8(1):9–37.

Miriam Eckert and Michael Strube. 2000. Dialogue acts, synchronizing units, and anaphora resolution. *Journal of Semantics*, 17(1):51–89.

Yulia Grishina and Manfred Stede. 2015. Knowledge-lean projection of coreference chains across languages. In *Proceedings of the 8th Workshop on Building and Using Comparable Corpora*, Beijing, China. Association for Computational Linguistics.

Barbara J. Grosz, Aravind K. Joshi, and Scott Weinstein. 1995. Centering: A framework for modeling the local coherence of discourse. *Computational Linguistics*, 21.

Jeanette Gundel, Nancy Hedberg, and Ron Zacharski. 1993. Cognitive status and the form of referring expressions in discourse. *Language*, pages 274–307.

Jeanette Gundel, Michael Hegarty, and Kaja Borthen. 2003. Cognitive status, information structure, and pronominal reference to clausally introduced entities. *Journal of Logic, Language and Information*, 12(3):281 – 299.

M.A.K. Halliday and Ruqaiya Hasan. 1976. *Cohesion in English*. Longman, London, New York.

Silvia Hansen-Schirra, Stella Neumann, and Erich Steiner. 2012. *Cross-linguistic Corpora for the Study of Translations. Insights from the Language Pair English-German*. de Gruyter, Berlin, New York.

Sanda M. Harabagiu and Steven J. Maiorano. 2000. Multilingual coreference resolution. In *Proceedings of the Sixth Conference on Applied Natural Language Processing*, ANLC '00, pages 142–149, Stroudsburg, PA, USA. Association for Computational Linguistics.

Thorsten Joachims. 1998. Text categorization with support vector machines: Learning with many relevant features. In *Proceedings of the European Conference on Machine Learning (ECML)*, pages 137–142, London, UK. Springer.

Andrej A. Kibrik. 2011. *Reference in Discourse*. Oxford University Press.

Manfred Klenner and Don Tuggener. 2011. An incremental model for coreference resolution with restrictive antecedent accessibility. In *Proceedings of the Fifteenth Conference on Computational Natural Language Learning: Shared Task, CoNLL 2011, Portland, Oregon, USA, June 23-24, 2011*, pages 81–85.

Sandra Kübler and Desislava Zhekova. 2016. Multilingual coreference resolution. *Language and Linguistics Compass*, 10(11):614–631.

Kerstin Kunz, Stefania Degaetano-Ortlieb, Ekaterina Lapshinova-Koltunski, Katrin Menzel, and Erich Steiner. 2017. Gecco – an empirically-based comparison of English-German cohesion. In Gert De Sutter, Marie-Aude Lefer, and Isabelle Delaere, editors, *Empirical Translation Studies: New Methodological and Theoretical Traditions*, volume 300 of *TILSM series*, pages 265–312. Mouton de Gruyter. TILSM series.

Kerstin Kunz and Ekaterina Lapshinova-Koltunski. 2015. Cross-linguistic analysis of discourse variation across registers. *Special Issue of Nordic Journal of English Studies*, 14(1):258–288.

Kerstin Kunz and Erich Steiner. 2012. Towards a comparison of cohesive reference in English and German: System and text. In M. Taboada, S. Doval Suárez, and E. González Álvarez, editors, *Contrastive Discourse Analysis. Functional and Corpus Perspectives*. Equinox, London.

Shalom Lappin and Herbert J. Leas. 1994. An algorithm for pronominal anaphora resolution. *Computational Linguistics*, pages 535–561.

Ekaterina Lapshinova-Koltunski, Kerstin Kunz, and Marilisa Amoia. 2012. Compiling a multilingual spoken corpus. In *Proceedings of the VIIth GSCP International Conference: Speech and corpora*, pages 79–84, Firenze. Firenze University Press.

Ruslan Mitkov, Richard Evans, and Constantin Orsan. 2002. A new, fully automatic version of Mitkov's knowledge-poor pronoun resolution method. In *Computational Linguistics and Intelligent Text Processing, Third International Conference, CICLing 2002, Mexico City, Mexico, February 17-23, 2002, Proceedings*, pages 168–186.

Michal Novák, Anna Nedoluzhko, and Zdeněk Žabokrtský. 2017. Projection-based coreference resolution using deep syntax. In *Proceedings of the 2nd Workshop on Coreference Resolution Beyond OntoNotes (CORBON 2017)*, pages 56–64, Valencia, Spain. Association for Computational Linguistics.

Michal Novák and Anna Nedoluzhko. 2015. Correspondences between Czech and English coreferential expressions. *Discours: Revue de linguistique, psycholinguistique et informatique*, 16.

Sameer Pradhan, Alessandro Moschitti, Nianwen Xue, Olga Uryupina, and Yuchen Zhang. 2012. CoNLL-2012 shared task: Modeling multilingual unrestricted coreference in OntoNotes. In *Joint Conference on EMNLP and CoNLL-Shared Task*, pages 1–40. Association for Computational Linguistics.

Ellen F. Prince. 1981. Towards a taxonomy of given-new information. In P. Cole, editor, *Radical Pragmatics*, pages 223–255. Academic Press, New York.

Altaf Rahman and Vincent Ng. 2012. Translation-based projection for multilingual coreference resolution. In *Proceedings of the 2012 Conference of the North American Chapter of the Association for Computational Linguistics: Human Language Technologies*, NAACL HLT '12, pages 720–730, Stroudsburg, PA, USA. Association for Computational Linguistics.

Marta Recasens, Luís Màrquez, Emili Sapena, Toni Martí, Mariona Taulé, Veronique Hoste, Massimo Poesio, and Yannick Versley. 2010. Semeval-2010 task 1: Coreference resolution in multiple languages. In *Proceedings of the 5th International Workshop on Semantic Evaluation*, pages 1–8. Association for Computational Linguistics.

Marta Recasens and Sameer Pradhan. 2016. Evaluation campaigns. In *Anaphora Resolution – Algorithms, Resources, and Applications*, pages 165–208. Springer.

Danny Roobaert, Grigoris Karakoulas, and Nitesh V. Chawla. 2006. Information Gain, Correlation and Support Vector Machines. In Isabelle Guyon, Masoud Nikravesh, Steve Gunn, and Lotfi A. Zadeh, editors, *Feature Extraction: Foundations and Applications*, pages 463–470. Springer Berlin Heidelberg, Berlin, Heidelberg.

Ina Rösiger and Simone Teufel. 2014. Resolving coreferent and associative noun phrases in scientific text. In *Proceedings of the EACL 2014 Student Research Workshop*, pages 45–55, Gothenburg, Sweden. Association for Computational Linguistics.

Olga Uryupina and Massimo Poesio. 2012. Domain-specific vs. uniform modeling for coreference resolution. In *Proceedings of the Eighth International Conference on Language Resources and Evaluation (LREC'12)*, pages 187–191, Istanbul, Turkey. European Language Resources Association (ELRA).

Vladimir Naumovich Vapnik and Alexey Yakovlevich Chervonenkis. 1974. *Theory of Pattern Recognition*. Nauka, Moscow.

Jian Bo Yang, Qi Mao, Qiao Liang Xiang, Ivor Wai-Hung Tsang, Kian Ming Adam Chai, and Hai Leong Chieu. 2012. Domain adaptation for coreference resolution: An adaptive ensemble approach. In *Proceedings of the 2012 Joint Conference on Empirical Methods in Natural Language Processing and Computational Natural Language Learning*, EMNLP-CoNLL '12, pages 744–753, Stroudsburg, PA, USA. Association for Computational Linguistics.

David Yarowsky, Grace Ngai, and Richard Wicentowski. 2001. Inducing multilingual text analysis tools via robust projection across aligned corpora. In *Proceedings of the First International Conference on Human Language Technology Research*, HLT '01, pages 1–8, Stroudsburg, PA, USA. Association for Computational Linguistics.

Amir Zeldes. 2018. A predictive model for notional anaphora in English. In *Proceedings of the First Workshop on Computational Models of Reference, Anaphora and Coreference*, pages 34–43, New Orleans, Louisiana. Association for Computational Linguistics.

A Appendix

type & form	examples
pers. head	*he/er, she/sie, they/sie*
pers. modifier	*her/ihr, his/sein, their/ihr*
it-endophoric	*it/es*
demonstr. head	*this/dies/das, that/jenes*
demonstr. modifier	*this/diese(r/s), that/jene(r/s)*
local	*here/hier, there/da*
temporal	*now/jetzt, then/dann*
pronadv	*herewith/hiermit, dagegen, damit*
comparat. particular	*bigger/grösser, better/besser*
comparat. general	*other/andere, such/solche*

Table 8: Anaphors and their subtypes annotated in GECCo.

type	example
pronoun	he wrote back saying if <this> is what i think *it* is...
np	*This set of euro coins will cost <20 marks>. For this, you get 20 coins...*
event-vp	<calculating the number of cannonballs in piles> for him, but this sparked...
fact-s	*<At the same time, we need to double the current level of prosperity>...this is the most urgent moral challenge we face.*
other	longer segments

Table 9: Types of antecedents annotated in GECCo.

feature	score
ana-dem-pronadv	0.8024
ana-pers-it	0.2351
ana-dem-local	0.1641
ana-comp-partic	0.1031
ana-comp-general	0.1031
ana-dem-temp	0.0833
ana-is-subj	0.0696
ant-fact-s	0.0677
srate4.2	0.0662
ana-obj	0.0496

Table 10: Features selected for language prediction with their IG scores.

feature	score
ana-dem-head	0.4672
ana-dem-local	0.2472
ana-pers-it	0.1337
ant-event-vp	0.1272
srate1	0.1247
srate4.1	0.1237
ana-pers-head	0.1194
ana-p-start	0.1181
ant-other	0.1166
ant-fact-s	0.1072
mention	0.1064
chain	0.1045
ana-pers-mod	0.0997
anaphor	0.0915
srate3	0.0825
ana-obj	0.0794
antecedent	0.0743
ant-np	0.0643
length	0.0602
ana-dem-temp	0.0580
ant-ttr	0.0577

Table 11: Features selected for mode prediction with their IG scores.

feature	score
ana-subj	0.557
ana-pers-head	0.547
ant-np	0.538
ana-dem-head	0.524
ana-pers-mod	0.497
anaphor	0.438
mention	0.430
chain	0.412
antecedent	0.408
ana-obj	0.368
length	0.321
ana-dem-mod	0.316
ant-ttr	0.306
ant-obj	0.297
ant-subj	0.294
ana-dem-local	0.248
ana-pers-it	0.230
ant-pronoun	0.225
ant-event-vp	0.216
ant-other	0.207
srate3	0.187
srate4.1	0.181
dist-t	0.166
ant-fact-s	0.162

Table 12: Features selected for register prediction with their IG scores.

a	b	c	d	e	f	g	⇐ classified as
50	0	0	0	2	0	0	a = ESSAY
0	**17**	0	3	0	0	0	b = FICTION
12	1	**9**	2	0	0	0	c = INSTR
6	0	1	**11**	3	0	0	d = POPSCI
11	2	3	2	**7**	0	0	e = WEB
	0	0	0	1	**13**	5	f = ACADEMIC
4	0	0	0	0	1	**21**	g = INTERVIEW

Table 13: Confusion matrix for the SVM register classification.

Contextualized Embeddings for Connective Disambiguation in Shallow Discourse Parsing

René Knaebel
Applied Computational Linguistics
Department of Linguistics
University of Potsdam
Germany
rknaebel@uni-potsdam.de

Manfred Stede
Applied Computational Linguistics
Department of Linguistics
University of Potsdam
Germany
stede@uni-potsdam.de

Abstract

This paper studies a novel model that simplifies the disambiguation of connectives for explicit discourse relations. We use a neural approach that integrates contextualized word embeddings and predicts whether a connective candidate is part of a discourse relation or not. We study the influence of those context specific-embeddings. Further, we show the benefit of training the tasks of connective disambiguation and sense classification together at the same time. The success of our approach is supported by state-of-the-art results.

1 Introduction

Coherence is crucial for humans to be able to interpret text. The area of discourse parsing models this by identifying certain phrases (arguments) within a text and using discourse relations to unfold their underlying connections. These discourse relations and their understanding are important for tasks such as machine translation (Sim Smith, 2017), abstractive summarization (Wu and Hu, 2018), and text simplification (Zhong et al., 2020). A subset of these relations is signaled by specific words, so-called *discourse connectives* (or discourse markers or cues), and thus referred to as *explicit discourse relations*. However, such cues can be ambiguous, as they may signal more than one relation type or may not always function as a relation indicator. Two challenges arise[1]—first, distinguishing connectives from words with mere sentential meaning:

1. Mr. Perkins believes, **however**, that the market could be stabilized.

2. "The 1987 crash was a false alarm **however** you view it," says university of Chicago economist.

Here, example 1 shows a discourse relation, while example 2 uses 'however' in its sentential reading. The second challenge consists in classifying a connective's sense (described in detail in Section 2):

3. She owns a bike, **while** her brother drives a car. (Comparison.Contrast)

4. You should take the deal **or** even try to negotiate this price down. (Expansion.Alternative)

5. **If** things work out, **then** everybody will be happy. (Contingency.Condition)

6. **While** it is raining outside, I clean the dishes. (Temporal.Synchronous)

Shallow discourse parsing (SDP) is the area that builds models to uncover such discourse structures within texts. SDP consists of the main tasks of identifying connectives, demarcating their arguments, assigning senses to them, and finding the senses of so-called implicit relations (which hold between adjacent text spans without a lexical signal being present). In this work, we focus in particular on the binary *connective disambiguation* of explicit discourse relations and, further, integrate explicit *sense prediction* into our model, as those two tasks are highly related.

Word embeddings provide dense token representations in a low-dimensional vector space pretrained on large unannotated text corpora. First, we use fastText (Bojanowski et al., 2017), which is based on the skip-gram model (Mikolov et al., 2013) and integrates character *n*-grams into its representation. Second, we use GloVe (Pennington et al., 2014); as opposed to fastText, those embeddings were calculated through co-occurrence statistics rather than trained by a neural network. Recently, models were introduced that provide *contextualized* word embeddings (Peters et al., 2018; Devlin et al., 2019) on

---

[1]Examples 1–2 are from PDTB (see Section 2); examples 3–6 are artificially constructed; senses follow PDTB2 style.

Proceedings of the First Workshop on Computational Approaches to Discourse, pages 65–75
Online, November 20, 2020. ©2020 Association for Computational Linguistics
https://doi.org/10.18653/v1/P17

demand and thus tackle the problem of identical representations for homonymous words with different senses, which had been indistinguishable in older models. For our experiments, we use BERT (Devlin et al., 2019), which was successful in many areas of NLP (Liu and Lapata, 2019; Liu et al., 2019).

In this work, we present a novel approach to identifying explicit relations in shallow discourse parsing. We introduce a simple yet powerful model that outperforms previous research on the binary disambiguation of connective candidates. Furthermore, we adopt connective sense classification as an auxiliary task to improve performance and generalization capabilities and study the benefits of jointly training the auxiliary task in addition to the main task. This is because, in various cases, training neural models on multiple related tasks has shown beneficial for the learned representation (Caruana, 1993), as it introduces inductive bias and, thereby, reduces the possible hypothesis space (Baxter, 2000). Specifically, the work of Collobert et al. (2011) has pointed out the advantages of multitask learning on NLP tasks. We compare our results with state-of-the-art SDP components that took part at the CoNLL Shared Task in 2016.[2] The contributions of this paper are as follows:

1. We design a simple neural architecture that eliminates the need for hand-engineered features. To the best of our knowledge, this work is the first to provide state-of-the-art performance on word-embedding-based connective disambiguation.

2. We present a novel approach that successfully combines the two tasks of connective disambiguation and explicit sense classification into one single model. In contrast to previous work, we introduce a more sensitive measure and, with its help, demonstrate improved stability of the jointly trained model.

In the following, Section 2 describes the corpus for the experiments; Section 3 explains our method. The experiments and results are presented in Section 4 and Section 5; Section 6 discusses relevant related work, followed by conclusions in Section 7.

2 Penn Discourse Treebank

Shallow discourse parsing is a challenging task that was promoted by the development of the second

---

Coarse Class	Absolute	Relative
NoConn	34174	69.90
Expansion	5007	10.24
Comparison	4382	8.96
Temporal	2752	5.63
Contingency	2578	5.27
Fine Class		
NoConn	34174	70.44
Expansion.Conjunction	4323	8.91
Comparison.Contrast	2956	6.09
Contingency.Condition	1147	2.36
Temporal.Sync	1133	2.34
Comparison.Concession	1079	2.22
Contingency.Cause.Reason	943	1.94
Temporal.Async.Succession	842	1.74
Temporal.Async.Precedence	770	1.59
Contingency.Cause.Result	487	1.00
Expansion.Instantiation	236	0.49
Expansion.Alternative	195	0.40
Expansion.Restatement	121	0.25
Expansion.Alternative.Chosen	95	0.20
Expansion.Exception	13	0.03

Table 1: Class distribution of the training data.

version of the Penn Discourse Treebank (PDTB2) (Prasad et al., 2008). This corpus provides about 43,000 annotated discourse relations, of which roughly 18,000 are signalled by explicit discourse connectives. Those relations are further annotated with a three-level sense hierarchy (one or two senses per relation). All discourse relations consist of two arguments and are associated with one of various types; the focus of our work is on relations of the *explicit* type.

The Shared Tasks at CoNLL 2015 and 2016 (Xue et al., 2015, 2016) used PDTB2 with minor changes. Successful systems were Wang et al. (2015); Wang and Lan (2016); Oepen et al. (2016). They largely follow a pipeline architecture (Lin et al., 2014), which consists of successive tasks of connective identification, argument labeling, and sense classification for both explicit and implicit relations.

Recently, PDTB3 (Prasad et al., 2018) was published, which extends the previous work with more available relations and corrects several former annotations. The authors also adjusted the relations' sense labels for a more balanced class distribution. For the sake of comparison with previous work on SDP, we stick to the PDTB2 corpus and assume to achieve similar results with PDTB3.

Table 1 summarizes the distribution regarding sense classes, where we denote candidate words with sentential reading by NoConn. In both settings, NoConn dominates other classes and, thus, serves as the majority baseline. The first setting shows the four *coarse* sense classes provided by PDTB2. The second setting describes the *fine* senses as defined in the Shared Task. In contrast to the first setting, the distribution slightly changes, as rare training samples were removed or combined with other classes. Although the exact numbers for NoConn are the same in both settings, the ratios are different, which can be explained by the small modifications made to PDTB2 in the competitions.

3 Method

This work introduces a first, simple neural architecture for shallow discourse connective disambiguation. The system builds upon previous observations that a word's context could be used as a strong indicator for the presence of a discourse relation (Lin et al., 2014).[3] Our work investigates the limitations of knowledge free approaches and introduces a simple yet flexible model without domain knowledge.

We assume that word embeddings contain information about the discourse that can be used for the disambiguation task. We study standard noncontextualized embeddings (in particular, GloVe embeddings and Wikipedia-based fastText embeddings) and compare those to the recently developed contextualized embeddings (represented by BERT). We first hypothesize that contextualized embeddings yield better results than their noncontextualized counterpart. Second, we expect the context span to influence the model's performance, as the context may indicate a word's function more clearly.

In addition, we propose a second model based on the first one, which successfully combines connective disambiguation with sense classification as an auxiliary task. We follow the idea of previous work that sense classification can be performed without extracting the connectives' arguments (Pitler and Nenkova, 2009; Lin et al., 2014; Qin et al., 2016). Further, it has been previously shown that, for the identification of an explicit relation's sense, the connective itself as well as its context already provide significant information (Pitler and Nenkova, 2009; Lin et al., 2014; Wang and Lan, 2015; Ghosh et al., 2011). Consequently, we assume the necessary information for sense classification to be already accessible by our neural connective disambiguation model to some degree. Also, this approach elim-

inates the error propagation and the performance of our joint model stays as is without relying on previous predictions. The reason for adding sense classification as an auxiliary task in the first place is that joint training with auxiliary tasks has shown benefits in earlier work, as mentioned in Section 1. We could validate that this is the case with our connective disambiguation task as well, as later demonstrated in our experiments (see Section 4.2).

In the following sections, we explain in more detail our binary connective disambiguation approach and the joint sense classification model.

3.1 Embedding-Based Connective Disambiguation

For parsing explicit discourse relations, the first task usually involves the identification of possible connective *candidates*. For this purpose, we use a list of candidate patterns based on PDTB2. Some candidates might look like discourse connectives, however, they might only be in sentential use.

Connective annotation in PDTB2 is quite flexible. Connectives can be individual words ('indeed'), multiple consecutive words ('in the end'), or distant words that function together ('neither … nor'). In addition, they can contain adverbial modifications ('at least when,' 'even when,' 'usually when'), which vastly increases the number of possible connectives. Regarding this problem, the CoNLL Shared Task introduced a mapping that normalizes instances of connectives to their *head* by removing adverbial modifiers. For example, the three full connectives above all normalize to their head 'when.' For our studies, we follow this approach and focus on the disambiguation of connective head candidates rather than fully annotated connectives as in the original corpus.

We introduce a simple neural architecture (see Figure 1) that relies on pretrained word embeddings instead of hand-engineered features. The network consists of a multilayer perceptron with a single hidden layer. As the network's input, we use the candidate word's embeddings and its context.

A continuous token sequence of length n is encoded as an embedding sequence $(e_1, e_2, \ldots, e_n)$. We define our input with regards to the candidate's positions within the sentence (denoted as C) and use *cmin* and *cmax* for the first and last occurrence of the candidate, respectively. Finally, with a con-

---

[3]Note that a word's *context* refers to the words immediately preceding and succeeding it, which is not to be confused with contextualized or noncontextualized word *embeddings*.

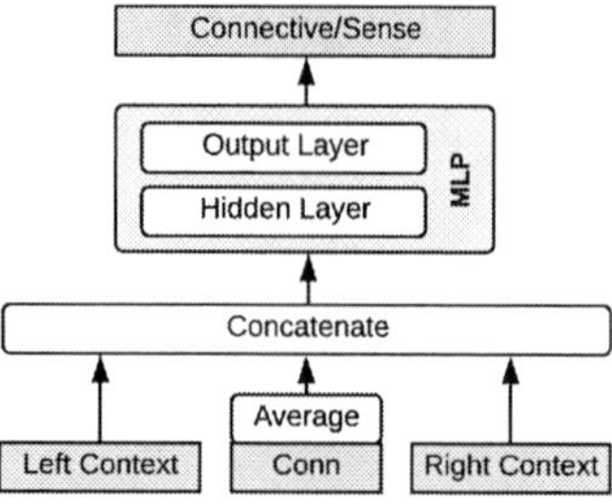

Figure 1: Model overview. The average of the connective embeddings and their context serve as input, a single hidden layer is used for transformation, and the final layer outputs either the connective probability or sense classes.

text size of s, our input looks as follows:

$$ctx_{left} = (e_{cmin-s}, \ldots, e_{cmin-1})$$
$$conn = (e_c : c \in C)$$
$$ctx_{right} = (e_{cmax+1}, \ldots, e_{cmax+s})$$

Because the candidate might consist of multiple words ('in particular'), we simply average all candidate embeddings and concatenate remaining embeddings to build the network's input x:

$$x = ctx_{left} + \overline{conn} + ctx_{right}$$

Thus, independent of the number of words describing a connective candidate, the input always has the same dimension. We do not average the embeddings of the context because this would lead to unwanted information loss.

For the transformation of candidates and their context into word embeddings, we use the tokenization provided by the CoNLL Shared Tasks. No other annotations such as POS, constituent trees, and dependencies are used for our experiments. GloVe and fastText are used for noncontextualized embeddings and BERT for contextualized embeddings. For contextualized embeddings, we noticed a difference in the tokenization of contractions. Therefore, we simply replaced occurrences of the token 'n't' by 'not' without changing the overall meaning.

The usage of embeddings is straightforward. Each token in a document is mapped to its embedding representation. In contrast, the contextualized embeddings are generated sentence-wise before extracting context and candidate embeddings. The input for BERT is prepared with special tags for sentence beginnings and ends. Further, original tokens might be split into smaller tokens based on the WordPiece tokenizer (Wu et al., 2016) before feeding them into BERT's encoder. This possibly leads to a higher number of BERT subtoken embeddings than tokens defined on the original corpus. Based on the alignment of original tokens and BERT subtokens, only the first BERT subtoken embedding of a corresponding token is used as its embedding. This selection follows the original BERT publication (Devlin et al., 2019), where features were extracted and the finally predicted classes only rely on the first subtoken's position.

3.2 Joint Disambiguation and Sense Classification

For the reasons explained in the beginning of Section 3, we combine binary connective disambiguation and sense classification into a single, second model. Thus, the model jointly learns whether a connective candidate serves as a discourse signal and, if so, determines its sense. We use the same model as in our previous experiment (see Figure 1) but introduce a novel prediction scheme for the joint classification. As both tasks have exclusive classes, our model either predicts whether a candidate is without sense, which is equivalent to having sentential reading, or predicts one of the desired sense classes. Combining multiple tasks into a single model is called multitask learning (see Section 6).

4   Evaluation

For our experiments, we use PDTB2 (Prasad et al., 2008), especially the version provided for the CoNLL Shared Task. We distinguish between *coarse* senses, which come from the original PDTB, and *fine* senses as defined by the Shared Task. Also, an official split is provided that makes comparisons to other systems more reliable. In particular, this means that we used folders 02–22 for training, folders 00 and 01 as a development set, and folders 23 and 24 for testing. We downloaded word embeddings for GloVe[4] and fastText[5] from their corresponding websites. For the contextualized embeddings, we extracted token embeddings that we had previously transformed using BERT.[6]

As we work with highly imbalanced data, we present our results using precision, recall, and F1 score. Typically, there is a natural inverse rela-

---

[4]`nlp.stanford.edu/data/glove.6B.zip`
[5]`dl.fbaipublicfiles.com/fasttext/`
`vectors-english/wiki-news-300d-1M.vec.zip`
[6]We use the `bert-base-uncased` model provided by Huggingface's transformer (Wolf et al., 2019).

Model	Conn Disambiguation	Coarse Sense Classification		Fine Sense Classification	
	$F1_{conn}$	$F1_{conn}$	$F1_{sense}$	$F1_{conn}$	$F1_{sense}$
Standard WSJ Test (Section 23)					
bert-ctx-1	**97.32** (99.20)	96.98 (99.77)	**93.03**	96.63 (99.78)	84.17
bert-ctx-0	97.20 (99.29)	**97.45** (99.81)	92.12	**97.18** (99.76)	**86.26**
bert-ctx-2	96.97 (99.08)	95.96 (99.71)	89.57	95.81 (99.72)	81.94
baseline	95.46 (97.11)	—	—	—	—
fasttext-ctx-1	92.09 (94.95)	92.26 (98.61)	87.51	92.63 (98.45)	80.39
glove-ctx-2	92.02 (94.58)	92.03 (98.52)	85.56	90.13 (98.20)	82.35
glove-ctx-1	91.76 (94.69)	91.90 (98.44)	87.22	91.30 (98.18)	78.17
fasttext-ctx-2	91.29 (94.98)	92.51 (98.86)	88.66	91.77 (98.47)	78.18
glove-ctx-0	84.99 (80.98)	84.33 (92.36)	75.53	84.80 (92.62)	66.19
fasttext-ctx-0	84.79 (80.72)	84.20 (92.27)	77.62	84.23 (92.59)	68.79
Wikipedia Blind Test					
bert-ctx-0	**97.03** (98.52)	**96.75** (99.74)	88.79	96.28 (99.72)	**71.69**
bert-ctx-1	96.98 (98.38)	96.18 (99.65)	**90.41**	**96.31** (99.69)	71.51
bert-ctx-2	96.40 (97.29)	95.09 (99.56)	87.92	94.01 (99.54)	66.97
baseline	94.50 (95.06)	—	—	—	—
fasttext-ctx-2	88.99 (90.31)	89.34 (97.95)	82.05	88.26 (97.42)	59.81
fasttext-ctx-1	88.74 (90.10)	88.01 (97.56)	78.46	89.74 (98.06)	62.74
glove-ctx-1	87.86 (88.80)	87.39 (96.95)	77.85	87.78 (97.19)	62.92
glove-ctx-2	87.54 (87.61)	87.63 (97.45)	78.31	87.01 (97.10)	61.15
glove-ctx-0	81.86 (73.77)	82.36 (90.66)	64.16	81.87 (90.91)	40.46
fasttext-ctx-0	81.76 (73.64)	82.98 (90.70)	67.61	82.28 (90.87)	45.68

Table 2: Experimental results for various embedding types (GloVe, fastText, BERT) and context sizes (*ctx*). Evaluation involves Section 23 of WSJ and the blind data set proposed for CoNLL Shared Task. All tasks are measured using F1 scores. Average precision is calculated for connective disambiguation and shown in parentheses. Results are ordered by primary task and separated with regards to the groups highlighted in Figure 2.

tion between precision and recall—as one increases, the other decreases. Depending on the final usage, either one could be optimized. While in previous work, scores were usually reported for one specific threshold only, we decided to use precision–recall curves for our experimental results. These give a better understanding of the models' sensitivity to the selected threshold in our binary disambiguation task. To approximate the area under the precision–recall curve, we compute the average precision (AP) score. While F1 score indicates performance for a single threshold only, the AP score helps to compare the precision–recall curves of various models.

In our experiments, we study different embedding types (GloVe, fastText, BERT) with a varying context size ($ctx \in \{0, 1, 2\}$). The dimension (*emb*) of the noncontextualized word embeddings is 300 and 768 for contextualized embeddings, which results in an input size of $(2 * ctx + 1) * emb$. The size of the hidden layer is 2048. All models were trained for at most 50 epochs using early stopping (Prechelt, 1998) when validation loss did not improve over 10 epochs, a batch size of 128, and the Adam (Kingma and Ba, 2015) optimizer with

a learning rate of 0.001. For comparison, we also provide a baseline from a reimplementation of Lin et al. (2014). Table 2 reports the performances of our models per experimental setting for each data partition (test and blind) and highlights best performances. In the remainder of this section, we discuss the experimental results obtained for the models presented in Sections 3.1 and 3.2.

4.1 Embedding-Based Connective Disambiguation

Table 2 shows that for contextualized word embeddings, our model generally outperforms the baseline, in particular, the `bert-ctx-1` configuration. This confirms our hypothesis that it is possible to disambiguate connectives to a good extent by using word embeddings. Further, certain groups of experiments can be visually distinguished (see Figures 2a). The weakest performance was achieved when using noncontextualized word embeddings and zero context. This is probably due to the ambiguity of words that have multiple senses. Models that take context into account clearly outperform those with standalone embeddings. From this, we

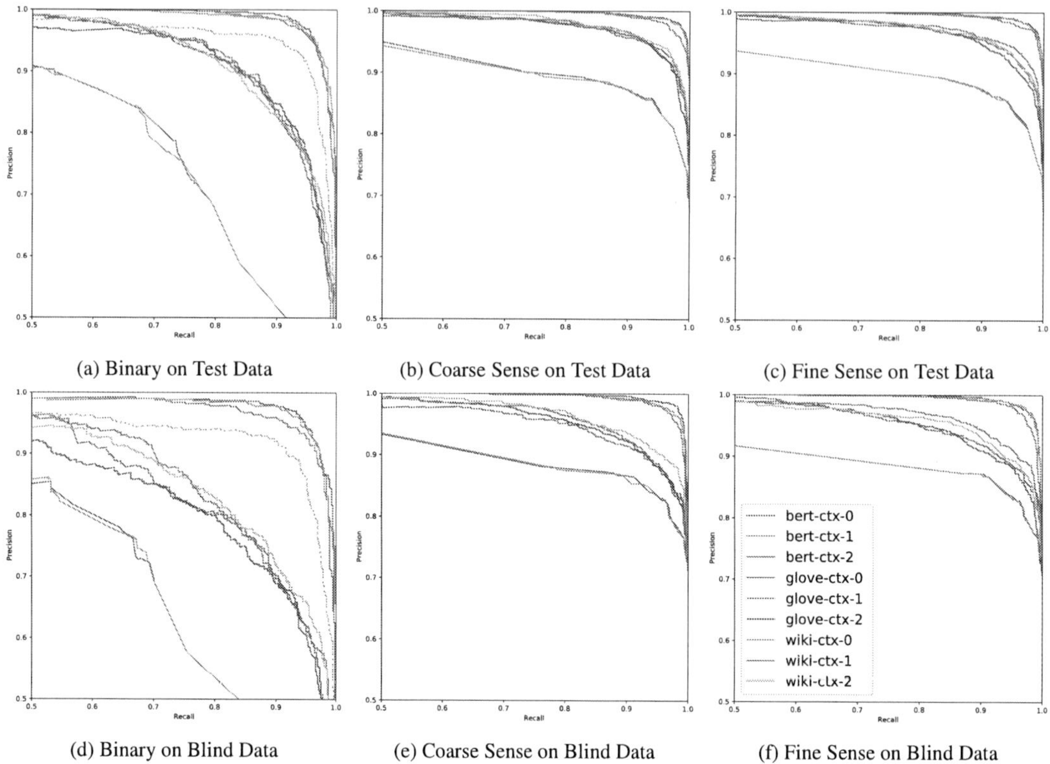

<table>
<tr><td>(a) Binary on Test Data</td><td>(b) Coarse Sense on Test Data</td><td>(c) Fine Sense on Test Data</td></tr>
<tr><td>(d) Binary on Blind Data</td><td>(e) Coarse Sense on Blind Data</td><td>(f) Fine Sense on Blind Data</td></tr>
</table>

Figure 2: Precision–recall curves for connective disambiguation for the different models—binary disambiguation (left), joint coarse sense (middle), joint fine sense (right)—and data sets—test (top) and blind (bottom). The baseline is shown as a dashed line.

conclude that single noncontextualized word embeddings do not contain enough discourse information but that a model can compensate the missing information with the connective's context. Finally, contextualized embeddings seem to already contain this discourse information, as varying context sizes did not lead to clearly different results. Also, these embeddings may have outperformed noncontextualized embeddings because their features are already based on full sentences. As shown in Figure 2, the baseline exhibited a high level of performance, between that of noncontextualized embeddings with context and contextualized embeddings.

Comparing the results on the test (Figures 2a) and blind (Figures 2d) data sets, we notice the usual drop in performance, as both data sets differ in their distribution. The test set comes from news articles, while the blind set is based on Wikipedia. With other feature-based models submitted to the Shared Tasks, we expect this performance drop to be higher, so that our model would generalize better.

We carried out a further analysis on the test data in order to characterize weaknesses of using word embeddings for connective disambiguation. Therefore, we examined our contextualized embedding model without context (`bert-ctx-0`), as it yielded high performance despite its low complexity. For most of the rare classification mistakes made by our model, we found that there existed similar embeddings to those that were misclassified, which naturally made them hard to distinguish for our model.

4.2 Joint Disambiguation and Sense Classification

For our second experimental setting, we study the influence of jointly training connective disambiguation and sense classification (coarse and fine senses shown in Figures 2b and 2c, respectively). As our hypothesis, we assumed generalization to improve with increasing task complexity. For the commonly evaluated F1 score, we do not see a vast improvement between connective disambiguation and the joint training approach. In addition to the previous metric, we use the average precision score that better summarizes the overall ratio of precision and

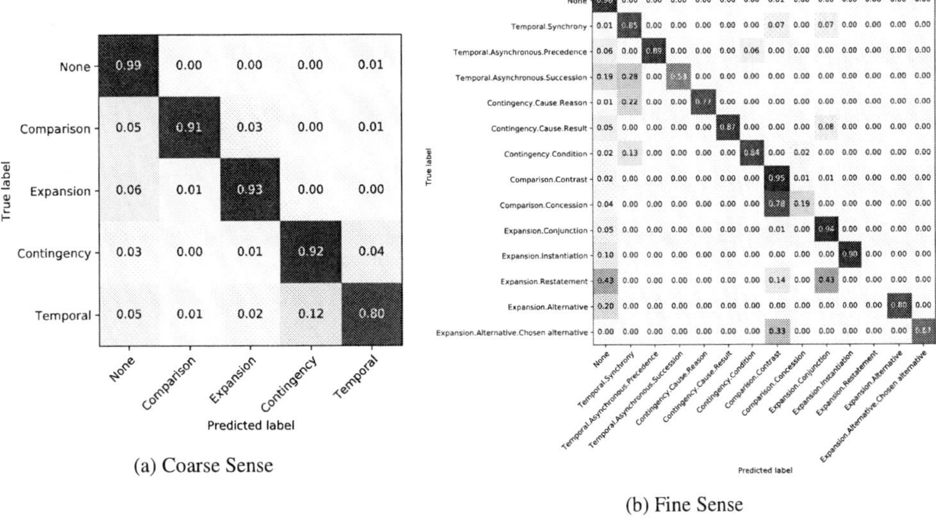

(a) Coarse Sense

(b) Fine Sense

Figure 3: Confusion matrix of `bert-ctx-0` on test data for joint disambiguation and sense classification. Relative class values are reported for coarse and fine senses. The label None represents an absence of connectives.

recall for a single model. With respect to this metric, we notice higher values for both kinds of sense classification in contrast to connective disambiguation. This confirms that, although the single F1 score might not change that much, more complex tasks indeed improve model generalization and result in more stable models. Further, it appears that training our model on fine senses is somewhat less effective for the main disambiguation task, as training on coarse senses often slightly outperforms it.

Finally, we studied the predictions of our contextualized embedding model (see Figure 3) as before. Here, we compare both sense levels and notice a change of performance in Contingency and Expansion. While the coarse model works better on the second class than the first one, this turns around for the fine-sense model. Especially for the fine-sense model, we observe an overall drop of performance, which could be related to the smaller number of samples per class.

5 Discussion

In our final comparison, Table 3 shows our best-performing models for each category (standard vs. contextualized embeddings and connective disambiguation vs. joint training for sense classification). For comparison, we included test results from successful submissions to the CoNLL 2016 Shared Task (Xue et al., 2016)—in particular, results that were achieved for connective disambiguation in the first part of the Shared Task and results for explicit sense classification taken from the second part. As Table 3 shows, when using contextualized embeddings, our model outperformed the other systems with F1 scores of up to 97.32. The authors of the models (Stepanov and Soochow) unfortunately submitted results only for the first task, and thus, we cannot compare their performance on sense classification to our model's performance. The numbers for sense classification of our proposed contextualized embedding approach are slightly below those of the compared systems. But it is important to note that the other systems are prone to error propagation—errors made early throughout the pipeline negatively affect all subsequent steps. However, in the competitions, error propagation was eliminated by providing preprocessed data to the competing systems. This can be considered an unfair advantage over our system, which performed all tasks simultaneously and thus had to operate on raw data.

6 Related Work

In this section, we discuss work relevant to the area of discourse parsing, in particular, connective disambiguation and sense classification. Finally, recent work on word embeddings and multitask learning with regard to discourse parsing is outlined.

For *connective disambiguation*, Pitler and Nenkova (2009) defined a set of syntactic features extracted from constituency trees. Beside the connective's surface and category information from related tree nodes (parent, siblings), they also used

Model	Test		Blind	
	$F1_{conn}$	$F1_{sense}$	$F1_{conn}$	$F1_{sense}$
Ecnuc	93.96	90.13	91.34	77.41
OPT	94.43	90.13	91.79	77.17
Stepanov	92.43	—	88.56	—
Soochow	94.74	—	91.04	—
ctx-embd (bert-ctx-1)	97.32	—	96.98	—
ctx-embd-mtl (bert-ctx-0)	97.18	86.26	96.28	71.69
embd (wiki-ctx-1)	92.09	—	88.74	—
embd-mtl (wiki-ctx-1)	92.63	80.39	89.74	62.74

Table 3: Task-related F1 scores. Results are taken from the CoNLL 2016 Shared Task website (`http://www.cs.brandeis.edu/~clp/conll16st/results.html`) for the following parsers: OPT (Oepen et al., 2016), Ecnuc (Wang and Lan, 2016), Stepanov (Stepanov and Riccardi, 2016a), Soochow (Fan et al., 2016). The ending `-mtl` refers to the results for fine-sense classification in Table 2.

binary features that check whether categories are contained by the nodes' traces and pairwise interaction features. In addition to these features, Lin et al. (2014) propose a set of lexicosyntactic features, as they observe that a connective's immediate context and part of speech is already a strong indicator for disambiguation. The authors further extend those features by category paths from the connective to the root. Wang and Lan (2015) further extend the previous two works and add similar features for more syntactic context information of the connective. Oepen et al. (2016) combine previous feature sets with work on identifying expressions of speculation and negation (Velldal et al., 2012). Recent work of Webber et al. (2019) highlights the complexity of several kinds of ambiguity when working with discourse connectives.

The connective and its *explicit sense* have a strong correlation as shown by Pitler and Nenkova (2009), who report accuracy higher than the interannotator agreement for their connective disambiguation features on coarse-grained level senses. Lin et al. (2014) use only context features and evaluate their work on second-level senses. Wang and Lan (2015) extend previous features and develop a model for the CoNNL Shared Task. Oepen et al. (2016) use an ensemble of three types of classifiers that are mainly based on previous features (Wang and Lan, 2015). Stepanov and Riccardi (2016b) use chained information extracted from syntactical trees and chunk tags. Qin et al. (2016) use convolutional neural networks on word-level embedded sentence pairs but a linear model with additional dependency features for sense classification.

Braud and Denis (2015) have shown that word embeddings outperform sparse features for implicit sense classification. They compare word pair features with Brown clusters and low-dimensional word embeddings. Bai and Zhao (2018) use different levels of input representations, ranging from character level to contextualized word embeddings. Kishimoto et al. (2020) adapt BERT to perform implicit discourse sense classification. They show promising results by adding tasks, such as connective prediction, for pretraining.

Multitask learning is also successfully applied to implicit sense classification (Liu et al., 2016). The authors combine four different tasks related to discourse parsing, but in contrast to our work, they rely on previously extracted argument spans. Qin et al. (2017) propose a model that, in addition to their main task (implicit sense classification), also learns to predict a possible connective that could be inserted. Lan et al. (2017) introduce various models that perform multitask learning, and their focus also lies on implicit sense classification.

7 Conclusions

In this work, we studied the value of discourse information in different kinds of word embeddings. We first presented a novel feature-free approach to connective disambiguation that achieves state-of-the-art results on this task. Then, this approach was extended by explicit sense classification to study the influence of jointly training both tasks. While our second approach does not directly outperform previous approaches on explicit sense classification, our model can be directly applied to raw input without being subject to error propagation, which is an advantage of our approach.

As our work indicates that combining multiple subtasks avoid error propagation issues, a future direction could be to investigate what other kinds of subtasks could be combined in order to benefit from this. Also, word embeddings have shown to be very flexible, and they are useful even for out-of-domain data. It is worth investigating whether they are suitable for language transfer. This is particularly interesting because data sets of a similar quality to PDTB do not exist for many languages other than English.

References

Hongxiao Bai and Hai Zhao. 2018. Deep enhanced representation for implicit discourse relation recognition. In *Proceedings of the 27th International Conference on Computational Linguistics*, pages 571–583, Santa Fe, New Mexico, USA. Association for Computational Linguistics.

Jonathan Baxter. 2000. A model of inductive bias learning. *Journal of artificial intelligence research*, 12:149–198.

Piotr Bojanowski, Edouard Grave, Armand Joulin, and Tomas Mikolov. 2017. Enriching word vectors with subword information. *Transactions of the Association for Computational Linguistics*, 5:135–146.

Chloé Braud and Pascal Denis. 2015. Comparing word representations for implicit discourse relation classification. In *Proceedings of the 2015 Conference on Empirical Methods in Natural Language Processing*, pages 2201–2211, Lisbon, Portugal. Association for Computational Linguistics.

Richard A. Caruana. 1993. Multitask learning: A knowledge-based source of inductive bias. In *Machine Learning Proceedings 1993*, pages 41 – 48. Morgan Kaufmann, San Francisco (CA).

Ronan Collobert, Jason Weston, Léon Bottou, Michael Karlen, Koray Kavukcuoglu, and Pavel Kuksa. 2011. Natural language processing (almost) from scratch. *J. Mach. Learn. Res.*, 12(null):2493–2537.

Jacob Devlin, Ming-Wei Chang, Kenton Lee, and Kristina Toutanova. 2019. BERT: Pre-training of deep bidirectional transformers for language understanding. In *Proceedings of the 2019 Conference of the North American Chapter of the Association for Computational Linguistics: Human Language Technologies, Volume 1 (Long and Short Papers)*, pages 4171–4186, Minneapolis, Minnesota. Association for Computational Linguistics.

Ziwei Fan, Zhenghua Li, and Min Zhang. 2016. Finding arguments as sequence labeling in discourse parsing. In *Proceedings of the CoNLL-16 shared task*, pages 150–157. Association for Computational Linguistics.

Sucheta Ghosh, Richard Johansson, Giuseppe Riccardi, and Sara Tonelli. 2011. Shallow discourse parsing with conditional random fields. In *Proceedings of 5th International Joint Conference on Natural Language Processing*, pages 1071–1079, Chiang Mai, Thailand. Asian Federation of Natural Language Processing.

Diederik P. Kingma and Jimmy Ba. 2015. Adam: A method for stochastic optimization. *CoRR*, abs/1412.6980.

Yudai Kishimoto, Yugo Murawaki, and Sadao Kurohashi. 2020. Adapting BERT to implicit discourse relation classification with a focus on discourse connectives. In *Proceedings of the 12th Language Resources and Evaluation Conference*, pages 1152–1158, Marseille, France. European Language Resources Association.

Man Lan, Jianxiang Wang, Yuanbin Wu, Zheng-Yu Niu, and Haifeng Wang. 2017. Multi-task attention-based neural networks for implicit discourse relationship representation and identification. In *Proceedings of the 2017 Conference on Empirical Methods in Natural Language Processing*, pages 1299–1308, Copenhagen, Denmark. Association for Computational Linguistics.

Ziheng Lin, Hwee Tou Ng, and Min-Yen Kan. 2014. A pdtb-styled end-to-end discourse parser. *Natural Language Engineering*, 20:151–184.

Xiaodong Liu, Pengcheng He, Weizhu Chen, and Jianfeng Gao. 2019. Multi-task deep neural networks for natural language understanding. In *Proceedings of the 57th Annual Meeting of the Association for Computational Linguistics*, pages 4487–4496, Florence, Italy. Association for Computational Linguistics.

Yang Liu and Mirella Lapata. 2019. Text summarization with pretrained encoders. In *Proceedings of the 2019 Conference on Empirical Methods in Natural Language Processing and the 9th International Joint Conference on Natural Language Processing (EMNLP-IJCNLP)*, pages 3730–3740, Hong Kong, China. Association for Computational Linguistics.

Yang Liu, Sujian Li, Xiaodong Zhang, and Zhifang Sui. 2016. Implicit discourse relation classification via multi-task neural networks. In *Proceedings of the Thirtieth AAAI Conference on Artificial Intelligence*, AAAI'16, page 2750–2756. AAAI Press.

Tomas Mikolov, Kai Chen, Greg Corrado, and Jeffrey Dean. 2013. Efficient estimation of word representations in vector space. In *1st International Conference on Learning Representations, ICLR 2013, Scottsdale, Arizona, USA, May 2-4, 2013, Workshop Track Proceedings*.

Stephan Oepen, Jonathon Read, Tatjana Scheffler, Uladzimir Sidarenka, Manfred Stede, Erik Velldal, and Lilja Øvrelid. 2016. OPT: Oslo–Potsdam–teesside. pipelining rules, rankers, and classifier ensembles for shallow discourse parsing. In *Proceedings of the CoNLL-16 shared task*, pages 20–26, Berlin, Germany. Association for Computational Linguistics.

Jeffrey Pennington, Richard Socher, and Christopher Manning. 2014. GloVe: Global vectors for word representation. In *Proceedings of the 2014 Conference on Empirical Methods in Natural Language Processing (EMNLP)*, pages 1532–1543, Doha, Qatar. Association for Computational Linguistics.

Matthew Peters, Mark Neumann, Mohit Iyyer, Matt Gardner, Christopher Clark, Kenton Lee, and Luke Zettlemoyer. 2018. Deep contextualized word representations. In *Proceedings of the 2018 Conference of the North American Chapter of the Association for Computational Linguistics: Human Language Technologies, Volume 1 (Long Papers)*, pages 2227–2237, New Orleans, Louisiana. Association for Computational Linguistics.

Emily Pitler and Ani Nenkova. 2009. Using syntax to disambiguate explicit discourse connectives in text. In *Proceedings of the ACL-IJCNLP 2009 Conference Short Papers*, pages 13–16, Suntec, Singapore. Association for Computational Linguistics.

Rashmi Prasad, Nikhil Dinesh, Alan Lee, Eleni Miltsakaki, Livio Robaldo, Aravind Joshi, and Bonnie Webber. 2008. The penn discourse treebank 2.0. In *In Proceedings of LREC*.

Rashmi Prasad, Bonnie Webber, and Alan Lee. 2018. Discourse annotation in the PDTB: The next generation. In *Proceedings 14th Joint ACL - ISO Workshop on Interoperable Semantic Annotation*, pages 87–97, Santa Fe, New Mexico, USA. Association for Computational Linguistics.

L. Prechelt. 1998. Automatic early stopping using cross validation: quantifying the criteria. *Neural networks : the official journal of the International Neural Network Society*, 11 4:761–767.

Lianhui Qin, Zhisong Zhang, and Hai Zhao. 2016. Shallow discourse parsing using convolutional neural network. In *Proceedings of the CoNLL-16 shared task*, pages 70–77, Berlin, Germany. Association for Computational Linguistics.

Lianhui Qin, Zhisong Zhang, Hai Zhao, Zhiting Hu, and Eric Xing. 2017. Adversarial connective-exploiting networks for implicit discourse relation classification. In *Proceedings of the 55th Annual Meeting of the Association for Computational Linguistics (Volume 1: Long Papers)*, pages 1006–1017, Vancouver, Canada. Association for Computational Linguistics.

Karin Sim Smith. 2017. On integrating discourse in machine translation. In *Proceedings of the Third Workshop on Discourse in Machine Translation*, pages 110–121, Copenhagen, Denmark. Association for Computational Linguistics.

Evgeny Stepanov and Giuseppe Riccardi. 2016a. Unitn end-to-end discourse parser for conll 2016 shared task. In *Proceedings of the CoNLL-16 shared task*, pages 85–91. Association for Computational Linguistics.

Evgeny Stepanov and Giuseppe Riccardi. 2016b. UniTN end-to-end discourse parser for CoNLL 2016 shared task. In *Proceedings of the CoNLL-16 shared task*, pages 85–91, Berlin, Germany. Association for Computational Linguistics.

Erik Velldal, Lilja Øvrelid, Jonathon Read, and Stephan Oepen. 2012. Speculation and negation: Rules, rankers, and the role of syntax. *Computational Linguistics*, 38(2):369–410.

Jianxiang Wang and Man Lan. 2015. A refined end-to-end discourse parser. In *Proceedings of the Nineteenth Conference on Computational Natural Language Learning - Shared Task*, pages 17–24, Beijing, China. Association for Computational Linguistics.

Jianxiang Wang and Man Lan. 2016. Two end-to-end shallow discourse parsers for english and chinese in conll-2016 shared task. In *Proceedings of the CoNLL-16 shared task*, pages 33–40. Association for Computational Linguistics.

Longyue Wang, Chris Hokamp, Tsuyoshi Okita, Xiaojun Zhang, and Qun Liu. 2015. The dcu discourse parser for connective, argument identification and explicit sense classification. In *Proceedings of the Nineteenth Conference on Computational Natural Language Learning - Shared Task*, pages 89–94. Association for Computational Linguistics.

Bonnie Webber, Rashmi Prasad, and Alan Lee. 2019. Ambiguity in explicit discourse connectives. In *Proceedings of the 13th International Conference on Computational Semantics - Long Papers*, pages 134–141, Gothenburg, Sweden. Association for Computational Linguistics.

Thomas Wolf, Lysandre Debut, Victor Sanh, Julien Chaumond, Clement Delangue, Anthony Moi, Pierric Cistac, Tim Rault, R'emi Louf, Morgan Funtowicz, and Jamie Brew. 2019. Huggingface's transformers: State-of-the-art natural language processing. *ArXiv*, abs/1910.03771.

Yonghui Wu, Mike Schuster, Zhifeng Chen, Quoc V. Le, Mohammad Norouzi, Wolfgang Macherey, Maxim Krikun, Yuan Cao, Qin Gao, Klaus Macherey, Jeff Klingner, Apurva Shah, Melvin Johnson, Xiaobing Liu, Lukasz Kaiser, Stephan Gouws, Yoshikiyo Kato, Taku Kudo, Hideto Kazawa, Keith Stevens, George Kurian, Nishant Patil, Wei Wang, Cliff Young, Jason Smith, Jason Riesa, Alex Rudnick, Oriol Vinyals, Greg Corrado, Macduff Hughes, and Jeffrey Dean. 2016. Google's neural machine translation system: Bridging the gap between human and machine translation. *CoRR*, abs/1609.08144.

Yuxiang Wu and Baotian Hu. 2018. Learning to extract coherent summary via deep reinforcement learning. *CoRR*, abs/1804.07036.

Nianwen Xue, Hwee Tou Ng, Sameer Pradhan, Rashmi Prasad, Christopher Bryant, and Attapol Rutherford. 2015. The conll-2015 shared task on shallow discourse parsing. In *Proceedings of the Nineteenth Conference on Computational Natural Language Learning - Shared Task*, pages 1–16. Association for Computational Linguistics.

Nianwen Xue, Hwee Tou Ng, Sameer Pradhan, Attapol Rutherford, Bonnie Webber, Chuan Wang, and Hongmin Wang. 2016. Conll 2016 shared task on multilingual shallow discourse parsing. In *Proceedings of the CoNLL-16 shared task*, pages 1–19. Association for Computational Linguistics.

Yang Zhong, Chao Jiang, Wei Xu, and Junyi Jessy Li. 2020. Discourse level factors for sentence deletion in text simplification. In *AAAI*.

DSNDM: Deep Siamese Neural Discourse Model with Attention for Text Pairs Categorization and Ranking

Alexander Chernyavskiy and **Dmitry Ilvovsky**

National Research University Higher School of Economics

Moscow, Russia

`alschernyavskiy@gmail.com`; `dilvovsky@hse.ru`

Abstract

In this paper, the utility and advantages of the discourse analysis for text pairs categorization and ranking are investigated. We consider two tasks in which discourse structure seems useful and important: automatic verification of political statements, and ranking in question answering systems. We propose a neural network based approach to learn the match between pairs of discourse tree structures. To this end, the neural TreeLSTM model is modified to effectively encode discourse trees and DSNDM model based on it is suggested to analyze pairs of texts. In addition, the integration of the attention mechanism in the model is proposed. Moreover, different ranking approaches are investigated for the second task. In the paper, the comparison with state-of-the-art methods is given. Experiments illustrate that combination of neural networks and discourse structure in DSNDM is effective since it reaches top results in the assigned tasks. The evaluation also demonstrates that discourse analysis improves quality for the processing of longer texts.

1 Introduction

The growing popularity of social networks and the widespread use of social media contributed to the emergence of many NLP tasks associated with the processing of statements. It can be analyzed from an emotional point of view (sentiment analysis), opinion and argumentation mining, text summarization and so forth.

Despite the success of the transformer-based neural networks, such as BERT (Devlin et al., 2018) and its modifications, in various NLP tasks, they also have disadvantages since they frequently analyze only the plain text that can be quite long and complex. At the same time, discourse structure contains important knowledge for solving these tasks, and several researchers demonstrated its significance (Galitsky et al., 2015; Bhatia et al., 2015; Ji

and Smith, 2017). However, the value of discourse have been already investigated only for some single text categorization tasks.

In this study, we demonstrate the utility and advantages of the matching of discourse tree structures of text pairs. Discourse analysis seems effective in textual entailment, text simplification and paraphrase detection tasks. However, it is necessary to analyze texts on the sentence level in most cases. We consider typical NLP tasks in which input texts are quite long and paragraphs are given initially.

One of such tasks is automatic verification of factual texts. Politicians may utilize unreliable statements for their own purposes. Due to the fact that there are plenty of such statements, it should be automatically evaluated for reliability and the possibility of manipulation of public opinion. In most cases, it is possible to extract some confirmation or refutation for a given factual text. In this way, we investigate the utility of discourse analysis in the classification of pairs of texts: statements and their justifications. Discourse structure may contain crucial knowledge even for the classification of the statements alone but can be even more effective in the case of analyzing additionally the confirmations and refutations.

Apart from that, one of the most appropriate tasks is the ranking in question answering systems. It was shown that discourse structure of questions and correct answers should correlate (Galitsky et al., 2015). Companies are interested in QA systems development in order to maximize the ease of interaction with customers. All questions can be divided into two groups: factoid and non-factoid. It is important to answer factoid questions to provide some specific information and non-factoid ones to maintain a dialogue. It is worth to emphasize that the second task is more challenging because there is no single correct answer for each question. We

Proceedings of the First Workshop on Computational Approaches to Discourse, pages 76–85

Online, November 20, 2020. ©2020 Association for Computational Linguistics

https://doi.org/10.18653/v1/P17

consider the non-factoid questions asked on Internet forums since the discourse analysis seems to be more helpful in this case.

The main technical idea of this paper is to combine discourse analysis and recursive neural network TreeLSTM (Tai et al., 2015), which previously obtained the state-of-the-art results in some single text classification tasks.

Our contributions can be formulated as the following:

- We propose a neural network approach to learn the match between pairs of the discourse tree structures. To this end, we modify the basic TreeLSTM model to effectively encode the discourse structure and propose DSNDM (Deep Siamese Neural Discourse Model) to analyze pairs of texts.

- We suggest the way of integration of the attention mechanism in the DSNDM model.

- We investigate the value of the proposed approach considering two tasks and experimentally confirm the utility and importance of discourse analysis for the text pairs processing.

Our paper is organized as follows. Firstly, we summarize related work and introduce some base concepts. We continue with the description of the base model and its modifications. Then, we discuss the obtained results, error analysis and propose directions for further research.

2   Related Work

There are several approaches to solve the fact-checking problem. The best models presented in the FEVER competition (Thorne et al., 2018) allocate a stage of extracting supporting or refuting information and a classification stage. Justifications have already been extracted in our case. Therefore, there is no need to use the first stage. The BERT model (Devlin et al., 2018) is frequently used as the main model of the approach (Nie et al., 2019; Alonso-Reina et al., 2019). It is worth to emphasize that BERT cannot process long texts (the sequence is limited to 512 tokens). Therefore, it is necessary to extract the key information from the given justification paragraph. Besides, BERT can not efficiently store and process discourse features.

Another approach uses knowledge graphs. Clancy et al. (2019) proposed the use of relations between the entities of the graph in order to confirm

some "distill" information extracted from the statement. Ciampaglia et al. (2015) suggested Knowledge Linker, the main idea of which is that if the path between entities in the knowledge graph is short, then the factual text containing them is reliable. It should be mentioned that this approach is generally applicable only to factoid statements since the entities must exist within knowledge graphs.

Finally, we distinguish the third approach which considers structural information extracted from texts (Wu et al., 2017; Galitsky and Ilvovsky, 2016). Galitsky et al. (2015) proposed to match discourse trees and solved the categorization task using Tree Kernel-based SVM. However, this approach does not utilize any modern neural networks. At the same time, recursive neural networks are gaining popularity (Ji and Smith, 2017; Bhatia et al., 2015; Tai et al., 2015). The main goal of them is to encode tree-like structures, such as syntax and discourse trees. These models achieved superior results in the single text categorization tasks, but researchers did not investigate the value of discourse analysis for processing pairs of texts. However, this approach is promising for the assigned task since frequently not only unreliable texts have a similar discourse structure, but the discourse structure of texts refuting them is also similar.

The main baselines for the question-answering problem are models that utilize keywords for ranking: using TF-iDF, BM25 and its modifications (Okapi BM25, BM25F). Frequently, their results are bad enough and need to be re-ranked using more complex methods. Neural network models, such as BERT, allow obtaining state-of-the-art results (Hashemi et al., 2020). It should be mentioned here that different training techniques of ranking are often not investigated.

In addition, some fact-checking approaches can be applied in question answering systems. For instance, Cui et al. (2017) and Liu et al. (2019) considered the possibility of using knowledge graphs. Galitsky (2019) investigated the value of discourse analysis in QA systems, but did not utilize any neural network approaches.

3   Methods

3.1   Discourse Tree Structure

Any text can be represented as a tree using the Rhetorical Structure Theory (RST) proposed by Mann and Thompson (1987). The tree is con-

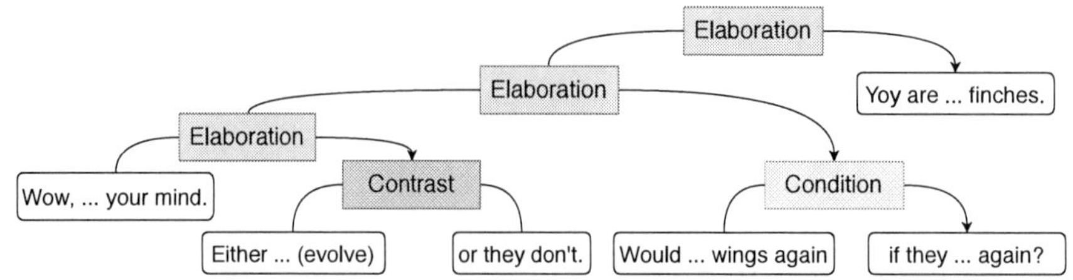

Figure 1: Discourse tree for text from an Internet forum.

structed step by step from the leaves to the root.

Initially, the text is divided into several intervals, called elementary discourse units (EDUs). Each of them contains a single thought, which cannot be broken more. Further, these intervals are connected by discourse relations such as "Elaboration", "Joint" and "Condition". After the unification of the elementary units, there are formed larger intervals of the text, which can be also connected by the corresponding discourse relations. This process can be continued until the only one node will remain (the root of the tree).

RST identifies two types of vertices: "Nucleus" and "Satellite". Vertices of the first type contain the crucial parts of the text, whereas, vertices of the second type provide some additional information.

Figure 1 demonstrates an example of a discourse tree for a text from an Internet forum.

3.2 EDU Embeddings

The pretrained Deep Averaging Network was chosen to construct embeddings of elementary discourse units (text spans). This model is a variation of the Universal Sentence Encoder, proposed by Cer et al. (2018). DAN averages word embeddings and applies a stack of fully-connected layers to get the final vector representation of the text.

We also consider parts-of-speech tags as additional information about the text. We embed POS-tags as vectors using one-hot encoding.

The final vector representation of an EDU is the concatenation of a semantic embedding from DAN and syntactic embedding constructed due to the POS-tags.

3.2.1 Recursive Neural Network

A recursive neural network encodes a tree as a vector of a fixed dimension. Similar to the tree construction in RST, the encoding occurs recursively along subtrees from leaves to root. The process of

obtaining an embedding of a subtree with the root in the node i can be described as follows.

Let x_i denote the text embedding corresponding to the node i.

$$x_i = \begin{cases} \text{EDU embedding, if } i \text{ is the leaf} \\ \text{Embedding of the empty text, else} \end{cases}$$

Text Encoder applies a fully-connected layer to this pre-trained vector:

$$\text{Text\_Enc}(i) = \text{FC}(x_i) \tag{1}$$

Let nodes denoted as j and k be children indices for the node i, and r be the name of the discourse relation that characterizes the link between them. Dummy child vertices containing empty text are added for the leaves. The vector representation of the input associated with i concatenates four vectors as follows:

$$t_i = \text{Concat}[\mathbb{I}[j \text{ is Nucleus}], \mathbb{I}[k \text{ is Nucleus}],$$
$$\text{OneHot}(r), \text{Text\_Enc}(i)] \tag{2}$$

In (2) $\mathbb{I}$ is the indicator function.

An embedding of the tree which has root in the node i is computed based on embeddings of its left and right subtrees due to the binary TreeLSTM model (Tai et al., 2015).

$$h_i = \text{TreeLSTM}(t_i, h_j, h_k) \tag{3}$$

We use TreeLSTM with dropout regularization of recurrent networks suggested by Semeniuta et al. (2016). Formally, the model is expressed with equations (4), (5) and (6).

$$\begin{pmatrix} \boldsymbol{i}_i \\ \boldsymbol{f}_{i0} \\ \boldsymbol{f}_{i1} \\ \boldsymbol{o}_i \\ \boldsymbol{u}_i \end{pmatrix} = \begin{pmatrix} \sigma(W_i[t_i, h_j, h_k] + b_i) \\ \sigma(W_{f_0}[t_i, h_j, h_k] + b_{f_0}) \\ \sigma(W_{f_1}[t_i, h_j, h_k] + b_{f_1}) \\ \sigma(W_o[t_i, h_j, h_k] + b_o) \\ D(\tanh(W_u[t_i, h_j, h_k] + b_u), \alpha) \end{pmatrix} \tag{4}$$

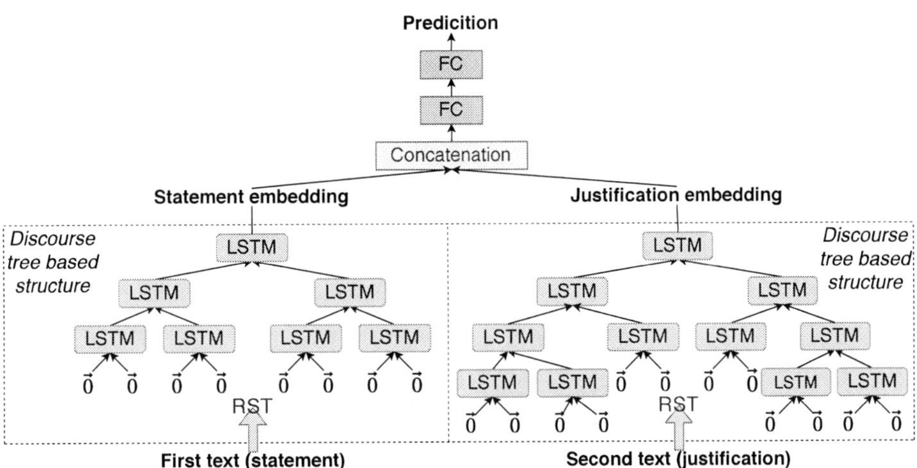

Figure 2: DSNDM model. Here, "LSTM" applies the TreeLSTM cell. Cells with the same color use the same weights. Each cell applied to EDUs receives zero vectors as embeddings of its children.

$$c_i = c_j * \boldsymbol{f}_{i0} + c_k * \boldsymbol{f}_{i1} + \boldsymbol{i}_i * \boldsymbol{u}_i \tag{5}$$

$$h_i = \boldsymbol{o}_i * c_i \tag{6}$$

Here, σ is the sigmoid function, D is the Dropout function, α is the dropout rate and $*$ is the element-wise multiplication. The memory cell is denoted as c. There are two forget outputs since the trees are binary.

The embedding received at the root of the tree is the vector representation of the entire text.

3.3 DSNDM

We propose DSNDM - siamese model based on the recursive neural network. There are two stages of the final model.

Firstly, the embeddings of the discourse trees for each of the input texts are calculated. The trainable parameters for both texts are the same. At the next stage, the resulting embeddings are aggregated for solving the categorization task. Here, the model concatenates the calculated trees embeddings and applies a sequence of two fully-connected layers to it. The last layer utilizes the Softmax function to map input features to the class probability space.

The main advantage of the proposed model is that it is capable of end-to-end learning. Figure 2 shows the architecture of the model. In this case, it solves the fact-checking problem. At the same time, it is almost the same for question-answer systems, except its inputs: the first text is a question, and the second is an answer.

3.4 Integration of the Attention Mechanism

We suggest a way of the integration of the attention mechanism (Vaswani et al., 2017), which has gained popularity in many NLP tasks. The main idea is that a constructed embedding of a question/statement can be used to filter information while constructing an embedding of an answer/justification. Thus, at each step, the model decides information from which subtree is more useful. The attention module can be integrated into the equations of the TreeLSTM model as follows.

Let us consider the Attention module, in which the key is the vector k and the values are represented by the matrix Q. In our case, the key is the embedding of the first text. The matrix Q is composed of vectors $q_1 = c_j * \boldsymbol{f}_{i0}$ and $q_2 = c_k * \boldsymbol{f}_{i1}$ and has the dimension $2 \times d$, where d is the dimension of the memory vector. Then, instead of equation (5), the memory cell vector is recalculated using attention matrices:

$$c_i = 2 \cdot \mathrm{Att}(k, Q) + \boldsymbol{i}_i * \boldsymbol{u}_i \tag{7}$$

$$\mathrm{Att}(k, Q) = \mathrm{SM}\left(\sum_{j=1}^{|Q|} \langle W_K k, W_Q q_j \rangle W_V q_j \right) \tag{8}$$

Here, SM is the Softmax layer which is used for normalization. In (7), multiplication by 2 is necessary to maintain a balance with equation (5). In (8), matrices W_K, W_Q and W_V are trainable matrices of parameters of the Attention module.

Equation (7) is utilized instead of (5) only to construct the embedding of the second text.

3.5 Training Techniques for Ranking

DSNDM can be used both in the text classification task and in the ranking task. In this paper, we investigate three ranking techniques.

1) Classification-based

All pairs in the dataset can be divided into two groups based on relevance. The suggested model can be applied to solve the binary classification of text pairs with these groups. The ranking of the answers for each question is carried out using the class probabilities predicted by the model. The architecture of the model completely coincides with the base one in this case, and cross-entropy loss is used to train it.

2) Pointwise ranking

In this case, the main task is the regression problem. Let $\{(q_i, a_i)_{i=1..N}\}$ is the set of the given pairs, and $\{r_i\}$ are the corresponding relevance scores. Let the proposed model is denoted as $\text{DSNDM}(q, a, w)$, where w are model parameters. Then, the model minimizes the following loss:

$$\sum_{i=1}^{N} (\text{DSNDM}(q_i, a_i, w) - r_i)^2 \to \min_{w} \qquad (9)$$

3) Pairwise ranking

Here, the input are triplets $\{(q_i, a_i^+, a_i^-)_{i=1..M}\}$, where the relevant and irrelevant answer are selected for each question. These triplets can be generated from pairs using relevance scores. The ranking model solves the regression problem and minimizes the loss from (11).

$$\text{PN(w)} = \text{DSNDM}(q_i, a_i^+, w) - \text{DSNDM}(q_i, a_i^-, w) \qquad (10)$$

$$\sum_{i=1}^{M} \frac{1}{1 + \exp(\text{PN(w)})} \to \min_{w} \qquad (11)$$

4 Results

4.1 Automatic Fact Verification

4.1.1 LIAR-PLUS dataset

This dataset (Alhindi et al., 2018) contains the statements of politicians collected from politifact.com and labeled by experts, depending on the veracity on a 6-point scale. Binary classification is also possible when all labels less than four indicate lie and the rest indicate truth. The LIAR-PLUS dataset is an extension of the LIAR dataset. It contains automatically extracted justification for each statement.

The dataset also contains metadata with information about the politician and the global context of the statement. The LIAR-PLUS dataset can be used in four scenarios, depending on the restriction on the available data: S (only statement is used), S + M (statement and metadata), SJ (pairs: statement and justification), and S + JM (all available data). The model proposed in this paper is applied to pairs in the SJ scenario. At the same time, the model can be also used in the S scenario utilizing only the recursive neural network.

The dataset contains 12,782 statements which were split into the train, validation and test samples in the ratio of 10:1:1. This dataset is balanced, and the accuracy metric can be used to compare results.

4.1.2 Implementation Details

Firstly, text preprocessing was applied. We converted texts to lower case, removed extra characters and stop words. The open-source discourse parser ALT (Joty et al., 2012) was applied to the prepossessed texts to obtain discourse trees. Finally, the constructed trees were converted to the format described in section 3.1.

We used the DyNet python library to implement our model. The size of the hidden layer in LSTM cells was established at 100, the dropout rate α at 0.1, the learning rate at 0.004 and the number of units in the fully-connected layer in the Text Encoder at the dimension of x_i. We chose the Adagrad optimizer which is less prone to overfitting for the assigned task. The optimal number of epochs is 4-9. The model was trained by mini-batches of 150 pairs of texts.

4.1.3 Experiments

The parser identified 18 unique discourse relations. The most popular relations are "Elaboration" (is chosen by default), "Attribution", "Joint" and "Same-Unit". Usually, the trivial relations are popular in texts, and the ALT parser tends to use it in uncertain cases.

We investigated the difference between relation distributions for the instances in "true" and "pantsfire" classes. The "Joint" relation is less common for truthful statements than for misleading statements (relative frequencies are 0.064 and 0.073). Thus, politicians tend to construct longer, complex sentences in the case of the deceptive statements. Besides, the "Attribution" relation is used more

Model	Binary		Six-way	
	valid	test	valid	test
LR	0.68	0.67	0.37	0.37
SVM	0.65	0.66	0.34	0.34
BiLSTM	0.70	0.68	0.34	0.31
P-BiLSTM	0.69	0.67	0.36	0.35
DSNDM	**0.71**	0.69	**0.40**	0.40
DSNDM + Att.	0.70	**0.71**	**0.40**	**0.41**

Table 1: Model performance (macro-avg. F1-score) on the LIAR-PLUS dataset.

often for truthful statements (frequencies are 0.17 and 0.15). In the biggest part of cases, it indicates a link to the source. Thus, the relations contain some important information by themselves.

We compared the model with the methods proposed in (Alhindi et al., 2018). In addition to well-known baselines (such as linear regression and SVM), BiLSTM and P-BiLSTM are considered. The last one is the siamese model based on the BiLSTM architecture. Table 1 demonstrates the results for the 6-class and binary categorization tasks.

The table shows that the DSNDM model significantly improves the results of baselines, especially in the case of the multiclass classification.

The fully-connected layer in the Text Encoder is crucial since it adds up to 0.02 to accuracy. The usage of the POS-tags embeddings also improves the overall quality approximately by 0.003-0.01.

The DSNDM model with the integrated attention module (denoted as DSNDM + Att.) reached the best results for the test set. This improvement is not significant because of the binary structure of trees (the attention module re-weights only two vectors at each node).

4.1.4 Error Analysis

It is worth emphasizing that in some case trees for statements contain only one node. Therefore, discourse analysis does not suffice to categorize it. For the deepest trees which contain more than 45 nodes in the statement and justification in total (there are 89 such instances in the dataset), the F1-score metric is higher than 0.46.

The confusion matrix is shown in Figure 3. It demonstrates that DSNDM mainly intermingles close labels. However, at the same time, it confuses the classes "false" and "true" in some cases.

We distinguish several types of such instances which are demonstrated in Table 3 (see Appendix

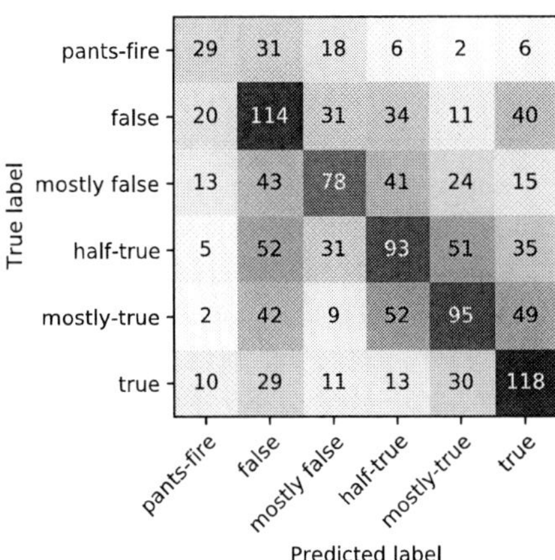

Figure 3: Confusion matrix for DSNDM + Att. model for the LIAR-PLUS dataset.

A). Firstly, there are some cases when refutation partly repeats the statement. Then, the model with attention focuses mainly on the repeated part and marks the misleading statement as "true". Secondly, the justification text can be extracted inaccurately and be not sufficient to estimate the veracity of the statement. Apart from that, the justification can be complex and contain only one useful sentence like in the third example. Finally, in the last pair, justification indicates that the statement can be labeled as "false" in some general cases, but has the label "true" in the considered case. Therefore, this justification contains useless thoughts and can be provided more accurately.

Thus, the quality of the proposed model is limited by several factors: the size of the discourse trees, the quality of the discourse parser, and the quality of the provided justifications.

4.2 Question Answering Systems

4.2.1 ANTIQUE Dataset

This dataset (Hashemi et al., 2020) contains non-factoid questions with a set of possible answers for each of them. The authors selected questions from the Yahoo! Webscope L6 (nfL6) database. The questions were preliminary filtered: short questions, duplicates, and some complex cases were removed.

The corpus contains 2,426 questions in the training sample and 200 in the test sample. Answers for each question were selected both from the question forum thread and from other threads using the BM25 algorithm. In this way, 27,422 answers were allocated for training, and 6,589 instances for testing.

The resulting QA pairs were labeled on a 4-point scale depending on the relevance of answers using the crowdsourcing procedure. The authors also proposed a binary classification task where instances with labels 1 and 2 can be considered as irrelevant, and instances with labels 3 and 4 can be considered as as relevant. Thus, the most common ranking metrics such as MAP and MRR can be used in the second task. At the same time, the multiclass metric nDCG can be also considered. The number of the best answers for questions differs, but on average it is approximately equal to 8.

The dataset is not balanced: the number of relevant answers is almost twice bigger than irrelevant ones. The authors used a negative sampling procedure to train baseline models, increasing the size of the dataset several times. However, it is important to emphasize that these additional QA pairs were not included in the publicly available dataset.

Questions are not very long and contain about 11 words on average. At the same time, the answers are much longer and contain more than 47 words on average. Therefore, it can be problematic to use the standard BERT model, but it is an advantage for the discourse analysis.

4.2.2 Implementation Details

The implementation details are almost the same as described in Sect. 4.1.2 except for some hyperparameters. It is better to choose the smaller dimension of the hidden vectors. The dimension of vectors in TreeLSTM was set to 100, and in the TextEncoder layer was set to 64. It takes 1-3 epochs to achieve optimal quality. A tenth of the training set was used as a validation sample during training.

4.2.3 Experiments

The discourse parser identified 18 different discourse relations like in the first task. However, in this case, the frequency statistics of relations are very similar for different classes. It is due to the fact that in this task the second text (answer) is not auxiliary.

We compared the suggested model with the baselines presented in (Hashemi et al., 2020). It should be highlighted that these baselines were trained on the extended dataset. The authors additionally performed the negative sampling procedure. Therefore, it is not correct to compare the results ob-

	Model	MRR	P@1
1	BM25	0.4885	0.3333
	DRMM-TKS (2016)	0.5774	0.4337
	aNMM (2016)	0.6250	0.4847
	BERT (2018)	*0.7968*	*0.7092*
2	ConvKNRM [pairwise]	0.4920	0.3650
	BERT [pointwise]	0.6694	0.5550
	BERT [pairwise]	*0.6999*	*0.5850*
	Tuned BM25	0.5802	0.4550
	Tuned SDM	0.5377	0.4400
3	Base [classif.]	0.6792	0.5350
	+ Att. [classif.]	0.6830	0.5350
	Base [pointwise]	0.6864	0.5300
	+ Att. [pointwise]	0.7098	0.5650
	Base [pairwise]	0.7120	0.5800
	+ Att. [pairwise]	**0.7267**	**0.6000**

Table 2: Model performance on the ANTIQUE test set. 1: Models presented in (Hashemi et al., 2020), 2: Models presented in (MacAvaney et al., 2020), 3: DSNDM

tained on the available base dataset with the results obtained on the extended dataset.

Apart from that, we considered several models discussed in (MacAvaney et al., 2020). In this paper, several negative examples were also added for each question. However, they were most likely selected only from the training corpus, since the authors were unable to reproduce the BERT results from the original paper.

MacAvaney et al. (2020) proposed various modifications of the training loss by adding a weight for each pair. We do not compare with the results obtained with a modified curriculum since we consider only the basic pointwise and pairwise losses.

The comparison results are presented in Table 2. It shows that DSNDM + Att. model trained using pairwise loss achieves high MRR and P@1 metrics. Its results are superior to the results of the best BERT model presented in (MacAvaney et al., 2020). We also trained BERT ourselves and obtained results close to it, and we could not reproduce the results from the original paper too. Also, the pointwise ranking performed better than the classification-based method.

The attention mechanism improved quality in all cases, especially for the pointwise and pairwise techniques.

4.2.4 Error Analysis

We investigated the mistakes of DSNDM trained for the classification problem. Figure 4 shows the

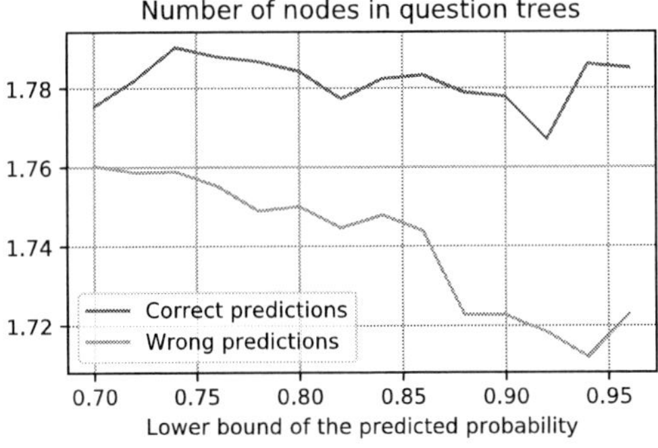

Number of nodes in question trees

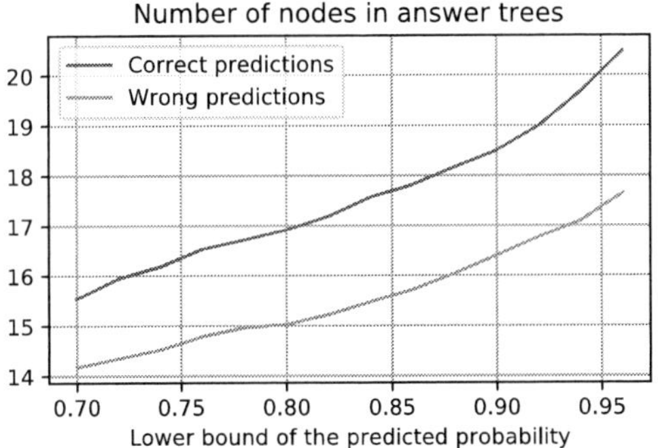

Number of nodes in answer trees

Figure 4: Dependence of the number of nodes in the discourse trees of questions (on the top) and answers (on the bottom) on the confidence of DSNDM in cases of correct and wrong predictions.

dependence of the average number of nodes in questions/answers on the confidence of the model. Thresholds are moved along the horizontal axis. Statistics are calculated only for pairs for which the model predicts a probability that exceeds the selected threshold. One can see that for both questions and answers, the number of nodes in discourse trees for correctly classified pairs is greater than for incorrectly classified ones. Thus, DSNDM makes wrong predictions mostly for small trees. Also, the plot for questions demonstrates that the model's greater confidence in the wrong answer is frequently triggered by the smaller size of the question tree. Therefore, the quality of the proposed model is closely related to the size of the discourse trees for this task too.

In this case, we distinguish several typical mistakes which are demonstrated in Table 4 (see Appendix A). In the first pair, the question contains only a few significant keywords, and the model focuses mainly on them. Despite the fact that the answer is irrelevant and unrelated to the question area, it often uses the same keywords. Thus, similar EDU embeddings do not contribute to the correct classification. In the second example, the meaning of the answer and the question is the opposite. That is, despite the correctness of the answer, its text refutes the information in the question. If the question contains only one node, then such instance is one of the most difficult for analysis. Finally, the last example demonstrates that in some cases the correct answers may be formulated in the way not expected by the authors of the questions. Thus, the quality of the model is also limited by the variability of possible answers.

5   Conclusion and Future Work

In this paper, we investigated the utility and importance of the discourse analysis for text pairs categorization and ranking. We considered two typical tasks in which discourse analysis seems promising: automatic verification of political statements and ranking in question answering systems.

We modified TreeLSTM to effectively encode discourse trees and proposed DSNDM which is capable of processing pairs of texts. In addition, the integration of the attention mechanism in the proposed model was suggested to obtain more useful embeddings of subtrees. Moreover, we investigated three training techniques for the ranking task.

The experiments were performed on the LIAR-PLUS and ANTIQUE datasets. DSNDM efficiently learned the match between discourse tree structures and achieved high quality in both tasks. Besides, the attention module improved the metrics of the base model in all cases. The error analysis showed that the model processes deeper trees more successfully.

There are possible directions for future work: the use of trees not only of a binary structure, the modification of vector representations of EDUs, as well as the investigation of the performance of DSNDM in other various tasks where discourse analysis may be helpful, e.g. machine translation, chat-bots and other QA systems. Apart from that, we will experiment with other hierarchical structures (e.g. syntactic) for deeper analysis of the importance of the RST-based structure in the proposed model.

Acknowledgments

The article was prepared within the framework of the HSE University Basic Research Program and funded by the Russian Academic Excellence Project '5-100'.

References

Tariq Alhindi, Savvas Petridis, and Smaranda Muresan. 2018. Where is your evidence: Improving fact-checking by justification modeling. pages 85–90.

Aimée Alonso-Reina, Robiert Sepúlveda-Torres, Estela Saquete, and Manuel Palomar. 2019. Team GPLSI. approach for automated fact checking. In *Proceedings of the Second Workshop on Fact Extraction and VERification (FEVER)*, pages 110–114, Hong Kong, China. Association for Computational Linguistics.

Parminder Bhatia, Yangfeng Ji, and Jacob Eisenstein. 2015. Better document-level sentiment analysis from RST discourse parsing. *CoRR*, abs/1509.01599.

Daniel Cer, Yinfei Yang, Sheng-yi Kong, Nan Hua, Nicole Limtiaco, Rhomni St. John, Noah Constant, Mario Guajardo-Cespedes, Steve Yuan, Chris Tar, Yun-Hsuan Sung, Brian Strope, and Ray Kurzweil. 2018. Universal sentence encoder. *CoRR*, abs/1803.11175.

Giovanni Luca Ciampaglia, Prashant Shiralkar, Luis Mateus Rocha, Johan Bollen, Filippo Menczer, and Alessandro Flammini. 2015. Computational fact checking from knowledge networks. *PLoS ONE*, 10.

Ryan Clancy, Ihab F. Ilyas, and Jimmy Lin. 2019. Scalable knowledge graph construction from text collections. In *Proceedings of the Second Workshop on Fact Extraction and VERification (FEVER)*, pages 39–46, Hong Kong, China. Association for Computational Linguistics.

Wanyun Cui, Yanghua Xiao, Haixun Wang, Yangqiu Song, Seung-won Hwang, and Wei Wang. 2017. Kbqa: Learning question answering over qa corpora and knowledge bases. *Proceedings of the VLDB Endowment*, 10:565–576.

Jacob Devlin, Ming-Wei Chang, Kenton Lee, and Kristina Toutanova. 2018. BERT: pre-training of deep bidirectional transformers for language understanding. *CoRR*, abs/1810.04805.

Boris Galitsky. 2019. *Learning Discourse-Level Structures for Question Answering*, pages 177–219.

Boris Galitsky and Dmitry Ilvovsky. 2016. Discovering disinformation: discourse level approach. In *15th National Conference on Artificial Intelligence with International Participation (CAI)*, pages 23–32.

Boris Galitsky, Dmitry Ilvovsky, and Sergei O. Kuznetsov. 2015. Text classification into abstract classes based on discourse structure. In *RANLP*, pages 200–207.

Jiafeng Guo, Yixing Fan, Qingyao Ai, and W. Croft. 2016. A deep relevance matching model for ad-hoc retrieval. pages 55–64.

Helia Hashemi, Mohammad Aliannejadi, Hamed Zamani, and W. Bruce Croft. 2020. Antique: A non-factoid question answering benchmark. In *Advances in Information Retrieval*, pages 166–173, Cham. Springer International Publishing.

Yangfeng Ji and Noah A. Smith. 2017. Neural discourse structure for text categorization. *CoRR*, abs/1702.01829.

Shafiq Joty, Giuseppe Carenini, and Raymond Ng. 2012. A novel discriminative framework for sentence-level discourse analysis. In *Proceedings of the 2012 Joint Conference on Empirical Methods in Natural Language Processing and Computational Natural Language Learning*, pages 904–915, Jeju Island, Korea. Association for Computational Linguistics.

Aiting Liu, Ziqi Huang, Hengtong Lu, Xiaojie Wang, and Caixia Yuan. 2019. *BB-KBQA: BERT-Based Knowledge Base Question Answering*, pages 81–92.

Sean MacAvaney, Franco Maria Nardini, Raffaele Perego, Nicola Tonellotto, Nazli Goharian, and Ophir Frieder. 2020. Training curricula for open domain answer re-ranking. pages 529–538.

William Mann and Sandra Thompson. 1987. Rhetorical structure theory: A theory of text organization.

Yixin Nie, Haonan Chen, and Mohit Bansal. 2019. Combining fact extraction and verification with neural semantic matching networks. In *AAAI*.

Stanislau Semeniuta, Aliaksei Severyn, and Erhardt Barth. 2016. Recurrent dropout without memory loss. *CoRR*, abs/1603.05118.

Kai Sheng Tai, Richard Socher, and Christopher D. Manning. 2015. Improved semantic representations from tree-structured long short-term memory networks. *CoRR*, abs/1503.00075.

James Thorne, Andreas Vlachos, Oana Cocarascu, Christos Christodoulopoulos, and Arpit Mittal. 2018. The fact extraction and VERification (FEVER) shared task. In *Proceedings of the First Workshop on Fact Extraction and VERification (FEVER)*, pages 1–9, Brussels, Belgium. Association for Computational Linguistics.

Ashish Vaswani, Noam Shazeer, Niki Parmar, Jakob Uszkoreit, Llion Jones, Aidan Gomez, Lukasz Kaiser, and Illia Polosukhin. 2017. Attention is all you need.

You Wu, Pankaj K. Agarwal, Chengkai Li, Jun Yang, and Cong Yu. 2017. Computational fact checking through query perturbations. *ACM Transactions on Database Systems (TODS)*, 42:1 – 41.

Liu Yang, Qingyao Ai, Jiafeng Guo, and W. Croft. 2016. anmm: Ranking short answer texts with attention-based neural matching model. pages 287–296.

A Appendix

Appendix contains typical examples of pairs for which DSNDM got wrong predictions.

Statement	Justification	Label
In rural Virginia, Sen. Warner ran 8 - 10 points ahead of a traditional Democrat – ahead of Senator Kaine, ahead of Governor McAuliffe.	Hallock said Warner, in this fall's Senate election, ran 8 - 10 points ahead of past performances by fellow Democrats McAuliffe and Kaine in rural Virginia. McAuliffe's portion of the rural vote, in his 2013 gubernatorial victory, was 3.6 percentage points below Warner's. Kaine's slice of the rural vote, in his 2012 Senate win, was 2.4 percentage points above Warner's.	false
In the U. S. Constitution, theres a little section in there that talks about life, liberty and the pursuit of happiness.	No court makes a legal decision based on the Declaration of Independence, Wilkes said. With his first speech as a bona fide candidate, Cain joins a long, bipartisan line of presidential hopefuls who have succumbed to foot - in - mouth disease. They include Cain's foe, President Barack Obama, who accidentally said there were 57 states during the 2008 campaign and U. S. Sen. John McCain, who said in an interview he was unsure how many houses he owned. Welcome to the 2012 presidential election season, folks.	false
In the Illinois Legislature, Barack Obama voted present, instead of yes or no on seven votes involving abortion rights.	Two other large groups, NARAL Prochoice America and Planned Parenthood, are not endorsing. Planned Parenthood, however, has given both candidates 100 percent ratings for their records on abortion. We stipulate that there are clearly different interpretations of the significance of Obama s present votes. But there s no doubt he made them.	true
As a result of climate change, ice fishermen in Wisconsin are already noticing fewer days they can be out on our ice covered lakes.	Not what is going to happen this year. Our rating It's been a longer and colder winter than in recent years. But that doesn't erase a trend that's been well - established. The number of days that the lakes have ice on them – making them safe for ice fishing – has declined.	true

Table 3: Typical mistakes of DSNDM on the LIAR test set where the model confuses "true" and "false" instances.

Question	Answer	Label
how does disneyland make it snow?	Well if you are using snow, just lay on you back in it and move your arms from your sides to the top of you head and open and close you legs a few times... to make snow angels!!!!	Out of context
Why cant teenagers vote?	Teens can vote. When theyre 18 and 19... Teens still have ALOT to learn. There is nothing wrong or demeaning about this. Even most ADULTS have alot to learn about politics. They go into a voting booth having no idea what party stands for what, or what candidate believes in what, and vote Democrat when their beliefs are Republican, or vote Republican when their beliefs are Democrat.	Correct answer
Why is Gordon Ramsey so popular?	Is he that popular? what little I have seen of him every second word is a swear word, if that makes him popular then it says a lot about what is wrong in this country... the man is a cretin.	Correct answer

Table 4: Typical mistakes of DSNDM on the ANTIQUE test set where the model confuses "Correct answer" and "Out of context" instances. .

Do Sentence Embeddings Capture Discourse Properties of Sentences from Scientific Abstracts ?

Laurine Huber[1]**, Chaker Memmadi**[1]**, Mathilde Dargnat**[2] **and Yannick Toussaint**[1]**,**
[1] Université de Lorraine, CNRS, Inria, LORIA (UMR 7503), F-54000 Nancy, France
{laurine.huber, yannick.toussaint}@loria.fr
chaker.memmadi@outlook.fr
[2] ATILF, Université de Lorraine, CNRS (UMR 7118), Nancy, France
et Institut des Sciences Cognitives Marc Jannerod, CNRS (UMR 5304), Bron, France
mathilde.dargnat@univ-lorraine.fr

Abstract

We introduce four tasks designed to determine which sentence encoders best capture discourse properties of sentences from scientific abstracts, namely coherence between clauses of a sentence, and discourse relations within sentences. We show that even if contextual encoders such as BERT or SciBERT encodes the coherence in discourse units, they do not help to predict three discourse relations commonly used in scientific abstracts. We discuss what these results underline, namely that these discourse relations are based on particular phrasing that allow non-contextual encoders to perform well.

1 Introduction

This paper compares the ability of different sentence encoders at representing coherence of sentences from scientific abstracts, and more specifically discourse relations between clauses.

Our first hypothesis is that BERT (Devlin et al., 2019) and SciBERT (Beltagy et al., 2019) models enable to produce sentence representations that take coherence into account thanks to their training done on Next Sentence Prediction. Our second hypothesis is that this training should also enable to capture discourse relations between clauses.

Discourse relations (DRs) represent the semantic and pragmatic links between discourse units (DUs), that are either clauses, sentences or groups thereof, within a hierarchical structure that represents the whole text. In this work, we focus on sentences that are defined as textual sequences separated by a period. Sentences may comprise one or more DUs, and when they have at least two DUs, the coherence links between them is represented through DRs. These DRs are either explicitly signaled, or left implicit. For example, the sentence *"By wearing a mask, we can protect the others."* conveys an `enablement` relation between the action

"wearing a mask" and the event *"protecting the others"*, which is here lexicalized by the connective **"by"**. DRs can be used to extract new knowledge, especially in scientific abstracts which are highly structured (Liddy, 1991).

Sentence embeddings (SE) represent the meaning of a sentence in a fixed-size vector space, and recent contextual approaches such as BERT have shown promising results for downstream tasks such as Semantic Textual Similarity (STS) or Natural Language Inference (NLI) (Reimers and Gurevych, 2019). When further trained on downstream tasks, these models have shown promising results. However, their performance also rely on linguistic knowledge acquired at pre-training. For example, BERT and SciBERT are trained on both Masked Language Model and Next Sentence Prediction tasks, in order to capture general linguistic properties that are then transferred to learn more specific representations.

In this work, we want to understand if discourse properties are embedded in sentence representations that are built before further training on downstream tasks.

We design probing tasks, that are classification tasks whose goals are to predict discourse properties of the sentences from their embedding. Our goal is to highlight if discourse properties of sentences are captured by those vectors without fine-tuning. We rely on the corpus SciDTB (Yang and Li, 2018) to build four datasets used to probe if embeddings capture some discourse properties of the sentences. The two first datasets probe the coherence of sentences, and the two others probe the presence of DRs. We use four different sentence encoders to produce sentence embeddings, that we then use as input vectors for two classification models. If the classifier succeeds, it means that the vectors stores the discourse property that is probed. We evaluate the classifiers, thus high-

86

Proceedings of the First Workshop on Computational Approaches to Discourse, pages 86–95
Online, November 20, 2020. ©2020 Association for Computational Linguistics
https://doi.org/10.18653/v1/P17

lighting encoders that best encode the properties we probe.

This paper is organized as follows. We first provide background to our work. Second, we detail the tasks that we design to detect discourse properties. Third, we present our experimental setup, including the different SE that we evaluate and the choices that are specific to the corpus on which we rely. Finally, we present our results and discuss some issues.

2 Background

Coherence and cohesion are two key notions in the perception of a text as a unified whole.

Coherence refers to logical and semantic relations between clauses and sentences in a text, while cohesion refers to grammatical or lexical devices such as pronouns, verb tense or connectives, that form external relations of a text (Halliday and Hasan, 1976). While the former may stand without the latter and vice versa, the connectivity model of Renkema (2009) mixes coherence and cohesion cues. In this work we follow this approach, and will refer to as coherence the properties of both coherence and cohesion.

DRs may either explicitly signal coherence relations by discourse connectives, or left them implicit. In this latter case, the reader infers the relations based on coherence links between clauses. For example, the marker "**to**" is frequently used to links an action X and a way Y to realize X, signaling that Y is the `manner-means` to do X. However, even if some relations are explicitly signaled with discourse connectives such as "**to**" or "**by**", others are less salient. For example in *"We propose a novel extension of this work using target context information."*, the ellipsis of "**by**" make it harder to infer the relation. Some of them (e.g `enablement`, `manner-means` or `attribution`) express a logical link between the content of the clauses they relate, while others (e.g `elaboration` or `progression`) only express a continuation or additive relation. In scientific abstracts especially, DRs that convey a logical link are often lexically marked.

Several theories such as Rhetorical Structure Theory (RST) (Taboada and Mann, 2006) or Segmented Discourse Representation Theory (SDRT) (Lascarides and Asher, 2007) help to build text discourse structures, by providing both sets of DRs that are defined based on the content of the DUs and a framework for attaching the DUs by means of DRs. The RST defines a set of relations[1] that are either mononuclear (if for two DUs, one is more salient than the other) or multinuclear (if two or more DUs have the same importance). They serve to build the hierarchical discourse structure of the text, either as a constituency tree, or, more recently, with dependency trees (Morey et al., 2018), which are used to annotate scientific abstracts from SciDTB (Yang and Li, 2018).

SE have shown promising results for a wide variety of NLP tasks (Conneau and Kiela, 2018), but are not interpretable independently of the others, making it unclear what linguistic information they contain and what is the *meaning* that they represent exactly. Previous works (Shi et al., 2016; Adi et al., 2016; Conneau et al., 2018) intended to clarify what linguistic information are contained in SE by designing auxiliary tasks that take a single sentence vector as input and tries to predict a simple linguistic property of the sentence. They showed that some syntactic properties (e.g word order or syntactic tree depth) and some properties that they defined as semantic[2] (e.g the tense of the main verb or the number of the subject) are well captured by SE. We then hypothesize that the latter may also capture discourse coherence and DRs in sentences from scientific abstracts, thus being the first step to extracting information at a semantic-pragmatic level.

3 Probing tasks

In this section, for each probing task, we explain how we build a dataset of sentences tagged with discourse properties. They are then encoded by various methods and used to train and evaluate classifiers. We introduce two tasks designed to check if coherence between clauses of a sentence is encoded (3.1, 3.2), and two tasks to check if DRs in sentences are encoded (3.3, 3.4).

3.1 Swapped units detection

Ordering of clauses fully participates to sentences coherence. We evaluate if coherence is captured by SE by evaluating the ability of a classifier to distinguish between coherent sentences and incoherent ones. We produce incoherent sentences by swap-

---

[1] `https://www.sfu.ca/rst/01intro/definitions.html`

[2] They admit however that the boundary they propose between syntactic and semantic tasks is somewhat arbitrary.

ping two adjacent discourse units from sentences originally correct.

The dataset for this probing task thus consists of original multi-clausal sentences and of their incoherent equivalent obtained by swapping two random adjacent DUs. By doing so, we however do not ensure that new sentences are always incoherent. For example, swapping units 0 and 1 in the sentence *"[Word alignment] [using recency-vector based approach] [has recently become popular.]"* produces the new coherent sentence *"[Using recency-vector based approach] [word alignment] [has recently become popular.]"*.

The resulting task is a binary classification task into $\{yes, no\}$, where yes corresponds to swapped sentences, and no to the original sentences.

3.2 Scrambled sentence detection

Topic incoherence may emerge when a topic T_1 is involved in the context of another topic T_2, leading to incoherence because of the incompatibility between T_1 and T_2.

The dataset used to probe this property is built as follows. Starting from original multi-clausal sentences splitted in DUs, we replace a randomly chosen DU by another randomly chosen DU from a different document, thus changing the context of a DU. Here again, the new sentence might be still coherent. For example, replacing the second DU in the sentence *"[But these methods cannot be used][to obtain the estimates of causal effects-the quantity of interest for applied researchers.]"* produces a new coherent sentence *"[But these methods cannot be used] [using a two-phase approach.]"*.

The resulting task is a binary classification task into $\{yes, no\}$, where yes corresponds to scrambled sentences, and no to the original sentences.

3.3 Relation detection

A sentence may either be composed of a single DU, or of multiple DUs. In the last case, the DUs may be links through additive or continuation DRs (in bold in Table 1), or through logical relations (in italics in Table 1). We distinguish them and evaluate if SE can be used to predict whether a sentence contains a logical DR.

We rely on the discourse annotations provided in SciDTB, from which we extract the subtrees corresponding to the discourse structures of the sentences. Sentences that contain only one DU and sentences made of multiple DUs whose subtree contains no logical DRs are classified as *norel*.

Attribution	*Background*	*Cause-effect*
Comparison	*Condition*	*Contrast*
Elaboration	*Enablement*	*Evaluation*
Explain	**Joint**	*Manner-means*
Progression	**Same-unit**	*Summary*
	Temporal	

Table 1: Discourse relations in SciDTB corpus

Others are classified as rel regardless of the type of the logical DR they contain.

The resulting task is a binary classification task into $\{rel, norel\}$.

3.4 Relation semantics detection

Being able to precisely identify which logical discourse relation is involved in a sentence may be useful as a first step toward knowledge extraction from texts. This task thus evaluates if the semantics of the DRs involved in sentences are represented in their embedding.

We rely again on the annotations to classify sentences based on the DR they contain. Sentences that contain only one DU and sentences made of multiple DU whose subtree contains no logical DRs are classified as *norel*. Others are classified based on the relation r they contain, if and only if they contain only one of these relations. The sentences that contain two or more logical relations are not tackled in our approach, and are thus not considered in the dataset.

The resulting task is a K-classes classification task where K is the number of relations that are considered.

4 Experiments

4.1 Data

SciDTB[3] is a corpus of 798 scientific abstracts from ACL Anthology[4]. Abstracts are segmented into DUs in a semi-automatic way, following the guidelines of (Carlson et al., 2003), and annotated by discourse structure in dependency with DRs from the RST relations set, which was slightly modified and extended to be adapted to scientific abstracts[5].

The majority of documents contain between 5 and 7 sentences (minimum 2, maximum 14, mean

---

[3]https://github.com/PKU-TANGENT/SciDTB
[4]https://www.aclweb.org/anthology/
[5]We refer the reader to the paper (Yang and Li, 2018) to get explanations on the adaptations and annotation procedure. The relations set is recalled in Table 1.

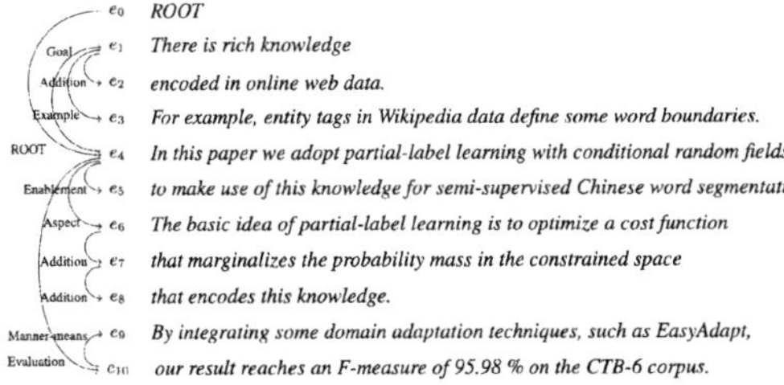

Figure 1: Example of dependency annotation from SciDTB.

6), resulting in a set of 4196 sentences in total. Among them, 787 are made of a single DU, thus containing no relation, and 3409 contain more than one DU, and thus at least one DR. We use the segmentation into DUs to produce the datasets for coherence detection tasks (swapped and scrambled). We use the inter-clausal DRs to produce the datasets for DR detection tasks (binRel and semRel)[6].

For swapped and scrambled, each sentence that has more than one DU is classified as *no*, and is used to produce a new sentence that is classified as *yes*, resulting in a dataset of 6818 sentences. For each sentence (original and modified), we ensure that punctuation and case do not bias the experiment by removing capitalization, periods and commas.

For binRel and semRel, we need to form classes that are broad enough to train the classifiers. It leads us to make choices because of the limited size of the corpus. Fig. 2 shows the number of sentences having one of the given DRs. Most of the DRs are involved in less than 200 sentences, which is not enough for training a classifier. Among the others, three relations are additive relations: `Same-Unit` links two segments of a DU broken into two parts, `Joint` links two DUs which are in conjunction, and for `Elaboration-addition` one DU gives additional information to another DU[7]. Moreover, the latter are involved in most of sentences made of more than 3 DUs, and are thus often used together with logical DRs. We decide to ignore them, which allows us to build a sufficiently

large dataset of sentences, tagged with the three relations: `enablement`, `manner-means` or `attribution`. We assume that the classifier will therefore learn to predict one of these relations.

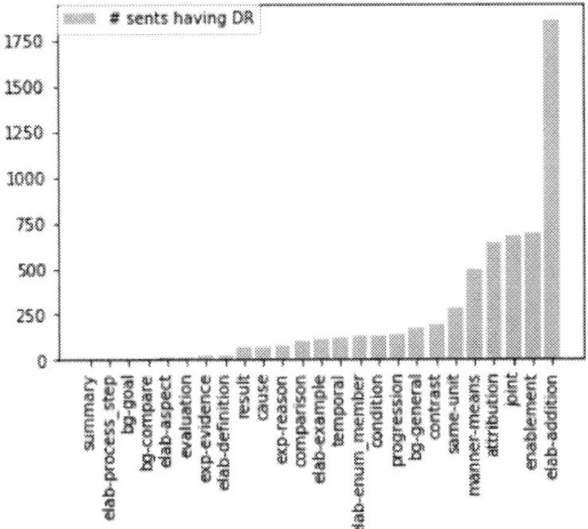

Figure 2: Distribution of relations in sentences.

For binRel, each sentence which has no DR or only DRs from {`joint`, `elaboration-addition`, `same-unit`} is classified as *norel*, and the others as *rel*. For semRel, the *norel* classification is done in the same way, and sentences that involve one and only one relation from {`attribution`, `enablement`, `manner-means`} are classified according to the relation they contain. Table 2 summarizes the datasets used for each probing task, where the classes for each task are balanced.

	classes	# sent	# sent / class
binRel	*rel*	2894	1447
	norel		
semRel	*attribution*	1432	358
	enablement		
	manner − means		
	norel		
swapped	*yes*	6818	3409
	no		
scrambled	*yes*	6818	3409
	no		

Table 2: Datasets description.

4.2 Sentence embeddings

In this section, we present the different SE that we study, most of them being obtained by using pre-trained models available on HuggingFace's (Wolf et al., 2019) website[8]. We compare SE obtained

---

[6]We make the resulting datasets available at `https://gitlab.com/laurinehu/scidtb_expe/-/tree/master/probing_datasets`.

[7]We admit however that saying that `Elaboration-addition` does not contain an interesting semantics is somehow arbitrary, but can be understood by comparison with the semantics of other DRs.

[8]https://huggingface.co/

by averaging non-contextual word vectors (bag-of-vectors), and SE obtained by using more recent language contextual models based on transformers that have shown promising results for various tasks. Comparing the last to bag-of-vectors enables us to determine whether coherence or DRs are only captured because of linguistic cues, or because of implicit links between clauses.

Global word Vectors (Pennington et al., 2014) are word representations obtained from aggregated global word-word co-occurrence statistics from a large crawled corpus. Training objective is to learn word vectors such that their dot product is the log of the word's probability of co-occurrences. We use the largest pre-trained model available, constituted of a vocabulary of 2.2M words, and containing vectors of dimension 300. We build sentence vectors by computing the mean of the word vectors, thus producing bag-of-vectors (BoV) of dimension 300.

Google USE (Cer et al., 2018) uses a Deep Averaging Network that is first trained in an unsupervised way as in Skip-Thoughts (Kiros et al., 2015), and whose output is transferred to be further trained on a supervised way on Natural Language Inference task. This encoder was the state-of-the-art before more recent contextual approaches with which we compare it. We use the largest model, which encodes sentences into vectors of dimension 512.

BERT (Devlin et al., 2019) is the current state-of-the-art for most NLP tasks. It produces contextual word representations, from training a bi-directional encoder on two tasks: the first called Masked LM (MLM) predicts a masked word from its left and right context, and the second called Next Sentence Prediction (NSP) predicts whether from two sentences A and B, B is the actual sentence that follows A. BERT thus represents the meaning of a word according to its immediate context, but also on the basis of relationships between sentences. We use BERT-base model, from which we recover the last hidden state after having processed the sentence in the model, thus producing vectors of dimension 768.

SciBERT (Beltagy et al., 2019) is a BERT model specifically trained on full papers from the corpus of Semantic Scholar, thus seeking to provide a better representation of scientific vocabulary. We use SciBERT-base and proceed in the same way as for BERT, obtaining vectors of the same dimension.

For GloVe, BERT and SciBERT, we calculate the embedding e(S) of the sentence S by calculating the mean of each word vector as defined in 1.

$$e(S) = \frac{1}{|S|} \sum_{w \in S} e(w) \qquad (1)$$

4.3 Classification

Because we deal with datasets of different size and vectors made of latent variables, we train and evaluate two different classifiers for each task, namely a Logistic Regression (LR) and a Multi-Layer-Perceptron (MLP) with one hidden layer and three hidden units. On the one hand, the datasets are small in size, which can make the training of the MLP hard and a good LR performance possible. On the other hand, the properties that we probe may not be linearly separable, which would make them hard to tackle with a LR classifier. The comparison of two classifiers thus gives us a fine-grained analysis of both the results obtained and the way in which the properties are encoded.

Experimental set-up We use the evaluation toolkit Senteval[9] (Conneau and Kiela, 2018), and keep the parameters as defined in it, namely the optimizer is RmsProp (Tijmen and Geoffrey, 2012), the batch size is 164 and the loss function is cross-entropy. Because the number of sentences that we have is quite small, we proceed with 5-fold cross validation. We compute the mean of accuracies at each fold. To compute the test accuracy, we keep the best model and test it on the testing set (10%) of the data. We compare both results to ensure that the model is not overfitting.

5   Results

In this section, we comment the results obtained for each probing tasks. Table 3 shows the test accuracy and the mean accuracy of 5-fold cross validation. We only comment the latter, as it is more relevant due to the small datasets we have.

The LR classifier obtains better results than the MLP for all tasks. Although losses in accuracy when using MLP can be explained by the lack of data, LR gives good results with BERT and SciBERT for binRel, swapped and scrambled, suggesting that those properties may be encoded linearly in the vectors.

Relation detection DR are almost as well encoded by BoV than by BERT and SciBERT, which

---

[9]https://github.com/facebookresearch/SentEval

Model	Encoder	binRel		semRel		swapped		scrambled	
		Test	Mean 5-fold	Test	Mean 5-fold	Test	Mean 5-fold	Test	Mean 5-fold
LR									
	BoV-Glove	**73.45**	73.83	**67.36**	61.3	50	51	52.2	51.9
	Google USE	**71.22**	71.03	**47.92**	50.07	58.8	63.3	50.4	59.8
	Bert-base uncased	70.69	74.97	61.81	59.8	75.22	76.49	**78.59**	77.53
	cased	**71.38**	74.84	**61.11**	55.65	**73.31**	77.33	78.3	76.30
	SciBert uncased	76.55	77.98	50.69	60.16	77.71	77.74	**80.06**	79.77
	cased	**78.28**	76.76	**63.19**	59.22	**77.71**	79.64	81.09	79.53
MLP									
	BoV-Glove	72.76	71.53	60.42	51.82	49.85	50.87	52.49	52.06
	Google USE	67.59	66.64	48.61	45.67	60.26	60.82	56.01	57.31
	Bert-base uncased	69.31	68.47	36.81	28.16	77.57	67.71	75.22	64.27
	cased	50	52.62	25	25.85	78.15	67.85	75.66	54.39
	SciBert uncased	73.45	74.13	38.89	37.23	75.81	68.49	79.91	65.76
	cased	71.38	68.72	43.75	33.83	78.01	70.09	78.01	64.59

Table 3: Test and 5-fold mean accuracies of LR and MLP classifiers on each task for each sentence representation.

can be explained by the fact that they are most of the time lexicalized. Contextual embeddings slightly improve the results for binRel (from $\approx$ 73% for BoV to 76.4 ± 1.5), but not for semRel (61.3% for BoV to 57.9 ± 2.2).

By comparing two by two the results of BoV, BERT, and SciBERT encoders for binRel, we highlight that those models nearly give the same predictions (see Table. 4). Among the 290 sentences used as test, 94 are predicted differently by BERT and BoV, 85 by SciBERT and BoV, and 67 by SciBERT and BERT. Among the sentences that are similarly predicted, less than 20% correspond to common mistakes, and the others to common good predictions. For BERT and SciBERT, around 70% of the predictions are similar, showing that the models capture similar information for this task. For BERT and SciBERT with BoV respectively, more than 50% are common, but still they make a lot of different predictions, showing that they do not capture same aspects of the sentence.

For semRel however, the models make very different predictions. Among the 144 examples used as test, 47 are predicted differently by BERT and BoV, 78 by SciBERT and BoV, and 71 by SciBERT and BERT. The results of Table 5 are consonant with this variation, showing that all encoders have in fact different abilities for the prediction.

We show both precision and recall obtained for SemRel in Table 5. For `attribution` detection, BoV, BERT-uncased and SciBERT-cased gives the best recall (81%), for `enablement` it is BERT-uncased (67%), for `manner-means` it is BoV (78%), and for `norel` it is SciBERT-uncased

(75%). These good recalls obviously result in lower precisions. However, as we want to find as many instances of a relation R, rather than maximizing the number of instances that are correctly found, we are still satisfied.

Coherence detection Representations build from BoV fail at predicting if units have been swapped ($51\%^{10}$), and perform badly for predicting if units have been scrambled ($\approx 51.9\%$). Google Universal Sentence Encoder improves swapped only by 10% and scrambled by 4%. Representations built from contextual embeddings improve accuracy for swapped by almost 26% for BERT and 27.5% for SciBERT and for scrambled by almost 25% for BERT and 27.8% for SciBERT. This shows that training on STS, on which Google USE is trained, is not enough to capture coherence links between clauses, and that the "Next Sentence Prediction" (NSP) task on which both BERT and SciBERT are trained seems indeed to help a lot. This task enables somehow to account for the order of the units in the sentence. Even if BERT and SciBERT are not trained at clause level, the corpus on which they are trained is large and therefore contains a large number of sentences that are made of a single clause. This enables the model to learn clause level contingency relations, which are in fact the task that we probe here.

---

[10]We consider that an accuracy close or less than 50% corresponds to random prediction, because a classifier predicting each class with a probability of 0.5 would have an accuracy of 50%.

	binRel			semRel		
	BERT-BoV	SciBERT-BoV	SciBERT-BoV	BERT-BoV	SciBERT-BoV	SciBERT-BoV
# common predictions	196	205	223	97	66	73
# different predictions	94	85	67	47	78	71
# common errors	162	175	180	64	54	73

Table 4: Two-by-two comparison of the predictions obtained by different encoders for binRel and semRel.

6 Discussion

In this section, we discuss potential biases in the probing tasks that we designed, how we control them, and the possible improvements that could be further done.

Relation prediction   A bias that could affect DR detection is the length of the sentence. In particular, Conneau et al. (2018) showed that BoV obtain 66.6% accuracy for predicting the length of the sentence, and get up to 99% with other more elaborated encoders such as BiLSTM or gated convolutional networks. We took that into account when selecting the different sentence sets. By including sentences that have more than one DU (sentences that only have relations with weak semantics) in the `norel` class , we somehow control the size of the sentences and ensure that the distributions of words per sentence are not specific to each class. The distributions are given in Fig. 3 , and are close enough to guarantee that the Sentence Length does not bias our predictions for binRel.

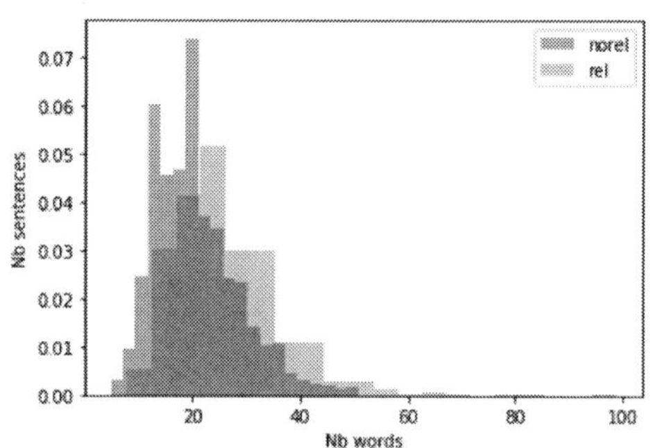

Figure 3: Distribution of the number of words per sentences for binRel.

Similarly, we ensured that the length of the sentence does not affect the detection of the relation semantics. The distributions which are given in Fig. 4 are close and, so, cannot be the only parameter involved in the good quality of the prediction.

However, good performances of BoV for this task are influenced by the fact that most of them are linguistically signalled. Even if this bias is in fact

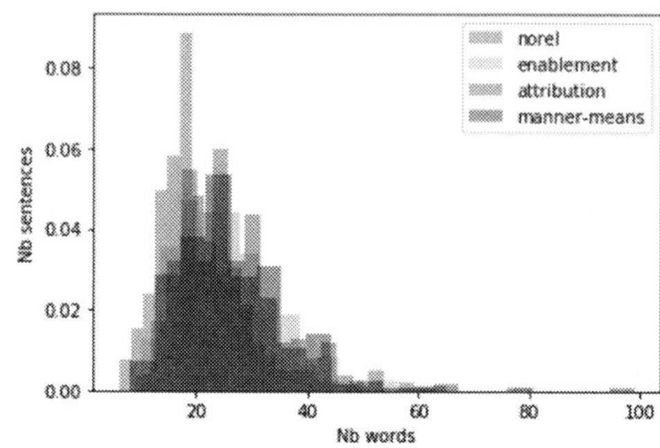

Figure 4: Distribution of the number words per sentences for semRel.

related to the specific genre of the corpus that we study, we discuss here the linguistic properties that play a role in the various encodings and predictions.

Verbs such as *"we show"* or *"we demonstrate"* typically occur in sentences which contain an `attribution` relation. Conjunctions such as **"to"** or **"in order to"** express `enablement` relations. Finally, `manner-means` are often signalled by verb forms such as **"(by) +ing"**. We think that these signals play an important role in the good performances of BoV especially for `attribution` and `manner-means`.

Manner-means   The sentence *"Most sentence embedding models typically represent each sentence only using word surface, which makes these models indiscriminate for ubiquitous homonymy and polysemy"* is a typical example of the sentences whose relation is predicted well with BoV encoders but neither by BERT, which predicts an `attribution`, nor by SciBERT, which predicts `noRel`. The verb "using" seem to be responsible for this good prediction. This underlies the good recall that BoV gets for the prediction of this DR, which gets a very bad recall for BERT and SciBERT.

Attribution   The sentence *"[Most studies on statistical Korean word spacing do not utilize the information]_1 [provided by the input sentence]_2 [and assume]_3 [that it was completely concate-*

		BoV	Google USE	BERT uncased	BERT cased	SciBERT uncased	SciBERT cased
Precision	**Attribution**	66	62	78	85	96	74
	Enablement	70	44	48	46	100	71
	Manner-Means	65	36	73	55	43	58
	NoRel	70	69	55	70	38	53
Recall	**Attribution**	**81**	78	**81**	78	61	**81**
	Enablement	58	19	**67**	58	14	47
	Manner-Means	**78**	69	53	64	53	58
	NoRel	53	25	47	44	**75**	67

Table 5: Precision and Recall for SemRel.

nated]_4.” is well predicted by all encoders, except SciBERT. Here, the captured relationship is a `manner-means` between units 3 and 4, which is in fact the deepest DR in the full structure of the sentence, and thus the less important. The second part (3+4) of the sentence is in conjunction with the first (1+2) and refers to it. The `manner-means` between 3 and 4 is thus not the more salient in the RST, but is however well predicted. This suggests that the choices that we did to ignore non-logical DRs work well and that the training made on sufficient data suffice to make the classifier focus on the relations that we consider.

Enablement With BERT, most of the sentences that contain the connective “**to**” are well detected as an `enablement` relation. Among those that are not well classified, most of them are classified as `attribution` or `norel`. One common characteristic to the sentences that are classified as `norel`, is that they are often long and contain more than 2 DUs and several discourse connectives, including “**to**” or “**for**”. It is thus harder for the model to understand and distinguish the role of the connectives, as they are drowned in a lot of lexical information, leading to errors because of the difficulty of the task. For sentences that are wrongly classified as `attribution`, we observe a similar behaviour. The sentence *“[Recent work has shown success] [in using continuous word embeddings] [to improve supervised NLP systems.]”* contains an `enablement` between segments 1 and 2, but is classified as an `attribution`. This errors seems to be due to the verb “shown” that appears a lot in sentences that contain an attribution. This shows that even if BERT improves a sort of coherence detection, it in fact relies a lot on lexical cues for detecting the semantics of relations.

Swapped and scrambled We admit that the tasks designed for probing coherence are somehow arbitrary, and produces different biases that could be better controlled. We present two major issues, and propose solutions for future work.

The first issue concerns the swapped task, where modifications of sentences may produce other coherent sentences, which are thus tagged as incoherent in the training set and used as it by the classifier. Those cases specifically correspond to sentences that are formed by two DUs and linked by a particle (such as “**by**”, “**for**” or “**to**”), which are thus swapped and still coherent. For example, the sentence *“[By incorporating textual information,][RCM can effectively deal with data sparseness problem.]”* becomes *“[RCM can effectively deal with data sparseness problem][by incorporating textual information.]”*. We expect such sentences to be poorly predicted, but it is not the case, showing that BERT and SciBERT probably rely on other indices.

Conneau et al. (2018) also created acceptable sentences for three of their probing tasks, and filtered them by crowd-sourcing, asking people to rate sentences according to their acceptability. This method would be the best suited to solve this issue, as it may be hard to control coherence automatically with syntactic parsers.

Secondly, we did not ensure that the property captured does not rely on syntax, because sentence modifications may also produce sentences that are syntactically incorrect and that we did not filter out. Here the problematic cases mostly come from two clauses sentences containing a conjunction such as “**that**” or “**and**”. For example the sentence *“[We present a human judgments dataset] [and an adapted metric for evaluation of Arabic machine translation.]”* becomes *“[And an adapted metric for evaluation of Arabic machine translation] [we present a human judgments dataset.]”*, thus being obviously syntactically incorrect, and possibly captured as incoherent based on this syntactic property. A possible solution to that issue could be to forbid the swap of the first and last DU, thus inducing another different bias and in our case reducing the size of the corpus. Another possibility is to introduce rules based on the syntactic tree of new sentences in order to filter those cases. In this preliminary work, we introduced the second coherence detection task (scrambled) with the aim of reducing those biases.

7   Conclusion

We introduced four tasks for probing the discourse properties involved in sentences from scientific abstracts. We evaluated the ability of a classifier to predict a discourse property of a sentence from its embedding. The performance of the classifier highlights the extent to which discourse properties are encoded in those representations.

We showed that coherence links are captured by vectors made from contextual models, as well as DRs, but that those models in fact do not encode the semantics of those DRs. We highlighted that BoV embeddings perform nearly as good as contextual embeddings for both DRs detection tasks, highlighting the fact that these relations are most of the time explicitly signalled in scientific abstracts.

This confirms our hypothesis that BERT and SciBERT training suffice to encode coherence to some extent. We think that the Next Sentence Prediction task is the reason for this performance, as it allows the model to learn adjacency properties of sentences, and thus of clauses. The second hypothesis however is not confirmed, as we concluded from the experiments that semantics of DRs are as well captured by BoV, as BERT or SciBERT.

The present work opens various possibilities, for improving the tasks as well as the analysis of the results. We decided here to focus on the detection of three specific relations that occur within sentences. We adopted strategies to make this possible, for example by ignoring DRs that are of continuation or additive and not logical. We could however go further by considering all relations involved in the sentences. A multi-label classification could be a solution to the problem of predicting all DRs of a sentence from its embedding. A Sequence-to-Sequence model could be a solution to the problem of predicting the discourse structure (or sequence of relations) from its embedding. For coherence prediction, we also plan to determine to what extent the tasks we introduced (swapped and scrambled) depend on syntactic properties. A statistical analysis of the syntactic structures involved could help to clarify the possible biases coming from the syntax. We also plan to further check the datasets that we introduce for those tasks, as we have raised that our method created coherent sentences, labeled as incoherent in our training dataset.

Other corpora such as RST-DT (Carlson and Okurowski, 2002) or PDTB (Webber et al., 2005), which could be combined, could be used to produce other datasets for probing DRs, enabling to evaluate how other DRs (such as `contrast` or `reason`) are encoded in sentence embeddings.

Acknowledgments

We want to thank the reviewers for their constructive comments and suggestions.

This work was supported partly by the french PIA project "Lorraine Université d'Excellence", reference ANR-15-IDEX-04-LUE.

References

Yossi Adi, Einat Kermany, Yonatan Belinkov, Ofer Lavi, and Yoav Goldberg. 2016. Fine-grained analysis of sentence embeddings using auxiliary prediction tasks. *CoRR*, abs/1608.04207.

Iz Beltagy, Kyle Lo, and Arman Cohan. 2019. SciBERT: A pretrained language model for scientific text. In *Proceedings of the 2019 Conference on Empirical Methods in Natural Language Processing and the 9th International Joint Conference on Natural Language Processing (EMNLP-IJCNLP)*, pages 3615–3620, Hong Kong, China. Association for Computational Linguistics.

Daniel Marcu Carlson, Lynn and Mary Ellen Okurowski. 2002. Rst discourse treebank.

Lynn Carlson, Daniel Marcu, and Mary Ellen Okurowski. 2003. Building a Discourse-Tagged Corpus in the Framework of Rhetorical Structure Theory. *Current Directions in Discourse and Dialogue*, pages 85–112.

Daniel Cer, Yinfei Yang, Sheng-yi Kong, Nan Hua, Nicole Limtiaco, Rhomni St. John, Noah Constant, Mario Guajardo-Cespedes, Steve Yuan, Chris Tar, Yun-Hsuan Sung, Brian Strope, and Ray Kurzweil. 2018. Universal sentence encoder. *CoRR*, abs/1803.11175.

Alexis Conneau and Douwe Kiela. 2018. SentEval: An evaluation toolkit for universal sentence representations. In *Proceedings of the Eleventh International Conference on Language Resources and Evaluation (LREC 2018)*, Miyazaki, Japan. European Language Resources Association (ELRA).

Alexis Conneau, German Kruszewski, Guillaume Lample, Loïc Barrault, and Marco Baroni. 2018. What you can cram into a single $&!#* vector: Probing sentence embeddings for linguistic properties. In *Proceedings of the 56th Annual Meeting of the Association for Computational Linguistics (Volume 1: Long Papers)*, pages 2126–2136, Melbourne, Australia. Association for Computational Linguistics.

Jacob Devlin, Ming-Wei Chang, Kenton Lee, and Kristina Toutanova. 2019. BERT: Pre-training of deep bidirectional transformers for language understanding. In *Proceedings of the 2019 Conference of the North American Chapter of the Association for Computational Linguistics: Human Language Technologies, Volume 1 (Long and Short Papers)*, pages 4171–4186, Minneapolis, Minnesota. Association for Computational Linguistics.

M.A.K Halliday and Ruqaiya Hasan. 1976. Cohesion in english. *Longman*.

Ryan Kiros, Yukun Zhu, Ruslan Salakhutdinov, Richard S. Zemel, Antonio Torralba, Raquel Urtasun, and Sanja Fidler. 2015. Skip-thought vectors. *CoRR*, abs/1506.06726.

Alex Lascarides and Nicholas Asher. 2007. Segmented Discourse Representation Theory: Dynamic Semantics With Discourse Structure. In Harry Bunt and Reinhard Muskens, editors, *Computing Meaning*, volume 3. Springer Netherlands, Dordrecht.

Elizabeth DuRoss Liddy. 1991. The discourse-level structure of empirical abstracts: An exploratory study. *Information Processing & Management*, 27(1):55–81.

Mathieu Morey, Philippe Muller, and Nicholas Asher. 2018. A dependency perspective on RST discourse parsing and evaluation. *Computational Linguistics*, 44(2):197–235.

Jeffrey Pennington, Richard Socher, and Christopher Manning. 2014. GloVe: Global vectors for word representation. In *Proceedings of the 2014 Conference on Empirical Methods in Natural Language Processing (EMNLP)*, pages 1532–1543, Doha, Qatar. Association for Computational Linguistics.

Nils Reimers and Iryna Gurevych. 2019. Sentence-BERT: Sentence embeddings using Siamese BERT-networks. In *Proceedings of the 2019 Conference on Empirical Methods in Natural Language Processing and the 9th International Joint Conference on Natural Language Processing (EMNLP-IJCNLP)*, pages 3982–3992, Hong Kong, China. Association for Computational Linguistics.

Jan Renkema. 2009. *The Texture of Discourse*. John Benjamins Publishing Company.

Xing Shi, Inkit Padhi, and Kevin Knight. 2016. Does string-based neural MT learn source syntax? In *Proceedings of the 2016 Conference on Empirical Methods in Natural Language Processing*, pages 1526–1534, Austin, Texas. Association for Computational Linguistics.

Maite Taboada and William C Mann. 2006. Rhetorical structure theory: Looking back and moving ahead. *Discourse studies*, 8(3):423–459.

Tieleman Tijmen and Hinton Geoffrey. 2012. Lecture 6.5-rmsprop: Divide the gradient by a running average of its recent magnitude. *COURSERA: Neural networks for machine learning*, 4:26–31.

Bonnie Webber, Aravind K Joshi, Eleni Miltsakaki, Rashmi Prasad, Nikhil Dinesh, Alan Lee, and Katherine Forbes. 2005. A short introduction to the penn discourse treebank. *Copenhagen Working Papers in Language and Speech Processing*.

Thomas Wolf, Lysandre Debut, Victor Sanh, Julien Chaumond, Clement Delangue, Anthony Moi, Pierric Cistac, Tim Rault, Rémi Louf, Morgan Funtowicz, et al. 2019. Huggingface's transformers: State-of-the-art natural language processing. *ArXiv*.

An Yang and Sujian Li. 2018. SciDTB: Discourse dependency TreeBank for scientific abstracts. In *Proceedings of the 56th Annual Meeting of the Association for Computational Linguistics (Volume 2: Short Papers)*, pages 444–449, Melbourne, Australia. Association for Computational Linguistics.

Joint Modeling of Arguments for Event Understanding

Yunmo Chen   Tongfei Chen   Benjamin Van Durme
Johns Hopkins University
{yunmo,tongfei,vandurme}@jhu.edu

Abstract

We recognize the task of event *argument linking* in documents as similar to that of intent *slot resolution* in dialogue, providing a Transformer-based model that extends from a recently proposed solution to resolve references to slots. The approach allows for joint consideration of argument candidates given a detected event, which we illustrate leads to state-of-the-art performance in multi-sentence argument linking. [1]

1 Introduction

Given an event recognized in text, we are concerned with finding its associated arguments. Significant work has focused at the level of single sentence contexts, such as in *semantic role labeling* (SRL; Gildea and Jurafsky, 2000; He et al., 2017; Ouchi et al., 2018, *inter alia*). Unfortunately even perfect performance in SRL will be limited by the existence of arguments outside the sentence boundary, leading to prior work (Das et al., 2010; Silberer and Frank, 2012; Ebner et al., 2020) on an alternative paradigm variously called *implicit role resolution* or *argument linking*, where an event trigger (e.g. "attack") evokes a set of roles (e.g. AT-TACKER, TARGET) to be filled, and they are linked to explicit argument mentions found in text. In argument linking, possible candidate arguments are first detected, then linked to specific roles of detected events. This bears similarity to coreference resolution, where document-level context can be aptly utilized. For an example, see Figure 1.

This formulation is similar to the resolution of referring expressions in conversational dialogues (Çelikyilmaz et al., 2014), where a current utterance is considered to invoke an *intent* (e.g. BUY-BOOK), accompanied by a number of *slots* (e.g.

NAME, AUTHOR, PUBLISHER, etc.). Even more than in event argument linking, in dialogue systems the sentence-level (utterance-level) context often fails to contain all salient arguments (slots): slots from previous rounds of dialogue may often be relevant to the current intent.[2]

We propose a novel model for joint modeling of potential arguments inspired by Chen et al. (2019) for slot-filling in dialogue systems, which proposed to jointly predict spans that are relevant to the intent of the current round of dialogue. Over detected arguments, a Transformer (Vaswani et al., 2017) encoder is placed upon the event trigger and potential *arguments* to jointly learn the relations between the event trigger and its arguments. The input to this Transformer is no longer *tokens* but *spans*: given the Transformer output of each span, a classification loss is utilized to perform argument role classification. We demonstrate this leads to state-of-the-art performance on the RAMS argument linking dataset introduced by Ebner et al. (2020),[3] showing the benefits of joint modeling when linking arguments to roles of events.

Dialogue	Events
Intent type	Event type
BUY-BOOK	ATTACK
Slot key	Role type
NAME, AUTHOR	ATTACKER, TARGET
Slot value	Argument
1984, George Orwell	*Russia, Ukraine*

Table 1: Mapping between terminologies in intent slot resolution and event argument linking, with examples.

---

[1] Our code can be found at https://github.com/wanmok/joint-arglinking.

[2] E.g., from Chen et al. (2019): *What's the weather in San Francisco? ... Any good Mexican restaurants there?*

[3] https://nlp.jhu.edu/rams.

Proceedings of the First Workshop on Computational Approaches to Discourse, pages 96–101
Online, November 20, 2020. ©2020 Association for Computational Linguistics
https://doi.org/10.18653/v1/P17

2 Background

Implicit role resolution Palmer et al. (1986) treated unfilled semantic roles as special cases of anaphora and coreference resolution. Starting from the SemEval 2010 Task 10: Linking Roles (Ruppenhofer et al., 2010), there have been more recent modeling efforts on this task. Chen et al. (2010) approached this with their SRL system SE-MAFOR (Das et al., 2010), casting the task as extended SRL by admitting constituents (potential arguments) from context larger than sentence boundaries. Silberer and Frank (2012) considered the problem as an anaphora resolution task within the discourse context. Ebner et al. (2020) similarly considered the task as related to anaphora resolution, and introduced a new dataset, RAMS, for exploring non-local argument linking. See O'Gorman (2019) and Ebner et al. (2020) for further background.

Event extraction In event extraction there are historically three subtasks: detecting event triggers, detecting entity mentions, and then *argument role prediction*, where relations between mentions and triggers are predicted in accordance to the event type's predefined set of roles under a closed ontology. Prior work has proposed pipeline system of the subtasks (Ji and Grishman, 2008; Li et al., 2013; Yang and Mitchell, 2016, *inter alia*), or as a joint model over the three tasks (Nguyen and Nguyen, 2019; Lin et al., 2020, *inter alia*). Our work could be seen as a version of argument role prediction, but which operates beyond sentence boundaries.

Frame-based SLU In dialogue systems, semantic frame based spoken language understanding (SLU) is one of the most commonly applied SLU technologies for human-computer interaction. Such systems often output an interpretation of dialogues represented as *intents* and *slots* (Wang et al., 2011). Çelikyilmaz et al. (2014) and Bapna et al. (2017) proposed models to resolve references to slots in the dialogue, tracking conversation states across multiple dialogue turns. Dhingra et al. (2017) augmented such methods with external knowledge bases (KBs) to create a multi-turn dialogue agent which helps users search KBs. Chen et al. (2019) proposed joint models over potential slots in dialogue to output which contextual slots should be carried over to the most recent utterance. Our approach is inspired by this work, by drawing analogies between concepts in SLU (intents / slots) and those in IE (events / arguments) (see Table 1).

3 Problem Formulation

Following Ebner et al. (2020) we consider argument linking as the task of choosing amongst detected mention span candidates given detected event trigger spans. Given a document $d = (w_1, \cdots, w_n)$ where each w_i is a word, entity mention set M (candidate arguments) containing mentions $m_i = d[l_i : r_i] \in M$ where l_i and r_i demarcates the left and right boundary (both inclusive), and a event trigger span $t = d[l_t : r_t]$, an argument linking model predicts the role (or absence) of each mention with respect to the event.

An event ontology can be formulated as a set of event types $\mathcal{T}$, where each type $e \in \mathcal{T}$ is associated with a set of *roles* $R(e)$,[4] while other roles are non-permissible. We denote the union of all roles for all event types, plus an empty ε role (a dummy role denoting an argument is not part of the event structure) as $\mathcal{R} = \bigcup_{e \in \mathcal{T}} R(e) \cup \{\varepsilon\}$.

4 Approach

Argument and trigger representation We compute a fixed-length vector with dimension d for each argument and trigger span as their representations. To compute this, we first pass the document through a pre-trained contextualizing model (BERT (Devlin et al., 2019) here).[5] We split documents into sentences and feed each sentence to BERT for encoding. Each token w_i might be split into more than 1 subword units—in this case we take the average of these subword representations so that each token w_i has 1 vector representation $\mathbf{w}_i \in \mathbb{R}^{d_{\text{tok}}}$, following Zhang et al. (2019).

For an argument span $m = (w_l, \cdots, w_r)$, we follow Lee et al. (2017) to generate a span embedding.[6] The span embedding $\mathbf{m}$ for mention span m comprises of three parts, the representation of its left boundary, its right boundary, and a learned pooling over the tokens in the span. This learned pooling utilized a global attention query vector $\mathbf{q} \in \mathbb{R}^{d_{\text{tok}}}$, and computes the weighted sum of all tokens with respect to the attention scores derived from $\mathbf{q}$:

$$a_i = \frac{\exp \mathbf{q}^{\mathsf{T}} \mathbf{w}_i}{\sum_{j=l}^{r} \exp \mathbf{q}^{\mathsf{T}} \mathbf{w}_j} \; ; \quad \mathbf{c} = \sum_{i=l}^{r} a_i \cdot \mathbf{w}_i \,, \quad (1)$$

---

[4] For example, in the ACE 2005 dataset, $R(\text{ATTACK}) = \{\text{ATTACKER}, \text{TARGET}, \text{INSTRUMENT}, \text{TIME}, \text{PLACE}\}$.

[5] Documents are chuncked into max-length 512 segments while respecting sentence boundaries, and each is fed to BERT respectively.

[6] The width embeddings in Lee et al. (2017) are not used.

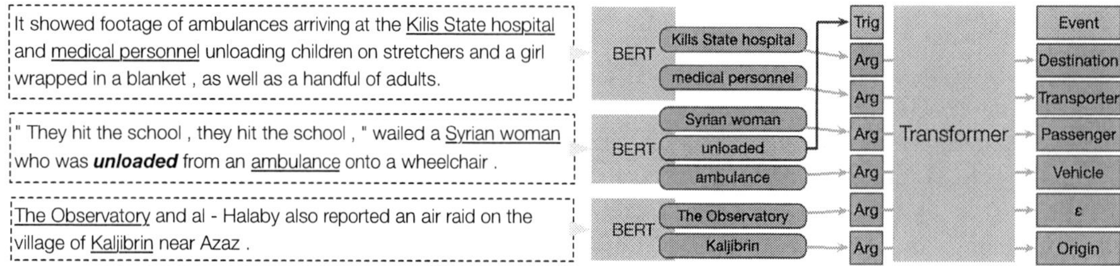

Figure 1: An example of our model running over a paragraph. Trigger and argument span representations are computed from BERT, then later fed to a Transformer for jointly modeling the spans to predict their roles.

and pass that through a 2-layer feed-forward neural network to yield a fixed-length vector $\mathbf{m}_i \in \mathbb{R}^{d_\text{span}}$ for each argument span m_i:

$$\mathbf{m} = \text{FFNN}_\text{arg}\left([\mathbf{w}_l \; ; \; \mathbf{w}_r \; ; \; \mathbf{c}]\right) . \tag{2}$$

Similarly, for any trigger span $t = [l : r]$, we employ a different set of parameters:

$$\mathbf{t} = \text{FFNN}_\text{trig}\left([\mathbf{w}_l \; ; \; \mathbf{w}_r \; ; \; \mathbf{c}]\right) . \tag{3}$$

Joint modeling of arguments We propose a joint model for all the arguments with respect to the given event trigger with event type e (see Figure 1). We form a sequence $(\mathbf{t}, \mathbf{m}_1, \mathbf{m}_2, \cdots, \mathbf{m}_n)$ with the trigger span encoding as the prefix, then followed by the representations of all the candidate mentions, then fed to a *Transformer* encoder (Vaswani et al., 2017). A Transformer, by its self-attention mechanism, naturally models the relation between every trigger-argument and argument-argument pair. Note two major differences as compared to a Transformer that runs on tokens: (1) each input to the Transformer represents a *span* instead of a token, following Chen et al. (2019); (2) since the arguments do not take an explicit sequential order, we forgo the positional embeddings in Transformers, effectively modeling the input as a *set* of spans instead of a *sequence* (self-attention exhibits the property of permutation invariance without positional embeddings (Lee et al., 2019)).

For each argument span input $\mathbf{m}_i$, we pass the output from the Transformer encoder $\hat{\mathbf{m}}_i$ to linear layer with the output size being the size of the role set $\mathcal{R}$. Softmax is applied to the output of size $|\mathcal{R}|$, with the non-permissible roles masked out, yielding a distribution over the set of roles designated by the given event type, plus the non-argument ε role:

$$P(r|t, m) = \frac{\exp \mathbf{w}_r^\mathsf{T} \hat{\mathbf{m}}}{\sum_{r' \in R(e) \cup \{\varepsilon\}} \exp \mathbf{w}_{r'}^\mathsf{T} \hat{\mathbf{m}}} \tag{4}$$

The model could hence be trained using a cross-entropy loss function to maximize such likelihood.

5 Experiments

As we draw the connections between SLU in dialogue systems and argument linking in information extraction, we focus primarily on evaluating the model a discourse-level dataset, RAMS (Ebner et al., 2020). First however we look at a more established dataset, ACE 2005 (Walker et al., 2006)[7], to verify if our model can reasonable performance compared to prior work in event understanding. While ACE 2005 is annotated only at the sentence-level, our model may still be applied in this setting. For detailed experimental setup, see Appendix A.

Baseline Aside from joint modeling of arguments, we also include an **independent** model as a case in ablation studies (while our proposed method labeled as **joint**). The independent model removes the Transformer encoder (cf. Equation 4), but directly applies a feed-forward neural network atop of the trigger representation and each argument representation to classify the role (or absence) of the argument with respect to the event trigger. [8]

$$P(r|t, m) = \frac{\exp \mathbf{w}_r^\mathsf{T} F_\text{ind}([t; m])}{\sum_{r' \in R(e) \cup \{\varepsilon\}} \exp \mathbf{w}_{r'}^\mathsf{T} F_\text{ind}([t; m])}$$

The result from model would show the difference between the proposed joint argument modeling approach v.s. a simpler, independent model.

____

[7] https://catalog.ldc.upenn.edu/LDC2006T06.

[8] This scoring function for triples (r, t, m) is similar to Ebner et al. (2020)'s model. However, their model is trained to maximize the posterior probability of the correct argument given a trigger and a role, whereas in our independent baseline here the probability of the correct role given a trigger and an argument candidate is maximized.

	Split	**ACE 2005**	**RAMS**
#Event types		33	139
#Role types		22	65
	train	4202/4859	7329/17026
#Events/#Args	dev	450/605	924/2188
	test	403/576	871/2023

Table 2: Dataset statistics.

Model	P	R	F_1
Lin et al. (2020)	*48.8*	*53.9*	*56.8**
Lin et al. (2020) PoE	-	-	*58.6**
Independent	48.0	76.7	59.0
Joint	56.0	79.2	65.6

Table 3: We verify our model achieves similar performance to recent work on ACE 2005. PoE denotes "product of experts", an ensemble model in Lin et al. (2020). * Results not directly comparable as we are exploring argument linking only.

Metrics We use precision, recall, and F_1-score as metrics. A link between the trigger and an argument is considered correct, if and only if the predicted argument span offsets and role matches the gold reference. We report using micro-average among F_1-scores across different roles.

5.1 ACE 2005

We use ACE 2005 as a sanity check for our discourse-context model to verify its ability to perform sentence-context extraction. We follow Lin et al. (2020)'s pre-processing and dataset splits for event extraction task (statistics see Table 2). Table 3 reports the experimental results on ACE 2005. Although the results are not directly comparable since our model has access to gold trigger/argument spans (Lin et al. (2020) does not), we can observe similar levels of performance, suggesting our method may be competitive when applied to event understanding beyond sentence boundaries.

5.2 RAMS

Roles Across Multiple Sentences (RAMS; Ebner et al., 2020) is an event extraction dataset that considers discourse-level, non-local arguments in document-level context. We follow the train/dev/test split provided in the dataset, with statistics shown in Table 2. Experiments setup follow the configuration employed for ACE 2005.

Table 4 shows the performance of our models on

Model	P	R	F_1
Ebner et al. (2020)	62.8	74.9	68.3
Ebner et al. (2020) TCD	78.1	69.2	73.3
Independent	73.5	73.0	73.3
Joint	**79.6**	**80.2**	**79.9**

Table 4: Experimental results on RAMS. TCD designates the use of ontology-aware type-constrained decoding, which is similar to our independent model.

Dist.	# Gold args.	RAMS-TCD	Ours
−2	79	75.7	**77.2**
−1	164	73.7	**74.4**
0	1,811	75.0	**79.6**
+1	87	76.5	**77.0**
+2	47	**79.1**	78.7

Table 5: Breakdown of the models' performance across sentence distances on the RAMS dev set. RAMS-TCD refers to Ebner et al. (2020)'s type-constrained decoding approach (see Table 4).

RAMS. Following the same conditions as Ebner et al. (2020), our joint model outperforms that work, and our independent baseline, by a substantial margin of 6.6%, illustrating the benefit of modeling potential arguments jointly.

We analyze the performance of our model on non-local arguments, i.e., arguments that are not in the same sentence as the event trigger (Table 5). Our model's performance on non-local arguments is on par with local arguments, demonstrating the ability to handle non-local argument linking.

Case study We here show one example where the joint model performs better than the independent model. The joint model correctly labeled all the roles, while the independent model failed on two. We hypothesize that joint modeling of the arguments will avoid these cases where multiple spans are labeled with the same role.

... Stratfor analyst Sim Tack:" This was indeed an *Islamic State* **attack**, rather than an accidental *explosion*." New satellite imagery appears to reveal extensive damage to a strategically significant *airbase* in *central Syria* used by Russian forces ...

Argument	**Independent**	**Joint**	**Gold**
Islamic State	Attacker	Attacker	Attacker
explosion	~~Attacker~~	Instrument	Instrument
airbase	~~Attacker~~	Victim	Victim
central Syria	Place	Place	Place

6   Conclusion

We proposed a joint modeling approach for argument linking that considers the interdependent relationships among argument mentions conditioning on a specific event. Our approach extends from recent work in dialogue systems, viewing a document as essentially a single-side discourse, and where event arguments are recognized as similar to slots that potentially carryover across utterances. Experimental results show our approach achieves superior performance on a recently introduced dataset for modeling discourse-level contexts.

Acknowledgments

This research was supported by the JHU HLTCOE, DARPA AIDA, and IARPA BETTER. The U.S. Government is authorized to reproduce and distribute reprints for Governmental purposes. The views and conclusions contained in this publication are those of the authors and should not be interpreted as representing official policies or endorsements of DARPA or the U.S. Government.

References

Ankur Bapna, Gökhan Tür, Dilek Hakkani-Tür, and Larry P. Heck. 2017. Sequential dialogue context modeling for spoken language understanding. In *Proceedings of the 18th Annual SIGdial Meeting on Discourse and Dialogue*, pages 103–114.

Asli Çelikyilmaz, Zhaleh Feizollahi, Dilek Hakkani-Tür, and Ruhi Sarikaya. 2014. Resolving referring expressions in conversational dialogs for natural user interfaces. In *Proceedings of the 2014 Conference on Empirical Methods in Natural Language Processing*, pages 2094–2104.

Desai Chen, Nathan Schneider, Dipanjan Das, and Noah A. Smith. 2010. SEMAFOR: frame argument resolution with log-linear models. In *Proceedings of the 5th International Workshop on Semantic Evaluation*, pages 264–267.

Tongfei Chen, Chetan Naik, Hua He, Pushpendre Rastogi, and Lambert Mathias. 2019. Improving long distance slot carryover in spoken dialogue systems. In *Proceedings of the First Workshop on NLP for Conversational AI*, pages 96–105. Association for Computational Linguistics.

Dipanjan Das, Nathan Schneider, Desai Chen, and Noah A. Smith. 2010. Probabilistic frame-semantic parsing. In *Human Language Technologies: Conference of the North American Chapter of the Association of Computational Linguistics, Proceedings*, pages 948–956.

Jacob Devlin, Ming-Wei Chang, Kenton Lee, and Kristina Toutanova. 2019. BERT: pre-training of deep bidirectional transformers for language understanding. In *Proceedings of the 2019 Conference of the North American Chapter of the Association for Computational Linguistics: Human Language Technologies*, pages 4171–4186.

Bhuwan Dhingra, Lihong Li, Xiujun Li, Jianfeng Gao, Yun-Nung Chen, Faisal Ahmed, and Li Deng. 2017. Towards end-to-end reinforcement learning of dialogue agents for information access. In *Proceedings of the 55th Annual Meeting of the Association for Computational Linguistics*, pages 484–495.

Seth Ebner, Patrick Xia, Ryan Culkin, Kyle Rawlins, and Benjamin Van Durme. 2020. Multi-sentence argument linking. In *Proceedings of the 58th Annual Meeting of the Association for Computational Linguistics, ACL 2020, Online, July 5-10, 2020*, pages 8057–8077.

Daniel Gildea and Daniel Jurafsky. 2000. Automatic labeling of semantic roles. In *38th Annual Meeting of the Association for Computational Linguistics*, pages 512–520.

Luheng He, Kenton Lee, Mike Lewis, and Luke Zettlemoyer. 2017. Deep semantic role labeling: What works and what's next. In *Proceedings of the 55th Annual Meeting of the Association for Computational Linguistics*, pages 473–483.

Dan Hendrycks and Kevin Gimpel. 2016. Gaussian error linear units (gelus). *CoRR*, abs/1606.08415.

Heng Ji and Ralph Grishman. 2008. Refining event extraction through cross-document inference. In *ACL 2008, Proceedings of the 46th Annual Meeting of the Association for Computational Linguistics*, pages 254–262.

Juho Lee, Yoonho Lee, Jungtaek Kim, Adam R. Kosiorek, Seungjin Choi, and Yee Whye Teh. 2019. Set transformer: A framework for attention-based permutation-invariant neural networks. In *Proceedings of the 36th International Conference on Machine Learning*, pages 3744–3753.

Kenton Lee, Luheng He, Mike Lewis, and Luke Zettlemoyer. 2017. End-to-end neural coreference resolution. In *Proceedings of the 2017 Conference on Empirical Methods in Natural Language Processing*, pages 188–197.

Qi Li, Heng Ji, and Liang Huang. 2013. Joint event extraction via structured prediction with global features. In *Proceedings of the 51st Annual Meeting of the Association for Computational Linguistics*, pages 73–82.

Ying Lin, Heng Ji, Fei Huang, and Lingfei Wu. 2020. A joint neural model for information extraction with global features. In *Proceedings of the 58th Annual Meeting of the Association for Computational Linguistics, ACL 2020, Online, July 5-10, 2020*, pages 7999–8009.

Ilya Loshchilov and Frank Hutter. 2019. Decoupled weight decay regularization. In *7th International Conference on Learning Representations*. OpenReview.net.

Trung Minh Nguyen and Thien Huu Nguyen. 2019. One for all: Neural joint modeling of entities and events. In *The Thirty-Third AAAI Conference on Artificial Intelligence, AAAI 2019*, pages 6851–6858.

Timothy J. O'Gorman. 2019. *Bringing Together Computational and Linguistic Models of Implicit Role Interpretation*. Ph.D. thesis, University of Colorado at Boulder.

Hiroki Ouchi, Hiroyuki Shindo, and Yuji Matsumoto. 2018. A span selection model for semantic role labeling. In *Proceedings of the 2018 Conference on Empirical Methods in Natural Language Processing*, pages 1630–1642.

Martha S. Palmer, Deborah A. Dahl, Rebecca J. Schiffman, Lynette Hirschman, Marcia Linebarger, and John Dowding. 1986. Recovering implicit information. In *24th Annual Meeting of the Association for Computational Linguistics*, pages 10–19.

Josef Ruppenhofer, Caroline Sporleder, Roser Morante, Collin Baker, and Martha Palmer. 2010. Semeval-2010 task 10: Linking events and their participants in discourse. In *Proceedings of the 5th International Workshop on Semantic Evaluation*, pages 45–50.

Carina Silberer and Anette Frank. 2012. Casting implicit role linking as an anaphora resolution task. In *Proceedings of the First Joint Conference on Lexical and Computational Semantics*, pages 1–10.

Ashish Vaswani, Noam Shazeer, Niki Parmar, Jakob Uszkoreit, Llion Jones, Aidan N. Gomez, Lukasz Kaiser, and Illia Polosukhin. 2017. Attention is all you need. In *Advances in Neural Information Processing Systems 30: Annual Conference on Neural Information Processing Systems*, pages 5998–6008.

Christopher Walker, Stephanie Strassel, Julie Medero, and Kazuaki Maeda. 2006. ACE 2005 multilingual training corpus (LDC2006T06). *Philadelphia: Linguistic Data Consortium*.

Ye-Yi Wang, Li Deng, and Alex Acero. 2011. *Semantic Frame Based Spoken Language Understanding*, pages 35–80. Wiley.

Bishan Yang and Tom M. Mitchell. 2016. Joint extraction of events and entities within a document context. In *NAACL HLT 2016, The 2016 Conference of the North American Chapter of the Association for Computational Linguistics: Human Language Technologies*, pages 289–299.

Sheng Zhang, Xutai Ma, Kevin Duh, and Benjamin Van Durme. 2019. AMR parsing as sequence-to-graph transduction. In *Proceedings of the 57th Conference of the Association for Computational Linguistics*, pages 80–94.

A Appendix

Experimental Details We use BERT (BERT-BASE-CASED here) as the encoder for text embedding. The models are setup with $d_{\text{tok}} = d_{\text{span}} = 768$, and are trained using AdamW optimizer (Loshchilov and Hutter, 2019) with learning rate of 3×10^{-5} for 200 epochs, and the tolerance $\epsilon = 1 \times 10^{-8}$. We employ gradient clipping to avoid exploding gradients with maximum gradient norm 5.0. We also use a linear learning rate scheduler to warmup models for the first 200 iterations.

The Transformer encoder has 3 layers with 64 attention heads[9], and its feed-forward neural networks (FFNNs) for computing the argument / trigger representations are set to have the dim of 2,048. For mention representations, we use two-layer FFNNs with hidden size of 768. Note there are two different sets of parameters for constructing trigger representations and argument representations. All non-linearities used in the paper are GELU (Hendrycks and Gimpel, 2016). Dropout with rate 0.2 is applied in each levels in the feed-forward neural network for argument / trigger representation computation, and also in each layer in the Transformer encoder.

For model selection, we pick the best performing model on the dev set and then run it on the test set. Early stopping is used with patience $p = 10$, i.e., if the performance on the dev set did not increase after p epochs, stop training.

In terms of hyperparameter sweep, we perform grid search over a combination of hyperparameters shown in Table 6, and choose the set performed best on the dev set.

Our models are trained on one Nvidia GTX 1080 Ti GPU. For the joint model, the training time is around 30 mins/epoch, and it takes 70 epochs (around 20 hours) to converge on average. For the independent model, it takes 15mins/epoch and converges in 5 epochs (around 50 mins) on average.

Hyperparameter	Range
# Encoder layers	$\{1, 2, 3, 4, 5, 6\}$
# Attention heads	$\{12, 64, 128\}$
Learning rate	$\{1 \times 10^{-5}, 3 \times 10^{-5}, 5 \times 10^{-5}\}$
Warmup steps	$\{0, 100, 200, \cdots, 500, 1000\}$

Table 6: Ranges for hyperparameter sweeps.

---

[9] According to Chen et al. (2019), increasing the number of attention heads substantially improves the model performance, so we prefer more attention heads over more encoder layers.

Analyzing Neural Discourse Coherence Models

Youmna Farag[1,2]   **Josef Valvoda**[1]   **Helen Yannakoudakis**[3]   **Ted Briscoe**[1,2]

[1]Department of Computer Science and Technology, University of Cambridge, United Kingdom
[2]The ALTA Institute, Cambridge, United Kingdom
{youmna.farag,jv406,ted.briscoe}@cl.cam.ac.uk
[3]Department of Informatics, King's College London, United Kingdom
helen.yannakoudakis@kcl.ac.uk

Abstract

In this work, we systematically investigate how well current models of coherence can capture aspects of text implicated in discourse organisation. We devise two datasets of various linguistic alterations that undermine coherence and test model sensitivity to changes in syntax and semantics. We furthermore probe discourse embedding space and examine the knowledge that is encoded in representations of coherence. We hope this study shall provide further insight into how to frame the task and improve models of coherence assessment further. Finally, we make our datasets publicly available as a resource for researchers to use to test discourse coherence models.

1 Introduction

Coherence refers to the properties of a text that indicate how meaningful (sub-)sentential constituents are connected to convey document-level meaning. Different theories have been proposed to describe the properties that contribute to discourse coherence and some have been integrated with computational models for empirical evaluation. A popular approach is the entity-based model which hypothesizes that coherence can be assessed in terms of the distribution of and transitions between entities in a text – by constructing an entity-grid (Egrid) representation (Barzilay and Lapata, 2005, 2008), building on Centering Theory (Grosz et al., 1995). Subsequent work has adapted and further extended Egrid representations (Filippova and Strube, 2007; Burstein et al., 2010; Elsner and Charniak, 2011; Guinaudeau and Strube, 2013). Other research has focused on syntactic patterns that co-occur in text (Louis and Nenkova, 2012) or semantic relatedness between sentences (Lapata and Barzilay, 2005; Soricut and Marcu, 2006; Somasundaran et al., 2014) as key aspects of coherence modeling. There have also been attempts to model coherence

by identifying rhetorical relations that connect textual units (Mann and Thompson, 1988; Lin et al., 2011; Feng et al., 2014) or capturing topic shifts via Hidden Markov Models (HMM, Barzilay and Lee, 2004). Other work has combined approaches to study whether they are complementary (Elsner et al., 2007; Feng et al., 2014). More recently, neural networks have been used to model coherence. Some models utilize structured representations of text (e.g. Egrid representations, Tien Nguyen and Joty, 2017; Joty et al., 2018) and others operate on unstructured text, taking advantage of neural models' ability to learn useful representations for the task (Li and Jurafsky, 2017; Logeswaran et al., 2018; Farag and Yannakoudakis, 2019; Xu et al., 2019; Moon et al., 2019).

Coherence has typically been assessed by a model's ability to rank a well-organized document higher than its noisy counterparts created by corrupting sentence order in the original document (*binary discrimination task*), and neural models have achieved remarkable accuracy on this task. Recent efforts have targeted additional tasks such as recovering the correct sentence order (Logeswaran et al., 2018; Cui et al., 2018), evaluating on realistic data (Lai and Tetreault, 2018; Farag and Yannakoudakis, 2019) and focusing on open-domain models of coherence (Li and Jurafsky, 2017; Xu et al., 2019). However, less attention has been directed to investigating and analyzing the properties of coherence that current models can capture, nor what knowledge is encoded in their representations and how it might relate to aspects of coherence.

In this work, we systematically examine what properties of discourse coherence current coherence models can capture. We devise two datasets that exhibit various kinds of incoherence and analyze model ability to capture syntactic and semantic aspects of text implicated in discourse organisation. We furthermore investigate a set of probing tasks to

102

Proceedings of the First Workshop on Computational Approaches to Discourse, pages 102–112
Online, November 20, 2020. ©2020 Association for Computational Linguistics
https://doi.org/10.18653/v1/P17

better understand the information that is encoded in their representations and how it might relate to aspects of coherence. We hope this study shall provide further insight into how to frame the task and improve models of coherence assessment further. Finally, we release our evaluation datasets as a resource for the community to use to test discourse coherence models.[1]

2   Neural Coherence Models

We experiment with a number of existing and state-of-the-art neural approaches to coherence assessment, that have publicly available implementations, and present details of the models below. Across all the BERT-based models, we use bert-large-uncased and layer 16 following Liu et al. (2019) and Hewitt and Manning (2019).

Multi-task learning (MTL, Farag and Yannakoudakis, 2019): The model applies a Bi-LSTM on input GloVe word embeddings (Pennington et al., 2014) followed by attention to build sentence representations; then builds a second Bi-LSTM with attention to compose a document vector. A linear operation followed by a sigmoid function is applied to the document representation to predict an overall coherence score as the main objective. Inspired by the Egrid approaches, the model is also optimized to predict the grammatical roles of the input words at the bottom layer of the network as an auxiliary task.

MTL with BERT embeddings (MTL_{bert}): We replicate the previous MTL model but now use BERT embeddings (Devlin et al., 2019) to initialize the input words.

Single-task learning (STL, Farag and Yannakoudakis, 2019): This model has the same architecture as MTL but only performs the coherence prediction task, excluding the grammatical role auxiliary objective.

STL with BERT (STL_{bert}): This is the same as STL but uses BERT embeddings.

Local Coherence Discriminator with Language modeling (LCD_{rnnlm}, Xu et al., 2019): The model generates sentence representations via an RNN language model, where word embeddings are initialized using GloVe. It then generates a representation for two consecutive sentences via concatenating the output of a set of linear transformations applied to the two sentences: concatenation, element-wise dif-

ference, element-wise product and absolute value of element-wise difference. This representation is fed to an MLP layer to predict a *local* coherence score.[2] The overall coherence of a document is the average of its local scores.

LCD with BERT (LCD_{bert}): We create a variant of the LCD_{rnnlm} model where instead of using an RNN language model encoder, we encode each sentence as the average BERT vectors of the words it contains. Everything else remains the same.

Local Coherence (LC, Li and Jurafsky, 2017): The model generates sentence vectors via an LSTM over GloVe-initialized word embeddings; then a window approach is applied over adjacent sentences to get embeddings of groups of sentences and predict local coherence scores. The final document score is calculated by averaging its local scores.

Egrid CNN ($Egrid_{cnn}$, Tien Nguyen and Joty, 2017): The model applies a CNN over Egrid representations across groups of consecutive sentences; the CNN slides multiple filters of weights to extract feature maps that represent high-level entity-transition features, followed by a max pooling function to focus on the important features. Furthermore, additional entity-related features are integrated such as salience, proper mentions and named entity type.

3   Binary Discrimination Task

Binary discrimination is a typical approach to assessing neural coherence models where a well-organized document should be ranked higher than its permuted counterparts created by corrupting sentence order. Following previous work, we train and test[3] the coherence models on the WSJ[4] and evaluate them using Pairwise Ranking Accuracy (PRA), which is calculated based on the fraction of correct pairwise rankings between a coherent document and its incoherent counterparts.

In Table 1, we present the performance of all coherence models. The high accuracy of the models demonstrates their efficacy for the task of selecting a maximally coherent sentence order from a set of candidate permutations. We note that the LCD and

---

[1]https://github.com/Youmna-H/coherence-analysis

[2]Gold local scores $\in \{0, 1\}$ represent whether a sequence of two sentences is coherent (i.e. extracted from a coherent document) or not (i.e. created via negative sampling).

[3]All models are run 5 times and the test predictions are averaged across the runs.

[4]We use the same train and test splits as Tien Nguyen and Joty (2017) and the same test set permuted counterparts as Farag and Yannakoudakis (2019).

MTL	MTL_{bert}	STL	STL_{bert}	LCD_{rnnlm}	LCD_{bert}	LC	Egrid_{cnn}
93.2	96.1	87.7	95.4	94.5	**97.1**	74.1	87.6

Table 1: PRA results of coherence models based on the binary discrimination task on the WSJ.

MTL BERT variants achieve a new state-of-the-art on the WSJ. The remarkable accuracy on this task may render this problem fully solved.

Herein, we seek to investigate how well these models of coherence can capture aspects of text implicated in discourse organisation. We devise a set of datasets and systematically test model susceptibility to syntactic or semantic changes.

4 Cloze Coherence (CC) Dataset

We compile a large-scale dataset, to which we refer as Cloze Coherence (CC), of coherent and incoherent examples, where the former are intact well-written texts while the latter are the result of applying syntactic or semantic perturbations to the coherent ones.

4.1 Coherent examples

For the sake of specifically testing for coherence, we avoid complex linguistic structures. Specifically, we focus on coherent examples that consist of two short sentences that are coreferential and exhibit a rhetorical relation (such properties can be manipulated to create incoherent counterparts). Furthermore, we focus on examples that are self-contained, meaning that they do not reference or rely on an outer context to be interpreted. We find that narrative texts are good candidates to satisfy these criteria and therefore create our coherent examples from the ROCStories Cloze dataset[5] (Mostafazadeh et al., 2016).

ROCStories Cloze contains short stories of 5 sentences manifesting a sequence of causal or temporal events that have a shared protagonist. A story usually starts by introducing a protagonist in the first sentence, then subsequent sentences describe events that happen to them in a logical / rhetorically plausible manner. The dataset was designed for commonsense reasoning by testing the ability of machine learning models to select a plausible ending for the story out of two alternative endings. Here, our main aim is to challenge the models and investigate whether they truly understand inter-sentential relations and coherence-related features. We specifically utilize the first two sentences in the

stories to compose the coherent examples in our dataset.[6]

Selecting the first two sentences helps make the examples self-contained since there is no preceding context to refer to, and no cataphoric relations to consequent sentences. Regarding rhetorical relations in these sentences, Mostafazadeh et al. (2016) conducted a temporal analysis to investigate the logical order of the events presented in a story, demonstrating, among others, that the first and second sentences in the stories are presented in a commonsensical temporal manner with logical links between them. In order to examine coreferential relations between the two sentences in each extracted pair, we gather a set of statistics. We adopt a heuristic approach[7] by simply counting the number of second sentences that contain at least one third person pronoun (either personal or possessive) and find that they constitute 80% of the examples.[8] Third person pronouns anaphorically refers to preceding items in text, which could occur in the same sentence or the previous one (i.e., the first sentence). We, therefore, randomly select, and manually inspect, 500 examples that contain third person pronouns in their second sentence and find that in 95% of them the referenced entity appears in the first sentence. Furthermore, third person pronouns are not the only coreferential relations in the examples. For instance, we find that 90% of the second sentences contain a personal or possessive pronoun (whether it is first, second or third person), which could also signal coreference, e.g., *'I was walking to school. Since I wasn't looking at my feet I stepped on a rock.'* There are also other coreferential devices such as: demonstrative references (e.g., 'this' and 'there'), 'the' + noun, proper names or nominal substitutions (e.g., 'one' or 'ones') to name a few (Halliday and Hasan., 1976), so the true proportion of coreferential pairs will be higher. Table 2 presents examples of different referential relations in our dataset.

---

[5] https://www.cs.rochester.edu/nlp/rocstories/

[6] We use NLTK for word tokenization; sentence boundaries are already marked in the stories.

[7] We initially used the spaCy and Stanford coreference resolution systems (Clark and Manning, 2016), but found their performance unreliable for the purposes of this experiment after manual inspection.

[8] If we exclude 'it' the percentage becomes 76%.

Type of reference	Example
Pronominal Reference	Rich was a musician. <u>He</u> made a few hit songs.
Proper Name	Dan's parents were overweight. <u>Dan</u> was overweight as well.
Nominal Substitution	My dog hates his treats. I decided to go buy some new <u>ones</u>.
Demonstrative Reference	My daughter wants to take her toddler to the Enchanted Village. <u>This</u> is a puppet show featuring early 20th century figurines.

Table 2: Examples of first two sentences extracted from the ROCStories Cloze dataset with different referential types (referring word underlined).

We use the same train/dev/test splits provided with ROCStories Cloze but only keep the first two sentences in each story. We exclude cases with erroneous sentence boundaries,[9] yielding $97,903$ examples for training, $1,871$ for development, and $1,871$ for testing, and a training vocabulary size of $29,596$ tokens. Each instance in our dataset contains two sentences that represent a coherent pair.

4.2 Incoherent examples

To assess model susceptibility to syntactic or semantic alterations, we construct incoherent examples by applying two different transformations to each coherent pair resulting in two different sets of data.

cloze_swap We create incoherent examples by swapping the two sentences in a coherent pair. This mostly breaks the coreference relation between them and/or the rhetorical relation (e.g. temporal or causal) by reversing the event sequence. The dataset, referred to as `cloze_swap`, is balanced, i.e., the number of incoherent examples is the same as the number of the coherent ones above. The way cloze_swap is created corrupts the syntactic patterns that co-occur in coherent texts (e.g. S $\rightarrow$ NP-SBJ VP | NP-SBJ $\rightarrow$ PRP) as demonstrated by Louis and Nenkova (2012).

cloze_rand Here we create incoherent examples by keeping the first sentence of a coherent pair intact and replacing the second with a randomly selected second sentence from (the same split of) our set of coherent examples. This dataset, referred to as `cloze_rand`, is also balanced (for each coherent pair, we compose one incoherent counterpart), and constitutes examples with changed semantics but with the main syntactic pattern intact. As the randomly-created pair may still be coherent, we address this by: 1) constraining random selection of the second sentence to not begin with the same

word as the second sentence in the original pair, or with the pronoun 'he' if the original starts with 'she', and vice-versa[10] (we note 70% of the second sentences in ROCStories Cloze start with a pronoun); 2) using human evaluation to further assess the validity of this data and get an estimate of upper-bound performance on the task. Specifically, we randomly select 100 coherent sentence pairs from our test split along with their own incoherent counterparts and ask two annotators (who are not authors of this paper), with high English proficiency levels, to *rank* each set of coherent–incoherent examples based on which one they considered to be more coherent and plausible. The average PRA of the annotators is 94.5%.

Table 3 shows examples from cloze_swap and cloze_rand. As our datasets are balanced (one incoherent counterpart per coherent pair), we have a total number of $195,806$, $3,742$ and $3,742$ instances in the train, dev, and test splits respectively for each cloze dataset (cloze_swap and cloze_rand have the same coherent examples, and the same number of coherent and incoherent examples).

We note that the gold labels in this data are not to be interpreted as (overall) binary indicators of coherence. We rather use these to test model performance using PRA, i.e. we only compare a coherent pair with *its own* incoherent counterpart.

5 Controlled Linguistic Alterations (CLA) Dataset

In order to further understand the properties of coherence that current coherence models capture, we manually construct a dataset of controlled sets of linguistic changes. We first identify a set of coherent, well-written texts of two consecutive sentences from business and financial articles in the BBC, the Independent and Financial Times (this allows us to stay in the same domain as the one used for training the models – the WSJ). We focus on sentence pairs where the subject of the first sentence is pronom-

---

[9]The training stories are in CSV format (separating sentences by comma delimiters) and we parse them using the Python CSV parser. We exclude the stories where the parser fails to detect 5 sentences.

[10]We do not find instances of 'they' as a third-person singular pronoun.

Coherent example	Incoherent example from cloze_swap	Incoherent example from cloze_rand
Tyrese joined a new gym. The membership allows him to work out for a year.	The membership allows him to work out for a year. Tyrese joined a new gym.	Tyrese joined a new gym. As children they hated being dressed alike.
Jasmine doesn't know how to play the guitar. She asked her dad to take her to guitar class.	She asked her dad to take her to guitar class. Jasmine doesn't know how to play the guitar.	Jasmine doesn't know how to play the guitar. May thought her milk was no good.
I wanted to play an old game one day. When I looked in the game's case the CD was missing.	When I looked in the game's case the CD was missing. I wanted to play an old game one day.	I wanted to play an old game one day. Jason pressed the buzzer since he knew the answer.

Table 3: Examples of coherent and incoherent pairs from the cloze_swap and cloze_rand datasets.

Original	A government paper on Monday found UK and EU firms would be faced with a "a significant new and ongoing administrative burden" in the event of a no-deal Brexit. It found large firms importing and exporting at scale would need to fill in forms taking one hour 45 minutes on average and cost £28 per form for each load imported.
Swap	It found large firms importing and exporting at scale would need to fill in forms taking one hour 45 minutes on average and cost £28 per form for each load imported. A government paper on Monday found UK and EU firms would be faced with a "a significant new and ongoing administrative burden" in the event of a no-deal Brexit.
Random	1- A government paper on Monday found UK and EU firms would be faced with a "a significant new and ongoing administrative burden" in the event of a no-deal Brexit. She spent over a decade at Swiss investment bank UBS before joining the UK Treasury's council of economic advisers in 1999. 2- Lady Vadera was born in Uganda and moved to the UK as a teenager. It found large firms importing and exporting at scale would need to fill in forms taking one hour 45 minutes on average and cost £28 per form for each load imported.
Lexical Substitution	The paper found large firms importing and exporting at scale would need to fill in forms taking one hour 45 minutes on average and cost £28 per form for each load imported. A government paper on Monday found UK and EU firms would be faced with a "a significant new and ongoing administrative burden" in the event of a no-deal Brexit.
Prefix Insertion	More Specifically, it found large firms importing and exporting at scale would need to fill in forms taking one hour 45 minutes on average and cost £28 per form for each load imported. A government paper on Monday found UK and EU firms would be faced with a "a significant new and ongoing administrative burden" in the event of a no-deal Brexit.
Lexical Perturbations	A government paper on Monday found UK and EU firms would be faced with a "a significant new and ongoing administrative burden" in the event of a no-deal Brexit. It found large firms importing and exporting at scale would need to fill in cups taking one hour 45 minutes on average and cost £28 per cup for each load imported.
Corrupt Pronoun	A government paper on Monday found UK and EU firms would be faced with a "a significant new and ongoing administrative burden" in the event of a no-deal Brexit. He found large firms importing and exporting at scale would need to fill in forms taking one hour 45 minutes on average and cost £28 per form for each load imported.

Table 4: Examples from our manually constructed CLA dataset. For 'Random' we create two incoherent instances: one where the first sentence is unchanged and the second is randomly selected (1-); and another where the first sentence is randomly selected and the second is kept intact (2-).

inalized in the second, and the second sentence begins with this pronoun. We select the examples so that they are self-contained and do not reference an outer context. We then manually create incoherent counterparts by modifying the coherent examples in a constrained way in order to systematically examine model performance. Specifically, we apply the following sets of perturbations to our set of coherent sentence pairs, examples of which are presented in Table 4.

Swap. We simply swap the two sentences.

Random. We keep the first sentence intact and select a second sentence randomly from our set of coherent examples. We constrain the selection so that the subject pronoun is different from the subject pronoun in the original sentence.[11] We also create another random pair with the same constraint but now changing the first sentence. Thus each original coherent example has two incoherent counterparts.

Lexical Substitution. We swap the two sentences in a coherent pair but replace the subject pronoun in the second sentence with *the + a general noun* that substitutes the subject in the first sentence (e.g.

the company, the woman, etc.).

Prefix Insertion. We analyze the WSJ training data and find that the average number of times the first sentence in a document starts with a pronoun is 0.02 (and never with 'he' or 'she') which is significantly less than the average number of times a sentence starts with a pronoun (regardless of its position) which is 0.07. This difference is not maintained in the randomly ordered documents in the WSJ training set and so this might give a signal to the models to detect that a swapped pair that starts with a pronoun is less coherent. To see if such positional information plays a role in model prediction, we insert a phrase, before the subject pronoun after swapping the sentences, that doesn't change the propositional content (e.g. 'More specifically', 'However', etc.). We can then observe whether this insertion will change the prediction of the model.

Lexical Perturbation. We investigate the robustness of the models to minor lexical changes that result in incoherent meaning, by replacing one word in either of the two sentences (if the word is repeated, we change that too). We choose a replacement word from the training vocabulary of the WSJ with the same part-of-speech tag. For example, in Table 4 'form' is replaced with 'cup' and 'forms' with 'cups'.

---

[11] We also take into account that some subjects could be referred to by 'he', 'she' or 'they' and thus factor that into the selection.

Corrupt Pronoun. We replace the subject pronoun in the second sentence with another pronoun that cannot reference anything in the first sentence. With this method, we test whether the models are capable of resolving coreferences or just rely on syntactic patterns.

Our dataset contains a total of 240 examples of coherent and incoherent pairs of sentences (30 coherent examples and 210 incoherent counterparts). Our constrained set of modifications ensures that all coherent examples are more coherent than any of the incoherent counterparts in the data.

6 Experiments

Table 5 (top) presents the PRA performance of the models trained on the WSJ (Section 3) when they are evaluated on the test sets of the CC datasets (rows 'cloze_swap' and 'cloze_rand'). We find that, overall, models are good at detecting syntactic alterations (cloze_swap; PRA ranging from 69.3 to 84.6) even though the test data is from a domain different than the training one. However, most models perform poorly on semantic alterations (cloze_rand; PRA ranging from 48.5 to 54.5), the only exception being LCD$_{bert}$ that achieves a PRA of 71. Specifically, models that use RNN-based sentence encoders (the first six models), even when initialised with BERT, or apply a CNN to capture entity transitions fall short in capturing semantic changes despite the fact that cloze_rand is from the same domain as cloze_swap. In contrast, LCD$_{bert}$ is more capable of detecting semantic changes where the model builds sentence representations by averaging BERT vectors then applies a set of linear transformations to increase its expressive power, surpassing its RNN-based counterpart (LCD_$rnnlm$) with 16.5% on cloze_rand. Additionally, across models, we observe that the use of contextualized (BERT) embeddings consistently improves performance on both cloze tasks, although performance on semantic alterations remains close to random.

We investigate domain shift effects and fine-tune the WSJ-trained models on each of the cloze_swap and cloze_rand training sets (Section 4) and re-evaluate performance on the respective test sets. Specifically, we use an MLP layer over the models' pre-prediction representation, followed by sigmoid non-linearity. The models are optimized using the mean squared error between the gold labels (0 or 1) and the predicted scores.[12] In this setup, only the MLP layer is fine-tuned and not the whole coherence model which allows us to create a fast efficient evaluation framework that can be applied as a further examination step after coherence models are developed and tuned on their respective datasets, instead of training the models from scratch. The results of the fine-tuned models are presented in Table 5 (CC; rows 'fine-tuned'). Although we can see that there is some domain effect, we nevertheless find that the results confirm our earlier observation: performance on semantic alterations is, overall, poor, in contrast to syntactic ones (cloze_swap).

In Table 5 (bottom), we can observe model performance (PRA) on our constrained set of manually devised examples (CLA). Again, we observe a similar result: across RNN-based models, performance is particularly low on random examples, which suggests that they struggle to detect topical or rhetorical shifts and unresolved references if the main syntactic pattern is maintained. The exception is LCD_$bert$ which is again the best performing model (PRA 78.3).

We furthermore observe that now Egrid$_{cnn}$ is the second best model on CLA Random (PRA 71.6). A sparser entity grid where entities in the two sentences are different allows the model to detect such cases (e.g. in the example in Table 4, 'firms' is mentioned in the two sentences, while in the two random examples, it is only mentioned in one). However, its substantial difference in PRA on CLA Random compared to cloze_rand (53.4) suggests that the lower performance observed in the latter is due to domain shift effects, something which we do not observe (to the same extent) with LCD$_{bert}$. Regarding the CLA Swap results, we can again confirm models' capability of detecting corrupted syntactic constructions. We furthermore observe that they are able to maintain good performance in the cases where a prefix is inserted ('Prefix Insertion') or the subject pronoun is substituted with a lexical item ('Lexical Substitution'). This suggests that they can capture the relevant syntactic patterns and do not rely solely on positional features.

Performance is overall low on lexical perturbations and corrupt pronouns which suggests that the models are not sensitive to minor lexical changes even if they result in implausible meaning and they also struggle to resolve pronominal references.

---

[12] We use Adam (Kingma and Ba, 2015), batch size 64, L2 regularization, and a learnable penalty rate (search space $\{0.00001, 0.0001, 0.001, 0.01\}$). We use early stopping and stop training if PRA does not improve on the dev set over 5 epochs (max epochs 200). MLP hidden unit size is 100.

	Dataset	# comparisons	Models							
			MTL	MTL_{bert}	STL	STL_{bert}	LC	LCD_{rnnlm}	LCD_{bert}	$Egrid_{cnn}$
CC	cloze_swap	1,871	69.3	73.5	74.2	75.3	70.7	74.5	75.4	**84.6**
	fine-tuned	1,871	88.8	88.5	83.5	84.7	76.3	88.4	**96.7**	88.1
	cloze_rand	1,871	51.3	53.3	48.5	52.5	50.5	54.5	**71.0**	53.4
	fine-tuned	1,871	65.7	54.2	53.7	56.1	51.3	65.2	**94.8**	68.8
CLA	Swap	30	90.0	**93.3**	83.3	90.0	80.0	**93.3**	86.6	83.3
	Random	60	56.6	45.0	50.0	51.6	51.6	61.6	**78.3**	71.6
	Lexical Substitution	30	83.3	**93.3**	80.0	90.0	86.6	83.3	86.6	76.6
	Prefix Insertion	30	83.3	**96.6**	76.6	90.0	76.6	86.6	93.3	80.0
	Lexical Perturbations	30	56.6	46.6	46.6	63.3	50.0	53.3	**80.0**	53.3
	Corrupt Pronoun	30	70.0	53.3	63.3	63.3	53.3	60.0	**76.6**	56.6
	All data	210	70.9	67.6	64.2	71.4	64.2	71.4	**82.8**	70.4
	All data (TPRA)	6,300	69.9	71.3	61.8	71.6	66.0	69.1	**72.2**	65.8

Table 5: PRA performance on the CLA (bottom) and CC datasets (top; 'fine-tuned' shows results for models tuned on the respective cloze training sets).

Task	Models								Human
	MTL	MTL_{bert}	STL	STL_{bert}	LC	LCD_{rnnlm}	LCD_{bert}	Best from Conneau et al. (2018)	
SubjNum	64.9	75.4	62.2	71.5	52.7	71.2	**88.0**	95.1 (Seq2Tree)	88.0
ObjNum	64.5	72.1	61.1	70.7	54.5	65.0	**86.5**	95.1 (Seq2Tree)	86.5
CoordInv	58.5	63.4	53.0	63.7	53.0	56.6	**78.4**	76.2 (NMT En-De)	85.0
CorruptAgr	53.2	69.7	57.7	68.6	52.2	64.2	**94.3**	-	-

Table 6: Classification accuracy on probing tasks. 'Human' shows the human upper bound on the task.

However, the exception is LCD_{bert} (with PRA 80 on lexical perturbations and 76.6 on corrupt pronoun) suggesting a better ability at capturing semantics and resolving references.

Across all six CLA datasets ('All data'; Table 5), we find that, overall, LCD_{bert} is the top performing model (average PRA). The 'All data' row reports the result of comparing a coherent example against its incoherent counterparts across the different alterations (i.e., in Table 4, the original example is compared against all the examples in the table and this is applied to all the original examples in the dataset). If we furthermore compare all the coherent examples against the incoherent ones in the whole dataset (rather than against their own incoherent counterparts), we find that a similar performance pattern is maintained (row 'All data (TPRA)', i.e., all data Total Pairwise Ranking Accuracy).

7 Probing Coherence Embedding Space

Inspired by previous work (Conneau et al., 2018), and to better understand the information that is encoded in the representations of coherence models, we investigate probing tasks that can capture coherence-related features.

We experiment with the following set of sentence-level tasks that are relevant to discourse coherence: 1) the subject number (SubjNum) task that detects the number of the subject of the main

clause; 2) the object number (ObjNum) task that detects the number of the direct object of the main clause; 3) the coordination inversion (CoordInv) task that contains sentences consisting of two coordinate clauses, where the two clauses are inverted in half of the sentences and kept intact in the other half (the task is to detect whether a sentence is modified or not); 4) the corrupt agreement (CorruptAgr) task where sentences are corrupted by inverting the verb number (the task is to identify corrupted sentences).

Tasks 1, 2 and 4 align with Centering theory as they probe for subject and object relevant information; the theory suggests that subject and object roles are indicators of entity salience. On the other hand, task 3 tests whether the models can capture intra-sentential coherence. For these tasks, we use the datasets from Conneau et al. (2018) (tasks 1,2 and 3) and Linzen et al. (2016) (task 4).

Probing model We adopt the SentEval framework of Conneau et al. (2018). Our probing model consists of an MLP layer over model sentence representations, followed by sigmoid non-linearity. We use the same training parameters as Conneau et al. (2018).[13]

Results Table 6 presents the results.[14] Overall, we observe that models are better at detecting Sub-

---

[13] https://github.com/facebookresearch/ SentEval

[14] $Egrid_{cnn}$ is based on entity transitions across sentences and therefore we cannot probe sentence representations.

jNum, and ObjNum (accuracy of at least 61% for all models except LC which is the odd one out) compared to CorruptAgr and CoordInv, with the last two being particularly challenging for most models (minimum accuracy of 53% excluding LC). For SubjNum and ObjNum the models can find hints in words other than the target word (as the majority of nouns in a sentence tend to have the same number, with 75.9% of SubjNum test sentences and 78.7% of ObjNum ones containing nouns of the same number in the same sentence (Conneau et al., 2018)). On the other hand, CorruptAgr examples are longer and with more syntactic variations and require the models to detect the dependency between verbs and their subjects. CoordInv is also a difficult task for the models particularly since they are pre-trained on the WSJ to focus on the order of sentences, not clauses.

Across all tasks, we find that LCD_{bert} achieves the best performance, outperforming all other approaches. We note, however, that LCD_{bert} does not fine-tune its sentence representations during coherence training in the WSJ but they are rather fixed and based on the average of BERT-based word embeddings (Section 2). This means the probing model fine-tunes averaged BERT-based word embeddings rather than actual sentence parameters from the LCD coherence model. Therefore, the level of performance observed is not representative of the maximum performance coherence models can achieve on these tasks.[15] We surmise that the comparatively lower performance observed with MTL_{bert} and STL_{bert} (whose sentence representations are fine-tuned during coherence training) is due to their coherence training objective. The models are optimized on the binary discrimination task, i.e. learning to rank a well-organized document higher than its permuted counterparts. This is an overly simplistic approach to coherence modeling that may be making models (and their representations) more susceptible to losing useful linguistic information. Having said that, though, MTL_{bert}, that has direct training signal with respect to the words' grammatical roles, is able to alleviate this issue to an extent and is the next best performing model on SubjNum, ObjNum and CorruptAgr.

Across tasks, LC is the odd one out, and the worst performing model. This can be explained partly by its comparatively lower performance on

the simpler binary discrimination task (Table 1) and partly by the simplicity of the approach: LC utilizes no attention mechanism as the MTL and STL family of models do, nor has expressive enough transformations as LCD_{rnnlm} does.

8 Discussion

Our evaluation experiments on two coherence datasets reveal that RNN- or EGrid-based coherence models are able to detect syntactic alterations that undermine coherence, but are less effecient at detecting semantic ones even after fine-tuning on the latter. We furthermore find that they particularly struggle with recognizing minor lexical changes even if they result in implausible meaning and resolving pronominal references. On the other hand, these models are particularly good at detecting cases where a prefix is inserted or the subject pronoun is substituted with a lexical item, suggesting that they are capable of capturing the relevant syntactic patterns and do not solely rely on positional features. We find that the best performing model overall is LCD_{bert} which does not use an RNN sentence encoder but rather builds sentence representations by averaging BERT embeddings then utilizes a number of linear transformations over adjacent sentences to facilitate learning richer representations.

Our probing experiments reveal that models are better at encoding information regarding subject and object number followed by verb number (CorruptAgr). These probing tasks align with Centering theory as they probe for subject and object relevant information. The task that tests for knowledge on coordination inversion is the lowest performing one overall, suggesting that there is little capacity at capturing information related to intra-sentential coherence. Excluding LCD_{bert}, MTL_{bert} is the best performing model; nevertheless, there is still scope for substantial improvement across all probing tasks and particularly on CoordInv and CorruptAgr.

9 Conclusion

We systematically studied how well current models of coherence can capture aspects of text implicated in discourse organisation. We devised datasets of various kinds of incoherence and examined model susceptibility to syntactic and semantic alterations. Our results demonstrate the models are robust with respect to corrupted syntactic patterns,

---

[15]Nevertheless, we observe that LCD_{bert} outperforms the best reported result on CoordInv by Conneau et al. (2018).

prefix insertions and lexical substitutions. However, they fall short in capturing rhetorical and semantic corruptions, lexical perturbations and corrupt pronouns. We furthermore find that discourse embedding space encodes subject and object relevant information; however, there is scope for substantial improvement in terms of encoding linguistic properties relevant to discourse coherence. Experiments on coordination inversion further suggest that current models have little capacity at encoding information related to intra-sentential coherence.

We hope this study shall provide further insight into how to frame the task of coherence modeling and improve model performance further. Finally, we make our datasets publicly available for researchers to use to test coherence models.

References

Regina Barzilay and Mirella Lapata. 2005. Modeling local coherence: An entity-based approach. In *Proceedings of the 43rd Annual Meeting on Association for Computational Linguistics*, pages 141–148. Association for Computational Linguistics.

Regina Barzilay and Mirella Lapata. 2008. Modeling local coherence: An entity-based approach. *Computational Linguistics*, 3(1):1–34.

Regina Barzilay and Lillian Lee. 2004. Catching the drift: Probabilistic content models, with applications to generation and summarization. In *Proceedings of the Human Language Technology Conference of the North American Chapter of the Association for Computational Linguistics: HLT-NAACL 2004*, pages 113–120, Boston, Massachusetts, USA. Association for Computational Linguistics.

Jill Burstein, Joel Tetreault, and Slava Andreyev. 2010. Using entity-based features to model coherence in student essays. In *Human Language Technologies: The 2010 Annual Conference of the North American Chapter of the Association for Computational Linguistics*, pages 681–684. Association for Computational Linguistics.

Kevin Clark and Christopher D. Manning. 2016. Deep reinforcement learning for mention-ranking coreference models. In *Proceedings of the 2016 Conference on Empirical Methods in Natural Language Processing*, pages 2256–2262, Austin, Texas. Association for Computational Linguistics.

Alexis Conneau, German Kruszewski, Guillaume Lample, Loïc Barrault, and Marco Baroni. 2018. What you can cram into a single $&!#* vector: Probing sentence embeddings for linguistic properties. In *Proceedings of the 56th Annual Meeting of the Association for Computational Linguistics (Volume 1: Long Papers)*, pages 2126–2136, Melbourne, Australia. Association for Computational Linguistics.

Baiyun Cui, Yingming Li, Ming Chen, and Zhongfei Zhang. 2018. Deep attentive sentence ordering network. In *Proceedings of the 2018 Conference on Empirical Methods in Natural Language Processing*, pages 4340–4349. Association for Computational Linguistics.

Jacob Devlin, Ming-Wei Chang, Kenton Lee, and Kristina Toutanova. 2019. BERT: Pre-training of deep bidirectional transformers for language understanding. In *Proceedings of the 2019 Conference of the North American Chapter of the Association for Computational Linguistics: Human Language Technologies, Volume 1 (Long and Short Papers)*, pages 4171–4186, Minneapolis, Minnesota. Association for Computational Linguistics.

Micha Elsner, Joseph Austerweil, and Eugene Charniak. 2007. A unified local and global model for discourse coherence. In *Human Language Technologies 2007: The Conference of the North American Chapter of the Association for Computational Linguistics; Proceedings of the Main Conference*, pages 436–443, Rochester, New York. Association for Computational Linguistics.

Micha Elsner and Eugene Charniak. 2011. Extending the entity grid with entity-specific features. In *Proceedings of the 49th Annual Meeting of the Association for Computational Linguistics: Human Language Technologies*, pages 125–129. Association for Computational Linguistics.

Youmna Farag and Helen Yannakoudakis. 2019. Multi-task learning for coherence modeling. In *Proceedings of the 57th Annual Meeting of the Association for Computational Linguistics*, pages 629–639, Florence, Italy. Association for Computational Linguistics.

Vanessa Wei Feng, Ziheng Lin, and Graeme Hirst. 2014. The impact of deep hierarchical discourse structures in the evaluation of text coherence. In *Proceedings of COLING 2014, the 25th International Conference on Computational Linguistics: Technical Papers*, pages 940–949. Dublin City University and Association for Computational Linguistics.

Katja Filippova and Michael Strube. 2007. Extending the entity-grid coherence model to semantically related entities. In *Proceedings of the Eleventh European Workshop on Natural Language Generation (ENLG 07)*, pages 139–142, Saarbrücken, Germany. DFKI GmbH.

Barbara J. Grosz, Scott Weinstein, and Aravind K. Joshi. 1995. Centering: A framework for modeling the local coherence of discourse. *Computational Linguistics*, 21(2).

Camille Guinaudeau and Michael Strube. 2013. Graph-based local coherence modeling. In *Proceedings of the 51st Annual Meeting of the Association for Computational Linguistics (Volume 1: Long Papers)*, pages 93–103. Association for Computational Linguistics.

M. A. K. Halliday and Ruqaiya Hasan. 1976. *Cohesion in English. Longman, London.*

John Hewitt and Christopher D Manning. 2019. A structural probe for finding syntax in word representations. In *Proceedings of the 2019 Conference of the North American Chapter of the Association for Computational Linguistics: Human Language Technologies, Volume 1 (Long and Short Papers)*, pages 4129–4138.

Shafiq Joty, Muhammad Tasnim Mohiuddin, and Dat Tien Nguyen. 2018. Coherence modeling of asynchronous conversations: A neural entity grid approach. In *Proceedings of the 56th Annual Meeting of the Association for Computational Linguistics (Volume 1: Long Papers)*, pages 558–568. Association for Computational Linguistics.

Diederik P. Kingma and Jimmy Ba. 2015. Adam: A method for stochastic optimization. In *3rd International Conference on Learning Representations, ICLR 2015, San Diego, CA, USA, May 7-9, 2015, Conference Track Proceedings*.

Alice Lai and Joel Tetreault. 2018. Discourse coherence in the wild: A dataset, evaluation and methods. In *Proceedings of the 19th Annual SIGdial Meeting on Discourse and Dialogue*, pages 214–223. Association for Computational Linguistics.

Mirella Lapata and Regina Barzilay. 2005. Automatic evaluation of text coherence: Models and representations. In *Proceedings of the 19th International Joint Conference on Artificial Intelligence*, IJCAI'05, pages 1085–1090, San Francisco, CA, USA. Morgan Kaufmann Publishers Inc.

Jiwei Li and Dan Jurafsky. 2017. Neural net models of open-domain discourse coherence. In *Proceedings of the 2017 Conference on Empirical Methods in Natural Language Processing*, pages 198–209. Association for Computational Linguistics.

Ziheng Lin, Hwee Tou Ng, and Min-Yen Kan. 2011. Automatically evaluating text coherence using discourse relations. In *Proceedings of the 49th Annual Meeting of the Association for Computational Linguistics: Human Language Technologies*, pages 997–1006, Portland, Oregon, USA. Association for Computational Linguistics.

Tal Linzen, Emmanuel Dupoux, and Yoav Goldberg. 2016. Assessing the ability of LSTMs to learn syntax-sensitive dependencies. *Transactions of the Association for Computational Linguistics*, 4:521–535.

Nelson F Liu, Matt Gardner, Yonatan Belinkov, Matthew Peters, and Noah A Smith. 2019. Linguistic knowledge and transferability of contextual representations. *arXiv preprint arXiv:1903.08855*.

Lajanugen Logeswaran, Honglak Lee, and Dragomir R. Radev. 2018. Sentence ordering and coherence modeling using recurrent neural networks. In *AAAI*, pages 5285–5292. AAAI Press.

Annie Louis and Ani Nenkova. 2012. A coherence model based on syntactic patterns. In *Proceedings of the 2012 Joint Conference on Empirical Methods in Natural Language Processing and Computational Natural Language Learning*, pages 1157–1168, Jeju Island, Korea. Association for Computational Linguistics.

William C Mann and Sandra A Thompson. 1988. Rhetorical structure theory: Toward a functional theory of text organization. *Text Interdisciplinary Journal for the Study of Discourse*, pages 243–281.

Han Cheol Moon, Tasnim Mohiuddin, Shafiq Joty, and Chi Xu. 2019. A Unified Neural Coherence Model. In *Proceedings of the 2019 Conference on Empirical Methods in Natural Language Processing and the 9th International Joint Conference on Natural Language Processing (EMNLP-IJCNLP)*, pages 2262–2272, Hong Kong, China. Association for Computational Linguistics.

Nasrin Mostafazadeh, Nathanael Chambers, Xiaodong He, Devi Parikh, Dhruv Batra, Lucy Vanderwende, Pushmeet Kohli, and James Allen. 2016. A corpus and cloze evaluation for deeper understanding of commonsense stories. In *Proceedings of the 2016 Conference of the North American Chapter of the Association for Computational Linguistics: Human Language Technologies*, pages 839–849, San Diego, California. Association for Computational Linguistics.

Jeffrey Pennington, Richard Socher, and Christopher D. Manning. 2014. GloVe: Global vectors for word representation. In *Empirical Methods in Natural Language Processing (EMNLP)*, pages 1532–1543.

Swapna Somasundaran, Jill Burstein, and Martin Chodorow. 2014. Lexical chaining for measuring discourse coherence quality in test-taker essays. In *Proceedings of COLING 2014, the 25th International Conference on Computational Linguistics: Technical Papers*, pages 950–961, Dublin, Ireland. Dublin City University and Association for Computational Linguistics.

Radu Soricut and Daniel Marcu. 2006. Discourse generation using utility-trained coherence models. In *Proceedings of the COLING/ACL 2006 Main Conference Poster Sessions*, pages 803–810, Sydney, Australia. Association for Computational Linguistics.

Dat Tien Nguyen and Shafiq Joty. 2017. A neural local coherence model. In *Proceedings of the 55th Annual Meeting of the Association for Computational Linguistics (Volume 1: Long Papers)*, pages 1320–1330. Association for Computational Linguistics.

Peng Xu, Hamidreza Saghir, Jin Sung Kang, Teng Long, Avishek Joey Bose, Yanshuai Cao, and Jackie Chi Kit Cheung. 2019. A cross-domain transferable neural coherence model. In *Proceedings of the*

57th Annual Meeting of the Association for Computational Linguistics, pages 678–687, Florence, Italy.
Association for Computational Linguistics.

Computational Interpretations of Recency for the Choice of Referring Expressions in Discourse

Fahime Same
University of Cologne
`f.same@uni-koeln.de`

Kees van Deemter
Utrecht University
`c.j.vandeemter@uu.nl`

Abstract

First, we discuss the most common linguistic perspectives on the concept of recency and propose a taxonomy of recency metrics employed in Machine Learning studies for choosing the form of referring expressions in discourse context. We then report on a Multi-Layer Perceptron study and a Sequential Forward Search experiment, followed by Bayes Factor analysis of the outcomes. The results suggest that recency metrics counting paragraphs and sentences contribute to referential choice prediction more than other recency-related metrics. Based on the results of our analysis, we argue that, sensitivity to discourse structure is important for recency metrics used in determining referring expression forms.

1 Introduction

Speakers use various linguistic forms such as pronouns, proper names, and common nouns, to refer to entities in discourse. A great number of studies have addressed the issue of referring, and the factors that play a role in speakers' choice of the form of referring expressions. These factors include grammatical function (Brennan, 1995), animacy (Fukumura and van Gompel, 2011), competition (Arnold and Griffin, 2007), frequency (Ariel, 1990) and recency (McCoy and Strube, 1999; Ariel, 2001), among others. The focus of this article is on recency.

Broadly speaking, we understand recency to be the distance between the current mention of a referent and its antecedent. Therefore, in this work, we employ recency metrics to predict the form of subsequent mentions, and are not interested in the choice of "first-mention" expressions.

Recency has received much attention in both linguistic and computational studies, but in many cases, the notion of recency itself has been left largely undefined even though, as we shall see, recency can be understood in different ways. This paper has three objectives. The first is to survey different computational "interpretations" of the notion of recency. The second goal is to determine which of these computational interpretations is most effective for predicting the form of a referring expression in discourse context. In other words, we will ask, "what is the best way to operationalize the notion of recency in computational and data-oriented studies?" And the final objective is to see to which extent the choice of recency metrics should depend on the corpus.

The structure of this paper is as follows: in section 2, we summarize how recency has been used in linguistic studies. In section 3, we provide a brief overview of the notion of recency in Machine Learning (ML) studies, with the purpose of creating a taxonomy of recency metrics discussed in section 4. Sections 5 and 6 report two new studies. The former analyzes single recency metrics, the latter takes their combination into account. Finally, section 7 gives a brief summary and review of the findings.

2 Different interpretations of the notion of recency/distance

There is a long tradition of work in linguistics considering recency as a factor influencing the salience of a referent. The general idea is that the greater the distance between the two mentions, the greater the chance of using a full noun phrase anaphor (Vonk et al., 1992; Givón, 1992; Arnold, 2010); conversely, the shorter the distance between the two mentions, the greater the chance of pronominalization. Some studies have kept the notion of recency or "distance to the previous mention" opaque by not defining what long and short distance mean; while others have presented different interpretations of the notion of distance. In this paper, we focus on the three most frequent interpretations that are found in the literature.

Proceedings of the First Workshop on Computational Approaches to Discourse, pages 113–123
Online, November 20, 2020. ©2020 Association for Computational Linguistics
https://doi.org/10.18653/v1/P17

2.1 Immediate context

In the studies where the main focus is on the pronominalization problem, the notion of distance is often concerned with whether or not the antecedent is present in the same or previous utterance (or clause). In a corpus study, Hobbs (1978) noticed that in 98% of the cases, the antecedent of a pronoun anaphor is in the previous or in the same sentence. Ariel (1990) used the same sentence metrics in her corpus study, where she focused on the distribution of pronouns, demonstratives and full NPs. She demonstrated that with respect to distance from the antecedent, in more than 80% of cases, pronouns favor short distances, where the antecedent is in the same sentence or only one sentence away. In centering-based studies such as Hitzeman and Poesio (1998), Poesio et al. (2004) and Henschel et al. (2000) too, long distance antecedents are those which are more than one utterance or one clause away.

2.2 Non-local context

In some other corpus-based studies, a larger span of text was taken into account. In a comprehensive work on topic continuity in discourse, Givón (1983) measured the distance to the previous mention up to 20 clauses back. The work by Givón is one of the first attempts in quantifying the role of distance in discourse. In a computational pronominalization study, McCoy and Strube (1999) hypothesized that "when the last mention of an item is several sentences back in the text, a definite description is preferred". For this study which was conducted on a corpus of The New York Times articles, they found out that in long-distance situations (where the antecedent is more than two sentences away), a definite description is almost always used. In a psycholinguistics experiment, Arnold et al. (2009) examined the choice of referring expressions made by high-functioning children and adolescents with autism. Arnold et al. grouped the distance to the antecedent into 4 categories and demonstrated that the participants in their experiment had sensitivity to the discourse context.

2.3 Unit boundary

While the distance patterns explained in the previous paragraphs account for a large number of pronominalization cases, according to Fox (1987), they cannot handle all various types of anaphoric patterns. She showed that pronouns can be used to refer to a referent over long stretches of distance until the goal of the narrative changes (cited in Smith (2003)). In line with this idea, Ariel (1990) proposed the notion of *unity*, meaning, the antecedent being in the same frame, segment or paragraph. Vonk et al. (1992) and Tomlin (1987) also emphasized the importance of episode or unit boundaries, mostly realized as paragraph boundaries in written text, as factors contributing to the recency of mention.

As explained, there are three different interpretations of recency in the literature. The first two interpretations are concerned with measuring the distance in sentences (or clauses), while the third one goes beyond the sentential level, and focuses on paragraphs. Which of these interpretations does best in algorithms to predict referential choice in discourse contexts?

3 Recency in ML studies

Within Natural Language Generation (Gatt and Krahmer, 2018), reference production is computationally modelled in an area known as Referring Expression Generation (REG) (Krahmer and van Deemter, 2019; van Deemter, 2016). REG models have various shapes and forms, with feature-based ML models playing a substantial role.

GREC (Belz and Kow, 2010) was a series of Shared Task Evaluation tasks that is still regarded as a natural starting point when it comes to the generation of referring expressions in context. Different ML algorithms were submitted to these shared tasks, a number of which have exploited recency metrics. Some of the metrics used in these algorithms are pursuant to the interpretations mentioned in section 2. For example, the recency feature in Greenbacker and McCoy (2009) resembles the metric defined in McCoy and Strube (1999). Another example is a binary feature used by Bohnet (2008), which captures whether or not the antecedent occurs in the same sentence. This metric is similar to the interpretation discussed above under the heading "Immediate Context". Some of the other recency metrics used in these algorithms, however, are not in accordance with the interpretations introduced in section 2. For instance, Bohnet (2008) and Jamison and Mehay (2008) used distance metrics measuring number of words between the two mentions. In a more recent ML study, Kibrik et al. (2016) stated that referential choice belongs to a large group of multifactorial processes. They used 7 different distance-related metrics in their study and concluded that these metrics are essential for successful prediction of referential choice, but there is no indication which metrics are the most relevant ones. Further studies that include recency metrics are Ferreira et al. (2016), Modi et al. (2017) and Saha et al. (2011), among others.

We saw that the metrics used in the ML studies are based on different units of measurement (e.g. word distance versus sentence distance). Likewise, different strategies are used to encode these metrics. For instance, some distances are measured in natural numbers while others are categorized in a smaller class of broader "bins". In the following example taken from the GREC-2.0 corpus (Belz et al., 2010), one could say that the distance between the expression "its" and its antecedent "Berlin" is 21 words (a natural number). Another solution would be, for instance, to follow Ferreira et al. (2016) in grouping the numerical distances into five groups consisting of 0-10 words, 11-20 words, 21-30 words, 31-40 words and more than 40 words. With this approach, the distance between "its" and its antecedent falls into the third bin, 21-30 words.

(1) **Berlin**$_{(1)}$ is$_{(2)}$ the$_{(3)}$ capital$_{(4)}$ city$_{(5)}$ and$_{(6)}$ one$_{(7)}$ of$_{(8)}$ the$_{(9)}$ sixteen$_{(10)}$ federal$_{(11)}$ states$_{(12)}$ of$_{(13)}$ Germany$_{(14)}$ ·$_{(15)}$ With$_{(16)}$ a$_{(17)}$ population$_{(18)}$ of$_{(19)}$ 3.4$_{(20)}$ million$_{(21)}$ in$_{(22)}$ **its**$_{(23)}$ city$_{(24)}$ limits$_{(25)}$,...

The question is which of these metrics work best in ML studies. The existing diversity motivated us to collect as many recency metrics as possible from the ML literature and create a taxonomy of recency metrics.

4 Methodology

This section begins with subsection 4.1 introducing recency metrics collected from different ML studies. Later, subsection 4.2 presents the two corpora used in our assessments and highlights their main differences. And finally, subsection 4.3 introduces the baseline algorithm and the ML method employed in our assessments.

4.1 Taxonomy of recency/distance metrics

Table 1 presents the metrics measuring the distance from the current expression to its antecedent [1]. As

mentioned in the previous section, recency metrics vary a great deal. The most important differences between these metrics are:

I. Antecedent type In most metrics, the antecedent is the nearest previous mention of the same entity. In one of the metrics (metric 14 in Table 1), however, instead of the distance to the nearest mention, the distance to the nearest full NP mention is measured.

II. Unit of measurement The units in which the distance is measured vary in the recency metrics. The units of measurements used in the metrics outlined in Table 1 include distance in number of:

- words [metrics 1-3]

- sentences [metrics 4-11]

- NPs [metric 12]

- markables, defined as the textual expressions, between which coreferential relations can be established (Chiarcos and Krasavina, 2005). [metrics 13-14]

- paragraphs [metric 15]

III. Type of encoding As shown in Example (1), the major difference between encoding of the metrics is whether the distance is reported as a numeric value or defined bins. Among the metrics presented below, metrics 2, 3, 5, 6, 7 and 10 are categorical, the rest are numeric.

Another difference in type of encoding concerns how numeric values are encoded. Of the metrics used in this assessment, metrics 1, 4 and 12-15 are reported as natural numbers (including 0), metric 8 is the natural logarithm of the number of intervening sentences, metric 9 is its exponential variant [2] and metric 11, which will be explained below, is the normalized distance.

Scaled/normalized sentence distance The distance between the mentions ranges from 0 to 19 sentences in MSR and 0 to 146 sentences in WSJ. To overcome this sparsity, we decided to bound

---

[1]Greenbacker and McCoy defined the recency metric in their study as: "Referring expressions which were separated from the most recent reference by more than two sentences were marked as long distance references" (2009, p. 101). We have two different interpretations of this sentence which are presented as metric 5 and metric 6.

[2]The exponential distance is not reported for WSJ in this study.

Metric	Type of encoding & description	Meas Unit	Reference
1	Numerical distance	word	Bohnet (2008)
2	Categorical distance (5 bins of 0-10, 11-20, 21-30, 31-40 and 40+ words)	word	Ferreira et al. (2016)
3	Categorical distance (3 bins of 0-5, 6-12 and 13+ words)	word	Jamison and Mehay (2008)
4	Numerical distance	sentence	Orăsan and Dornescu (2009) Hendrickx et al. (2008) Kibrik et al. (2016) Saha et al. (2011)
5	Categorical distance [1st interp] (+/-2 sentences)	sentence	Greenbacker and McCoy (2009)
6	Categorical distance [2nd interp] (4 bins of 0,1,2,+ 2 sentences)	sentence	Greenbacker and McCoy (2009)
7	Categorical distance (3 bins of 0, 1, 2+ sentences)	sentence	Jamison (2008) Saha et al. (2011)
8	Log distance	sentence	Saha et al. (2011)
9	Exponential distance	sentence	Modi et al. (2017)
10	Antecedent in the same sentence?	sentence	Bohnet (2008)
11	Normalized distance	sentence	Newly implemented
12	Numerical distance	NP	Hendrickx et al. (2008)
13	Numerical distance	markable	Kibrik et al. (2016) Saha et al. (2011)
14	Numerical distance to the nearest non-pronominal antecedent	markable	Kibrik et al. (2016)
15	Numerical distance	paragraph	Kibrik et al. (2016)

Table 1: List of metrics collected from different ML studies

the values between two numbers [0,1], using the following formula:

$$x_{norm} = \frac{x_i - x_{min}}{x_{max} - x_{min}} \tag{1}$$

In this section, we introduced 14 metrics from the ML literature, plus one additional metric we decided to include in the study. The assessment of these metrics will be presented in section 5.

4.2 Corpora used in this study

As indicated earlier, we are also interested to find out the extent to which the choice of recency metrics should take the corpus itself into account. Corpora can be different from each other in terms of, for instance, size, genre (e.g. Wikipedia article, newspaper articles and medical reports) and structure of their documents (e.g. length and sentence structure). For this study, we have chosen two corpora which are different from each other in terms of *text genre* and length-related attributes (which will be referred to as *text structure* in this article).

Considering that the GREC Shared Tasks were among the first systematic studies tackling the referential choice in context, we decided to start our assessment of the metrics with GREC-2.0 (henceforth MSR[3]), one of the underlying corpora of these Shared Tasks[4]. MSR consists of more than 1500 introductory sections of Wikipedia articles in 5 different classes (people, city, country, river and mountain). The major pitfall of MSR is that only mentions to the main reference of the article are annotated.

In addition to MSR, we decided to include the Wall Street Journal portion (henceforth WSJ) of the OntoNotes corpus (Hovy et al., 2006; Pradhan et al., 2013) in this study. The genres of the two

---

[3]As this corpus is used in the GREC-MSR Shared Tasks, we abbreviate its name to MSR.

[4]We decided to exclude GREC-People, the other corpus used in these Shared Tasks because after the exclusion of the first mention expressions, only 121 instances of common nouns (2.16% of the whole data) were left. In a pilot study, we found out that the data is not enough for a three-way referential choice prediction task.

corpora are different, with the former containing Wikipedia articles, and the latter having newspaper articles. Also, the structure of the documents, such as length of each document, number of sentences and number of paragraphs are radically different across both corpora. The existing differences between the two corpora make it possible to explore whether the choice of recency metrics should depend on the text structure. Table 2 illustrates the major differences between the two corpora. In order to apply the recency metrics to MSR, we conducted tokenization and sentence segmentation using the spaCy python library. The texts of WSJ were already segmented and tokenized.

It is also important to note that four referring expression types, namely common noun, proper name, pronoun and zero anaphor are annotated in MSR. In WSJ, zero cases are not annotated, and only realized expressions are considered. For this reason, we decided to include only realized expressions (namely common nouns, proper names and pronouns) in our study and exclude the covert references. Hence, as mentioned before, the task in this study is to predict whether a target referring expression is a pronoun, a proper name or a common noun. The total number of referring expressions is 9306 in MSR and 21565 in WSJ, of which we placed 70% in a training set and 30% in a test set.

Corpus features	MSR	WSJ
number (n) of documents	1655	589
mean n of words / doc	166.5	600.8
mean n of sentences / doc	7.1	25
mean n of paragraphs / doc	2.3	10.8
mean n of chains / doc	n/a	15
mean length of sentences	25.8	29.5
n of common nouns	1613	6917
n of proper names	2813	7695
n of pronouns	4880	6953

Table 2: Comparison of the MSR and WSJ corpora in terms of length-related features and number of different types of referring expressions. Mean n of chains, meaning mean number of different annotated referents in a document, is not reported for MSR because only one chain per document is annotated.

As shown in Table 2, the documents in WSJ are roughly 4 times longer than the documents in MSR. Also, each document has a greater number of sentences and paragraphs. We expect that in the ML studies, the WSJ algorithms overall have a lower accuracy than the MSR algorithms.

4.3 Baseline algorithms and ML method

In order to assess the recency metrics, the first step is to create a baseline algorithm which contains no recency metric. This enables us to compare the performance of the experimental algorithms incorporating recency metrics against the baseline. We could have chosen different features, but we chose grammatical role of the current mention and grammatical role of the previous mention as the features of the baseline system for the following reasons: Using grammatical role is a safe choice, because the same syntactic categories were used in both corpora, so any differences in performance between the two corpora will not be due to differences in the annotations. Furthermore, we wanted to make sure that the features in the baseline algorithm are not confounding with recency metrics. For example, a competition-based feature such as the number of competing discourse entities between the two mentions would be confounding because the more competition there is, the greater the distance between the referent and the antecedent is likely to be. For this reason, we chose an algorithm that did not use anything other than grammatical role.

In this study, we use Multi-Layer Perceptron (henceforth MLP), a class of feedforward artificial neural networks as our ML approach. The model has two hidden layers with respectively 16 and 8 units. While hidden layers use the rectified linear activation function (ReLU), the output layer uses the softmax activation function. The model will be fit for 50 training epochs, and 50 samples (batch size) are being propagated through the network. It is noteworthy that since MLP cannot handle categorical data, all categorical metrics have been one-hot encoded in this study.

5 Assessing recency metrics using MLP

This section firstly reports on the success of the baseline algorithms, and continues with the algorithms incorporating the recency metrics.

5.1 Baseline algorithms

We mentioned in the previous section that the baseline algorithms are made up of two features, the grammatical role of the current mention and the grammatical role of its antecedent. Table 3 shows the accuracy of the two baseline algorithms.

	MSR	WSJ
baseline	0.585	0.55

Table 3: Accuracy of the MSR and WSJ baseline algorithms

5.2 Assessing recency metrics

Each experimental algorithm is composed of two baseline features and one recency metric. For instance, model 4 includes grammatical role of the current mention and the antecedent plus metric 4, which is the numerical distance in sentences. Since there are 15 different recency metrics and two different corpora, the total number of experimental algorithms is 30. If, for instance, an experimental algorithm would have 2 recency metrics instead of one, we would not be able to firmly test whether both features contribute to the performance of the algorithm, or only one of them is involved. For this reason, each metric is tested individually, and not in combination with other recency metrics. The overall accuracy of the experimental algorithms incorporating different recency metrics is reported in Table 4.

Meas Unit	Name	MSR	WSJ
	model 1	0.60	0.576
Word	model 2	0. 594	0. 551
	model 3	0.592	0. 572
	model 4	0.607	0.62
	model 5	0. 588	0. 582
	model 6	0.608	0. 622
	model 7	0.602	0.622
Sentence	model 8	0.607	0.611
	model 9	0.609	-
	model 10	0.589	0.597
	model 11	0.602	0.604
NP	model 12	0.59	0.623
Markable	model 13	-	0.577
	model 14	0.594	0.561
Paragraph	model 15	0.625	0. 616

Table 4: Accuracy of the experimental algorithms. The first column, Meas(urement) Unit specifies metrics' units of measurement detailed in section 4.1, II. Unit of measurement

The reported accuracies are all higher than the baseline accuracy, but it is still unclear whether the recency metrics are strongly informative of the probability of the increase in the accuracy of the algorithms.

We conducted Bayes Factor (henceforth BF) analysis using a beta distribution to investigate whether the outcomes of the experimental and the baseline algorithms come from distributions with the same underlying probability parameter, or ones with different underlying parameters. Hence, in the case of our current assessment, BF is used to determine whether or not there is good evidence for saying that the difference in accuracy rates of the models is less or greater than 0.01 (henceforth threshold). If the difference in accuracy is below the threshold, the evidence is in favor of similar distributions; if it is above the threshold, there is good evidence that the outcomes come from different distributions. In case of being from different distributions, we infer that the inclusion of recency metrics leads to an improvement in the performance of experimental algorithms.

Additionally, the strength of evidence for each experimental model versus the baseline will be assessed according to the scale of Kass and Raftery (1995).

BF	Interpretation
1 to 3	Not worth more than a bare mention
3 to 20	Positive
20 to 150	Strong
>150	Very strong

Table 5: Interpretation of Bayes Factors according to Kass and Raftery (1995, p. 777)

For the sake of space, we only report the results suggesting that the outcomes of the experimental and the baseline algorithms come from different distributions.

5.2.1 BF analysis of the MSR models

Comparing the rate of correct predictions of each experimental model to that of the baseline shows *positive* evidence that the accuracy of model 15, the one incorporating *distance in paragraph* as its recency metric, comes from different distribution than the baseline (BF=3.286). The other models were doing better than the baseline too, but there is insufficient evidence to say they are different from the baseline. More research is needed to investigate why other experimental models are not statistically different from the baseline.

5.2.2 BF analysis of the WSJ models

In the case of WSJ, the accuracy rates of 8 models are different from the accuracy of the baseline.

Similar to MSR, the outcome of model 15, utilizing the paragraph-based recency metric, comes from distributions with different underlying probabilities than the baseline. Additionally, *except* the outcome of model 5, there is very strong evidence that the accuracy of all other models (6 models in total) incorporating sentence-based recency metrics are being shifted by more than 0.01 beyond the baseline. This means, 6 out of 7 sentence-based recency metrics have improved the performance of the algorithms over the baseline. The remaining model with a different accuracy than the baseline is model 12, having NP distance as its recency metric.

Name	Meas	Def	BF
model 4	sentence	num	54×10^8
model 6	sentence	cat (4)	19×10^9
model 7	sentence	cat (3)	37×10^9
model 8	sentence	log	78×10^5
model 10	sentence	binary	14×10^2
model 11	sentence	norm	12×10^4
model 12	NP	num	56×10^9
model 15	paragraph	num	16×10^7

Table 6: Bayes Factor analysis giving the ratio of probabilities that the underlying accuracy rates are within 1% of each other or not. According to the scale of Kass and Raftery (1995) presented in Table 5, there is very strong evidence that the accuracy rates of all these models are different from the baseline. The column `Def` presents very briefly the definition of the metrics according to Table 1. For instance, `cat(4)` means the categorical distance in 4 bins.

5.2.3 BF analysis of the best performing models

As a next step, we compare the best performing models of each unit of measurement with each other. Since the only difference between the models is in their recency metrics, if there is good evidence that the difference in the accuracy of the models is greater than the threshold, we conclude that this difference is due to the differences in the recency metrics. Table 7 illustrates the best performing algorithms of each unit of measurement.

I. MSR models We conducted a one to one comparison between the best performing models of each unit. The evidence suggests that these models are not statistically different from each other.

II. WSJ models The evidence suggests that models 7, 12 and 15 are not evidentially distinguishable

Meas Unit	MSR	WSJ
Word	Model 1	Model 1
Sentence	Model 9	Model 7
NP	Model 12	Model 12
Markable	Model 14	Model 13
Paragraph	Model 15	Model 15

Table 7: Best performing algorithms of each unit of measurement

from each other. In other words, if we only focus on the WSJ corpus, we do not have enough evidence to prefer one model over another, and we can conclude that the best performing models incorporating sentence, paragraph and NP level recency metrics are equally good. But when we did a one to one comparison between these three models and the best performing models of word and markable units, we found out that the accuracy rates of each of these models have been shifted by more than 0.01 beyond the accuracy rates of the word and markable models. This means, the models incorporating paragraph, sentence and NP level metrics are statistically different from the models incorporating word and markable level information.

As discussed in this section, the recency metrics clearly made a bigger improvement in the WSJ models. In the case of MSR, only one model had a distinguishable performance; while in the case of WSJ, 8 models performed statistically better than the baseline. Furthermore, sentence, paragraph and NP-based metrics evidentially improved the performance of the WSJ algorithms.

The results reported in this section were based on the assessment of single recency metrics; yet, there is no assessment of the combination of these metrics. In the next section, we report on a feature selection study we conducted to investigate which combinations of recency metrics lead to best results.

6 Sequential Forward Search

In order to investigate the extent to which the combination of different recency metrics improves the performance, we run a Sequential Forward Search (SFS) algorithm. The algorithm starts with an empty set and adds features to the model up to the point that no further improvement occurs. For this study, we used the R package mlr (Bischl et al., 2016) with the learner `classif.mlp`, and 5-fold cross-validation resampling strategy.

The result of the MSR experiment shows that the two recency metrics playing the most important roles are metric 15, distance in paragraph, and metric 9, exponential distance in sentences. Retraining the MLP algorithm on the new model, the accuracy is 0.637. The Bayes Factor analysis provides strong evidence that the outcome of this model is statistically different from the baseline (BF = 26.11).

In the WSJ SFS experiment, metric 15, distance in paragraphs, and metric 8, log distance in sentences, were chosen as the two recency features whose combination produced the best result. The model trained on the combination of these two metrics had the accuracy of 0.631. The Bayes Factor analysis finds very strong evidence that the outcomes of the baseline and this model are coming from different distributions.

What stands out in this experiment is that in the case of both MSR and WSJ, distance in paragraph is chosen as one of the recency metrics. The other chosen measures are exponential distance in MSR and logarithmic distance in WSJ. This could indicate that the algorithm is sensitive to the encoding of the sentence-based metrics. More experimentation in a more elaborated feature-based study is necessary to test this point.

7   Conclusion

Our goal was to shed light on different interpretations of recency, and to find out which of these interpretations are most effective for referential choice prediction. A subsidiary goal was to investigate whether the choice of recency metric should take corpus-specific features such as text genre and text structure into consideration.

The findings of this study should be of interest to theoretical and computational linguists alike, because both groups of researchers have studied the relation between recency and referential choice. In the linguistic tradition, the notion of recency has often been studied without a clear definition being offered (section 2). In the computational tradition, by contrast, researchers have dwelt less on theoretical justification but have had to provide precise definitions, to ensure that their algorithms are able to deal with a broad range of inputs. For example, Kibrik et al. (2016) defined 7 different implementations of the notion of recency taking different units of measurement into account; while Saha et al. (2011) employed various implementations of sentence-related metrics.

Another difference is that in the linguistic tradition, researchers usually think of recency as operating solely on the sentence or paragraph levels; while in computational works, less conventional metrics such as measuring the distance in words or NPs have been also practiced. We believe that the existence of a wider range of recency metrics in computational feature-based studies has the potential to open new windows into a better understanding of recency, and can encourage a re-evaluation of recency in the linguistic tradition. What is missing from many computational works is an explanation of why a certain metric or a certain way of encoding has been chosen over another. The findings from this study make the following contributions to the literature:

Creating a taxonomy of recency metrics   After providing an overview of the most prevalent interpretations of recency in the linguistic tradition, we scrutinized the feature-based ML studies and provided, for the first time as far as we know, a taxonomy of recency metrics. The importance of this taxonomy is firstly that we do not know of any available work classifying and analyzing this notion comprehensively, so this work could be a starting point for getting deeper into the notion of recency.

Secondly, we have shed light on the differences between these metrics. Knowing what the differences are, and where they stem from, could be the first step in dissecting various aspects of this notion and developing new, improved recency metrics.

Assessing a wide range of recency metrics   We have assessed individual metrics using the Multilayer Perceptron algorithm, and conducted a Bayes Factor analysis using a beta distribution to investigate whether there is evidence that the models incorporating recency metrics come from different distributions than the baseline algorithms. Additionally, we conducted a Bayes Factor analysis between the best performing models of each measurement unit to see whether there is enough evidence that the outcomes of models are different from each other.

The evidence reported in Table 6 for the models built on the WSJ corpus suggests that the outcome of the models incorporating NP, paragraph and sentence metrics have been shifted by more than 0.01 beyond the baseline's outcome. Also, we have strong evidence to believe that these models are statistically different from the models incorporating word and markable distance measures.

Additionally, the results of the Sequential Forward Search experiment show that, for both corpora, a combination of the paragraph-based and one of the sentence-based metrics leads to the best performance. This finding is important because it provides some direction in choosing recency metrics for feature-based computational studies. Furthermore, the Bayes Factor analysis and SFS combined suggest that "higher-level" metrics such as distance in paragraphs and sentences might result in greater changes in the performance of the algorithms than "lower-level" metrics based on counting words or markables. Finally, it raises the question of why a measurement such as distance in the number of sentences performs better than a measurement such as distance in the number of words. This is notable because the distance in words might be more indicative of the physical distance between the mentions, considering that sentences can vary enormously in length.

Another interesting observation is that some encoding solutions are more successful than others. For instance, the sentential distance in metric 5 is grouped into 2 bins of +/-2 sentences, while in metric 6, the distance is grouped into 4 bins of 0, 1, 2 or more than 2 sentences. While the former metric leads to a marginal difference in the performance of the algorithms, the latter contributes more to the improvement of the accuracy. These subtle differences in encoding and the great impact that they can make should be the focus of more experimentation.

Another major finding was the important role of distance measured in paragraphs. The Bayes Factor analysis showed that there is strong evidence for the differences between the performance of the baseline and the algorithms incorporating this metric. Also, using the SFS algorithm, this metric was selected in both MSR and WSJ as a feature contributing to the improvement of the results. The important role of paragraph information is in line with what we presented in section 2 under the topic "Unit boundary". According to Vonk et al. (1992), episode boundaries can decrease the accessibility of a referent, resulting in re-mentioning with full NPs. This might be the reason that including paragraph distance, and signaling whether or not the antecedent is in a different paragraph, makes the referential choice prediction simpler for the algo-

rithms. The surprising point is that despite the major role of paragraph information, the only study from subsection 4.1 which has used the paragraph distance metric is Kibrik et al. (2016). The results from the current study could motivate a greater focus on paragraph-based information in feature-based studies.

Importance of the choice of corpus Surprisingly, the results of this study showed that recency measures were of greater importance when applied to WSJ than to MSR. In case of the MSR models, the only metric which in isolation led to a distribution different from the baseline was distance in the number of paragraphs, while in the case of WSJ, 8 different recency metrics led to major differences. One possible reason for the different behavior of recency metrics could be that due to unbalanced number of referring expression types (more than 50% pronouns and less than 20% common names), MSR is, most likely, not a suitable corpus for a three-way referential choice task.

It can be seen from the data in Table 2 that except the length of the sentences which is almost equal in both corpora, other text structure features, such as the number of words, sentences and paragraphs are very different from each other (with WSJ having almost 4 times more words, sentences and paragraphs). One speculation is that length-related features modulate the importance of the recency metrics in the ML models.

Further research is needed to identify the causes of this difference. However, based on our study, one might conclude that the more complex the discourse structure, the greater the role of recency measures. If this is true, it would be of great importance to carefully inspect the characteristics of the textual source prior to deciding which features to include in the study, as apparently, the choice of recency metric should depend on text genre and structure.

References

Mira Ariel. 1990. *Accessing Noun-Phrase Antecedents.* Routledge.

Mira Ariel. 2001. Accessibility theory: An overview. *Text representation: Linguistic and psycholinguistic aspects*, 8:29–87.

Jennifer E Arnold. 2010. How speakers refer: The role of accessibility. *Language and Linguistics Compass*, 4(4):187–203.

Jennifer E Arnold, Loisa Bennetto, and Joshua J Diehl. 2009. Reference production in young speakers with and without autism: Effects of discourse status and processing constraints. *Cognition*, 110(2):131–146.

Jennifer E Arnold and Zenzi M Griffin. 2007. The effect of additional characters on choice of referring expression: Everyone counts. *Journal of memory and language*, 56(4):521–536.

Anja Belz and Eric Kow. 2010. The GREC challenges 2010: overview and evaluation results. In *Proceedings of the 6th international natural language generation conference*, pages 219–229. Association for Computational Linguistics.

Anja Belz, Eric Kow, Jette Viethen, and Albert Gatt. 2010. Generating referring expressions in context: The task evaluation challenges. In *Empirical methods in natural language generation*, pages 294–327. Springer.

Bernd Bischl, Michel Lang, Lars Kotthoff, Julia Schiffner, Jakob Richter, Erich Studerus, Giuseppe Casalicchio, and Zachary M Jones. 2016. mlr: Machine Learning in R. *The Journal of Machine Learning Research*, 17(1):5938–5942.

Bernd Bohnet. 2008. IS-G: The comparison of different learning techniques for the selection of the main subject references. In *Proceedings of the Fifth International Natural Language Generation Conference*, pages 192–193. Association for Computational Linguistics.

Susan E Brennan. 1995. Centering attention in discourse. *Language and Cognitive processes*, 10(2):137–167.

Christian Chiarcos and Olga Krasavina. 2005. Annotation guidelines. pocos-potsdam coreference scheme. *Unpublished manuscript*.

Kees van Deemter. 2016. *Computational models of referring: a study in cognitive science*. MIT Press.

Thiago Castro Ferreira, Emiel Krahmer, and Sander Wubben. 2016. Towards more variation in text generation: Developing and evaluating variation models for choice of referential form. In *Proceedings of the 54th Annual Meeting of the Association for Computational Linguistics (Volume 1: Long Papers)*, pages 568–577.

Barbara A. Fox. 1987. *Discourse Structure and Anaphora: Written and Conversational English*. Cambridge Studies in Linguistics. Cambridge University Press.

Kumiko Fukumura and Roger PG van Gompel. 2011. The effect of animacy on the choice of referring expression. *Language and cognitive processes*, 26(10):1472–1504.

Albert Gatt and Emiel Krahmer. 2018. Survey of the state of the art in natural language generation: Core tasks, applications and evaluation. *Journal of Artificial Intelligence Research*, 61:65–170.

Talmy Givón. 1983. Topic continuity in discourse: An introduction. *Topic continuity in discourse: A quantitative cross-language study*, 3:1–42.

Talmy Givón. 1992. The grammar of referential coherence as mental processing instructions. *Linguistics*.

Charles Greenbacker and Kathleen McCoy. 2009. Udel: generating referring expressions guided by psycholinguistic findings. In *Proceedings of the 2009 Workshop on Language Generation and Summarisation*, pages 101–102. Association for Computational Linguistics.

Iris Hendrickx, Walter Daelemans, Kim Luyckx, Roser Morante, and Vincent Van Asch. 2008. Cnts: Memory-based learning of generating repeated references. In *Proceedings of the Fifth International Natural Language Generation Conference*, pages 194–195. Association for Computational Linguistics.

Renate Henschel, Hua Cheng, and Massimo Poesio. 2000. Pronominalization revisited. In *Proceedings of the 18th conference on Computational linguistics-Volume 1*, pages 306–312. Association for Computational Linguistics.

Janet Hitzeman and Massimo Poesio. 1998. Long distance pronominalisation and global focus. In *COLING 1998 Volume 1: The 17th International Conference on Computational Linguistics*.

Jerry R Hobbs. 1978. Resolving pronoun references. *Lingua*, 44(4):311–338.

Eduard Hovy, Mitchell Marcus, Martha Palmer, Lance Ramshaw, and Ralph Weischedel. 2006. Ontonotes: the 90% solution. In *Proceedings of the human language technology conference of the NAACL, Companion Volume: Short Papers*, pages 57–60.

Emily Jamison. 2008. Using discourse features for referring expression generation. In *Proceedings of the 5th Meeting of the Midwest Computational Linguistics Colloquium (MCLC)*.

Emily Jamison and Dennis Mehay. 2008. Osu-2: Generating referring expressions with a maximum entropy classifier. In *Proceedings of the Fifth International Natural Language Generation Conference*, pages 196–197. Association for Computational Linguistics.

Robert E Kass and Adrian E Raftery. 1995. Bayes factors. *Journal of the american statistical association*, 90(430):773–795.

Andrej A Kibrik, Mariya V Khudyakova, Grigory B Dobrov, Anastasia Linnik, and Dmitrij A Zalmanov. 2016. Referential choice: Predictability and its limits. *Frontiers in psychology*, 7(1429).

Emiel Krahmer and Kees van Deemter. 2019. *Computational Generation of Referring Expressions: An Updated Survey*. Oxford University Press.

Kathleen F McCoy and Michael Strube. 1999. Generating anaphoric expressions: pronoun or definite description? In *The Relation of Discourse/Dialogue Structure and Reference*.

Ashutosh Modi, Ivan Titov, Vera Demberg, Asad Sayeed, and Manfred Pinkal. 2017. Modeling semantic expectation: Using script knowledge for referent prediction. *Transactions of the Association for Computational Linguistics*, 5:31–44.

Constantin Orăsan and Iustin Dornescu. 2009. WLV: A confidence-based machine learning method for the GREC-NEG'09 task. In *Proceedings of the 2009 Workshop on Language Generation and Summarisation (UCNLG+Sum 2009)*, pages 107–108. Association for Computational Linguistics.

Massimo Poesio, Rosemary Stevenson, Barbara Di Eugenio, and Janet Hitzeman. 2004. Centering: A parametric theory and its instantiations. *Computational linguistics*, 30(3):309–363.

Sameer Pradhan, Alessandro Moschitti, Nianwen Xue, Hwee Tou Ng, Anders Björkelund, Olga Uryupina, Yuchen Zhang, and Zhi Zhong. 2013. Towards robust linguistic analysis using ontonotes. In *Proceedings of the Seventeenth Conference on Computational Natural Language Learning*, pages 143–152.

Sriparna Saha, Asif Ekbal, Olga Uryupina, and Massimo Poesio. 2011. Single and multi-objective optimization for feature selection in anaphora resolution. In *Proceedings of 5th International Joint Conference on Natural Language Processing*, pages 93–101.

Carlota S. Smith. 2003. *Referring expressions in discourse*, Cambridge Studies in Linguistics, page 123–152. Cambridge University Press.

Russell S Tomlin. 1987. *Coherence and grounding in discourse: outcome of a symposium, Eugene, Oregon, June 1984*, volume 11. John Benjamins Publishing.

Wietske Vonk, Lettica GMM Hustinx, and Wim HG Simons. 1992. The use of referential expressions in structuring discourse. *Language and cognitive processes*, 7(3-4):301–333.

Do We Really Need That Many Parameters In Transformer For Extractive Summarization? Discourse Can Help !

Wen Xiao, Patrick Huber, Giuseppe Carenini
Department of Computer Science
University of British Columbia
Vancouver, BC, Canada, V6T 1Z4
{xiaowen3, huberpat, carenini}@cs.ubc.ca

Abstract

The multi-head self-attention of popular transformer models is widely used within Natural Language Processing (NLP), including for the task of extractive summarization. With the goal of analyzing and pruning the parameter-heavy self-attention mechanism, there are multiple approaches proposing more parameter-light self-attention alternatives. In this paper, we present a novel parameter-lean self-attention mechanism using discourse priors. Our new tree self-attention is based on document-level discourse information, extending the recently proposed "Synthesizer" framework with another lightweight alternative. We show empirical results that our tree self-attention approach achieves competitive ROUGE-scores on the task of extractive summarization. When compared to the original single-head transformer model, the tree attention approach reaches similar performance on both, EDU and sentence level, despite the significant reduction of parameters in the attention component. We further significantly outperform the 8-head transformer model on sentence level when applying a more balanced hyper-parameter setting, requiring an order of magnitude less parameters[1].

1 Introduction

The task of extractive summarization aims to generate summaries for multi-sentential documents by selecting a subset of text units in the source document that most accurately cover the authors communicative goal (as shown in red in Figure 1). As such, extractive summarization has been a long standing research question with direct practical implications. The main objective for the task is to determine whether a given text unit in the document is important, generally implied by multiple

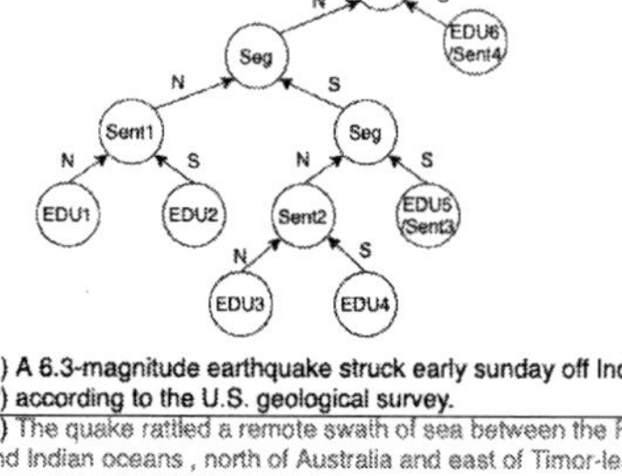

Sent 1
(1) A 6.3-magnitude earthquake struck early sunday off Indonesia,
(2) according to the U.S. geological survey.

Sent 2
(3) The quake rattled a remote swath of sea between the Pacific and Indian oceans, north of Australia and east of Timor-leste, some 5.6 miles (9 kilometers) deep,
(4) according to the U.S. agency.

Sent 3
(5) It was centered approximately 212 miles (340 kilometers) west-northwest of Saumlaki in Indonesia 's Tanimbar Islands, 217 miles east-northeast of Dili, Timor-leste, and 226 miles of Ambon, Indonesia.

Sent 4
(6) Neither the Pacific Tsunami Warning Center nor the Japan Meteorological Agency issued Tsunami Warnings or advisories immediately after the tremor.

Figure 1: News document (4 sentences / 6 EDUs), with both its discourse tree (top) and possible extractive summaries at the sentence/EDU level (extracted sentences and EDUs shown in boxes and red respectively).

factors, such as position, stance, semantic meaning and discourse.

Marcu (1999) already showed early on that discourse information, as defined in the Rhetorical Structure Theory (RST) (Mann and Thompson, 1988), are a good indicator of the importance of a text unit in the given context. The RST framework, one of the most elaborate and widely used theories of discourse, represents a coherent document (a discourse) as a constituency tree. The leaves are thereby called *Elementary Discourse Units* (EDUs), clause-like sentence fragments corresponding to minimal units of content (i.e. propositions). Internal tree nodes, comprising document sub-trees, represent hierarchically compound text spans (or constituents). An additional nuclearity attribute is assigned to each child, representing the importance of the subtree in the local constituent, i.e. the 'Nucleus' child plays a more important role than the 'Satellite' child in the parent's relation. Alternatively, if both children are equally important,

---

[1] Our code can be found here - http://www.cs.ubc.ca/cs-research/lci/research-groups/natural-language-processing/

Proceedings of the First Workshop on Computational Approaches to Discourse, pages 124–134
Online, November 20, 2020. ©2020 Association for Computational Linguistics
https://doi.org/10.18653/v1/P17

both are represented as Nuclei.

While other popular theories of discourse exist (most notably PDTB (Prasad et al., 2008)), RST along with its human-annotated RST-DT treebank (Carlson et al., 2002) have been leveraged in the past to improve extractive summarizations, with either unsupervised (Hirao et al., 2013; Kikuchi et al., 2014), or supervised (Xu et al., 2020) methods.

In this paper, we explore a novel, equally important application for discourse information in extractive summarization, namely to reduce the number of parameters. Instead of exploiting discourse trees as an additional source of information on top of neural models, we use the information as a prior to reduce the number of parameters of existing neural models. This is critical not only to reduce the risk of over-fitting but also to create smaller models that are easier to interpret and deploy.

Not surprisingly, reducing the number of parameters has become increasingly important in the last years, due to the deep-learning revolution. Generally speaking, the objective of reducing neural network parameters involves addressing two central questions: **(1)** What do these models really learn? Such that better priors can be provided and less parameters are required and **(2)** Are all the model parameters necessary? To identify which parameters can be safely removed.

Recently, researchers have explored these questions especially in the context of transformer models. With respect to what is learned in such models, several experiments reveal that the information captured by the multi-head self-attention in the popular BERT model (i.e., the learned attention weights) generally align well with syntactic and semantic relations within sentences (Vig and Belinkov, 2019; Kovaleva et al., 2019). Regarding the second question, building on previous work exploring how to prune large neural models while keeping the performance comparable to the original model (Michel et al., 2019), very recently Tay et al. (2020) has proposed the "Synthesizer" framework, comparing the performance when replacing the dot-product self-attention in the original transformer model with other, less parameterized, attention types.

Inspired by these two lines of research on transformer-based models, namely the identification of a close connection between learned attention weights and linguistic structures, and the potential for safely reducing attention parameters, we propose a document-level discourse-based attention method for extractive summarization. With this new, discourse-inspired approach, we reduce the size of the attention module, the core component of the transformer model, while keeping the model-performance competitive to comparable, fully parameterized models on both EDU and sentence level.

2 Related Work
2.1 Attention Methods

Attention mechanisms have become a widely used component of many modern neural NLP models. Originally proposed by Bahdanau et al. (2014) and Luong et al. (2015) for machine translation, the general idea behind attention is based on the intuition that not all textual units within a sequence contribute equally to the result. Thus, the attention value is introduced to learn how to assess the importance of a unit during training.

In recent years, the role of attention within NLP further solidified with researchers exploring new variants, such as multi-head self-attention, as used in transformers (Vaswani et al., 2017). Generally, larger transformer models with more attention-heads (and therefore more parameters) achieve better performance for many tasks (Vaswani et al., 2017). In the context of explaining the internal workings of neural models, Kovaleva et al. (2019) has recently focused on transformer-style models, investigating the role of individual attention-heads in the BERT model (Devlin et al., 2019). Analyzing the capacity to capture different linguistic information within the self-attention module, they find that information represented across attention-heads is oftentimes redundant, thus showing potential to prune those parameters.

Following these findings, Raganato et al. (2020) define a combination of fixed, position-based attention heads and a single learnable dot-product self-attention head. They empirically show that this hybrid approach reduces the spatial complexity of the model, while retaining the original performance. In addition, the hybrid model improves the performance in the low-resource case. Broadening these results, Tay et al. (2020) further investigate the contribution of the self-attention mechanism in their proposed "Synthesizer" model, they present a generalized version of the transformer, exploring alternative attention types, generally requiring less parameters, but achieving competitive performances on multiple tasks.

In this paper, instead of pruning the redundant

heads of the transformer model empirically or exclusively based on position, we reduce the number of parameters by incorporating linguistic information (i.e. discourse) in the attention computation. We compare our setup for extractive summarization against alternative attention mechanisms, defined in the Synthesizer (Tay et al., 2020).

2.2 Discourse and Summarization

Marcu (1999) was the first to explore the application of RST-style discourse to the task of extractive summarization. In particular, he showed that discourse can be used directly to improve summarization, by simply extracting EDUs along the paths with more nuclei as the document summary.

Later on, researchers started to explore unsupervised methods for discourse-tree-based summarization. Hirao et al. (2013) for example propose a trimming-based method on dependency trees, previously converted from the RST constituency trees, aiming to generate a more coherent summary. Based on this idea of trimming the dependency-tree, Kikuchi et al. (2014) propose another method of trimming nested trees, composed into two levels: a document-tree considering the structure of the document and a sentence-tree considering the structure within each sentence.

More recently, further work along this line started to incorporate discourse structures into supervised summarization with the goal to better leverage the (linguistic) structure of a document. Xiao and Carenini (2019) and Cohan et al. (2018) thereby use the natural structure of scientific papers (i.e. sections) to improve the inputs of the sequence models, better encoding long documents using a structural prior. They empirically show that such structure effectively improves performance.

Moreover, Xu et al. (2020) propose a graph-based discourse-aware extractive summarization method incorporating the dependency trees converted from RST trees on top of the BERTSUM model (Liu and Lapata, 2019) and the document co-reference graph. The results show consistent improvements, implying a close, bidirectional relationship between downstream tasks and discourse parsing. Huber and Carenini (2019, 2020) show that sentiment information can be used to infer discourse trees with promising performance. They further mention extractive summarization as another important downstream task with strong potential connections to the document's discourse, motivating the bidirectional use of available information.

This paper employs a rather different objective from aforementioned work combining discourse and summarization. Instead of leveraging additional discourse information to enhance the model performance, we strive to create a summarization model with significantly less parameters, hence being less prone to over-fitting, smaller, and easier to interpret and deploy.

3 Synthesizer-based Self-Attention Evaluation Framework

Aiming to answer the two guiding questions stated in section 1, Tay et al. (2020) propose a suite of alternative self-attention approaches besides the standard dot-product self-attention, as used in the original transformer model. In their "Synthesizer" framework, they show that parameter-reduced self-attention mechanisms can achieve competitive performance across multiple tasks, including abstractive summarization. While the experiments in the original "Synthesizer" framework are on token level, employing an sequence-to-sequence architecture, we adapt the framework to explore different attention mechanisms on EDU-/sentence-level for the extractive summarization task.

To evaluate the effect of different attention types in our scenario, we apply the general system shown in Figure 2, using the pretrained BERT model as our unit encoder. Each unit is thereby represented as the hidden state of the first token in the last BERT layer. Subsequently, we feed the BERT representations into the "Synthesizer" document-encoder (Tay et al., 2020) with different attention types and employ a Multi-Layer Perceptron (MLP) with Sigmoid activation to retrieve a confidence score for each unit, indicating its predicted likelihood to be part of the extractive summary.

The "Synthesizer" document encoder is essentially a transformer encoder with alternative attention modules, other than the dot-product self-attention. As commonly done, we employ multiple self-attention heads, previously shown to improve the performance of similar models (Vaswani et al., 2017). For each attention head, the input is defined as $X \in R^{l \times d}$ where l is the length of the input document (i.e. the number of units), and d represents the hidden dimension of the model. The self-attention matrix is accordingly defined as $A \in R^{l \times l}$, where A_{ij} is the attention-value that unit i pays to unit j. We further force the sum of the incoming attentions to each unit (as commonly done) to add up to 1, i.e. $\sum_j A_{ij} = 1$. The pa-

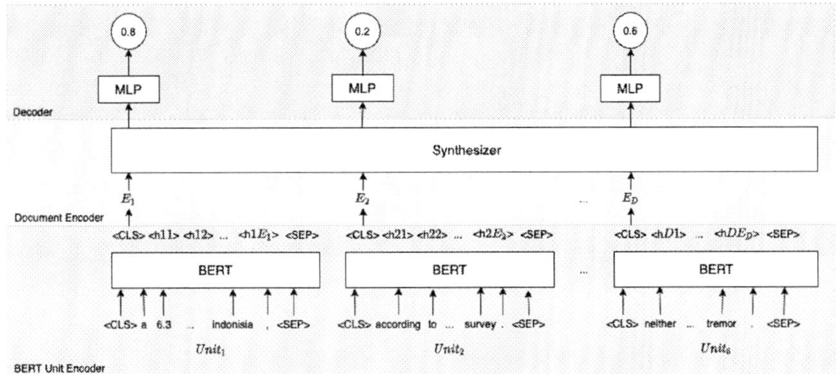

Figure 2: Structure of the extractive summarization framework containing the Synthesizer module

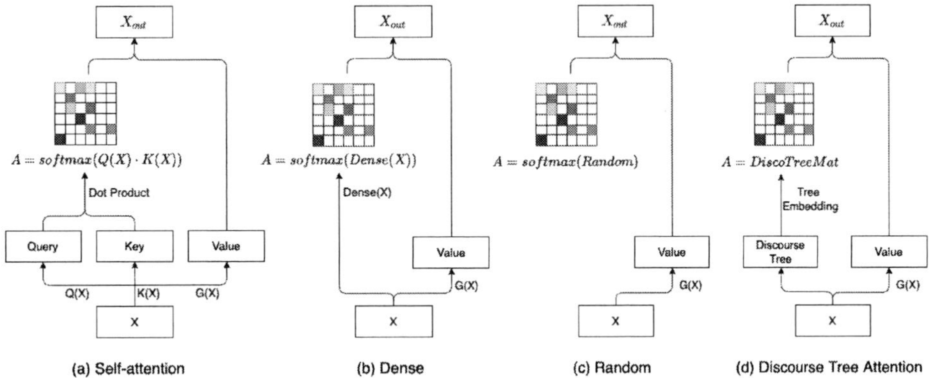

Figure 3: Comparison of attention methods. (a),(b) and (c) taken from (Tay et al., 2020), (d) proposed in this paper.

rameterized function G, calculating the *Value*, is multiplied with the attention matrix for the attention output: $X_{out} = A \cdot G(X)$. Here, we evaluate the three self-attention methodologies proposed by Tay et al. (2020) as our baselines:

Dot Product: As used in the original transformer model, this self-attention calculates a key, a value and a query representation for each textual unit. The attention value is learned as the relationship between the key- and the query-vector defined as $A = softmax(K(X) \cdot Q(X))$

Dense: Instead of using the relationship between units, encoded as keys and values, the dense self-attention $A = softmax(Dense(X))$ is solely learned based on the input unit, where $Dense(\cdot)$ is a two-layer fully connected layer mapping from $R^{l \times d}$ to $R^{l \times l}$, which can be represented as $Dense(X) = W_1 \sigma(W_2 X + b_2) + b_1$.[2]

Random: A random attention matrix is generated for each attention-head, shared across all data points, i.e. $A = softmax(R)$. R can thereby be either updated (referred as *Learned Random* in Sec. 5) or fixed (*Fixed Random*) during training.

---

[2]We use the inner dimension as 512 for all experiments.

4 Discourse Tree Attention

We propose a fourth self-attention candidate: a fixed, discourse-dependent self-attention matrix taking advantage of the strong, tree-structured discourse prior. (see Figure 3 for a comparison of all the self-attention methods). The justification for our new self-attention is two-fold: **(1)** RST-style discourse trees represent document-level semantic structures of coherent documents, which are important semantic markers for the summarization task **(2)** RST discourse-trees, especially the nuclearity attribute, has been shown to be closely related to the summarization task (Marcu, 1999; Hirao et al., 2013; Kikuchi et al., 2014).

To explore a diverse set of RST-style discourse tree attributes, we propose three distinct tree-to-matrix encodings focusing on: the nuclearity-attribute, through a dependency-tree transformation; the plain discourse-structure, derived from the original constituency structure; and a nuclearity-augmented discourse structure, obtained from the constituency representation.

4.1 Dependency-based Nuclearity Attributes (D-Tree)

Inspired by previous work using dependency trees to support the summarization task (Marcu, 1999; Hirao et al., 2013; Xu et al., 2020), we first convert the original constituency-tree, obtained with the RST-DT trained discourse parser (Wang et al., 2017), into the respective dependency tree and subsequently generate the final matrix-representation.

In the first step, we follow the constituency-to-dependency conversion algorithm proposed by Hirao et al. (2013) (shown superior for summarization in Hayashi et al. (2016)). While this algorithm ensures a near-bijective conversion (see Morey et al. (2018)), the resulting dependency trees do not necessarily have single-rooted sentence sub-trees. To account for this, we apply the post-editing method proposed in Hayashi et al. (2016).

To use the newly generated dependency tree in the "Synthesizer" transformer model, we generate the self-attention matrix from the tree structure by following a standard Graph Theory approach (Xu et al., 2020). Head-dependent relations in the tree are represented as binary values (1 indicating a relation, 0 representing no connection) in the self-attention matrix, where each column of the matrix identifies the head and each row represents dependents. The root is considered head and dependent of itself, ensuring all row-sums to be 1. Figure 4 shows the inferred dependency-tree and the generated self-attention matrix for our running example.

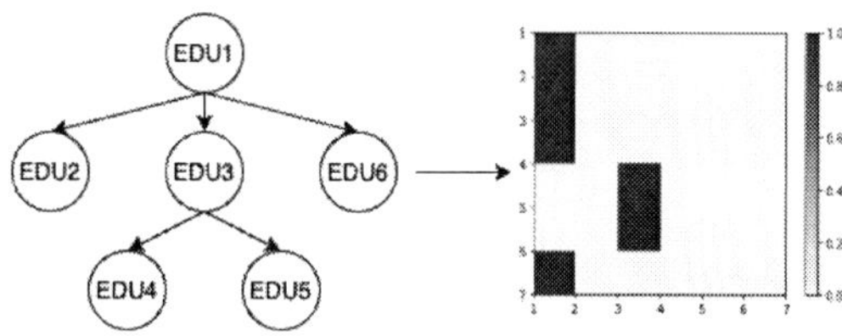

Figure 4: Dependency tree-to-matrix conversion.

4.2 Constituency-based Structure Attributes (C-Tree)

Arguably, there are aspects of the constituency tree-structure that may not be captured adequately by the corresponding dependency-tree. These aspects, defining the compositional structure of the document, may contain valuable information for the self-attention. In particular, the inter-EDU relationships encoded in the constituency tree can be used to define the relatedness of textual units, implying that the closer the units are in the discourse tree,

the more related they are, and the more attention they should pay to each other. Further inspired by the ideas of aggregation (Nguyen et al., 2020) and splitting (Shen et al., 2019), we define the attention between EDUs based on the depth of the constituency-tree on which they are assigned to the same constituent (Left in Figure 5).

More specifically, we compute the attention between every two nodes in the self-attention matrix as follows. Suppose the height of the constituency-tree is H, then for each level L of the tree, there is a binary matrix $M^L \in R^{l \times l}$ with $M^L_{ij} = 1$ if EDU i and EDU j are in the same constituent and $M^L_{ij} = 0$ otherwise. The final self-attention matrix A is defined as the normalized aggregate matrices of all levels: $A = normalize(\sum_L M^L)$

The resulting self-attention matrix A is exclusively based on the discourse structure-attribute, without taking the nuclearity into account, representing a rather different approach from the previously described one based on the dependency-tree.

4.3 Constituency-based Structure and Nuclearity Attributes (C-Tree w/Nuc)

With the previous sections focusing on either exploiting the nuclearity attribute, by converting the RST-style constituency tree into a dependency representation, or the constituency-tree structure itself, we now propose a third, hybrid approach, using both attributes to generate the self-attention matrix. Plausably, the combination could further enhance the quality of the self-attention matrix. The combined approach is closely related to the structural approach presented in section 4.2, but extends the binary self-attention matrix computation to the ternary case. At each level, $M^L_{ij} = 2$ if the node rooting the local sub-tree containing EDU i and EDU j is the nucleus in its relation[3], $M^L_{ij} = 1$ for the satellite case. Unchanged from section 4.2, if EDUs i and j are not sharing a common sub-tree on level L, $M^L_{ij} = 0$. For example, $M^1_{3:4,3:4} = 2$, as the sub-tree containing EDU 3 & 4 is the nucleus in it's relation with the sub-tree containing EDU 5.

4.4 Sentence-based Discourse Self-Attention

The natural granularity-level for a discourse-related summarization model is Elementary Discourse Units (EDUs). Besides using EDUs as our atomic elements, we also explore similar models on sentence-level, the more standard approach in the

---

[3]The weight of Nucleus and Satellite is set hard-coded, and will be tuned in the future.

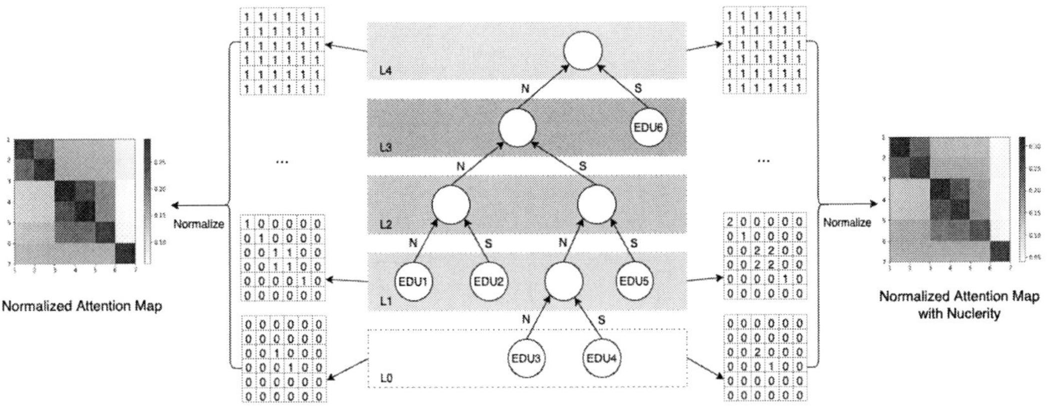

Figure 5: Constituency tree-to-matrix conversion. Left: Structure only, Right: Structure and Nuclearity

area of extractive summarization, using a BERT sentence-encoder instead of the previously used BERT EDU-encoder.

To obtain the respective sentence-level self-attention matrix, given the EDU-level self-attention matrix A^e of the three matrix-generation approaches defined above, we define an indicator-matrix $I \in R^{NS \times NE}$. NS and NE are thereby the number of sentences and EDUs in the document. $I_{ij} = 1$ if and only if EDU j belongs to sentence i. The sentence-level self-attention matrix A^s is then defined as

$$A^s = I A^e I^T$$

Generating the sentence-level self-attention matrices directly from the EDU-level self-attention matrices, instead of the tree-representation itself, avoids the problem of potentially leaky EDUs (Joty et al., 2015), as sentences with leaky EDUs (having naturally high attention values between them) will continue to be tightly connected.

5 Experiments

5.1 Experimental Setup

Dataset: We use the popular CNN/DM dataset (Nallapati et al., 2016), a standard corpus for extractive summarization. Key dimensions of the dataset with corresponding statistics are in Table 1. Based on the average number of units selected

#token	#EDU	#Sent	#EDU(O.)	#Sent(O.)
546	70.2	27.2	6.4	3.1

Table 1: Statistics of the CNNDM dataset. O. means the average number of units in the oracle

by the oracle[4] on EDU- and sentence-level, we de-

---

[4]The oracle summary contains the units greedily picked according to the ground-truth summary, which is built follow Kedzie et al. (2020).

fine the summarization task to choose the top 6 EDUs or the highest scoring 3 sentences, depending on the task granularity. Please further note that the original corpus does not contain any EDU-level markers (as presented in Table 1). The EDU segmentation process employed for EDU-related dataset dimensions is described below.

Discourse Augmentation: To obtain high-quality discourse representations for the documents in the CNN/DM training corpus we use the pre-trained versions of the top-performing discourse-segmenter (Wang et al., 2018) and -parser (Wang et al., 2017), reaching an F1-score of 94.3%, 86.0% (span) and 72.4% (nuclearity) respectively on the RST-DT dataset.[5] In line with previous work exploring the combination of discourse and summarization, we follow the "dependency-restriction" strategy proposed in Xu et al. (2020) to enhance the coherence and grammatical correctness of the summarization. Such strategy requires that all ancestors of a selected EDU within the same sentence should be recursively added to the final summary.

Hyper-Parameters: To stay consistent with previous work, we set the dimensions of the attention key(d_k), value(d_v) and query vector(d_q) to 64 for each head, and the inner dimension of the position-wise feed-forward layer (d_{inner}) to 3072. Similar to the synthesizer model (Tay et al., 2020), we only alter the attention part of the transformer model, which contains a small portion of the overall parameters. Additionally, we explore a more balanced, setting, with $d_v = d_k = d_q = 512$ and $d_{inner} = 512$ for all models. During training, we use a scheduled learning-rate ($lr = 1e - 2$) with standard warm-up steps for the Adam opti-

---

[5]We use the publicly available implementation by the original authors at //github.com/yizhongw/StageDP

Model	Rouge-1	Rouge-2	Rouge-L	# Heads	# Params(attn)	# Params
Lead6	37.99	15.56	34.08	-	-	-
Oracle	62.08	38.20	58.86	-	-	-
DiscoBERT(5 EDUs)	43.77	20.85	40.67	-	-	-
Default Models ($d_k = d_v = d_q = 64, d_{inner} = 3072$)						
Dot Product(8)	**41.02**	**18.78**	**37.96**	8	3.2M	12.7M
Dot Product(1)	**40.92**‡	**18.69**‡	**37.85**‡	1	0.4M	9.9M
Dense	40.70	18.65†	37.74†	1	1.5M	11.0M
Learned Random	40.24	18.28	37.32	1	0.7M	10.3M
Fixed Random	40.36	18.35	37.40	1	0.2M	9.7M
No attention	39.89	17.98	36.99	1	0.2M	9.7M
D-Tree	40.43	18.32	37.45	1	0.2M	9.7M
C-Tree	40.80†	18.56	37.74†	1	0.2M	9.7M
C-Tree w/Nuc	40.76	18.59†	37.73	1	0.2M	9.7M
Balanced Models ($d_k = d_v = d_q = 512, d_{inner} = 512$)						
Dot Product(8)	**40.95**	**18.52**	**37.78**	8	25.2M	27M
Dot Product(1)	40.64	18.33	37.54	1	3.2M	4.8M
Dense	**40.87**‡	**18.59**‡	**37.79**‡	1	2.9M	4.5M
Learned Random	40.32	18.22	37.31	1	2.1M	3.8M
Fixed Random	40.18	18.13	37.19	1	1.6M	3.2M
No attention	40.21	18.17	37.22	1	1.6M	3.2M
D-Tree	40.29	18.17	37.29	1	1.6M	3.2M
C-Tree	40.28	18.13	37.28	1	1.6M	3.2M
C-Tree w/Nuc	40.70	18.46† ‡	37.63	1	1.6M	3.2M

Table 2: Overall Performance of the models on the EDU level with the number of heads each layer, as well as the number of parameters to train in the attention module and in the whole model. The dashed line splits the models with **learnt attentions** and with **fixed attentions**. † indicates that corresponding result is **NOT** significantly worse than the best result of single-head models with $p < 0.01$ with the bootstrap test, and ‡ indicates that the corresponding result is **NOT** significantly worse than the result of the 8-head Dot Product with same setting.

mizer (Kingma and Ba, 2014), following the hyper-parameter setting in the original transformer paper (Vaswani et al., 2017).

Baseline Models: We compare our new, parameter-reduced Tree Attention approach against a variety of competitive baselines. Based on the standard Dot Product Attention, as used in the original transformer, we explore two settings: A single head and an 8-head Dot Product Attention. Inspired by the "Synthesizer"-framework, we further compare our approach against the Dense and Random Attention computation, as mentioned in Section 3. To better show the effect of different attention methods, we use a 'No Attention Model' as an additional baseline, in which each input can only attend to itself, i.e. $A = I$. Please note, (1) as our goal is to explore possible parameter reductions, we ensure that all heads contain similar dimensions across models. (2) The attention matrices in the "Fixed Random", "No Attention" and all three Tree Attention models (D-Tree, C-Tree and C-Tree w/Nuc) are fixed, while they are learned for other models.

5.2 Results and Analysis

We present and discuss three sets of experimental results. First, the natural task for discourse-related extractive summarization on EDU-level. Second, the most common task of extractive summarization on sentence-level and, finally, further experiments regarding the low resource case.

Tables 2 and 3 show our experimental results on EDU and Sentence level, respectively. Each row thereby contains the Rouge-1, -2 and -L scores of the model, along with the number of self-attention heads and the amount of trainable parameters in the attention module and in the complete model[6]. For readability, the results in either table are divided into three sub-tables. The first sub-table contains the commonly used Lead-baseline (Lead6 on EDU level and Lead3 on sentence level), along with the Oracle, representing the performance upper-bound, and the current state-of-the-art models (DiscoBERT (Xu et al., 2020) on EDU level, BERT-SUM (Liu and Lapata, 2019) on sentence level). Please note, both SOTA models finetune BERT as a token-based document encoder, to learn additional cross-unit information of tokens. However, this requires additional training resources (as the BERT model itself contains 108M learnable parameters). Furthermore, both SOTA models use

---

[6]The BERT EDU/sentence encoder is fixed and the parameters therefore not included.

Model	Rouge-1	Rouge-2	Rouge-L	# Heads	# Params(attn)	# Params
Lead3	40.30	17.52	36.54	-	-	-
Oracle	56.04	33.10	52.29	-	-	-
BERTSUM(w/Tri-Block)	43.25	20.24	39.63	-	-	118M
Default Models ($d_k = d_v = d_q = 64$, $d_{inner} = 3072$)						
Dot Product(8)	**41.82**	**19.18**	**38.18**	8	3.2M	12.7M
Dot Product(1)	**41.71‡**	**19.08‡**	**38.08‡**	1	0.4M	9.9M
Dense	41.69†	19.07‡ †	38.08‡ †	1	1.5M	11.0M
Learned Random	41.21	18.86	37.67	1	0.7M	10.3M
Fixed Random	41.27	18.91	37.72	1	0.2M	9.7M
No attention	40.97	18.64	37.44	1	0.2M	9.7M
D-Tree	41.44	18.87	37.83	1	0.2M	9.7M
C-Tree	41.64†	19.04†	38.03†	1	0.2M	9.7M
C-Tree w/Nuc	41.64†	19.05†	38.03†	1	0.2M	9.7M
Balanced Models ($d_k = d_v = d_q = 512$, $d_{inner} = 512$)						
Dot Product(8)	41.45	18.88	37.84	8	25.2M	27M
Dot Product(1)	41.51	18.95	37.94	1	3.2M	4.8M
Dense	41.63†	19.05†	38.01†	1	2.9M	4.5M
Learned Random	41.26	18.83	37.70	1	2.1M	3.7M
Fixed Random	41.17	18.81	37.61	1	1.6M	3.2M
No attention	41.25	18.75	37.68	1	1.6M	3.2M
D-Tree	41.31	18.80	37.75	1	1.6M	3.2M
C-Tree	**41.68**	**19.11**	**38.12**	1	1.6M	3.2M
C-Tree w/Nuc	41.64†	19.02†	38.06†	1	1.6M	3.2M

Table 3: Overall Performance of the models on the sentence level. † represents that it is **NOT** significantly worse than the best result of the single-head models with $p < 0.01$ with the bootstrap test, and ‡ indicates that the corresponding result is **NOT** significantly worse than the result of 8-head Dot Product with same setting (‡ for Default Models only).

'Trigram-Blocking', which has been shown to be able to greatly improve summarization results (Liu, 2019). The second sub-table shows our experimental results using the default parameter setting, as proposed in the original transformer, and the last sub-table presents the results when using a balanced parameter setting. Within each sub-table, we further differentiate models by the number of heads, either containing a single attention head or the original 8-head self-attention. As each document only contains a single discourse tree, there is only one fixed self-attention matrix for each document, making the single-head model equivalent to the multi-head approach.

EDU Level Experiments: are shown in Table 2. When comparing the single head models using the default setting (second sub-table), it appears that both, C-Tree and C-Tree w/Nuc achieve competitive performance with the single head Dot Product model, despite the Dot product using twice as many parameters in the attention module ($0.4M$ vs. $0.2M$). This is an important advantage because, even though the non attention related parameters in the complete model outweigh the number of attention parameters in this setting, the attention however resembles the core component of the transformer model, and so saving attention parameters is arguably more critical. In addition, the difference would become large with the increment of the number of heads. Furthermore, when comparing models with fixed attention or no attention, the effect of the attention module becomes clear, showing superior performance of the C-Tree and C-Tree /w Nuc approaches, indicating that discourse structure can indeed help for the task of extractive summarization. In contrast, the D-Tree inspired self-attention does not perform as well. The drop in performance when using this tree-attention might be caused by the rather strict, binary attention computation, potentially pruning too much valuable discourse information. Examining the models with learnt attentions, we observe that the Dense model reduces the number of parameters compared to the best performing 8-head Dot Product, however, still contains far more parameters than the single-head Dot Product. Despite the large difference in the number of parameters, the single-head Dot Product Attention performs comparable to the Dense model, suggesting the necessity to synthesize the Dense attention (see (Tay et al., 2020)). Regarding the Balanced model (bottom sub-table), we put additional emphasis on the attention component, showing trends when using larger attention computation modules. The results in this sub-table suggest that the benefits of our tree attention models are improving over-proportionally for more balanced models, with the C-tree /w Nuc even outperforming the single-head Dot Product and achieving competitive performance to the 8-head Dot Product model, which contains an order of magnitude more parameters in this setting.

Sentence Level Experiments: Our sentence level experiments, presented in Table 3, are mostly akin to the EDU level experiments. However, a relative performance improvement of fixed attention models compared to learned attention approaches can be observed, leading to a smaller performance gap on sentence level. We believe that this over-proportional improvement might be due to the position bias on sentence level, which tends to be larger than on EDU level, generally making the sentence level task easier to learn. In line with this trend, we also observe that the difference between the Lead-baseline (40.30/17.53/36.54) and the Oracle (56.04/33.10/52.29) on sentence level is relatively small when compared to the EDU level Lead-baseline(37.99/15.56/34.08) and Oracle(62.08/38.20/58.86). As a result, the fixed tree attention models are statistically equivalent to the learned single-head Dot Product in the default sentence level setting, and significantly outperform the 8-head Dot Product model in the balanced setting.

Low Resource Experiments: Complementing our previous experiments, showing consistently competitive results of the parameter-sparse models using tree priors, we further explore the robustness of our tree self-attention methods in additional low resource experiments on EDU level. Therefore, we randomly generate 5 small subsets of the training dataset, each containing $1,000$ datapoints, training the same models as shown in Tables 2 and 3 on each subset. However, contrasting our initial expectation, the tree-inspired C-Tree w/Nuc model only improves the performance on the low-ressource experiments under the balanced setting, with no significant improvements under the default setting.

Overall: Comparing the results in Tables 2 and 3, it becomes obvious that the sentence level models are consistently better than the EDU level models, despite the opposite trend holding between sentence Oracle and EDU Oracle, as well as the respective SOTA models. One possible reason for this result is that the BERT model is originally trained on the sentences, which might potentially impair the subsentential (EDU) representation generation ability of the model.

Furthermore, when comparing the single head and 8 head Dot Product models in both tables and in both settings, we find that the improvement gains of adding additional heads is rather limited, even impairing the performance in the balanced setting on sentence level. We therefore believe that the balance between the performance and the number of parameters is worth of further exploration for the task of extractive summarizarion.

6 Conclusion and Future Work

We extend and adapt the "Synthesizer" framework for extractive summarization by proposing a new tree self-attention method, based on RST-style consitituency and dependency trees. In our experiments, we show that the performance of the tree self-attention is significantly better than other fixed attention models, while being competitive to the single-head standard dot product self-attention in the transformer model on both, the EDU-level and sentence-level extractive summarization task. Furthermore, our tree attention is better than the 8-head dot product in the balanced setting. Besides these general results, we further investigate low-resource scenarios, where our parameter-light approaches are assumed to be especially useful. However, contrary to this expectation, they do not seem to be more stable and robust than other solutions. In addition, we also find that the multi-head Dot product model is not always significantly better than the single-head approach. This, combined with the previous finding, suggest that more research is needed on the balance between the number of parameter and the performance of the summarization model.

In the future, we plan to explore ways to also incorporate rhetorical relations into self-attention, in addition to discourse structure and nuclearity. Further, we want to replace the hard-coded weight trade-off between Nucleus and Satellite in the C-Tree w/Nuc approach, using instead the confidence score from the discourse parser as the weight. Finally, since the current two-level encoder performs generally worse than a single token-based encoder (e.g. BERTSUM(Liu and Lapata, 2019)), we intend to explore tree self-attention in combination with the BERTSUM model.

Acknowledgments

We thank reviewers and the UBC-NLP group for their insightful comments. This research was supported by the Language & Speech Innovation Lab of Cloud BU, Huawei Technologies Co., Ltd.

References

Dzmitry Bahdanau, Kyunghyun Cho, and Yoshua Bengio. 2014. Neural machine translation by jointly learning to align and translate. *arXiv preprint arXiv:1409.0473*.

Lynn Carlson, Mary Ellen Okurowski, and Daniel Marcu. 2002. *RST discourse treebank*. Linguistic Data Consortium, University of Pennsylvania.

Arman Cohan, Franck Dernoncourt, Doo Soon Kim, Trung Bui, Seokhwan Kim, Walter Chang, and Nazli Goharian. 2018. A discourse-aware attention model for abstractive summarization of long documents. *NAACL HLT 2018 - 2018 Conference of the North American Chapter of the Association for Computational Linguistics: Human Language Technologies - Proceedings of the Conference*, 2:615–621.

Jacob Devlin, Ming-Wei Chang, Kenton Lee, and Kristina Toutanova. 2019. BERT: Pre-training of deep bidirectional transformers for language understanding. In *Proceedings of the 2019 Conference of the North American Chapter of the Association for Computational Linguistics: Human Language Technologies, Volume 1 (Long and Short Papers)*, pages 4171–4186, Minneapolis, Minnesota. Association for Computational Linguistics.

Katsuhiko Hayashi, Tsutomu Hirao, and Masaaki Nagata. 2016. Empirical comparison of dependency conversions for rst discourse trees. In *Proceedings of the 17th Annual Meeting of the Special Interest Group on Discourse and Dialogue*, pages 128–136.

Tsutomu Hirao, Yasuhisa Yoshida, Masaaki Nishino, Norihito Yasuda, and Masaaki Nagata. 2013. Single-Document Summarization as a Tree Knapsack Problem. Technical report.

Patrick Huber and Giuseppe Carenini. 2019. Predicting discourse structure using distant supervision from sentiment. In *Proceedings of the 2019 Conference on Empirical Methods in Natural Language Processing and the 9th International Joint Conference on Natural Language Processing (EMNLP-IJCNLP)*, pages 2306–2316.

Patrick Huber and Giuseppe Carenini. 2020. Mega rst discourse treebanks with structure and nuclearity from scalable distant sentiment supervision. In *Proceedings of the 2020 Conference on Empirical Methods in Natural Language Processing*.

Shafiq Joty, Giuseppe Carenini, and Raymond T Ng. 2015. Codra: A novel discriminative framework for rhetorical analysis. *Computational Linguistics*, 41(3):385–435.

Chris Kedzie, Kathleen McKeown, and Hal Daumé. 2020. Content selection in deep learning models of summarization. *Proceedings of the 2018 Conference on Empirical Methods in Natural Language Processing, EMNLP 2018*, pages 1818–1828.

Yuta Kikuchi, Tsutomu Hirao, Hiroya Takamura, Manabu Okumura, and Masaaki Nagata. 2014. Single document summarization based on nested tree structure. *52nd Annual Meeting of the Association for Computational Linguistics, ACL 2014 - Proceedings of the Conference*, 2:315–320.

Diederik P Kingma and Jimmy Ba. 2014. Adam: A method for stochastic optimization. *arXiv preprint arXiv:1412.6980*.

Olga Kovaleva, Alexey Romanov, Anna Rogers, and Anna Rumshisky. 2019. Revealing the dark secrets of BERT. In *Proceedings of the 2019 Conference on Empirical Methods in Natural Language Processing and the 9th International Joint Conference on Natural Language Processing (EMNLP-IJCNLP)*, pages 4365–4374, Hong Kong, China. Association for Computational Linguistics.

Yang Liu. 2019. Fine-tune BERT for extractive summarization. *CoRR*, abs/1903.10318.

Yang Liu and Mirella Lapata. 2019. Text Summarization with Pretrained Encoders. *EMNLP-IJCNLP 2019 - 2019 Conference on Empirical Methods in Natural Language Processing and 9th International Joint Conference on Natural Language Processing, Proceedings of the Conference*, pages 3730–3740.

Minh-Thang Luong, Hieu Pham, and Christopher D Manning. 2015. Effective approaches to attention-based neural machine translation. *arXiv preprint arXiv:1508.04025*.

William C. Mann and Sandra A. Thompson. 1988. Rhetorical Structure Theory: Toward a functional theory of text organization.

Daniel Marcu. 1999. Discourse Trees are Good Indicators of Importance in Text. *Advances in Automatic Text Summarization*, pages 123–136.

Paul Michel, Omer Levy, and Graham Neubig. 2019. Are sixteen heads really better than one? In H. Wallach, H. Larochelle, A. Beygelzimer, F. dAlché-Buc, E. Fox, and R. Garnett, editors, *Advances in Neural Information Processing Systems 32*, pages 14014–14024. Curran Associates, Inc.

Mathieu Morey, Philippe Muller, and Nicholas Asher. 2018. A dependency perspective on rst discourse parsing and evaluation. *Computational Linguistics*, 44(2):197–235.

Ramesh Nallapati, Bowen Zhou, Cicero dos Santos, Çağlar Gulçehre, and Bing Xiang. 2016. Abstractive text summarization using sequence-to-sequence RNNs and beyond. In *Proceedings of The 20th SIGNLL Conference on Computational Natural Language Learning*, pages 280–290, Berlin, Germany. Association for Computational Linguistics.

Xuan-Phi Nguyen, Shafiq Joty, Steven C. H. Hoi, and Richard Socher. 2020. Tree-structured Attention with Hierarchical Accumulation. pages 1–15.

Rashmi Prasad, Nikhil Dinesh, Alan Lee, Eleni Miltsakaki, Livio Robaldo, Aravind Joshi, and Bonnie Webber. 2008. The penn discourse treebank 2.0. *LREC*.

Alessandro Raganato, Yves Scherrer, and Jörg Tiedemann. 2020. Fixed Encoder Self-Attention Patterns in Transformer-Based Machine Translation.

Yikang Shen, Shawn Tan, Alessandro Sordoni, and Aaron Courville. 2019. Ordered neurons: Integrating tree structures into recurrent neural networks. *7th International Conference on Learning Representations, ICLR 2019*, pages 1–14.

Yi Tay, Dara Bahri, Donald Metzler, Da-Cheng Juan, Zhe Zhao, and Che Zheng. 2020. Synthesizer: Rethinking self-attention in transformer models.

Ashish Vaswani, Noam Shazeer, Niki Parmar, Jakob Uszkoreit, Llion Jones, Aidan N. Gomez, Łukasz Kaiser, and Illia Polosukhin. 2017. Attention is all you need. *Advances in Neural Information Processing Systems*, 2017-Decem(Nips):5999–6009.

Jesse Vig and Yonatan Belinkov. 2019. Analyzing the structure of attention in a transformer language model. In *Proceedings of the 2019 ACL Workshop BlackboxNLP: Analyzing and Interpreting Neural Networks for NLP*, pages 63–76, Florence, Italy. Association for Computational Linguistics.

Yizhong Wang, Sujian Li, and Houfeng Wang. 2017. A two-stage parsing method for text-level discourse analysis. In *Proceedings of the 55th Annual Meeting of the Association for Computational Linguistics (Volume 2: Short Papers)*, pages 184–188.

Yizhong Wang, Sujian Li, and Jingfeng Yang. 2018. Toward fast and accurate neural discourse segmentation. *arXiv preprint arXiv:1808.09147*.

Wen Xiao and Giuseppe Carenini. 2019. Extractive summarization of long documents by combining global and local context. In *Proceedings of the 2019 Conference on Empirical Methods in Natural Language Processing and the 9th International Joint Conference on Natural Language Processing (EMNLP-IJCNLP)*, pages 3011–3021, Hong Kong, China. Association for Computational Linguistics.

Jiacheng Xu, Zhe Gan, Yu Cheng, and Jingjing Liu. 2020. Discourse-aware neural extractive text summarization. In *Proceedings of the 58th Annual Meeting of the Association for Computational Linguistics*, pages 5021–5031, Online. Association for Computational Linguistics.

Extending Implicit Discourse Relation Recognition to the PDTB-3

Li Liang[1]   **Zheng Zhao[2]**   **Bonnie Webber[2]**

[1]Dept of Linguistics and English Language, University of Edinburgh
[2]School of Informatics, University of Edinburgh
`L.Liang-7@sms.ed.ac.uk`
`zheng.zhao@ed.ac.uk` `bonnie@inf.ed.ac.uk`

Abstract

The PDTB-3 contains many more implicit discourse relations than the previous PDTB-2. This is in part because implicit relations have now been annotated *within* sentences as well as *between* them. In addition, some now co-occur with explicit discourse relations, instead of standing on their own. Here we show that while this can complicate the problem of identifying the *location* of implicit discourse relations, it can in turn simplify the problem of identifying their *senses*. We present data to support this claim, as well as methods that can serve as a non-trivial baseline for future state-of-the-art recognizers for implicit discourse relations.

1 Introduction

Most readers will be familiar with the PDTB-2 (Prasad et al., 2008). At the time of its creation, it was the largest public repository of annotated discourse relations (over 43K), including over 18.4K signalled by explicit discourse connectives (coordinating or subordinating conjunctions, or discourse adverbials). In the corpus, discourse relations comprise two arguments labelled *Arg1* and **Arg2**, with each relation anchored by either an explicit discourse connective or adjacency. In the latter case, annotators inserted one or more *implicit connectives* to signal the sense(s) they inferred to hold between the arguments. The size and availability of the PDTB-2 spawned work on *shallow discourse parsing*, as in the 2015 and 2016 CoNLL shared tasks (Xue et al., 2015, 2016).

With the release of the PDTB-3[1], there are now ~12.5K additional intra-sentential relations annotated (i.e., relations that lie wholly within the projection of a top-level S-node) and ~1K additional inter-sentential relations (Webber et al., 2019).

Work on *shallow discourse parsing* (including the CoNLL shared tasks, as well as (Bai and Zhao, 2018; Dai and Huang, 2018; Rutherford et al., 2017; Shi and Demberg, 2017)) consistently shows that recognizing and sense labelling implicit discourse relations poses more of a challenge than doing so for explicit discourse relations. Hence, implicit relations are the focus of the current work.

But there is another reason as well: Work on the PDTB-2 has assumed (correctly) that non-explicit discourse relations (i.e., implicit relations, *AltLex relations* (Prasad et al., 2010) and entity relations) only hold between *adjacent sentences* as they did in the PDTB-2, so that a sentence boundary is the only position that needs to be checked for the presence of a non-explicit relation. The difficult problem lay in assigning sense-labels to implicit relations.

In Section 2, we show that, with the PDTB-3, this is no longer the case because non-explicit relations can hold *within* sentences as well as *between* them. This in turn motivates a new approach to handle implicit discourse relations in shallow discourse parsing, involving both finding them as well as identifying their senses (Section 3). After showing that the sense-distribution of implicit relations *within* sentences differs from that *between* them (cf. Section 4), we argue that one should be able to take advantage of this fact in sense-labelling these relations.[2] Section 5 describes two different ways of doing so, along with a way of dealing with another difference in sense distribution — that of implicit relations that co-occur with explicit relations and implicit relations that do not. While the particular methods used here for sense-labelling may not advance the state-of-the-art, it is the way we use them

---

[1]`https://catalog.ldc.upenn.edu/LDC2019T05`

[2]Some previous approaches to discourse parsing have also distinguished relations that occur within a sentence from those that occur across sentences (Joty et al., 2013, 2015), but it was not felt to be needed in the PDTB-2, where implicit relations only appeared across sentences.

Proceedings of the First Workshop on Computational Approaches to Discourse, pages 135–147
Online, November 20, 2020. ©2020 Association for Computational Linguistics
https://doi.org/10.18653/v1/P17

that should deliver a new baseline for recognizing a fuller range of implicit relations and contribute to the next generation of shallow discourse parsers.[3]

2 Discourse Annotation in PDTB-3

Discourse annotation in the PDTB-3 differs from that in the PDTB-2 in two major ways: (1) many more discourse relations are annotated *within* sentences, and (2) there are changes in the sense hierarchy used in annotating them. While only the first requires changes to shallow discourse parsing, presenting changes to the senses used in annotating relations will allow us to show differences in the distribution of senses associated with different types of implicit discourse relations.

2.1 Additional Annotation in PDTB-3

It was a consequence of the way that the PDTB-2 was annotated, that there were over twice as many discourse relations annotated across sentences than within them. The former were either explicit relations associated with discourse adverbials or sentence-initial coordinating conjunctions[4], or implicit relations between paragraph-internal adjacent sentences not otherwise linked by a discourse connective. Within sentences, only annotated were explicit relations associated with subordinating conjunctions, sentence-internal coordinating conjunctions, and discourse adverbials (both of whose arguments were in the same sentence). So it should not be surprising that there were many more inter-sentential relations than intra-sentential relations in the PDTB-2.

In contrast, of the over 13K additional discourse relations annotated in the PDTB-3, over 95% of them occur *within* individual sentences. Of the new relations, 5780 are implicit, some standing alone (like the implicit relations between sentences), with others co-occuring with an explicit discourse relation. Within a sentence, implicit relations occur at the boundaries of syntactic forms — for example, at the boundary between a *free adjunct* and its matrix clause (Ex. 1), or at the boundary between a *to-clause* and its matrix clause (Ex. 2), or between two punctuation-marked conjuncts (Ex. 3).

(1) *Treasury bonds got off to a strong start,* **advancing modestly during overnight trading on foreign markets**. Conn=*specifically* (ARG2-AS-DETAIL) [wsj_0351]

(2) *After a bad start, Treasury bonds were buoyed by a late burst of buying,* **to end modestly higher**. Conn=*therefore* (RESULT) [wsj_0400]

(3) Father McKenna moves through the house *praying in Latin,* **urging the demon to split**. (CONJUNCTION) [wsj_0413]

Because implicit relations within sentences don't all occur at a single, well-defined position, this adds to the problems of shallow discourse parsing.

In addition to stand-alone implicits in the PDTB-3, annotators were allowed to indicate implicit relations that co-occur with explicit relations (Rohde et al., 2017, 2018), as a way of indicating a relation that did not derive from the explicit connective, but rather from what the annotator inferred from the arguments themselves, as in Ex. 4–6:

(4) We've got to *get out of the Detroit mentality* **and** Implicit=instead **be part of the world mentality,** declares Charles M. Jordan, GM's vice president for design . . . [wsj_0956] (EXPANSION.CONJUNCTION, EXPANSION.SUBSTITUTION.ARG2-AS-SUBST)

(5) . . . Exxon Corp. *built the plant* **but** (Implicit=then) **closed it in 1985.** [wsj_1748] (COMPARISON.CONCESSION.ARG2-AS-DENIER, TEMPORAL.ASYNCHRONOUS.PRECEDENCE)

(6) . . . which [i.e., the line item veto] would enable him *to kill individual items in a big spending bill* **without** (Implicit=however) **having to kill the entire bill.** [wsj_1133] (EXPANSION.MANNER.ARG2-AS-MANNER, COMPARISON.CONCESSION.ARG2-AS-DENIER)

In Ex. 4, the annotators indicated that they inferred ARG2-AS-SUBST from the pair of arguments conjoined with *and*. The annotators took *and* itself to convey only that its arguments played the same role with respect to the prior text. It is the arguments themselves that led them to conclude that the second conjunct is meant to substitute for the first.

Similarly, in Ex. 5, the annotators indicated that they inferred the temporal relation PRECEDENCE from the pair of arguments conjoined with *but*. The annotators took *but* itself to convey CONCESSION. It is the arguments themselves that led the annotators to conclude that the second conjunct follows the first in time.

Finally, in Ex. 6, the annotators indicated that they inferred a CONCESSION relation from the pair of arguments linked by *without*. The annotators took *without* itself (like its positive version *with*) to

---

[3]It would not make sense to have separate processors for explicit discourse relations, as the decision process takes account of the discourse connective, thereby already learning whether the arguments are likely to occur across vs. within sentences.

[4]Despite what people may have been taught, there are over 2100 tokens of sentence-initial "But" in the Penn *WSJ* corpus and over 660 tokens of sentence-initial "And".

convey MANNER. It is only the arguments that led them to conclude that Arg2 denies an expectation raised by Arg1.

In the PDTB-3, when two relations co-occur, they are explicitly **linked** through a shared index. The consequence for shallow discourse parsing is that explicit relations now need to be checked for co-occurence with an implicit relation.

2.2 Changes to the Sense Hierarchy

The sense hierarchy used in annotating the PDTB-3 differs from that used in annotating the PDTB-2 in three ways:

1. Rare and/or difficult to annotate senses were dropped, as with the different types of conditional senses;

2. Sense relations at Level-3 now only encode *directionality* — for example, distinguishing ARG1-AS-SUBST (Ex. 7) from ARG2-AS-SUBST (Ex. 8)

3. New senses were added that were found to be needed for annotating relations within sentences.

(7) ARG1-AS-SUBST: <u>instead of</u> **featuring a major East Coast team against a West Coast team,** *it pitted the Los Angeles Dodgers against the losing Oakland A's* [wsj_0443]

(8) He *could develop the beach through a trust,* **but** <u>instead</u> **is trying have his grandson become a naturalized Mexican so his family gains direct control.** [wsj_0300]

More about the senses used in annotating the PDTB-3 can be found in Webber et al. (2019). Senses are relevant to this discussion of implicit relations in shallow discourse parsing because (as set out in Section 4) implicit relations have been found to have different sense distributions depending on where they occur.

2.3 Stand-off annotation in the PDTB-3

Both the PDTB-2 and PDTB-3 use stand-off annotation. What is relevant with respect to the experiments we report here, is what information is explicit in the annotation, as opposed to having to be computed. This information includes (1) the type of the relation (Explicit, Implicit, AltLex, AltLexC, Entity, Hypophora, NoRel); (2) the byte spans of the two arguments of the relation; and (3) the explicit index (aka *link*) of relations that co-occur by virtue of sharing the same or nearly

the same arguments. The full field structure of discourse relations is set out in Section 8 of Webber et al. (2019). What has to be recovered from the argument spans and the span of the projection of the top node in each sentence-level parse tree is whether a relation occurs wholly within a single sentence or involves multiple sentences.

3 Basic Model Architecture

The sense classifiers for implicit relations used in this paper are based on a Basic Model whose properties reflect consideration of data size and the interaction between lexical information and structural information. (A full description of the Basic Model is given in Appendix A.)

The architecture of Basic Model is shown in Figure 1. It consists of two LSTMs (Hochreiter and Schmidhuber, 1997) and max-pooling layers, a hidden layer, a dense layer, and a softmax layer. Inputs to the model consist of pairs of discourse arguments, each represented as a sequence of word vectors. The output is a probability distribution of the senses between the discourse argument spans. The two sequences of word vectors are encoded by LSTMs in order to capture positional information within the sequential structure. Max-pooling on the output of the LSTMs is used to compose meaning and reduce parameters for the model, as it has been proven effective in Conneau et al. (2017). Modeling the interaction between discourse arguments follows Rutherford and Xue (2016), who argue that discourse relations can only be determined by jointly analyzing the arguments. In addition, Rutherford et al. (2017) observed the influence of different configurations on the performance of the model for the implicit sense classification task, suggesting an interaction between the lexical information in word vectors and the structural information encoded in the model itself. We follow them in adopting a 300-dimension word2vec (Mikolov et al., 2013b) word embedding and hidden size of 100 for the Basic Model.

4 Differences in the distribution of sense relations

To argue for separating the recognition of intra-sentential implicits from inter-sentential implicits, and the recognition of linked implicits from stand-alone implicits, we show how their sense distributions are different.

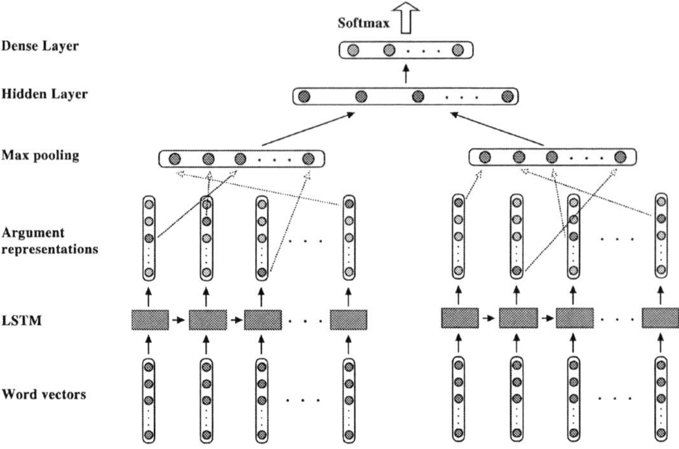

Figure 1: The overall model architecture for implicit sense classification

Table 1 compares the distribution of inter-sentential and intra-sentential implicit relations with respect to the PDTB-3's Level-2 sense labels, along with the proportion of each label to the total inter-sentential and intra-sentential implicit relations. Besides differences in frequency — for example, relations expressing PURPOSE constitute 21.76% of intra-sentential implicit relations, while only 0.12% of inter-sentential implicits, while relations expressing INSTANTIATION constitute 8.89% of inter-sentential implicits, while only 1.4% of intra-sentential implicits — the senses of inter-sentential implicits are more unequally distributed. That is, three senses — CONTINGENCY.CAUSE, EXPANSION.CONJUNCTION and LEVEL-OF-DETAIL cover 67.08% of the inter-sentential implicits. In contrast, except for CONTINGENCY.CAUSE and PURPOSE, most of the other intra-sentential implicits are more evenly distributed. As often happens with training on an imbalanced distribution, the unequal distribution of inter-sentential relations can lead the model to predict the majority class, ignoring minority classes.

As for the 1753 implicits that co-occur with explicit relations, Table 2 shows that their sense distribution differs sharply from that of stand-alone implicit relations. For example, over 70% convey either CAUSE or ASYNCHRONOUS, while this holds of only 28.7% of stand-alone implicit relations. As such, linked implicits should be more predictable than stand-alone implicit relations.

5 Inter- and intra-sentential Implicits

Differences in the distribution of implicit relations *within* sentences and *across* sentences suggest that we exploit this difference in sense-labelling implicit relations. In this section, we first assume that we know where implicit relations are located within a sentence, so that we can simply consider their arguments. We then present work we have done towards relaxing this assumption.

Task 1: Consider the location of implicit relations in classification. There are different ways to take the location of implicit relations into consideration. Here we present two models, **Model 1** (Section 5.2) and **Model 2** (Section 5.3), both based on the basic model architecture described in Section 3. We compare them with the **Basic Model**, which uses the same classifier on all tokens. We compare their performance not just using the standard training-development-test split, where the ratio of inter- to intra-sentential implicits in the training set, WSJ section 2-21, is 12787:5014. In addition, we follow Shi and Demberg (2017), who argue that evaluation through cross-validation is more predictive, given the wide variation in texts that appear in different sections of the Penn *Wall Street Journal* corpus. The average ratio of inter- to intra-sentential implicits in training sets of cross-validation is 12747:4992. The scores of 3 models are weighted by the proportion of inter- and intra-sentential tokens in the test set.

Task 2: Identify the location of implicit relations. To reduce the dependency on the gold standard annotations of where implicit discourse re-

		inter-sentential	intra-sentential
Comparison	Concession	1355 (8.70%)	136 (2.19%)
	Concession+SpeechAct	7 (0.04%)	3 (0.05%)
	Contrast	700 (4.50%)	156 (2.51%)
	Similarity	14 (0.09%)	14 (0.23%)
Contingency	Cause	4153 (26.67%)	1613 (25.97%)
	Cause+SpeechAct	21 (0.13%)	1 (0.02%)
	Cause+Belief	105 (0.67%)	94 (1.51%)
	Condition	1 (0.01%)	198 (3.19%)
	Condition+SpeechAct	1 (0.01%)	1 (0.02%)
	Purpose	19 (0.12%)	1351 (21.76%)
Expansion	Conjunction	3648 (23.43%)	733 (11.80%)
	Disjunction	9 (0.06%)	21 (0.34%)
	Equivalence	286 (1.84%)	48 (0.77%)
	Exception	4 (0.03%)	1 (0.02%)
	Instantiation	1385 (8.89%)	87 (1.40%)
	Level-of-detail	2644 (16.98%)	589 (9.48%)
	Manner	4 (0.03%)	223 (3.59%)
	Substitution	221 (1.42%)	145 (2.33%)
Temporal	Asynchronous	647 (4.15%)	608 (9.79%)
	Synchronous	348 (2.23%)	188 (3.03%)
total		15572	6210

Table 1: Distribution of inter-sentential/intra-sentential implicit relations among Level 2 labels and the proportion of each label with respect to inter-sentential/intra-sentential implicit relations

lations hold within sentences, two recognizers to identify implicit relations and find argument spans are provided. The first recognizer (Section 5.4) takes syntactic features to identify sentences that contain intra-sentential relations. The second recognizer (Section 5.5) exploits the properties that some explicit relations are linked with implicit relations, checking the explicit relations for co-occurrence with implicit relations to obtain the shared arguments.

5.1 Basic Model

The Basic Model uses the same classifier on all tokens. Since we know which tokens are inter-sentential and which are intra-sentential, we can compare how well the Basic Model does on each. To compute the F_1 scores for the overall performance of the model, the scores of the model are combined, weighted by the proportion of inter- or intra-sentential tokens in the test set. This is shown on the first line of Table 3, elaborated in the confusion matrix shown in Figure 2. A Chi-squared test on the results show the performance of the Basic Model appears to depend to a statistically significant extent on whether the sense appears inter- or intra-sententially (p=1.50e-03).

5.2 Model 1

Model architecture: The idea behind Model 1 is to separate the classification task into intra-sentential and inter-sentential implicit sense clas-sification, with separate classifiers for each. The model architecture and configuration of each classifier are the same as in the Basic Model (Section 3). We expect each classifier to capture different sense distributions of intra-sentential or inter-sentential implicits.

Training and evaluation: Based on their argument spans and the spans associated with each sentence in a file, tokens can be labeled as inter-sentential or intra-sentential. For the standard training-development-test framework, the tokens are allocated into separate inter-sentential/intra-sentential training, development, and test sets. The inter-sentential training set is used in training the inter-sentential implicit sense classifier, and similarly for intra-sentential classification. Test set tokens labeled as inter-sentential or intra-sentential are fed into the appropriate classifier.

Results: The second line of Table 3 presents F_1 scores for Model 1 evaluated on the main evaluation test set and by cross-validation. It shows that Model 1 improves on the Basic Model in predicting intra-sentential implicit relations. The performance of the model significantly depends on the location of relations (p = 2.41e-09). The confusion matrix for Model 1[5] (cf. Figure 2) shows that labels with a relatively larger sample size in each set are predicted more often, includ-

---

[5]combining results of the inter-sentential and intra-sentential classifiers

		stand-alone		linked	
Comparison	Concession	1401	(6.99%)	90	(5.13%)
	Concession+SpeechAct	10	(0.05%)	0	(0.00%)
	Contrast	795	(3.97%)	61	(3.48%)
	Similarity	18	(0.09%)	10	(0.57%)
Contingency	Cause	4943	(24.68%)	823	(46.95%)
	Cause+SpeechAct	22	(0.11%)	0	(0.00%)
	Cause+Belief	164	(0.82%)	35	(2.00%)
	Condition	199	(0.99%)	0	(0.00%)
	Condition+SpeechAct	2	(0.01%)	0	(0.00%)
	Purpose	1367	(6.83%)	3	(0.17%)
Expansion	Conjunction	4360	(21.77%)	21	(1.20%)
	Disjunction	30	(0.15%)	0	(0.00%)
	Equivalence	326	(16.28%)	8	(0.46%)
	Exception	4	(0.02%)	1	(0.06%)
	Instantiation	1456	(7.27%)	16	(0.91%)
	Level-of-detail	3172	(15.84%)	61	(3.48%)
	Manner	173	(0.86%)	54	(3.08%)
	Substitution	276	(1.38%)	90	(5.13%)
Temporal	Asynchronous	800	(3.99%)	455	(25.96%)
	Synchronous	511	(2.55%)	25	(1.43%)
total		20029		1753	

Table 2: Distribution of linked and stand-alone implicit relations among Level 2 labels and the proportion of each label with respect to the total linked/stand-alone implicit relations

	Main evaluation metric			Cross
	inter-sentential	intra-sentential	overall	validation
Basic model	35.791	47.154	38.608	41.463
Model 1	34.973	56.666	40.222	**43.418**
Model 2	37.701	50.410	**40.827**	42.174

Table 3: F_1 scores of the different models on inter-sentential and intra-sentential implicit relation at Level 2.

ing CONTINGENCY.PURPOSE (frequent in intra-sentential implicits), EXPANSION.CONJUNCTION (frequent in inter-sentential implicits) and CONTINGENCY.CAUSE (frequent in both). The confusion matrix also shows that less frequent senses are confused with these frequent labels more often. Model 1 also reduces the ignorance problem of the Basic Model, in that it correctly classifies some samples into TEMPORAL.SYNCHRONOUS, which is a label ignored by the basic model.

5.3 Model 2

Model architecture: Model 2 treats being inter-sentential or intra-sentential as a single binary feature. Model 2 is created by modifying the Basic Model to include this feature after obtaining the combined representations of the two arguments. We concatenate the binary feature f_S with the output of the dense layer before applying the softmax function, expecting it to affect the final prediction.

Training and evaluation: The data selection follows the standard and cross-validation data split process. The evaluation assumes that each token in the test set has been given an inter-sentential or intra-sentential feature. The scores are computed following the general process as the basic model.

Results: The third line of Table 3 shows that Model 2 improves over the Basic Model with respect to both inter- and intra-sentential implicit sense prediction, though the performance of the model still has a statistically significant dependence on the location of relations (p = 4.53e-04). The improvement of Model 2 on intra-sentential labels is not as dramatic as Model 1. Compared to the previous model, Model 2 doesn't sharpen its focus on those frequent labels in inter- or intra-sentential sets. Instead, the integrated feature in the representations distributes the benefits on the prediction ability of different labels more evenly. In addition, the confusion matrix in Figure 2 shows that Model 2 reduces the confusion between INSTANTIATION and LEVEL-OF-DETAIL, which Scholman and Demberg (2017) have hightlighted as a common source of confusion. The confusion matrix for Model 2 also shows some attention to less frequent labels such as COMPARISON.CONTRAST, which are not predicted in either the Basic Model or Model 1.

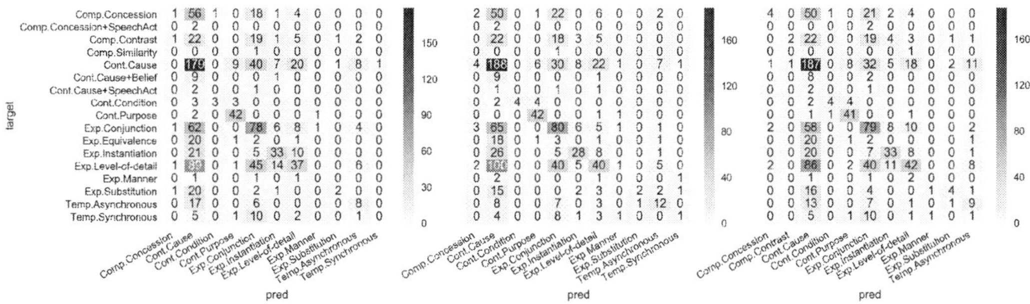

Figure 2: Confusion matrix of the Basic Model, Model 1 and Model 2

5.4 Towards finding implicits within sentences

The results presented above reflect "gold knowledge" of where implicit discourse relations hold within sentences. But in truth, their locations need to be identified before (or jointly with) labelling their senses. We have viewed this as a two-step process: Recognizing sentences that contain at least one implicit intra-sentential relation, and then recognizing the arguments to each relation. The first step has been implemented using a recognizer that takes a linearized parse tree of a sentences as the input. The second step is future work.

Model architecture: Similar to the Basic Model, inputs are represented as a sequence of word vectors, and word embeddings are initialized using pre-trained fastText (Bojanowski et al., 2017) vectors (16B tokens). These vectors are fed to a BiLSTM whose outputs are then fed to a linear layer to produce a binary label, indicating the existence of at least one implicit intra-sentential relation. Word embeddings are set to 200, hidden dimensions, to 256, and vocabulary size, to 25k.

Training and evaluation: To train our recognizer, we first created a dataset of triplets comprising a sentence from PDTB-3, its corresponding parse tree, and a binary label. We obtain the parse trees from the Penn TreeBank (PTB – Marcus et al. 1993) and set the binary label to 1 if there exist at least one implicit or AltLex relation in that sentence. For example, the sentence in Ex. 9 is labelled 1, while that in Ex. 10 is labelled 0.

(9) MARKET MOVES, these managers don't.
((S-HLN (S (NP-SBJ (NN MARKET)) (VP (VBZ MOVES))) (, ,) (S (NP-SBJ (DT these) (NNS managers)) (VP (VBP do) (RB n't) (VP (-NONE- *?*)))) (. .))) [wsj_1825]

(10) Oil-tool prices are even edging up.
((S (NP-SBJ (NN Oil-tool) (NNS prices)) (VP (VBP are) (ADVP (RB even)) (VP (VBG edging) (ADVP-DIR (RP up)))) (. .))) [wsj_0725]

Intra-sentential AltLex relations are included here because they are simply Implicit relations whose alternative lexicalization reliably signals its sense — for example, the phrases "resulting in", "avoiding", and "contributing to" are all taken to be alternative lexicalizations that reliably signal RESULT. This is not true of the earlier Examples 1–3, which are classed as Implicits. On the other hand, we do not label "linked" implicit relations as 1 because the visible evidence is an explicit connective signalling an explicit relation, and we don't want that to be taken *per se* as evidence for an implicit relation. For recognizing linked implicits, we have built a separate model which will be discussed in Section 5.5.

Our training used the Adam optimizer (Kingma and Ba, 2015) with a learning rate of 1e-4. We randomly split the dataset into training (60%), development (20%) and test (20%). To understand what happens if "gold parse trees" are not used, we also created variants of the dataset using parse trees from the widely used Berkeley parser (Kitaev and Klein, 2018) and Stanford parser (Manning et al., 2014).

Results: As the dataset is heavily imbalanced, we also added a simple baseline which predicts the most frequent label. Test set results of the recognizer on the three datasets are presented in Table 4. Even though the baseline achieved an accuracy of ∼0.9, it doesn't convey any useful information, as it labels all instances as 0. We can observe that the model with gold Penn TreeBank parse trees obtain the best performance, followed by the Berkeley parser. Stanford parse trees result in worst perfor-

141

Parse trees	Accuracy	Precision	Recall	F_1
Baseline	0.9028	0	0	0
Gold	0.9617	0.7799	0.8968	0.8343
Berkeley	0.9473	0.7814	0.6334	0.6997
Stanford	0.9349	0.7153	0.5537	0.6242

Table 4: Results on task of identifying sentences that contain at least one intra-sentential relation, comparing gold parse trees from the PTB with the parse trees output by the Berkeley parser and by the Stanford parser. Baseline refers to the model that predicts the most frequent label.

mance. Examining these trees led us to conclude that, while the Stanford parser does well for basic syntactic structures, which are the most common, it has trouble with challenging structures such as those associated with conjunction. An example is provided in Ex. 11. Here, "steps" has been incorrectly labelled NNS, when it is actually a VBZ, heading the second conjunct. If there were only two conjuncts, explicitly conjoined with "and", the sentence would not contain an implicit relation. With three conjuncts, however, the first two would normally be *comma-conjoined*, with the discourse relation between them taken to be implicit. But the error in PoS-tagging has eliminated evidence of a second conjunct, with an implicit discourse relation to the first conjunct. Errors in PoS-tagging and mis-parsing associated with rare constructions, means that the accuracy is lower than that of the Berkeley parser. However, as Precision, Recall, and F_1 are measured for 1 labels, these metrics are more adversely affected when compared to those of the Berkeley parser.

(11) With three minutes left on the clock, Mr. Aikman takes the snap, steps back and fires a 21-yard pass – straight into the hands of an Atlanta defensive back.

IN CD NNS VBD IN DT NN , NNP NNP VBZ DT NN , NNS RB CC VBZ DT JJ NN : RB IN DT NNS IN DT NNP NN RB .

((S (SBAR (IN With) (S (NP (CD three) (NNS minutes)) (VP (VBD left) (PP (IN on) (NP (DT the) (NN clock)))))) (, ,) (NP (NNP Mr.) (NNP Aikman)) (VP (VP (VBZ takes) (NP (NP (DT the) (NN snap)) (, ,) (NP (NNS steps))) (ADVP (RB back))) (CC and) (VP (VBZ fires) (NP (DT a) (JJ 21-yard) (NN pass)) (: –) (PP (RB straight) (IN into) (NP (NP (DT the) (NNS hands)) (PP (IN of) (NP (DT an) (NNP Atlanta) (NN defensive))))))) (ADVP (RB back))) (. .))) [wsj_1411]

5.5 Recognizing "linked" implicit relations

As noted in Section 2.1, implicit relations can co-occur with explicit relations. While the location of such implicits is not identified by the recognizer

	Precision	Recall	F_1	Proportion
stand-alone	0.951	0.905	0.928	93.67%
linked	0.193	0.329	0.243	6.33%

Table 5: Precision, Recall and F_1 scores of linked/stand-alone labels predicted by the recognizer using main evaluation metrics and their proportion in test data.

described in Section 5.4, we actually know the location of their arguments, because co-occurring (aka "linked") relations share their argument spans. Hence, recognizing explicit relations linked with implicit ones means that we also obtain argument spans of these implicits. Here we describe a first attempt to automatically discriminate explicit relations linked with implicit relations from ones that are not so linked. It comprises two steps: extracting sentences that contain explicit relations as our datasets, and then recognizing the ones linked with implicit relations.

Model architecture: To detect linked implicit relations from explicit relations, we use a naive Bayes classifier — specifically, the one provided in NLTK (Bird and Loper, 2004). Production rules are selected as input feature as it has been proven notably effective in feature-based implicit discourse relation recognition task among different features (Park and Cardie, 2012). Models trained in Task 1 will be adopted for linked sense classification.

Training and evaluation: We follow the standard split to select the training and test set. Each token in the training set consists of *Arg1*, connective and **Arg2**, and are parsed to extract syntactic productions used in parent-child nodes in the argument parse trees. The 100 most-frequent production rules are used to build a feature dictionary for input. A production rule feature is labeled as 1 in the dictionary if it appears in the parse tree of the token, otherwise it will be 0. The linked/stand-alone label is determined by whether the explicit relation shares the same index value with an implicit relation. The recognizer is evaluated by how well it distinguishes explicit relations that have a linked implicit relation from ones that don't. Classifiers are evaluated on the recognized implicit relations.

Results: The low Recall for linked relations in Table 5 shows that the recognizer performs better on predicting stand-alone relations, which are a majority of the data. Linked implicits in the test set (WSJ Section 23) are mostly linked to conjoined clauses or conjoined VPs, and are signaled by implicit connective like "and" (81.08%) or "but" or an adverbial. Most correctly recognized relations are VPs conjoined with "and". All the recognized linked implicit relations are found intra-sentential. We adopt the intra-sentential classifier in Model 1 and the Basic Model to test the classifier based on the recognized results. The intra-sentential classifier achieves an F_1 score of 75, compared with 68.182 using the Basic Model. This again emphasizes that knowing the location of implicit discourse relation would benefit sense identification.

6 Conclusion and future work

We have shown that recognizing implicit discourse relations as annotated in the PDTB-3 now requires finding them, as well as figuring out what sense relation(s) holds between the arguments. However, we have also shown that the latter task is simplified by differences in the sense distribution of different implicit relations. We still have to develop a way of recognizing precisely where implicit relations hold in those sentences that can be identified as containing them, and a more accurate approach to sense labelling implicit relations that co-occur with explicit ones. We are also interested in whether these different sense distributions hold in other news corpora and other genres. While it is likely not the case that all languages show the same difference in the sense distribution of discourse relations, we would not be surprised if the discourse relations realized within sentences differed from those realized across sentences. In conclusion, we hope that the current effort will contribute to future work on shallow discourse parsing as annotated in the PDTB-3.

Acknowledgments

We would like to thank the anonymous reviewers for their valuable comments. We would also like to thank Annie Louis for her contributions to the work on recognizing the presence of sentence-internal implicit discourse relations.

References

Hongxiao Bai and Hai Zhao. 2018. Deep enhanced representation for implicit discourse relation recognition. In *Proceedings of the 27th International Conference on Computational Linguistics*, pages 571–583, Santa Fe, New Mexico, USA. Association for Computational Linguistics.

Steven Bird and Edward Loper. 2004. NLTK: The natural language toolkit. In *Proceedings of the ACL Interactive Poster and Demonstration Sessions*, pages 214–217, Barcelona, Spain. Association for Computational Linguistics.

Piotr Bojanowski, Edouard Grave, Armand Joulin, and Tomas Mikolov. 2017. Enriching word vectors with subword information. *Transactions of the Association for Computational Linguistics*, 5:135–146.

Alexis Conneau, Douwe Kiela, Holger Schwenk, Loïc Barrault, and Antoine Bordes. 2017. Supervised learning of universal sentence representations from natural language inference data. In *Proceedings of the 2017 Conference on Empirical Methods in Natural Language Processing*, pages 670–680, Copenhagen, Denmark.

Zeyu Dai and Ruihong Huang. 2018. Improving implicit discourse relation classification by modeling inter-dependencies of discourse units in a paragraph. In *Proceedings of the 2018 Conference of the North American Chapter of the Association for Computational Linguistics: Human Language Technologies, Volume 1 (Long Papers)*, pages 141–151, New Orleans, Louisiana. Association for Computational Linguistics.

Sepp Hochreiter and Jürgen Schmidhuber. 1997. Long short-term memory. *Neural Comput.*, 9(8):1735–1780.

Shafiq Joty, Giuseppe Carenini, Raymond Ng, and Yashar Mehdad. 2013. Combining intra- and multi-sentential rhetorical parsing for document-level discourse analysis. In *Proceedings of the 51st Annual Meeting of the Association for Computational Linguistics*, pages 486–496, Sofia, Bulgaria.

Shafiq Joty, Giuseppe Carenini, and Raymond T. Ng. 2015. CODRA: A novel discriminative framework for rhetorical analysis. *Computational Linguistics*, 41(3):385–435.

Diederik P. Kingma and Jimmy Ba. 2015. Adam: A method for stochastic optimization. In *3rd International Conference on Learning Representations, ICLR 2015, San Diego, CA, USA, May 7-9, 2015, Conference Track Proceedings*.

Nikita Kitaev and Dan Klein. 2018. Constituency parsing with a self-attentive encoder. In *Proceedings of the 56th Annual Meeting of the Association for Computational Linguistics (Volume 1: Long Papers)*, pages 2676–2686, Melbourne, Australia. Association for Computational Linguistics.

Christopher D Manning, Mihai Surdeanu, John Bauer, Jenny Rose Finkel, Steven Bethard, and David McClosky. 2014. The stanford corenlp natural language processing toolkit. In *Proceedings of 52nd annual meeting of the association for computational linguistics: system demonstrations*, pages 55–60.

Mitchell P. Marcus, Beatrice Santorini, and Mary Ann Marcinkiewicz. 1993. Building a large annotated corpus of English: The Penn Treebank. *Computational Linguistics*, 19(2):313–330.

Tomas Mikolov, Kai Chen, G.s Corrado, and Jeffrey Dean. 2013a. Efficient estimation of word representations in vector space. *Proceedings of Workshop at ICLR*, 2013.

Tomas Mikolov, Ilya Sutskever, Kai Chen, Greg Corrado, and Jeffrey Dean. 2013b. Distributed representations of words and phrases and their compositionality. In *Proceedings of the 26th International Conference on Neural Information Processing Systems - Volume 2*, NIPS'13, page 3111–3119, Red Hook, NY, USA. Curran Associates Inc.

Joonsuk Park and Claire Cardie. 2012. Improving implicit discourse relation recognition through feature set optimization. In *Proceedings of the 13th Annual Meeting of the Special Interest Group on Discourse and Dialogue*, pages 108–112, Seoul, South Korea. Association for Computational Linguistics.

Rashmi Prasad, Nikhil Dinesh, Alan Lee, Eleni Miltsakaki, Livio Robaldo, Aravind Joshi, and Bonnie Webber. 2008. The penn discourse treebank 2.0. In *Proceedings of the Sixth International Language Resources and Evaluation (LREC'08)*, pages 2961–2968. European Language Resources Association (ELRA).

Rashmi Prasad, Aravind Joshi, and Bonnie Webber. 2010. Realization of discourse relations by other means: Alternative lexicalizations. In *Proceedings of the 23rd International Conference on Computational Linguistics (COLING)*, Beijing, China.

Hannah Rohde, Anna Dickinson, Nathan Schneider, Christopher Clark, Annie Louis, and Bonnie Webber. 2017. Exploring substitutability through discourse adverbials and multiple judgments. In *Proceedings, 12th International Conference on Computational Semantics (IWCS 2017)*, Montpellier, France.

Hannah Rohde, Alexander Johnson, Nathan Schneider, and Bonnie Webber. 2018. Discourse coherence: Concurrent explicit and implicit relations. In *Proceedings of the 56th Annual Meeting of the ACL*.

Attapol Rutherford, Vera Demberg, and Nianwen Xue. 2017. A systematic study of neural discourse models for implicit discourse relation. In *Proceedings of the 15th Conference of the European Chapter of the Association for Computational Linguistics (EACL 2017)*, pages 281–291.

Attapol Rutherford and Nianwen Xue. 2016. Robust non-explicit neural discourse parser in English and Chinese. In *Proceedings of the CoNLL-16 shared task*, pages 55–59, Berlin, Germany.

Merel Scholman and Vera Demberg. 2017. Examples and specifications that prove a point: Identifying elaborative and argumentative discourse relations. *Dialogue & Discourse*, 8:56–83.

Wei Shi and Vera Demberg. 2017. On the need of cross validation for discourse relation classification. In *Proceedings of the 15th Conference of the European Chapter of the Association for Computational Linguistics: Volume 2, Short Papers*, pages 150–156, Valencia, Spain. Association for Computational Linguistics.

Bonnie Webber, Rashmi Prasad, Alan Lee, and Aravind Joshi. 2019. The penn discourse treebank 3.0 annotation manual. https://catalog.ldc.upenn.edu/docs/LDC2019T05/PDTB3-Annotation-Manual.pdf.

Nianwen Xue, Hwee Tou Ng, Sameer Pradhan, Rashmi Prasad, Christopher Bryant, and Attapol Rutherford. 2015. The CoNLL-2015 shared task on shallow discourse parsing. In *Proceedings of the Nineteenth Conference on Computational Natural Language Learning - Shared Task*, pages 1–16, Beijing, China. Association for Computational Linguistics.

Nianwen Xue, Hwee Tou Ng, Sameer Pradhan, Attapol Rutherford, Bonnie Webber, Chuan Wang, and Hongmin Wang. 2016. CoNLL 2016 shared task on multilingual shallow discourse parsing. In *Proceedings of the CoNLL-16 shared task*, pages 1–19, Berlin, Germany. Association for Computational Linguistics.

A Specifics of the Basic Model

Here we describe the basic model architecture for implicit relation sense classification in PDTB-3. The configuration for the model is chosen based on consideration of data size and the interaction between lexical information and structural information. A further analysis on the predictive performance of the basic model on each labels is provided as well.

A.1 Model architecture

Figure 1 (repeated here as Figure 3) illustrates the overall model architecture of the neural implicit sense classifier that consists of two LSTM and max-pooling layers, a hidden layer, a dense layer, and a softmax layer. The input for the model is the discourse argument pairs with additional labels[6], and the output is a probability distribution of the senses between the discourse argument spans.

Word vectors: In our model, arguments $Arg1$ and $Arg2$ are viewed as two sequences of word vectors with length of n_1 and n_2. Word vectors for the word in arguments are taken from word embeddings.

$$Arg1 : [x_1^1, x_2^1, ..., x_{n_1}^1] \qquad (1)$$

$$Arg2 : [x_1^2, x_2^2, ..., x_{n_2}^2] \qquad (2)$$

Argument representations: The two sequences of word vectors are encoded by LSTM respectively. The hidden states H_{Arg1} and H_{Arg2} of LSTM are taken. The max-pooling function is employed to compose meaning in the hidden states and reduce parameters for the model, as it has been proven effective in (Conneau et al., 2017). As shown in eq. 6, it will select the maximum value along the sequence at each dimension of the hidden states. $a_j^1(a_j^2)$ represents a maximum value from all the values in a sequence with length of $n_1(n_2)$ at dimension j of the hidden states H_{Arg1} (H_{Arg2}). By concatenating the output of max-pooling function, we have abstract representations A_{Arg1} and A_{Arg2} of arguments $Arg1$ and $Arg2$ individually.

$$H_{Arg1} = [h_1^1, h_2^1, ..., h_{n_1}^1] \qquad (3)$$

$$H_{Arg2} = [h_1^2, h_2^2, ..., h_{n_2}^2] \qquad (4)$$

$$a_j^1 = \max_{k \in n_1}(H_{Arg2_{j_k}}) \qquad (5)$$

$$a_j^2 = \max_{k \in n_2}(H_{Arg1_{j_k}}) \qquad (6)$$

$$A_{Arg1} = [a_1^1, a_2^1, ..., a_{hidden\_size}^1] \qquad (7)$$

$$A_{Arg2} = [a_1^2, a_2^2, ..., a_{hidden\_size}^2] \qquad (8)$$

Inter-argument interaction modeling: The modeling of the interaction between two discourse argument representations follows (Rutherford and Xue, 2016), which argues that discourse relations can only be determined by jointly analyzing the arguments. In our model, argument representations A_{Arg1} and A_{Arg2} are weighted by W_1 and W_2 separately. The combination of the weighted argument representations is then transformed non-linearly with $tanh$ function in the first hidden layer H_{hid}. It is then fed into a dense layer H_{dense}[7]. Finally, we predict the discourse relation sense using a softmax function.

$$H_{hid} = tanh(W_1 \cdot A_{Arg1} + W_2 \cdot A_{Arg2} + b_{hid}) \quad (9)$$

$$H_{dense} = tanh(W_{dense} \cdot H_1 + b_{dense}) \qquad (10)$$

$$output = softmax(W_{output} \cdot H_{dense} + b_{output}) \qquad (11)$$

A.2 Configuration

Implementation: The model is implemented with PyTorch. The cost function is the standard cross-entropy loss function and Adam optimizer with an initial learning rate of 0.001 and a batch size of 32. We determine convergence if the performance of the model on the development set does not improve after more than 3 epochs.

One problem that challenges the training of the model is the limitation on the size of the data. We introduce other resources to overcome it and adopt different techniques to avoid overfitting. Word vectors are directly taken from Word2vec embeddings (Mikolov et al., 2013a) trained with the skip-gram algorithm on Brown corpus, and are fixed during training. To avoid overfitting, we apply a 0.25 dropout ratio to the input of the LSTM layer. Batch normalization is added to normalize the activation between the hidden layer and the dense layer to accelerate the training speed and further prevent overfitting with regularization.

---

[6]These labels are not used in the basic model described in this work, but serve for statistical tests and further experiments.

[7]The default size of the dense layer is $hidden\_size//5$.

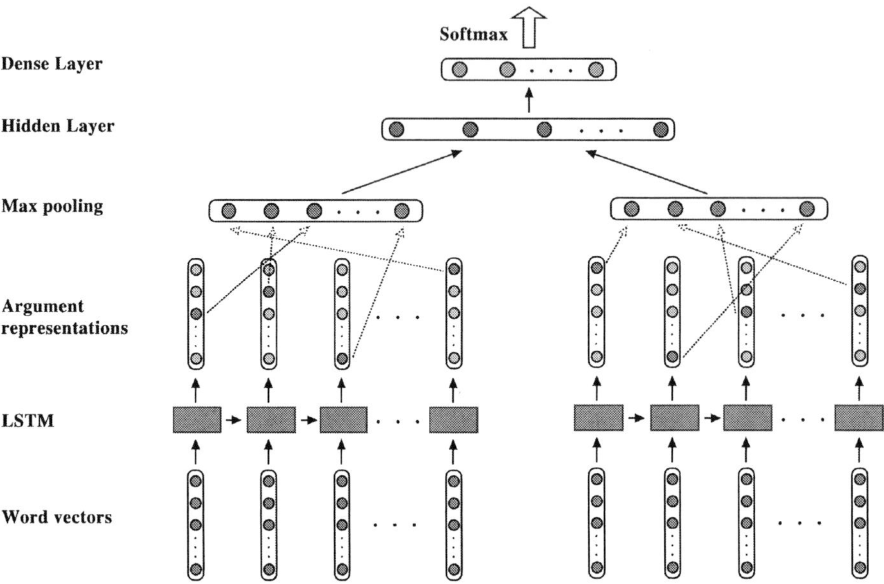

Figure 3: The overall model architecture for implicit sense classification

Hyperparameter Settings: (Rutherford et al., 2017) observed the influence of different configurations on the performance of the model for the implicit sense classification task, suggesting an interaction between the lexical information in word vectors and the structural information encoded in the model itself. To determine the configuration for our model, we trained our model with different combinations of the dimension of word embedding (50, 300) and hidden size (50, 100), and evaluate it on Level 2 labels on the WSJ section 23. Table 6 presents the performance of the model with different configurations. The baseline is Most Frequent Sense heuristic, using the most frequent sense CONTINGENCY.CAUSE in the training data for each target. Our result is in line with their finding of sequential LSTM model, showing larger hidden size 100 is effective when it is accompanied with 300-dimension word embedding. Based on the performance on Level 2 labels, we choose 300-dimension Word2vec word embedding and hidden size 100 as our configuration for the Basic Model.

Our model scores 34.778 at Level 3 (31-way classification). Using cross-validation, our model obtains 41.463 at Level 2.

A.3 Discussion

It is worth examining the performance of the model on each Level 2 label individually. Table 7 displays the precision, recall and F_1 scores of each label along with its proportion in the test data.

The classifier obtains relatively higher scores on some types of labels. The first type is senses with larger sample size in the corpus, suggesting the imbalanced classification problem. Two senses occur frequently in the corpus (CONTINGENCY.CAUSE and EXPANSION.CONJUNCTION) are recognized with high Recall, but low Precision. This could indicate a strong signal, but one that is likely to be ambiguous. Other less frequent labels are constantly misclassified into these frequent labels. For example, the amount of EXPANSION.MANNER samples is largely reduced by our method dealing with multi-label instances, and the classifier fails to recognize the minority class. Another type of senses achieving high scores are those occurring predominantly in intra-sentential relations (CONTINGENCY.PURPOSE and CONTINGENCY.CONDITION) or in inter-sentential relations (EXPANSION.INSTANTIATION and EXPANSION.LEVEL-OF-DETAIL). The model recognize these senses with high Precision, but different levels of Recall, which could be due to a difference in the strength of evidence signalling the relation. Additionally, TEMPORAL.ASYNCHRONOUS sense that associates with much higher proportion in linked relations than stand-alone ones obtain similar Recall and Precision scores.

	embedding size	hidden size	F_1
Our model	50	50	36.492
	50	100	37.097
	300	50	37.601
	300	100	**38.608**
Baseline	-	-	28.024

Table 6: F_1 scores of the model with different configurations on predicting Level 2 sense labels

	Precision	Recall	F_1	Proportion
Comparison.Concession	20.000	1.235	2.326	8.17%
Comparison.Concession+SpeechAct	0.000	0.000	0.000	0.20%
Comparison.Contrast	0.000	0.000	0.000	5.14%
Comparison.Similarity	0.000	0.000	0.000	0.10%
Contingency.Cause	35.098	67.547	46.194	26.71%
Contingency.Cause+Belief	0.000	0.000	0.000	1.01%
Contingency.Cause+SpeechAct	0.000	0.000	0.000	0.30%
Contingency.Condition	75.000	33.333	46.154	0.91%
Contingency.Purpose	73.684	93.333	82.353	4.54%
Expansion.Conjunction	34.211	48.750	40.206	16.13%
Expansion.Equivalence	0.000	0.000	0.000	2.42%
Expansion.Instantiation	51.562	47.826	49.624	6.96%
Expansion.Level-of-detail	42.045	19.171	26.335	19.46%
Expansion.Manner	0.000	0.000	0.000	0.30%
Expansion.Substitution	50.000	7.692	13.333	2.62%
Temporal.Asynchronous	27.586	25.806	26.667	3.12%
Temporal.Synchronous	0.000	0.000	0.000	1.92%

Table 7: Precision, Recall and F_1 scores of different labels predicted by the basic model using main evaluation metric and their proportions in test data

TED-MDB Lexicons: Tr-EnConnLex, Pt-EnConnLex

Murathan Kurfalı[†*]**, Sibel Özer**[‡*]**, Deniz Zeyrek**[‡*]**, Amália Mendes**[§]
[†]Linguistics Department, Stockholm University, Stockholm, Sweden
[‡]Graduate School of Informatics, Middle East Technical University, Ankara, Turkey
[§]Center of Linguistics, University of Lisbon, Lisbon, Portugal
`murathan.kurfali@ling.su.se e159606,dezeyrek@metu.edu.tr`
`amaliamendes@letras.ulisboa.pt`

Abstract

In this work, we present two new bilingual discourse connective lexicons, namely, for Turkish-English and European Portuguese-English created automatically using the existing discourse relation-aligned TED-MDB corpus. In their current form, the Pt-En lexicon includes 95 entries, whereas the Tr-En lexicon contains 133 entries. The lexicons constitute the first step of a larger project of developing a multilingual discourse connective lexicon.

1 Introduction

During the past decade or so the interest in discourse studies have dramatically increased following the release of the PDTB 2.0 corpus (Prasad et al., 2008) and, later, with the TextLink initiative[1]. In parallel to this interest, available resources annotated for various discourse-level phenomena have expanded, where discourse relational devices (DRDs) have received a special interest leading to the Connective-Lex database (Stede et al., 2019). ConnLex is a joint online database project, which is the first attempt to bring together connective lexicons of different languages. It currently hosts the connective lexicons of nine different languages providing a web-based interface together with a cross-linguistically applicable XML schema. The entries in the lexicons provide fundamental information about discourse connectives, such as orthography, syntactic category, and their senses. The ConnLex project pursues the aim of expanding the database both in coverage (by adding new languages) and depth of the information. However, except for a few resources, most of the previous effort on devising discourse connective lexicons has relied on monolingual resources and any multilingual links that were provided have not gone beyond offering English equivalents. Few exceptions involve the

bilingual Italian–German contrastive/concessive connective lexicon based on the cross-lingual projection of monolingual lexicons for Italian and German (Bourgonje et al., 2017), and the very recent GeCzLex, Anaphoric Connective Lexicon for Czech and German (Poláková et al., 2020).

The main contributions of the present study are (1) proposing an alternative way of producing bilingual lexicons, potentially applicable to building multilingual lexicons, (2) providing new bilingual discourse connective lexicons for European Portuguese-English and Turkish-English by (3) considering not only the explicit discourse relations but also the implicit relations in a recent multilingual discourse bank, namely TED-Multilingual Discourse Bank (TED-MDB) annotated in the PDTB style (Zeyrek et al., 2019). The lexicon entries are extracted from TED-MDB, where each relation in the source language is aligned to its semantic equivalent in the target languages (Turkish and European Portuguese) (see §2.1). In their current form, the Pt-En lexicon includes 95 entries covering 51 connectives in Portuguese and 57 connectives in English, while the Tr-En lexicon contains 133 entries with 72 connectives in Turkish and 56 in English.

The rest of the study is structured as follows: We firstly summarize the main data source, TED-MDB followed by the discourse relation alignment procedure (§2), the output of which is used as inputs to construct bilingual lexicons. §3 describes the construction of the bilingual lexicons in detail. In §4, we discuss issues concerning our lexicon construction procedure. §5 concludes the paper presenting some future directions.

2 TED-MDB

TED-MDB is a resource of TED talk transcripts comprising 7 languages manually annotated for discourse relations. It includes English, the source language (SL) along with transcribed texts in Ger-

---

*Authors contributed equally.
[1]http://textlink.ii.metu.edu.tr/

Proceedings of the First Workshop on Computational Approaches to Discourse, pages 148–153
Online, November 20, 2020. ©2020 Association for Computational Linguistics
https://doi.org/10.18653/v1/P17

man, Lithuanian, European Portuguese, Russian, Turkish and Polish (target languages, or TLs). [2] Following the rules and principles of the PDTB, it annotates five discourse relations types (henceforth, DRs) with respect to the PDTB-3 sense hierarchy (Webber et al., 2016) and ultimately aims to provide a clearly described level of discourse structure and semantics in multiple languages, thus engendering discourse parsing studies in multiple languages. TED-MDB currently involves 6 TED talk transcripts annotated with 5 DR types (Explicit, Implicit, AltLex, EntRel, NoRel), their senses and binary arguments, amounting to a total of 3649 tokens. The annotations have been carried out by native speaker annotators of the languages involved using the PDTB annotation tool. (Lee et al., 2016)[3] This tool stores the DR annotations in separate pipe-delimited files.

2.1 Alignment Procedure

To create TED-MDB, each monolingual team annotated the texts independently of the original texts to avoid the risk of the original language influencing the annotations. Yet, due to cross-lingual variation in rendering DRs, this design criterion led to tokens not existing in the original language (Zeyrek et al., 2019). As the extraction of bilingual DC lexicons requires aligned relations, in the present study, our pipeline starts with the alignment of DRs following Özer and Zeyrek (2019). Firstly, the DR annotations originally kept in pipe-delimited files were transferred onto the base text files of both TLs generating an ID for each. Then, word- and punctuation-tokenization as well as sentence alignment procedures were performed, followed by manual corrections of the latter. For DR alignment, all DRs in each bi-text unit were paired constructing DR matrices. The text pieces constituting discourse relations were translated into the SL using the Google Translate API and stop words were removed. Next, semantic similarity, taken in terms of cosine distance, was calculated between the source and target text segments using Word2Vec (Mikolov et al., 2013) within the range of 0 ("no similarity") to 1 ("perfect similarity"). DR pairs with a similarity over 0.7 were further evaluated for alignment.

For DR pairs with acceptable scores, the similarity of the DR sense and type was evaluated using a ranking algorithm which depends on the sense

tags on the DRs. A score that reflected the SL-TL match was added to the semantic similarity score, where the DR type and the

SL sense were both considered. The DR pair with the maximum score was marked as an aligned pair, and the same procedure was repeatedly applied until no DR pair was left in the matrices.

All the aligned pairs were manually checked by the authors.

The alignment algorithm has an F-score of 0.78 for Turkish-English and 0.81 for European Portuguese-English distributed over six documents accepting English annotations as the gold standard.

3 TED-MDB Lexicons

As shown in Poláková et al. (2020) and Bourgonje et al. (2017), preparing a bilingual lexicon of discourse connectives is not a straightforward task requiring a variety of resources to compute a translation candidate table including monolingual DC lexicons of the TLs and a large parallel corpus (with at least 2M parallel sentences). A monolingual discourse connective lexicon exists for Portuguese (Mendes and Lejeune, 2016) and one is being developed for Turkish (Zeyrek and Başıbüyük, 2019) but parallel corpora of the required size are absent for the language pairs under investigation. Thus, the current study is built on the observation that just as monolingual lexicons can be compiled from annotated resources, bilingual dictionaries of discourse connectives can be constructed from a similar though low scaled parallel corpus such as TED-MDB. This corpus includes 375 bi-sentence units for English-Turkish and 364 for English-European Portuguese. The rest of the section describes the method employed to create two such bilingual DC lexicons of English-Turkish and English-European Portuguese.

3.1 Populating lexicon entries automatically

Given the availability of TED-MDB, we propose an alternative way of building bilingual DC lexicons, which can be seen as the multilingual extension of extracting DC lexicons from annotated resources as in Mendes and del Río (2018); Das et al. (2018).

The method accepts a set of aligned DRs as input. For pre-processing, we firstly filter out all aligned pairs which contain a non-Explicit or non-Implicit relation followed by the removal of the pairs which are not annotated with exactly the same sense. This step helps us to eliminate the translation-based

---

[2]https://github.com/MurathanKurfali/Ted-MDB-Annotations

[3]https://www.cis.upenn.edu/ pdtb/annotator.html

Language	Explicit	Implicit	AltLex	EntRel	NoRel	Total
English	290 (44%)	198 (30%)	46 (7%)	78 (12%)	49 (7%)	661
Russian	237 (42%)	221 (39%)	20 (4%)	57 (10%)	30 (5%)	565
Polish	218 (37,5%)	195 (33,5%)	11 (2%)	104 (18%)	52 (9%)	580
Portuguese	269 (43%)	256 (41%)	29 (5%)	38 (6%)	33 (5%)	625
German	240 (43%)	214 (38%)	17 (3%)	59 (11%)	30 (5%)	560
Turkish	276 (42%)	202 (30,5%)	59 (9%)	70 (10,5%)	51 (8%)	658
Total	1530	1286	182	406	245	3649

Table 1: Distribution of discourse relation types in TED-MDB (Zeyrek et al., 2019)

noise in the corpus as it is not uncommon for the senses of DRs to be lost or modified during translation.

After the pre-processing step, the bilingual lexicons are constructed in the following way:

- For each connective in the SL, the list of senses in the input is computed.

- The translation equivalents of the given connective are found in the TL using the aligned DRs. The translations are grouped under the senses found in the first step. Hence, we create different entries for each sense conveyed by the connective in SL. For example, in Tr-En, the "but/ama" pair appears both under the Comparison:Concession:Arg2-as-denier sense and the Comparison:Contrast sense.

Due to the limited number of explicit DRs in TED-MDB (Table 1), we also include in our lexicon *implicit connectives* which are the connectives inserted to implicit DRs by the annotators (Prasad et al., 2008). An inserted *implicit connective* can be regarded as the most suitable overt marker for a given implicit relation; hence, the pair of implicit connectives extracted from an aligned implicit DR is as valid an entry for our lexicon just as a pair of explicit connectives extracted from an aligned explicit DR. However, in order to keep things separated and facilitate further research, we create different entries for explicit and implicit usages of connectives in our lexicon. The detailed statistics about the lexicons are provided in Table 2.

3.2 Post-process

The inspection of the automatically extracted connective pairs reveals several issues, which can mostly be attributed to translation strategies. In certain cases, translators use a completely different linguistic construction in the TL; yet, they manage to preserve the sense of the SL text (Example 1).

Since both relations are annotated with the same sense, our method erroneously assumes these different connectives form a valid pair.

(1)   by **investing sustainably,** *we're doing two things ..*

        Quando **investimos na sustentabilidade** *estamos a fazer duas coisas*

        '<u>When</u> **we invest in sustainability**, *we are doing two things..*'

In order to fix such cases, we firstly adopted a fully automatic approach where we tried to eliminate the unacceptable pairs by checking them against comprehensive bilingual dictionaries similar to Poláková et al. (2020). To this end, we used Treq (Škrabal and Vavřín, 2017) and the OPUS word alignment database.[4] However, both resources turned out to be unsuitable for our purposes. The translation candidate tables created from these resources eliminate a nontrivial amount of acceptable pairs as most of the time, valid translations are either absent in the databases or are assigned a very low probability, making it virtually impossible to determine an appropriate threshold between unacceptable and acceptable translations. That some of the Turkish connectives are suffixal connectives further render the use of dictionaries impractical. Therefore, we manually went through each entry in the lexicons in order to reach gold pairs. As the lexicons are not large and the task of deciding whether two words are translation equivalents is not too challenging, the manual control was completed within hours. The decision was made unanimously, which resulted in the removal of 9 pairs from Portuguese and only 2 from Turkish. It is also worth noting that the eliminated pairs overwhelmingly had the label Expansion:Level-of-detail:Arg2-as-detail, which "is used when Arg2 describes in more detail, the situation in Arg1"(Webber et al., 2019).

---

[4]http://opus.nlpl.eu/lex.php

Language	# of Connectives				# of Sense	# of Translations		
	Exp	Imp	Total (Unique)	Monolingual		Min	Max	Avg
English	26	31	57 (48)	142	1.23	1	6	1.36
Portuguese	26	25	51 (42)	-	1.49	1	4	1.36
English	24	32	56 (47)	142	1.29	1	7	1.83
Turkish	34	38	72 (62)	226	1.44	1	4	1.26

Table 2: Statistics regarding the constructed lexicons. "Exp" and "Imp" refers to the number of Explicit and Implicit connectives, respectively. The "Total" column represents the number of connectives when implicit and explicit connectives are counted as separate entries and when their type is disregarded (within parenthesis). The "Monolingual" column represents the number of connectives in the the respective language's monolingual lexicon (retrieved from (Stede et al., 2019)) . The last column presents the minimum, maximum and the average number of translation equivalents in the target language.

A close examination showed that this subsense was not conveyed by the annotated DC tokens in the SL but rather inferred from the arguments, leading the translator to render the DR almost freely with a mismatching token in the TL. The removed pairs are as follows:

- **Pt-En:** e - *rather*, e - *for that matter*, enquanto - *and*, assim - *that is*, de facto - *specifically*, e - *as well as*, e - *lastly*, isto é - *clearly*, assim - *specifically*

- **Tr-En:** özetle - *clearly*, yani - *clearly*, işte - *clearly*

3.3 The Structure of the Lexicons

Each entry in the TED-MDB lexicons corresponds to a specific connective in the TL and a list of its possible translations in the TL grouped under the sense the connective conveys. Specifically, an entry consists of the following components (illustrated in Figure 1):

- **Connective**: The head of each entry is a DC represented in its lemmatized form.

- **Dimlex link**: Each DC and its translations are accompanied with an URL to their respective connective-lex entry,[5] which serves as a bridge between the bilingual and monolingual lexicons.

- **Sense list:** The list of the senses that the head connective conveys in TED-MDB is displayed in the main screen of the interface sorted by the corpus frequencies of the senses.

- **List of translation candidates**: For each sense in the list, the translation candidates specified in TL texts are provided. The translation candidates also have their own entries and are accessible just by clicking.

- **Example sentence**: Each connective pair is accompanied with a randomly selected sentence pair from TED-MDB.

4 Discussion

To the best of our knowledge, the TED-MDB lexicons presented here constitute the first attempt to construct a bilingual connective lexicon directly from an annotated parallel resource. Compilation of bilingual lexicons in this way has a number of practical benefits, where the main advantage is being not dependent on external resources. It alleviates the need for parallel corpora required to extract the translation candidates to map the connectives in different languages onto each other and does not necessitate monolingual DC lexicons, a challenging and time consuming effort especially when started from scratch (Roze et al., 2012). Also, as all entries are populated from an annotated corpus, the lexicons are guaranteed to be symmetrical, and the bilingual examples provide an opportunity to observe the usage of connectives in context in two languages. It must also be noted that despite being compiled from a set of merely 300+ relations in each language set, our bilingual lexicons roughly account for 30% of the documented connectives of these languages; hence, their coverage is more impressive than it looks (Table 2).

As explained in Section 3.2, there are certain cases where the connectives from an aligned DR pair do not form valid lexicon entries. This issue revealed the larger problem that translational candidate tables, even those from a large parallel corpus like InterCorp (Škrabal and Vavřín, 2017) cannot

---

[5]http://connective-lex.info/

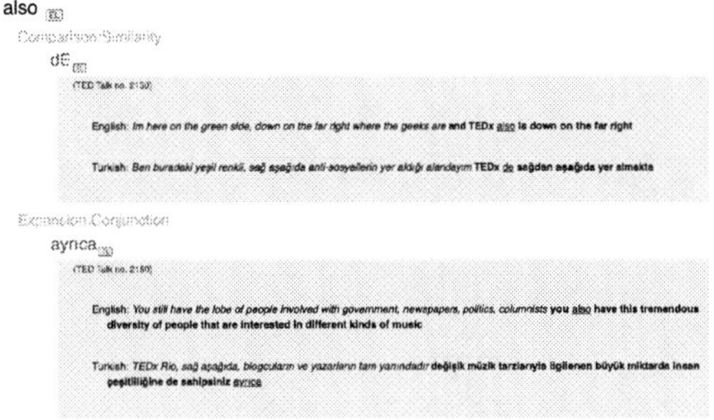

Figure 1: The entry for 'also'in Tr-En lexicon

adequately capture the translation equivalents of connectives. We believe this finding further highlights the need for such bilingual lexicons.

Finally, as the manual control of the DR alignments constitutes one of the two non-automatic steps of our pipeline, we investigated its effect on the final lexicons to guide future research. To our surprise, the automatic alignment procedure turns out to be more than satisfactory: we were able to fetch more than 96% of all entries in the gold lexicons, suggesting that even a multilingual lexicon involving all languages in TED-MDB can be automatically constructed. This is left for future work.

5   Conclusion

In translation, the choice of a DC that best conveys the sense of a relation and renders the relation in a natural way is not a trivial task. At a minimum, it requires careful consideration of the multiple senses of the connectives and their parts-of-speech. Even a bilingual dictionary is not always helpful for a translator. Bilingual lexicons built on the basis of naturalistic data is important to aid both machine and human translation as well as second language learners. In this study, we described a method of building two bilingual lexicons using aligned DR annotations. Both lexicons are available online as HTML web pages. [6] In contrast to previous bilingual lexicon studies, we did not use monolingual connective lexicons or dictionaries as the former was absent (at least for Turkish), and the latter caused loss of useful data. Although the alignment and the lexicon extraction procedures have been applied to two languages so far, this approach has the potential to be extended to other language pairs covered in the TED-MDB corpus, and this is what we plan to do as a future study.

---

[6]http://metu-db.info/mdb/ted/resources.jsf

References

Peter Bourgonje, Yulia Grishina, and Manfred Stede. 2017. Toward a bilingual lexical database on connectives: Exploiting a german/italian parallel corpus. In *Proceedings of the Fourth Italian Conference on Computational Linguistics–CLIC-IT*, pages 53–58.

Debopam Das, Tatjana Scheffler, Peter Bourgonje, and Manfred Stede. 2018. Constructing a lexicon of english discourse connectives. In *Proceedings of the 19th Annual SIGDIAL Meeting on Discourse and Dialogue*, pages 360–365.

Alan Lee, Rashmi Prasad, Bonnie Webber, and Aravind Joshi. 2016. Annotating discourse relations with the pdtb annotator. In *Proceedings of COLING 2016, the 26th International Conference on Computational Linguistics: System Demonstrations*, pages 121–125.

Amália Mendes and Pierre Lejeune. 2016. Ldm-pt-a portuguese lexicon of discourse markers. In *Conference Handbook of TextLink–Structuring Discourse in Multilingual Europe Second Action Conference*, pages 89–92. Debrecen University Press.

Amália Mendes and Iria del Río. 2018. Using a discourse bank and a lexicon for the automatic identification of discourse connectives. In *International Conference on Computational Processing of the Portuguese Language*, pages 211–221. Springer.

Tomas Mikolov, Ilya Sutskever, Kai Chen, Greg S Corrado, and Jeff Dean. 2013. Distributed representations of words and phrases and their compositionality. In *Advances in neural information processing systems*, pages 3111–3119.

Sibel Özer and Deniz Zeyrek. 2019. An automatic discourse relation alignment experiment on TED-MDB. In *Proceedings of the 2019 Workshop on Widening NLP*, pages 31–34, Florence, Italy. Association for Computational Linguistics.

Lucie Poláková, Kateřina Rysová, Magdaléna Rysová, and Jiří Mírovský. 2020. Geczlex: Lexicon of czech and german anaphoric connectives. In *Proceedings of The 12th Language Resources and Evaluation Conference*, pages 1089–1096.

Rashmi Prasad, Nikhil Dinesh, Alan Lee, Eleni Miltsakaki, Livio Robaldo, Aravind K Joshi, and Bonnie L Webber. 2008. The penn discourse treebank 2.0. In *LREC*. Citeseer.

Charlotte Roze, Laurence Danlos, and Philippe Muller. 2012. Lexconn: a french lexicon of discourse connectives. *Discours. Revue de linguistique, psycholinguistique et informatique. A journal of linguistics, psycholinguistics and computational linguistics*, (10).

Michal Škrabal and Martin Vavřín. 2017. The translation equivalents database (treq) as a lexicographer's aid. In *Electronic lexicography in the 21st century.*

Proceedings of eLex 2017 conference. Leiden: Lexical Computing.

Manfred Stede, Tatjana Scheffler, and Amália Mendes. 2019. Connective-lex: A web-based multilingual lexical resource for connectives. *Discours. Revue de linguistique, psycholinguistique et informatique. A journal of linguistics, psycholinguistics and computational linguistics*, (24).

Bonnie Webber, Rashmi Prasad, Alan Lee, and Aravind Joshi. 2016. A discourse-annotated corpus of conjoined vps. In *Proceedings of the 10th Linguistic Annotation Workshop held in conjunction with ACL 2016 (LAW-X 2016)*, pages 22–31.

Bonnie Webber, Rashmi Prasad, Alan Lee, and Aravind Joshi. 2019. The penn discourse treebank 3.0 annotation manual.

Deniz Zeyrek and Kezban Başıbüyük. 2019. Tcl-a lexicon of turkish discourse connectives. In *Proceedings of the First International Workshop on Designing Meaning Representations*, pages 73–81.

Deniz Zeyrek, Amália Mendes, Yulia Grishina, Murathan Kurfalı, Samuel Gibbon, and Maciej Ogrodniczuk. 2019. Ted multilingual discourse bank (ted-mdb): a parallel corpus annotated in the pdtb style. *Language Resources and Evaluation*, pages 1–27.

Evaluation of Coreference Resolution Systems
Under Adversarial Attacks

Haixia Chai[†] Wei Zhao[Φ] Steffen Eger[Φ] Michael Strube[†]
[†] Heidelberg Institute for Theoretical Studies
[Φ] Computer Science Department, Technische Universität Darmstadt
{haixia.chai, michael.strube}@h-its.org
{zhao,eger}@aiphes.tu-darmstadt.de

Abstract

A substantial overlap of coreferent mentions
in the CoNLL dataset magnifies the recent
progress on coreference resolution. This is
because the CoNLL benchmark fails to evaluate the ability of coreference resolvers that requires linking novel mentions unseen at train
time. In this work, we create a new dataset
based on CoNLL, which largely decreases
mention overlaps in the entire dataset and exposes the limitations of published resolvers
on two aspects—lexical inference ability and
understanding of low-level orthographic noise.
Our findings show (1) the requirements for embeddings, used in resolvers, and for coreference resolutions are, by design, in conflict and
(2) adversarial approaches are sometimes not
legitimate to mitigate the obstacles, as they
may falsely introduce mention overlaps in adversarial training and test sets, thus inflating
the performance.

1 Introduction

Resolution of coreferring expressions is a natural step for text understanding, but coreference
resolvers appear to have a negligible effect in
downstream NLP tasks (Yu and Ji, 2016; Durrett
et al., 2016; Voita et al., 2018). For instance, Durrett et al. (2016) rewrite pronouns with their antecedents (e.g., *he* is replaced by *Dominick Dunne*),
using the Berkeley Entity Resolution System (Durrett and Klein, 2014). However, this fails to improve the cross-sentence coherence of system summaries, although the resolver performs well on the
OntoNotes 4.0 dataset (Pradhan et al., 2011).

The CoNLL benchmark (Pradhan et al., 2012) reflects the recent advances of coreference resolution
systems. Nevertheless, previous work (Moosavi
and Strube, 2017) indicates that the progress on the
CoNLL benchmark is inflated, as the training and
test sets share a large size of mentions. This may

Test Example: Iraqi leader Saddam has given a speech to mark the tenth anniversary of **the Gulf war**. The Iraqi leader said **the Gulf war** was a confrontation...
Train Example: There were other signs today that Iraq's leaders have few regrets over the action that precipitated **the Gulf war**. **The Gulf war** began 10 years ago...

Table 1: Replacing "*the Gulf war*" with "*the Gulf war-
fare*" or "*the Gulf wärfäre*" addresses (1) exact match
in the test example; (2) mention overlaps across examples.

be the reason why coreference resolvers have little
effect in downstream tasks.

As opposed to evaluating on standard bench-
marks, recent work (Glockner et al., 2018; Pruthi
et al., 2019; Eger et al., 2019; Eger and Benz, 2020)
investigates the generalization ability of NLP systems under adversarial attacks. For instance, Glockner et al. (2018) show that natural language inference systems fail blatantly when lexical changes,
e.g., replacing a word by its synonym, occur in
premises and hypotheses. Pruthi et al. (2019) observe that spelling errors distract text classification systems from correct prediction. Inspired by
these works, we investigate published coreference
resolvers in two realistic adversarial setups, which
challenge (a) lexical inference ability to resolve
coreferent mentions, where one mention is, e.g.,
synonymous or in a type-of relationship with its
antecedent and (b) denoising ability against typo-
graphic (low-level) noise. To do so, we construct a
new benchmark dataset by modifying the mention
spans from CoNLL (Pradhan et al., 2012). This
can mitigate lexical overlaps between the CoNLL
training and test sets, as illustrated in Table 1.

Our analysis yields several findings: (1) We
show that the lexical inference ability of published
resolvers, including the state-of-the-art resolver
based on BERT, is poor, i.e., the failure to properly
resolve the coreference of a mention and its hy-

Proceedings of the First Workshop on Computational Approaches to Discourse, pages 154–159
Online, November 20, 2020. ©2020 Association for Computational Linguistics
https://doi.org/10.18653/v1/P17

pernymous (or hyponymous) antecedent within the same synset. (2) We identify an important reason for this failure: a mismatch, by design, between the requirements of coreference resolution and embeddings (used in resolvers). While a plausible coreference resolver anticipates ignoring the semantic difference of a word and its hypernym and linking them as coreferent mentions, embeddings capture the nuanced and fine-grained meanings well. (3) Further, we show that coreference resolvers fail to generalize to the CoNLL benchmark dataset with minor low-level (orthographic) noise. As a remedy, we use a common adversarial approach (Goodfellow et al., 2015) to incorporate lexical changes and low-level noise in coreferent mentions at train time, which appears to largely address the obstacles. However, we reveal that it introduces a large size of mention overlaps in the adversarial training and the test sets. This indicates an unrealistic situation where resolvers are only robust to what has been seen during training.

These findings indicate potential directions for future work, which may benefit coreference resolvers in downstream tasks and in real-world applications with natural occurring noise (e.g., user-generated texts).

2 Adversarial Data Collection

Our goal is to construct a benchmark dataset on which we evaluate the ability to resolve coreference that requires lexical inference and understanding of low-level noise.

2.1 Generating Adversarial Examples

Recent work for adversarial attacks concerning lexical changes and orthographic modification has shown deficiencies of NLP models for many tasks. To adapt previous approaches to coreference resolution, we design the following attack schemes where we focus on text changes occurring in mention spans. This setup also can address lexical overlap issue. To do so, we collect mentions from the training and test sets in the CoNLL benchmark dataset. We i.i.d. randomly attack each word in a mention with probability p and apply one of the below schemes. Table 2 shows examples of our modifications.

Lexical Changes. Modifiers and head words of noun phrases in a chain of mentions sometimes occur repeatedly. For instance, *president* both appears in the mention *the 44th president of the US* and its

Modification	Original $\rightarrow$ Modification
SWAP	people $\rightarrow$ peolpe
DELETE	rise $\rightarrow$ rse
VISUAL	emergency $\rightarrow$ emergeňcy
SYNONYM	next $\rightarrow$ upcoming
HYPONYM	people $\rightarrow$ workers
HYPERNYM	pigeon $\rightarrow$ bird

Table 2: Examples of text modification.

antecedent *the first African-American president of the US*. The CoNLL dataset involves many such lexical overlaps in coreferent mentions. Furthermore, Moosavi and Strube (2017) find a large size of mentions are overlapping in the CoNLL training and test examples. Together, this shows that the CoNLL evaluation setup does require only little lexical inference requirements. Subramanian and Roth (2019) remove named entities overlapping in the training and test sets. In contrast, we choose a word overlap randomly from mentions and substitute it with its hyponym, hypernym and synonym, as found in WordNet (Miller, 1995). To prevent the meaning of a word substitution deviated from the original word, we make the substitution only when two words share one word sense (synset), obtained from adapted LESK algorithm (Banerjee and Pedersen, 2002).

Orthographic Changes. Character-level ("low-level") text changes, e.g., random swapping of characters (Pruthi et al., 2019), create surface form noise that often does not affect humans. We investigate the impact of different forms of low-level noise, namely (a) swapping a pair of adjacent letters, (b) deleting letters, and (c) visual perturbation, i.e., changing characters in a word by visually similar ones. To make text changes less perceptible to humans, we restrict for (a) and (b) to: (1) an individual word is allowed to be modified only once, (2) the first and the last letter of a word cannot be modified—as human reading is more resilient to internal letter exchanges, as shown by psycholinguistic research (Davis, 2003), and (3) modifications to a word with less than four characters are not allowed. As for visual attacks (c), we obtain character 'embeddings' from descriptions of each character in the Unicode 11.0.0 final names list, and then determine a set of nearest neighbors by choosing those characters whose descriptions refer to the same letter. Such perturbations have been shown little effect on human text processing (Eger et al., 2019).

Systems	CLEAN	Avg	△	$\alpha(3)$	△	$\beta(3)$	△
Non-Neural Systems							
DETERMINISTIC	57.10	46.32	−10.78	41.24	−15.86	51.40	−5.70
STATISTICAL	66.83	55.17	−11.66	50.24	−16.59	60.10	−6.73
Neural Systems							
DEEP-RL	69.13	58.15	−10.98	51.17	−17.96	65.12	−4.01
COARSE-TO-FINE (C2F)	72.96	60.04	−12.92	55.08	−17.33	64.99	−7.97
C2F⊕BERT	73.38	61.59	−11.79	55.63	−17.75	67.54	−5.84
C2F⊕SPANBERT	77.43	64.62	−12.81	58.44	−18.99	70.80	−6.63

Table 3: Overall results of the published baselines, on the clean, α (orthographic noise) and β (lexical changes) test sets. Brackets denote the number of modified test sets per group (α or β). Results are averaged for each group. △ is the difference between the performance of the clean and average result per group.

3 Experiments

Benchmark Dataset. We collect the training, development and test documents in the CoNLL benchmark dataset and use the above-described adversarial schemes to generate 16,812 training, 2,058 development and 2,088 test documents. We note that there are only about 2.3 words per mention and about 2 mentions per sentence on average in the CoNLL dataset. Therefore, we set a relatively low modification probability $p = 0.5$, thus making about 2 words changes per sentence. The percents of the mentions in the CoNLL test set modified by lexical and orthographic changes are 24% and 46%, respectively. When applying text changes to the test set, the percent of mention overlaps in the training and the test sets are decreased from 56.7% to 34.3%.

Baselines. We investigate non-neural systems[1], namely the DETERMINISTIC (Lee et al., 2013) and STATISTICAL (Clark and Manning, 2015) systems together with neural systems, including DEEP-RL (Clark and Manning, 2016), COARSE-TO-FINE (C2F) (Lee et al., 2018), C2F⊕BERT and C2F⊕SPANBERT (Joshi et al., 2019). The results are reported using the CoNLL F1 score—the average of MUC (Vilain et al., 1995), B3 (Bagga and Baldwin, 1998) and CEAFe (Luo, 2005).

Overall Results. Despite the minor changes in text, Table 3 shows that, the drop in performance is consistently big on average (10-12 points CoNLL F-score) across systems. The systems appear to suffer the most from orthographic changes, however, the percent of the examples of low-level noises is twice as large as that of lexical changes. Together,

Training Set	CLEAN	SYNO	HYPO	HYPER
100% CLEAN	73.4	69.1	67.9	65.6
50% CLEAN and 50% SYNONYM	72.7	71.8	70.4	69.2

Table 4: Results of C2F⊕BERT on the test sets.

this exposes the limitation of non-neural and neural systems, including the systems based on BERT and SpanBERT, on lexical inference ability and understanding of low-level noise. Also, we note that the drop in non-neural baselines is smaller, which we believe is because linguistic features are primary predictors in them and have a positive effect.

4 Shielding via Adversarial Training

Shielding Setup. We measure to what extent adversarial training (Goodfellow et al., 2015) can improve lexical inference ability and the robustness to low-level noise for the baseline systems. We include the adversarial training set at train time, but do not augment the training data, i.e., only replace 50% clean examples using our text manipulations. We split our evaluation into two setups: (1) in-domain evaluation, e.g., the training and test set used for training and evaluation are modified by swapping characters and (2) out-of-domain evaluation, e.g., we use adversarial training that trains a baseline system from scratch on a modified training set of one noise, denoted as AT-NOISE, and evaluates on the adversarial test sets of the remaining noise.

Lexical Changes Analysis. Table 4 shows that the performance drops for C2F⊕BERT in the HYPONYM and HYPERNYM test sets are much bigger than that in the SYNONYM test set, but AT-SYNONYM considerably helps. To more thoroughly examine this, we randomly extract pairs of 1,000

---

[1] For non-neual systems, their linguistic features are extracted from our benchmark dataset using spaCy.

words and their synonyms, hyponyms and hypernyms from WordNet, as a form of coreferent mentions. We show histograms of the cosine similarity scores of word pairs, based on the last layer of BERT embeddings, used in C2F⊕BERT. Figure 1 (above) shows that a pair of a mention and its hypernymous/hyponymous antecedent is often assigned lower a cosine similarity score than a mention and its synonymous antecedent pair, suggesting that BERT embeddings capture the semantic differences of the three well. However, a plausible coreference resolver requires to ignore such fine-grained differences in meanings and links them all as coreferent mentions. This indicates the requirements for embeddings, used in resolvers, and for coreference resolvers, by design, are in conflict. However, this issue can be mitigated using AT-SYNONYM, as illustrated in Figure 1 (below). This is because a gold label can bridge a mention and its hypernymous/synonymous antecedent (within the same synset), thus omitting the semantic differences of them.

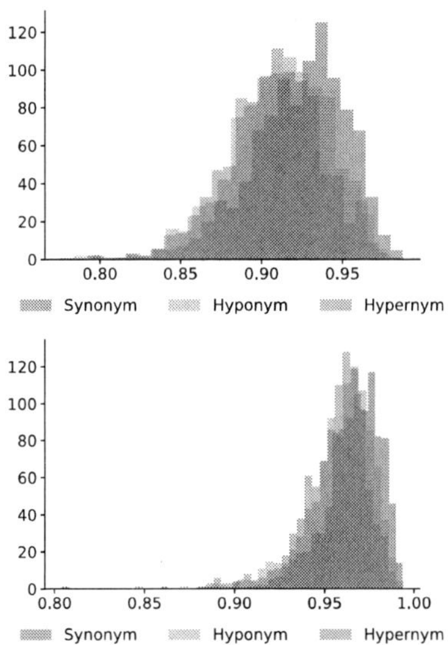

Figure 1: Histograms of cosine similarity scores of word pairs. C2F⊕BERT trained on the clean training set (above) and on SYNONYM training set (below).

In-domain and Out-of-domain Evaluations. Figure 2 shows that C2F⊕BERT via adversarial training appears to achieve consistent improvements in the in-domain evaluation setup, e.g., the gain achieved by AT-SWAP is 15.3 points on the SWAP test set. However, we observe that about 10% percent of mention are overlapping in the adversarial training and test sets, introduced by the

Training Set	SWAP	DELETE	VISUAL
100% CLEAN	56.8	55.4	54.5
100% SYNONYM	50.1	48.7	48.0
50% CLEAN and 50% SYNONYM	**58.1**	**57.1**	**55.6**

Table 5: Results of C2F⊕BERT trained via AT, on the training sets with synonym changes.

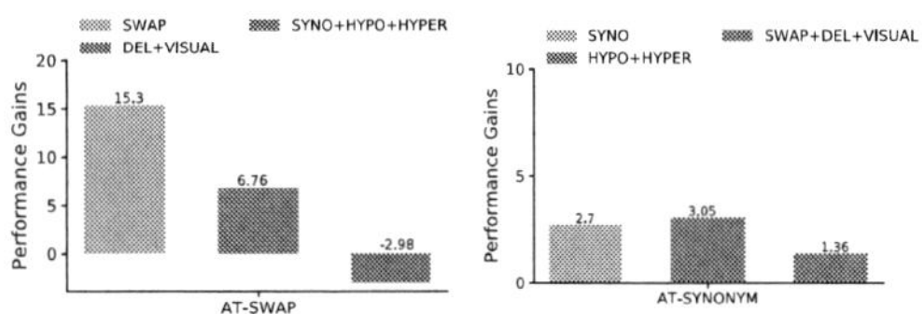

Figure 2: Performance gains (in points) in the in-domain and out-of-domain evaluation setup.

adversarial training approach. This may give a false and inflated impression for the improvements. Further, the effects for the out-of-domain evaluation are different. For instance, AT-SWAP obtains a large gain (+6.76 points) on the DELETE and VISUAL test sets, as the domain difference between the two and the SWAP test set is small. However, we note that AT-SWAP has a negative effect for the performance on the adversarial test sets involving lexical changes, since character-level noise and lexical replacement have little in common. In contrast, AT-SYNONYM appears to have a positive effect for the performance in the low-level noise domain. However, Table 5 shows that C2F⊕BERT trained on full SYNONYM training set causes a big performance drop on average across low-level noise. This indicates that enriching the system with lexical knowledge fails to improve its robustness to orthographic changes (similarly as for the negative effect of AT-SWAP to lexical changes). The gain on the test sets with low-level noise only appears when involving clean training examples at train time, as this substantially increases the size of mention overlaps, leading to a simpler coreference resolution task.

5 Conclusions

Coreference resolution have the potential to help downstream NLP systems solve problems that require text understanding. However, the performance scores on the CoNLL benchmark are inflated, because mentions are largely overlapping in the whole dataset, and the evaluation in a constrained domain fails to expose the limitations of coreference resolvers in the wild. Our experiments show that published resolvers fail to link coreferent mentions involving minor low-level noise and lexical changes. Beyond that, we show a caveat when mitigating the obstacles via adversarial approaches: lexical overlaps introduced by data augmentation must be removed from adversarial training and test sets so as to see how the approaches perform realistically.

Acknowledgments

The authors would like to thank Mark-Christoph Müller, Yufang Hou, Nafise Sadat Moosavi and the anonymous reviewers for their helpful comments and feedbacks. This work has been funded by the Klaus Tschira Foundation, Heidelberg, Germany. Haixia Chai has been supported by a Heidelberg Institute for Theoretical Studies PhD. scholarship. The contribution of Wei Zhao is supported by German Research Foundation as part of the Research Training Group Adaptive Preparation of Information from Heterogeneous Sources (AIPHES) at the Technische Universität Darmstadt under grant No. GRK 1994/1.

References

Amit Bagga and Breck Baldwin. 1998. Algorithms for scoring coreference chains. In *The first international conference on language resources and evaluation workshop on linguistics coreference*, volume 1, pages 563–566. Granada.

Satanjeev Banerjee and Ted Pedersen. 2002. An adapted lesk algorithm for word sense disambiguation using wordnet. In *International conference on intelligent text processing and computational linguistics*, pages 136–145. Springer.

Kevin Clark and Christopher D Manning. 2015. Entity-centric coreference resolution with model stacking. In *Proceedings of the 53rd Annual Meeting of the Association for Computational Linguistics and the 7th International Joint Conference on Natural Language Processing (Volume 1: Long Papers)*, pages 1405–1415.

Kevin Clark and Christopher D. Manning. 2016. Deep reinforcement learning for mention-ranking coreference models. In *Proceedings of the 2016 Conference on Empirical Methods in Natural Language Processing*, pages 2256–2262, Austin, Texas. Association for Computational Linguistics.

M Davis. 2003. Aoccdrnig to a rscheearch at cmabrigde uinervtisy. retrieved july 25, 2005.

Greg Durrett, Taylor Berg-Kirkpatrick, and Dan Klein. 2016. Learning-based single-document summarization with compression and anaphoricity constraints. In *Proceedings of the 54th Annual Meeting of the Association for Computational Linguistics (Volume 1: Long Papers)*, pages 1998–2008, Berlin, Germany. Association for Computational Linguistics.

Greg Durrett and Dan Klein. 2014. A joint model for entity analysis: Coreference, typing, and linking. *Transactions of the Association for Computational Linguistics*, 2:477–490.

Steffen Eger and Yannik Benz. 2020. From hero to zéroe: A benchmark of low-level adversarial attacks. In *Proceedings of the 1st Conference of the Asia-Pacific Chapter of the Association for Computational Linguistics*.

Steffen Eger, Gözde Gül Şahin, Andreas Rücklé, Ji-Ung Lee, Claudia Schulz, Mohsen Mesgar, Krishnkant Swarnkar, Edwin Simpson, and Iryna Gurevych. 2019. Text processing like humans do: Visually attacking and shielding NLP systems. In *Proceedings of the 2019 Conference of the North American Chapter of the Association for Computational Linguistics: Human Language Technologies, Volume 1 (Long and Short Papers)*, pages 1634–1647, Minneapolis, Minnesota. Association for Computational Linguistics.

Max Glockner, Vered Shwartz, and Yoav Goldberg. 2018. Breaking NLI systems with sentences that require simple lexical inferences. In *Proceedings of the 56th Annual Meeting of the Association for Computational Linguistics (Volume 2: Short Papers)*, pages 650–655, Melbourne, Australia. Association for Computational Linguistics.

Ian J. Goodfellow, Jonathon Shlens, and Christian Szegedy. 2015. Explaining and harnessing adversarial examples. In *3rd International Conference on Learning Representations, ICLR 2015, San Diego, CA, USA, May 7-9, 2015, Conference Track Proceedings*.

Mandar Joshi, Omer Levy, Luke Zettlemoyer, and Daniel Weld. 2019. BERT for coreference resolution: Baselines and analysis. In *Proceedings of the 2019 Conference on Empirical Methods in Natural Language Processing and the 9th International Joint Conference on Natural Language Processing (EMNLP-IJCNLP)*, pages 5802–5807, Hong Kong, China. Association for Computational Linguistics.

Heeyoung Lee, Angel Chang, Yves Peirsman, Nathanael Chambers, Mihai Surdeanu, and Dan Jurafsky. 2013. Deterministic coreference resolution based on entity-centric, precision-ranked rules. *Computational Linguistics*, 39(4):885–916.

Kenton Lee, Luheng He, and Luke Zettlemoyer. 2018. Higher-order coreference resolution with coarse-to-fine inference. In *Proceedings of the 2018 Conference of the North American Chapter of the Association for Computational Linguistics: Human Language Technologies, Volume 2 (Short Papers)*, pages 687–692, New Orleans, Louisiana. Association for Computational Linguistics.

Xiaoqiang Luo. 2005. On coreference resolution performance metrics. In *Proceedings of the conference on human language technology and empirical methods in natural language processing*, pages 25–32. Association for Computational Linguistics.

George A Miller. 1995. Wordnet: a lexical database for english. *Communications of the ACM*, 38(11):39–41.

Nafise Sadat Moosavi and Michael Strube. 2017. Lexical features in coreference resolution: To be used with caution. In *Proceedings of the 55th Annual Meeting of the Association for Computational Linguistics (Volume 2: Short Papers)*, pages 14–19, Vancouver, Canada. Association for Computational Linguistics.

Sameer Pradhan, Alessandro Moschitti, Nianwen Xue, Olga Uryupina, and Yuchen Zhang. 2012. CoNLL-2012 shared task: Modeling multilingual unrestricted coreference in OntoNotes. In *Joint Conference on EMNLP and CoNLL - Shared Task*, pages 1–40, Jeju Island, Korea. Association for Computational Linguistics.

Sameer Pradhan, Lance Ramshaw, Mitchell Marcus, Martha Palmer, Ralph Weischedel, and Nianwen Xue. 2011. CoNLL-2011 shared task: Modeling unrestricted coreference in OntoNotes. In *Proceedings of the Fifteenth Conference on Computational Natural Language Learning: Shared Task*, pages 1–27, Portland, Oregon, USA. Association for Computational Linguistics.

Danish Pruthi, Bhuwan Dhingra, and Zachary C. Lipton. 2019. Combating adversarial misspellings with robust word recognition. In *Proceedings of the 57th Annual Meeting of the Association for Computational Linguistics*, pages 5582–5591, Florence, Italy. Association for Computational Linguistics.

Sanjay Subramanian and Dan Roth. 2019. Improving generalization in coreference resolution via adversarial training. In *Proceedings of the Eighth Joint Conference on Lexical and Computational Semantics (*SEM 2019)*, pages 192–197, Minneapolis, Minnesota. Association for Computational Linguistics.

Marc Vilain, John Burger, John Aberdeen, Dennis Connolly, and Lynette Hirschman. 1995. A model-theoretic coreference scoring scheme. In *Proceedings of the 6th conference on Message understanding*, pages 45–52. Association for Computational Linguistics.

Elena Voita, Pavel Serdyukov, Rico Sennrich, and Ivan Titov. 2018. Context-aware neural machine translation learns anaphora resolution. In *Proceedings of the 56th Annual Meeting of the Association for Computational Linguistics (Volume 1: Long Papers)*, pages 1264–1274, Melbourne, Australia. Association for Computational Linguistics.

Dian Yu and Heng Ji. 2016. Unsupervised person slot filling based on graph mining. In *Proceedings of the 54th Annual Meeting of the Association for Computational Linguistics (Volume 1: Long Papers)*, pages 44–53, Berlin, Germany. Association for Computational Linguistics.

Coreference for Discourse Parsing: A Neural Approach

Grigorii Guz and Giuseppe Carenini
Department of Computer Science
University of British Columbia
Vancouver, BC, Canada, V6T 1Z4
{gguz, carenini}@cs.ubc.ca

Abstract

We present preliminary results on investigating the benefits of coreference resolution features for neural RST discourse parsing by considering different levels of coupling of the discourse parser with the coreference resolver. In particular, starting with a strong baseline neural parser unaware of any coreference information, we compare a parser which utilizes only the output of a neural coreference resolver, with a more sophisticated model, where discourse parsing and coreference resolution are jointly learned in a neural multitask fashion. Results indicate that these initial attempts to incorporate coreference information do not boost the performance of discourse parsing in a statistically significant way.

1   Introduction and Task Description

Discourse parsing is a very useful Natural Language Processing (NLP) task involving predicting and analyzing discourse structures, which represent the coherence properties and relations among constituents of multi-sentential documents. In this work, we investigate discourse parsing in the context of Rhetorical Structure Theory (RST) Mann and Thompson (1988), which encodes documents into complete constituency discourse trees. An RST tree is defined on the sequence of a document's EDUs (Elementary Discourse Units), which are clause-like sentences or sentence fragments (propositions), acting as the leaves of the tree. Adjacent EDUs and constituents are hierarchically aggregated to form (possibly non-binary) constituents, with internal nodes containing (1) a nuclearity label, defining the importance of that subtree (rooted at the internal node) in the local context and (2) a relation label, defining the type of semantic connection between the two subtrees (e.g., Elaboration, Background).

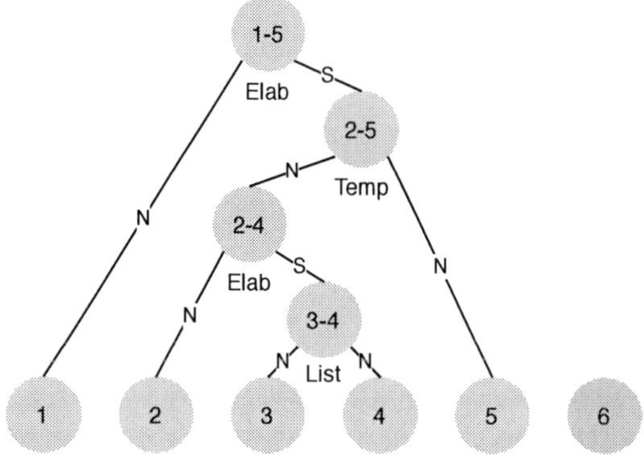

Figure 1: An example (Asher and Lascarides, 2003) of a discourse being ill-formed due to the invalid anaphoric link. The leaf EDUs are as follows: [Max had a great evening last night.]$_1$ [He had a great meal.]$_2$ [He ate salmon.]$_3$ [He devoured lots of cheese.]$_4$ [He then won a dancing competition.]$_5$ [It was a beautiful pink]$_6$

Previous research has shown that the use of RST-style discourse parsing as a system component can enhance important tasks, such as sentiment analysis, summarization and text categorization (Bhatia et al., 2015; Nejat et al., 2017; Hogenboom et al., 2015; Gerani et al., 2014; Ji and Smith, 2017). And more recently, it has been found that RST discourse structures can complement learned contextual embeddings (e.g., BERT (Devlin et al., 2018)), in tasks where linguistic information on complete documents is critical, such as argumentation analysis (Chakrabarty et al., 2019).

In this work, we present preliminary results of investigating the benefits of coreference resolution features for RST discourse parsing. From the theoretical perspective, it has long been established (Asher and Lascarides, 2003) that discourse structure can impose constraints on mention antecedent distributions, with these constraints being derived from the role of each discourse unit (sen-

Proceedings of the First Workshop on Computational Approaches to Discourse, pages 160–167
Online, November 20, 2020. ©2020 Association for Computational Linguistics
https://doi.org/10.18653/v1/P17

tence or EDU) with respect to the global discourse. The Veins theory (Cristea et al., 1998) is the most known formalization of anaphoric constraints with respect to RST tree structures, involving assigning to each EDU a subset of preceding EDUs defined by the nuclearity attributes of the EDU's parent nodes in the document's discourse tree (see Appendix A for the exact definition). These constrains act as a domain of referential accessibility where the antecedents must reside, for otherwise the discourse would be considered incoherent. As an example of this phenomenon, consider the discourse structure in Figure 1. In principle, a reader could apply commonsense knowledge to resolve the pronoun *it* in the last sentence to *salmon* in the third sentence, any proficient English speaker would call such a discourse ill-formed and incoherent, due to the fact that it breaks the discourse-imposed antecedent scope. In general, anaphora can only be resolved with respect to the most salient (sentence 1 in Figure 1) units of the preceding discourse (Asher and Lascarides, 2003). For our purposes, this means that having access to a document's coreference structure might be beneficial to the task of predicting the discourse structure, since the coreference structure can constrain the discourse parser's solution space. However, as shown in a corpus study by Zeldes (2017), the antecedent boundaries defined by Veins Theory are often too restrictive, suggesting that while discourse structures can be useful for predicting coreference structures and vice versa, these mutual constrains must be defined softly, at least in the context of RST theory.

To explore these ideas computationally with respect to modern neural models, we investigate the utility of automatically extracted coreference features and discourse-coreference shared representations in the context and for the benefit of neural RST discourse parsing. Our strong baseline SpanBERT-NoCoref utilizes SpanBERT (Joshi et al., 2020) as in the current SOTA coreference resolver, without utilizing any direct coreference information. Next, our SpanBERT-CorefFeats considers the output of coreference resolver as per Dai and Huang (2019), letting us test the benefit of predicted and so possibly noisy coreference features. Finally, our more sophisticated SpanBERT-Multitask model learns discourse parsing together with coreference resolution in the neural multitask learning fashion, sharing the SpanBERT contextual word encoder for both models.

2   Related Work

Dai and Huang (2019) have already explored the benefit of using coreference information for neural PDTB implicit discourse relation classification, in a way similar to our SpanBERT-CorefFeats model. In our study, we also explore the use of shared encoder architecture for both tasks to detect the additional possible synergy.

Modelwise, the most common approach to infer discourse trees is the linear bottom-up shift-reduce method, adopted from syntactic parsing. Wang et al. (2017) uses hand-crafted features and the shift-reduce method predicted by two separate Support-Vector-Machines (SVMs) for structure- and nuclearity-prediction and relation-estimation. The neural model by Yu et al. (2018) uses a similar topology, but instead relies entirely on LSTMs for automatic feature extraction and on a single multilayer-perceptron (MLP) for classifying all possible actions. Top-down approaches to discourse parsing are also quite promising, with recent work of Kobayashi et al. (2020) applying ELMO (Peters et al., 2018) for computing span representations and achieving the new absolute SOTA performance, reporting however the scores of an ensemble of five independent runs of their proposed model instead of single-model results. In this work we follow the shift-reduce strategy and apply SpanBERT-Base (Joshi et al., 2020; Wolf et al., 2020), which we introduce below, for encoding the document contents.

The field of coreference resolution has recently been dominated by deep learning models. The current SOTA model by Joshi et al. (2020) is built upon the neural coreference resolver of (Lee et al., 2018) by incorporating SpanBERT language model, which modifies the commonly used BERT (Devlin et al., 2019) architecture with a novel span masking pretraining objective. In our work, we re-implemented their coreference resolver in PyTorch (Paszke et al., 2019). Our code for both models is available[1].

3   Shift-Reduce Architecture

All our proposed parsers share the same basic shift-reduce architecture, consisting of a Queue, which is initially filled with documents EDUs in order

---

[1] `http://www.cs.ubc.ca/cs-research/lci/research-groups/natural-language-processing/index.html`

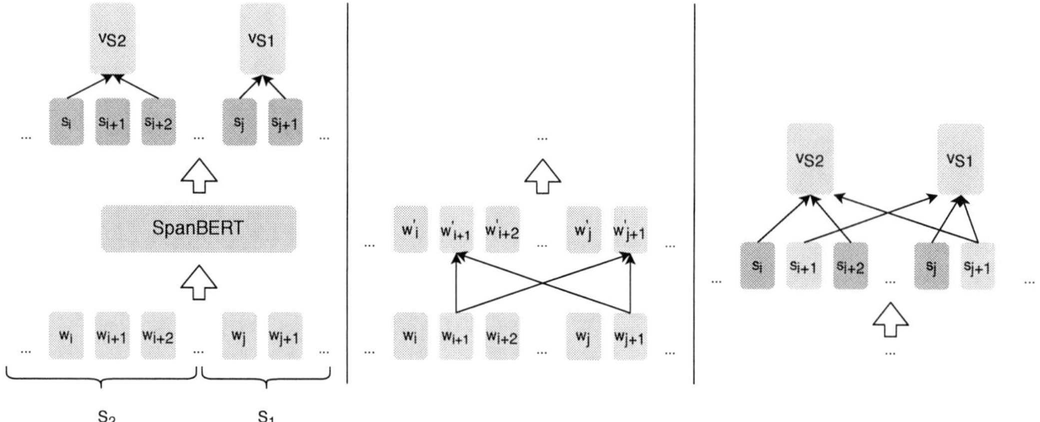

Figure 2: Overview of our models. For spans S_2 are S_1, the $w_{i:i+2}$ and $w_{j,j+1}$ respectively are the nuclear EDUs. (Left) All components of SpanBERT-NoCoref. (Middle) SpanBERT-CorefFeats modifies the initial SpanBERT embeddings according to predicted coreference clusters (in red). (Right) SpanBERT-MultiTask updates the final span representations with embeddings of mentions of shared entities.

from first to last one, and a Stack, which is initially empty, as well as the following actions on them:

The Shift delays aggregations of sub-trees at the beginning of the document by popping the top EDU Q_1 on the queue and pushing it onto the stack.

The Reduce-X aggregates the top subtrees (S_1, S_2) on the stack into a single subtree (S_{1-2}). Each reduce action further defines a nuclearity assignment $X_N \in \{$NN, NS, SN$\}$ to the nodes covered by S_{1-2} and a relation $X_R \in \{$Elaboration, Contrast, ...$\}$ holding between them.

3.1 Action Classifier Parametrization

Similarly to (Wang et al., 2017; Yu et al., 2018), all models under consideration utilize the information from top two elements S_1, S_2 of the stack, and top element Q_1 of the queue. In addition to word-/word+coreference-based representations $v_{S_2}, v_{S_1}, v_{Q_1}$ for these nodes, computed differently by each model as described below, we extract textual organization features of Wang et al. (2017). In particular, for each pair $S_2 - S_1$ and $S_1 - Q_1$, we extract indicator features representing whether the pair is within the same sentence or paragraph; for each of S_2, S_1 and Q_1 we compute whether each of them are at the start/end of a sentence/paragraph/document.

In accord with Wang et al. (2017), the parsing action at each timestep is chosen by two trainable classifiers, being multi-layer perceptrons (MLPs) in our system, where each classifier takes in the concatenation of $v_{S_2}, v_{S_1}, v_{Q_1}$, together with the dense embeddings for the aforementioned organizational features. The first classifier predicts the action and nuclearity assignment among $y_{Act,Nuc} \in \{Shift, Reduce_{NN}, Reduce_{NS}, Reduce_{SN}\}$, and in case the Reduce action is chosen, the second classifier predicts the discourse relation among 18 coarse-grained RST relation classes $y_{Rel} \in \{Attribution, Elaboration, ...\}$.

3.2 Action Classifier Training and Inference

Both classifiers are trained using the Cross-Entropy loss, computed for each Stack-Queue parsing step. At test time, we apply the greedy decoding strategy to predict the discourse structure.

4 Proposed Models

We now describe the three proposed discourse parsing models which differ in the levels of coupling with the coreference model. See Figure 2 for the visual comparison.

SpanBERT-NoCoref: in addition to the organizational features, our baseline system utilizes only the output SpanBERT-contextualized word embeddings. To predict each Stack-Queue action, a full document is passed through SpanBERT in a non-overlapping sliding window fashion, as per Joshi et al. (2020), so that the context of full document can be considered for each parsing action to account for possible context-sensitivity of discourse structures (Dai and Huang, 2018). The node representation v_{Q_1} for the first Queue element is computed as the mean of the first and the last word

162

Model	Structure	Nuclearity	Relation
HILDA(2010)	82.6	66.6	54.6
DPLP(2014)	82.0	68.2	57.8
CODRA(2015)	82.6	68.3	55.8
Two-Stage(2017)	86.0	72.4	59.7
Transition-Syntax(2018)	85.5	73.1	60.2
D2P2S2E (Ensemble)(2020)	87.0	74.6	60.0
SpanBERT-NoCoref	87.8 ± 0.2	75.8 ± 0.2	63.4 ± 0.3
SpanBERT-CorefFeats	88.1 ± 0.3	76.1 ± 0.6	63.6 ± 0.3
SpanBERT-MultiTask	87.9 ± 0.2	75.9 ± 0.6	63.3 ± 0.7
Human (2017)	88.3	77.3	65.4

Table 1: RST-Parseval micro precision for structure, nuclearity and relation prediction on RST-DT corpus. Scores for previous approaches are from either Morey et al. (2017) or the original papers.

embedding of the EDU that this Queue element represents. v_{S_1} and v_{S_2} are computed as the means of the first and the last word embeddings of the nuclear EDU of S_1 and S_2, as each non-leaf node in an RST structure encodes a relation between nuclear EDUs of its children (Morey et al., 2018).

SpanBERT-CorefFeats: with this architecture variant, we attempt to assess the benefit of coreference features generated by the coreference resolver for RST parsing. Given a document with n words, the coreference features will be used to update the initial (not contextualized) SpanBERT word embeddings $w_{1:n}$, which will later be passed to SpanBERT.

Specifically, for a given document we apply the pre-trained coreference parser of Joshi et al. (2020) to extract the document's coreference clusters $C_1, C_2, ...$, each of which are equivalence classes representing different mentions of the same entity. Afterwards, we compute the vector representation c_i for each cluster C_i by performing attention-based averaging over word-vectors corresponding to mentions in that cluster:

$$c_i = \sum_{k \in C_i} a_k w_k$$

where $w_k \in \mathbb{R}^d$ is the initial SpanBERT word embedding for word k and $a_k \in [0, 1]$ are attention scores. These cluster representations are then used for updating the document's word representations using the gating mechanism Lee et al. (2018): for each word $w_k \in D$,

$$f_k = \sigma(W[c_i; w_k])$$

$$w'_k = \begin{cases} f_k \circ w_k + (1 - f_k) \circ c_i & \text{if } w_k \in C_i \\ w_k & \text{otherwise} \end{cases}$$

Finally, the embeddings w'_k are passed to SpanBERT for contextualization, and the node representations $v_{S_1}, v_{S_2}, v_{Q_1}$ are computed as in SpanBERT-NoCoref.

SpanBERT-MultiTask: learns discourse parsing and coreference resolution in a multitask learning regime, weight-sharing the SpanBERT encoder module. The coreference resolver training step proceeds in the same fashion as in (Joshi et al., 2020). For updating the discourse parsing model, we use the pre-computed coreference clusters C_i obtained from the pretrained coreference model, as running it at every training step was prohibitively time-consuming. Using the contextualized SpanBERT word embeddings $s_{1:n}$ for all words in the document, we check these coreference clusters for overlaps: considering a pair of spans S_1, S_2, if a cluster C_i has entity mentions in the spans of both stack elements S_1 and S_2, so that if there are mentions $m_j, m_k \in C_i$ such that $m_j \in S_1$ and $m_k \in S_2$, we update the span representation v_{S_1} (computed as in SpanBERT-NoCoref) with the attention weighted sum of mentions $m_k \in C_i \cap S_2$ by applying the gating mechanism as in SpanBERT-CorefFeats, so that the span representation for S_1 can incorporate more relevant context from S_2. The representation for v_{S_2} is computed similarly using mentions $m_k \in C_i \cap S_1$, and the analogous computation is performed for $S_1 - Q_1$ pair.

For learning both tasks at the same time, we utilize the approach similar to (Sanh et al., 2018), where gradient updates are performed separately for each task and the probability of sampling a task is proportional to the relative size of each task's dataset. The initial shared SpanBERT encoder weights are set from the pretrained coreference resolver checkpoint.

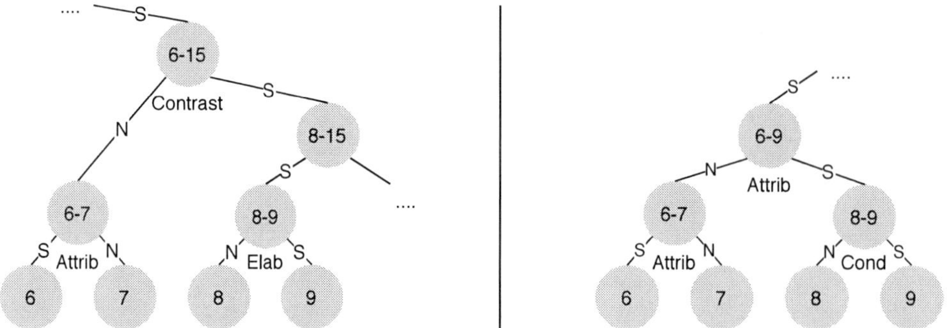

Figure 3: A subtree from SpanBERT-NoCoref prediction for *wsj_0631* (left) and gold-standard (right). Incorrect nodes are colored in purple. The EDUs are: [Finnair and SAS said]₆ [they plan to swap stakes in each other.]₇ [Neither discussed details]₈ [pending board meetings next month.]₉.

5   Experimental Settings and Results

All models were trained on the RST-DT (Carlson et al., 2002) and evaluated with RST-Parseval procedure (Marcu, 2000), with the coreference component of SpanBERT-MultiTask being trained on full OntoNotes 5.0 corpus (Weischedel et al., 2013). The details of the training procedure such as hyperparameter assignment are outlined in the Appendix B. The test results are presented in Table 1 and are the average and standard deviation single-model scores of five independent runs.

Firstly, we observe that our models strongly outperform all previous approaches, indicating huge benefit of pretrained language models for RST discourse parsing, with results approaching human performance. Then, with respect to coreference features, we notice that the models utilizing coreference information are statistically equivalent in performance to the SpanBERT-NoCoref baseline, while displaying higher variance of the test scores for Nuclearity and Relation prediction. This suggests four plausible (and not mutually exclusive) explanations: (1) the coreference information relevant to discourse parsing is already captured by SpanBERT, (2) or that coreference information is not a strong signal for discourse structure (Zeldes, 2017), or that (3) the coreference information extracted automatically is too noisy, or that (4) our specific ways of combining coreference with discourse parsing are not adequate and more work is needed to develop better solutions. It should also be noted that we only experimented on a single discourse parsing dataset, so the conclusions or generalizations should be considered preliminary.

In an attempt to shed some light on the results,

we compare the predicted and gold subtree from one of the documents in our development set on Figure 3. The trees were analyzed using the RST tree visualization tool by Huber (2019). According to Veins theory, the pronoun [*neither*] in EDU 8 is a mention that should have access to its mentions ([*Finnair and SAS*] or [*they*]) in preceding EDUs. However, accoding to the discourse structure predicted by SpanBERT-NoCoref, the vein for node (8) does not contain the EDUs (6) and (7) (and in fact any of its preceding EDUs), so that [*neither*] cannot be linked to any of its preceding mentions. On the other hand, according to the gold discourse structure, EDU 8 has EDU 7 on its vein, meaning that this anaphora can be resolved. This means that if one had access to gold coreference structure and applied Veins Theory strictly, the substructure produced by SpanBERT-NoCoref would not be permitted.

6   Conclusions and Future Work

We empirically compare different levels of coupling between a shift-reduce neural discourse parser and a neural coreference resolver. Remarkably, our baseline delivers SOTA performance on RST-DT, but does not seem to benefit from coreference features.

For future work, we plan to experiment with (1) alternative discourse parsing architectures and approaches for neural multitasking, along with more powerful coreference models (2) alternative ways of augmenting a neural discourse parser with coreference information and other tasks like summarization (3) improving the coreference resolution performance by leveraging information provided by a discourse parser.

References

Ralph Weischedel et al. 2013. Ontonotes release 5.0. *Linguistic Data Consortium.*

Nicholas Asher and Alex Lascarides. 2003. *Logics of Conversation.* Cambridge University Press.

Parminder Bhatia, Yangfeng Ji, and Jacob Eisenstein. 2015. Better document-level sentiment analysis from rst discourse parsing. In *Proceedings of the 2015 Conference on Empirical Methods in Natural Language Processing*, pages 2212–2218.

Lynn Carlson, Mary Ellen Okurowski, and Daniel Marcu. 2002. *RST discourse treebank.* Linguistic Data Consortium, University of Pennsylvania.

Tuhin Chakrabarty, Christopher Hidey, Smaranda Muresan, Kathleen McKeown, and Alyssa Hwang. 2019. Ampersand: Argument mining for persuasive online discussions. In *Proceedings of the 2019 Conference on Empirical Methods in Natural Language Processing and the 9th International Joint Conference on Natural Language Processing (EMNLP-IJCNLP)*, pages 2926–2936.

Dan Cristea, Nancy Ide, and Laurent Romary. 1998. Veins theory: A model of global discourse cohesion and coherence. In *36th Annual Meeting of the Association for Computational Linguistics and 17th International Conference on Computational Linguistics, Volume 1*, pages 281–285, Montreal, Quebec, Canada. Association for Computational Linguistics.

Zeyu Dai and Ruihong Huang. 2018. Improving implicit discourse relation classification by modeling inter-dependencies of discourse units in a paragraph. In *Proceedings of the 2018 Conference of the North American Chapter of the Association for Computational Linguistics: Human Language Technologies, Volume 1 (Long Papers)*, pages 141–151, New Orleans, Louisiana. Association for Computational Linguistics.

Zeyu Dai and Ruihong Huang. 2019. A regularization approach for incorporating event knowledge and coreference relations into neural discourse parsing. In *Proceedings of the 2019 Conference on Empirical Methods in Natural Language Processing and the 9th International Joint Conference on Natural Language Processing (EMNLP-IJCNLP)*, pages 2976–2987, Hong Kong, China. Association for Computational Linguistics.

Jacob Devlin, Ming-Wei Chang, Kenton Lee, and Kristina Toutanova. 2018. Bert: Pre-training of deep bidirectional transformers for language understanding. *arXiv preprint arXiv:1810.04805.*

Jacob Devlin, Ming-Wei Chang, Kenton Lee, and Kristina Toutanova. 2019. BERT: Pre-training of deep bidirectional transformers for language understanding. In *Proceedings of the 2019 Conference of the North American Chapter of the Association for Computational Linguistics: Human Language Technologies, Volume 1 (Long and Short Papers)*, pages 4171–4186, Minneapolis, Minnesota. Association for Computational Linguistics.

Shima Gerani, Yashar Mehdad, Giuseppe Carenini, Raymond T Ng, and Bita Nejat. 2014. Abstractive summarization of product reviews using discourse structure. In *Proceedings of the 2014 conference on empirical methods in natural language processing (EMNLP)*, pages 1602–1613.

Dan Hendrycks and Kevin Gimpel. 2016. Gaussian error linear units (gelus). *arXiv preprint arXiv:1606.08415.*

Hugo Hernault, Helmut Prendinger, Mitsuru Ishizuka, et al. 2010. Hilda: A discourse parser using support vector machine classification. *Dialogue & Discourse*, 1(3).

Alexander Hogenboom, Flavius Frasincar, Franciska De Jong, and Uzay Kaymak. 2015. Using rhetorical structure in sentiment analysis. *Commun. ACM*, 58(7):69–77.

Patrick Huber. 2019. Discourse-sentiment alignment tool (dsat).

Yangfeng Ji and Jacob Eisenstein. 2014. Representation learning for text-level discourse parsing. In *Proceedings of the 52nd Annual Meeting of the Association for Computational Linguistics (Volume 1: Long Papers)*, volume 1, pages 13–24.

Yangfeng Ji and Noah A Smith. 2017. Neural discourse structure for text categorization. In *Proceedings of the 55th Annual Meeting of the Association for Computational Linguistics (Volume 1: Long Papers)*, pages 996–1005.

Mandar Joshi, Danqi Chen, Yinhan Liu, Daniel S. Weld, Luke Zettlemoyer, and Omer Levy. 2020. Spanbert: Improving pre-training by representing and predicting spans. *Transactions of the Association for Computational Linguistics*, 8:64–77.

Shafiq Joty, Giuseppe Carenini, and Raymond T Ng. 2015. Codra: A novel discriminative framework for rhetorical analysis. *Computational Linguistics*, 41(3).

Naoki Kobayashi, Tsutomu Hirao, Hidetaka Kamigaito, Manabu Okumura, and Masaaki Nagata. 2020. Top-down rst parsing utilizing granularity levels in documents. *Proceedings of the AAAI Conference on Artificial Intelligence*, 34:8099–8106.

Kenton Lee, Luheng He, and Luke Zettlemoyer. 2018. Higher-order coreference resolution with coarse-to-fine inference. In *Proceedings of the 2018 Conference of the North American Chapter of the Association for Computational Linguistics: Human Language Technologies, Volume 2 (Short Papers)*, pages 687–692, New Orleans, Louisiana. Association for Computational Linguistics.

Ilya Loshchilov and Frank Hutter. 2019. Decoupled weight decay regularization. In *International Conference on Learning Representations*.

William C Mann and Sandra A Thompson. 1988. Rhetorical structure theory: Toward a functional theory of text organization. *Text-Interdisciplinary Journal for the Study of Discourse*, 8(3):243–281.

Daniel Marcu. 2000. *The Theory and Practice of Discourse Parsing and Summarization*.

Mathieu Morey, Philippe Muller, and Nicholas Asher. 2017. How much progress have we made on RST discourse parsing? a replication study of recent results on the RST-DT. In *Proceedings of the 2017 Conference on Empirical Methods in Natural Language Processing*, pages 1319–1324, Copenhagen, Denmark. Association for Computational Linguistics.

Mathieu Morey, Philippe Muller, and Nicholas Asher. 2018. A dependency perspective on rst discourse parsing and evaluation. *Computational Linguistics*, 44(2):197–235.

Bita Nejat, Giuseppe Carenini, and Raymond Ng. 2017. Exploring joint neural model for sentence level discourse parsing and sentiment analysis. In *Proceedings of the 18th Annual SIGdial Meeting on Discourse and Dialogue*, pages 289–298.

Adam Paszke, Sam Gross, Francisco Massa, Adam Lerer, James Bradbury, Gregory Chanan, Trevor Killeen, Zeming Lin, Natalia Gimelshein, Luca Antiga, Alban Desmaison, Andreas Kopf, Edward Yang, Zachary DeVito, Martin Raison, Alykhan Tejani, Sasank Chilamkurthy, Benoit Steiner, Lu Fang, Junjie Bai, and Soumith Chintala. 2019. Pytorch: An imperative style, high-performance deep learning library. In H. Wallach, H. Larochelle, A. Beygelzimer, F. dAlché-Buc, E. Fox, and R. Garnett, editors, *Advances in Neural Information Processing Systems 32*, pages 8026–8037. Curran Associates, Inc.

Matthew Peters, Mark Neumann, Mohit Iyyer, Matt Gardner, Christopher Clark, Kenton Lee, and Luke Zettlemoyer. 2018. Deep contextualized word representations. In *Proceedings of the 2018 Conference of the North American Chapter of the Association for Computational Linguistics: Human Language Technologies, Volume 1 (Long Papers)*, pages 2227–2237, New Orleans, Louisiana. Association for Computational Linguistics.

Victor Sanh, Thomas Wolf, and Sebastian Ruder. 2018. A hierarchical multi-task approach for learning embeddings from semantic tasks.

Yizhong Wang, Sujian Li, and Houfeng Wang. 2017. A two-stage parsing method for text-level discourse analysis. In *Proceedings of the 55th Annual Meeting of the Association for Computational Linguistics*

(Volume 2: Short Papers), pages 184–188, Vancouver, Canada. Association for Computational Linguistics.

Thomas Wolf, Lysandre Debut, Victor Sanh, Julien Chaumond, Clement Delangue, Anthony Moi, Pierric Cistac, Tim Rault, Rémi Louf, Morgan Funtowicz, Joe Davison, Sam Shleifer, Patrick von Platen, Clara Ma, Yacine Jernite, Julien Plu, Canwen Xu, Teven Le Scao, Sylvain Gugger, Mariama Drame, Quentin Lhoest, and Alexander M. Rush. 2020. Huggingface's transformers: State-of-the-art natural language processing.

Nan Yu, Meishan Zhang, and Guohong Fu. 2018. Transition-based neural rst parsing with implicit syntax features. In *Proceedings of the 27th International Conference on Computational Linguistics*, pages 559–570.

Amir Zeldes. 2017. A distributional view of discourse encapsulation: Multifactorial prediction of coreference density in RST. In *Proceedings of the 6th Workshop on Recent Advances in RST and Related Formalisms*, pages 20–28, Santiago de Compostela, Spain. Association for Computational Linguistics.

A Veins Theory Definitions

The following definitions are from Cristea et al. (1998). For each node in an RST tree, its head is defined as follows:

1. The head of the terminal (leaf) node is itself.

2. The head of a non-terminal node is the concatenation of the heads of its nuclear children.

Next, we define the vein expression of each node recursively top-down. When the node is a leaf, the preceding nodes on its vein correspond to its domain of referential accessibility.

1. The vein expression of the root is its head.

2. For each nuclear node, its vein expression is the union of its head with:

   - its parent's vein, if this node has no left siblings that are satellites.
   - its parent's vein and its left sibling's vein, if this sibling is a satellite.

3. For every satellite node, its vein expression is the union of its head with:

   - its parent's vein, if this node is a left child.
   - its parent's vein with heads of prior (up in the tree) satellite nodes removed.

B Hyperparameters and Training Settings

As RST-DT does not specify a standard training-validation split, we select 10% of the training documents for the validation set, stratifying the split by the number of EDUs in each document. Similarly to Joshi et al. (2020), we train all of our models with AdamW (Loshchilov and Hutter, 2019) optimizer with learning rate of $1e^{-5}$ for SpanBERT and $2e^{-4}$ for model-specific components, with the batch size of 5 and linear decay for 20 epochs. All of our MLPs consist of 2 linear layers, with a GeLU (Hendrycks and Gimpel, 2016) nonlinearity and a Dropout layer with a value of 0.3 between them. Each organizational feature of Wang et al. (2017) is represented using a learnable 10-dimentional embedding, or a vector of zeros if the feature is missing (for example, the feature specifying if the 2-top elements of the stack are in the same sentence when the stack contains only one element). With regards to multitask regime, the probability of discourse parsing task being sampled over coreference resolution was ≈ 0.72 (each Stack-Queue state was treated as a datapoint), but due to highly demanding computational requirements of the coreference resolver and time constrains, this probability was increased to 0.9. Nonetheless, the results for the correct task proportions will be provided through other sources.

Association for Computational Linguistics
209 N. Eighth Street
Stroudsburg, Pennsylvania 18360

ISBN 978-1-7138-1984-4